# THE SOCIOLOGY OF EDUCATION

second edition

*Robert James Parelius and Ann Parker Parelius*

*Rutgers, The State University of New Jersey*

PRENTICE-HALL, INC., Englewood Cliffs, New Jersey 07632

*Library of Congress Cataloging-in-Publication Data*

Parelius, Robert James [date]
The sociology of education.

Ann Parker Parelius's name appeared first on the earlier edition.
Includes index.
1. Educational sociology—United States.
I. Parelius, Ann Parker [date]. II. Sociology of education.
III. Title.
LC191.4P37 1987 370.19'0973 86-22627
ISBN 0-13-821125-6

Editorial/production supervision and
interior design: Dee Amir Josephson
Cover design: Wanda Lubelska Design
Manufacturing buyer: John Hall



PRINTED IN THE UNITED STATES OF AMERICA

10 9 8 7 6 5 4 3 2 1

ISBN 0-13-821125-6 01

PRENTICE-HALL INTERNATIONAL (UK) LIMITED, *London*
PRENTICE-HALL OF AUSTRALIA PTY. LIMITED, *Sydney*
PRENTICE-HALL CANADA INC., *Toronto*
PRENTICE-HALL HISPANOAMERICANA, S.A., *Mexico*
PRENTICE-HALL OF INDIA PRIVATE LIMITED, *New Delhi*
PRENTICE-HALL OF JAPAN, INC., *Tokyo*
PRENTICE-HALL OF SOUTHEAST ASIA PTE. LTD., *Singapore*
EDITORA PRENTICE-HALL DO BRASIL, LTDA., *Rio de Janeiro*

*To Jessie Helen Parelius,*

*and in loving memory of Martin Wells Parelius*

# CONTENTS

## CHAPTER THREE
## INDUSTRIALIZATION 46



## CHAPTER FOUR
## BUREAUCRATIZATION 90

## CHAPTER FIVE
## THE ORGANIZATON OF STUDENT LIFE



## CHAPTER SIX
## PROFESSIONALIZATION 177



## CHAPTER SEVEN
## CENTRALIZATION OF POWER 229

# PREFACE

It is not easy to provide an overview of American eduction. Statistics that describe our educational institutions as the decade of the eighties began suggest the difficulty of the task.* At that time, 54, 224 elementary schools, 11,593 middle schools, 16,285 secondary schools, 1,194 two-year colleges, and 1,957 four-year colleges were in operation. These institutions were diverse as well as numerous, varying with regard to type of control (public or private), size, student composition, and internal organization. Despite the fact that their number had been sharply reduced by decades of consolidation, 15,538 separate and distinct public school districts remained in operation. The schools, colleges, and universities employed 2,460,000 teachers and 846,000 college professors. Expenditures were impressive as well: $96,881,000,000 for public elementary and secondary schools and $65,584,000,000 for higher education (public and private). Furthermore, this system, if it can rightly be called a system, was highly dynamic. Both internal and external relationships changed in response to social, demographic, political, and economic trends. Sociologists have contributed a great deal to our understanding of education in these United States, but there is still so much we do not know.

*Source of data is Valena White Plisko, *The Condition of Education 1984* (Washington, D.C.: Government Printing Office, 1984), and Plisko, *The Condition of Education 1981* (Washington, D.C.: Government Printing Office, 1981).

This book is our second attempt to summarize sociological theory and research as it relates to education in America. Those who have read the first edition will notice much that is familiar yet much that is new in this edition. The original emphases on process as well as structure, on conflict as well as consensus, and on higher as well as elementary and secondary education have been retained. The basic organizational framework remains largely intact as well, the primary change being the deletion of the chapter dealing with school-community relationships.

The entire text has been updated, and large portions of several chapters have been rewritten. The chapter dealing with bureaucratization has been revised to emphasize *goal ambiguity* and *loose coupling*. Unions and collective bargaining have been given greater prominence in the discussion of professionalization. Finally, the chapter dealing with governance has been recast in order to focus on the most important overall trend—namely, the centralization of power. Our goal has been to produce a fresher, more complete book without diminishing the strengths of the first edition.

We wish to thank our editor, Bill Webber, for his quiet, patient support throughout the long period during which this revision took shape. We also want to thank Kathleen Dorman, Dee Josephson, and the other members of the Prentice-Hall staff who rushed this manuscript into production once it was finally received.

*Robert James Parelius*
*Ann Parker Parelius*

# THE SOCIOLOGY OF EDUCATION

# CHAPTER ONE SOCIOLOGY AND THE FIELD OF EDUCATION

## FROM EDUCATIONAL SOCIOLOGY TO THE SOCIOLOGY OF EDUCATION

During the late nineteenth and early twentieth centuries, sociologists and educators were caught up in the optimism of the Progressive Era. Rejecting the prevailing belief that human affairs are governed by destiny, they insisted instead that intellect could guide societal evolution toward the achievement of worthy goals. Among these advocates were such sociological pioneers as Lester Ward and Albion Small and such prominent educators as William James and John Dewey.

This was a time during which educators and sociologists worked closely together in an enterprise known as Educational Sociology. Their goal was the perfection of humanity and society. Their common belief was that the schools could contribute toward that perfection by developing human intellect and by inspiring students to devote themselves to reforming society.

Much of the work done by educational sociologists centered on the relationship between education and the larger society. Some of it was abstract and philosophical. For example, they argued that schools could develop our ability to shape the future by teaching us to approach all subjects scientifically. Some of their work was naively utopian, and argued that education was the key to the alleviation of all social ills. Some of it was narrowly pragmatic, and focused on details of school and classroom organization. There was much discussion of administrative problems and of methods for managing conflicts between schools and families, special interest groups, and problem students.[1]

However, the close cooperation between sociologists and educators did not last. The development of sociology was heavily influenced by the model of the German University, where the goal of scholarship was to contribute to the general body of theory and research upon which the development of sociology as a distinct academic discipline was based. It was assumed that the highest levels of scholarship were manifested in research that was empirical, methodologically sophisticated, value free, and tied to general theory. The ideal of value-free analysis was thought to demand the insulation of academia from practical, pragmatic, and political concerns. When judged according to these ideals, Educational Sociology appeared sadly wanting. Sociologists increasingly regarded the subject as an applied field, theoretically fragmented and devoid of adequate research methods.[2]

Educators also became disillusioned with Educational Sociology. The grand claims of perfecting society were not to be realized, and sociologists could offer few definitive solutions to educational problems. To many educators, sociologists appeared increasingly elitist, obsessed with highly technical research methods on the one hand, and grandiose and inapplicable theories on the other.

In time, Educational Sociology fell into disrepute. Educators and sociologists both turned inward toward their own diciplines, each attempting to develop their own unique body of theory and research.

Educational Sociology became a historical phenomenon. Its passing was marked officially in 1963 when the *Journal of Educational Sociology* became the journal of the *Sociology of Education* and when the American Sociological Association's section on Educational Sociology became its section on the Sociology of Education.

Today, the Sociology of Education closely approximates the scientific ideals of sociology as a whole, but it also profits significantly from the input of professional educators. A 1970 survey of the members of the Sociology of Education section of the American Sociological Association indicated that a substantial portion of the membership is closely connected with education.[3] These members hold teaching certificates, administrative posts, and teaching positions within departments of education at colleges and universities. Those with educational connections tend to emphasize the practical application of sociology to the daily operation of the schools. Among their primary concerns are equality of educational opportunity, school desegregation, curriculum content, intergroup relations in the school, and teaching as a career. There is some divergence in the research priorities of these members and those of other academic sociologists, but these differences should not be exaggerated. During the last two decades, a rapproachment has developed that has brought educators and sociologists closer together. This is evidenced by the increased number of sociologists employed within education departments and by organizational changes, such as that at the University of Chicago, which incorporated the Department of Education into the Social Sciences Division.[4] Furthermore, interdisciplinary cooperation was evident in recent federal commission reports on excellence in elementary, secondary, and higher education.[5] It has become obvious to many that sociological theory and research are relevant in the search for the solution to educational problems, and that experience with the operation of educational institutions can contribute to the development of social research and theory building. We hope this book will help further this favorable trend.

## THEORY IN THE SOCIOLOGY OF EDUCATION

Abstract concepts are helpful to students of educational institutions in the same way that a flashlight is helpful in the dark. Each illuminates certain aspects of reality and helps make sense of what is otherwise hidden and chaotic. We cannot deal with everything in our surroundings at once. Concepts help by focusing attention on certain phenomena while distracting us from others. By imposing a simplified order on the complexities of social life, they offer us a clearer intellectual path. At the same time, though, they keep some aspects of reality in the shadows and distort our perceptions of others.

At present, two contrasting conceptual paradigms are widely used by scholars in the Sociology of Education. The adherents of each proclaim the virtues of their own particular approach, and both have made important contributions. These paradigms are most commonly referred to as *consensus theory* and *conflict theory*. Historically, the consensus approach has been dominant, not only in the sociological study of education but also in virtually all other areas of sociology. Recently, however, there has been an outpouring of work using the conflict perspective, with a renewed appreciation of its usefulness.

Despite the fact that many sociologists actually use elements of both theoretical perspectives in their work, and although there are areas of overlap between them, it is possible to distinguish the key elements of these two schools of sociological thought. The consensus and conflict theorists offer alternative interpretations of the forces that bind societies together and the role of educational institutions in society. First, we will sketch the basics of consensus theory and illustrate its application to the analysis of schools and classrooms. Then we will follow a similar procedure with conflict theory. Our introductory discussion of theory in the Sociology of Education will conclude with certain cautions about the uses and limitations of grand theory and a few words about the importance of empirical research as an anchor for theoretical speculation.

### Consensus Theorists

Consensus theorists generally agree that societies are in some ways like biological organisms. Both are composed of many distinct, but interdependent parts, and each part makes some contribution to the survival of the whole. Both tend to maintain a state of relative equilibrium. When something disturbs one part of the system, or threatens to destroy it, all of the other parts react to bring the system back to an even keel. Our own bodies destroy threatening bacteria, keep body temperature within tolerable range, and maintain proper levels of oxygen in the blood. In an analogous fashion, societies adapt to the physical environment, maintain adequate levels of production, distribute essential goods and services, keep violence under control, and so on.

But the analogy must not be overdrawn. Social institutions are not biological organs and individuals are not biological cells. Human behavior is purposive and goal directed. We can all think, and our thinking, our perceptions of the world around us, our attitudes, and our values all affect our behavior. Consensus theorists point out that societies cannot survive unless their members share at least some common sets of perceptions, attitudes, and values. As their name implies, consensus theorists often stress the beliefs and interests that we share in common and give less attention to those beliefs and interests on which we differ. Let us look more formally at the key elements implicit here.[6]

*Structure and Function.* Consensus theorists, like many other social theorists, see societies as being made up of "parts." These "parts" make up the social structure of each society. There is some disagreement as to whether these "parts" are best thought of as social institutions, patterns of social behavior, social roles, or some other type of unit. In the remainder of this text, we will sometimes be talking about the institutional structure of society, especially when we look at the interrelationships between the school and such other institutions as the family or the economy. We will sometimes be talking about patterns of social behavior, such as in our discussions of school-community relations, and we will sometimes be talking about social roles, as when we talk about what constitutes being a "teacher" or a "student."

Consensus theorists are distinct from other social theorists in their emphasis on the contributions that each "part" of society makes to the survival of the whole. This contribution is its "function," and consensus theorists are concerned with showing how the recurrent survival needs of societies are met by their institutions, norms, and social roles. Consensus theorists are often criticized for exaggerating the positive contributions that various parts of society make to the functioning of the whole and for ignoring the destructive effects of other elements.

*Integration.* Consensus theorists also stress that the various parts of society, however they are defined, are integrated with each other. A change that occurs in one part of society will affect all the others. But these parts are not just interdependent—they are coordinated and complementary. They seldom stand in opposition or conflict with one another. Each part supports the workings of the others as well as the society as a whole. Even consensus theorists recognize that integration is never complete, however. Some parts may overlap or fail to mesh completely. In general, though, consensus theorists emphasize the ways in which the various elements of the social structure work together to maintain the overall social system.

*Stability.* No society is completely static, and consensus theorists recognize that at least some social change is inevitable. For example, events may occur outside a particular society that impinge upon it and force it to change in response. Nevertheless, consensus theorists stress the forces that keep societies relatively stable rather than those that press for radical and abrupt change. Consensus theorists point to the persistence of such basic institutions as the family and to similarities in the values and behavior of various generations as evidence of how slowly societies actually change.

*Consensus.* Agreement on important perceptions, sentiments, values, and beliefs is another theme of consensus theory. Of course, societies vary in terms of the nature and extent of consensus; it is easier to achieve consensus in small folk societies than in large modern industrial states. Consensus theorists point out, however, that in any society, modern or folk, large or small, there is a shared set of abstract and complex assumptions about the world without which social life would be impossible. This consensus is achieved through socialization, and, in modern societies, the function of socialization is primarily performed by the family and the schools. Consensus theorists have been criticized for overemphasizing similarities among people and ignoring the diversity of interests, values, and beliefs that exist in complex pluralistic societies.

### Durkheim's Sociology of Education

Like numerous social thinkers both before and after his own lifetime, Émile Durkheim was interested in the fundamental question of how societies are held together. This concern with the basis of social order is a central theme running through many of his works.

Durkheim's approach to the problem of social order emphasizes two basic ideas. First, Durkheim believed that complex societies are held together by the mutual interdependence of their members. Individuals do not and cannot meet all their needs by themselves. Instead, individuals specialize. There is an intricate division of labor such that each individual produces some portion of the goods or services required by the other members of society and exchanges them for the goods and services one needs but does not produce. In an advanced technological society such as our own, such exchanges are effected through a system involving labor, wages, markets, industrial enterprises, and so on. The complexity of our division of labor makes us all mutually interdependent, and, according to Durkheim, contributes to social stability.[7]

At the same time, however, Durkheim recognized that mutual economic interdependence was not enough. There must be some agreement among us about what we are doing and what we should do. Furthermore, we must all agree to participate and to subordinate our own personal interests to those of the larger society whenever this becomes necessary.

According to Durkheim, we are all born into society as asocial beings. Obviously, we do not know society's language, skills, or customs, and we must learn these to survive—both as individuals and as a group. But our learning must also include something else. We must develop a sense of commitment to society, and internalization of its most central values and ideas. We must change from being egoists, responding greedily to our own endless self-centered desires, into moral citizens, responding in terms of our duty to the state and our loyalty to something greater than ourselves.[8]

Durkheim did not doubt that there were central ideas and values in all societies: "respect for reason, for science, for ideas and sentiments which are at the base of democratic morality"[9] were some of the examples he gave for his own society. This is not to say that Durkheim totally ignored diversity, but he did not emphasize it. He recognized that the very division of labor in society requires some degree of differentiation of values and ideas. Different occupations require different aptitudes, practices, and modes of viewing the world.[10] But Durkheim stressed that there must be an underlying consensus regarding the central values and beliefs of society, or it could not survive.

If a consensus of values and beliefs is necessary, though, how is it to be achieved? How do we transform each new generation of asocial infants into responsible adults? The answer for Durkheim was through moral education.[11] For Durkheim, moral education consisted of socialization experiences that result in the internalization of society's central values and beliefs. Such internalization, when totally successful, is a powerful form of social control, because individuals then believe that their own society's norms represent the only right or moral way to behave. From then on, they will be self-policing. Even thinking about violating their internalized beliefs and values will arouse feelings of guilt and shame that will deter the potential violation.

But how is society to accomplish such socialization? According to Durkheim, each society must accomplish it in ways that are appropriate to the values and beliefs it needs to instill. In some societies, the family (especially the extended family) might play an important role. Durkheim argued that in the decades immediately preceding his writing, the Catholic Church performed this vital function in his own society, France. With increasing industrialization, urbanization, and secularization, however, the values and beliefs taught by the church and the manner in which it taught them no longer represented the central values and beliefs of French society and could no longer be the basis of its moral order. Some other mechanism for moral education had to be found, one more attuned to the needs of a modern state; for Durkheim, that mechanism was the schools. The schools could transform us. They could help us overcome our initial egoism and teach us discipline and self-control. They could encourage us to adopt the fundamental principles of our society as our own.

One can see that from Durkheim's perspective the task of the school is critical to society's survival. In line with this view, Durkheim believed that educational institutions must be closely guarded. The state, whose interest in survival the educational institutions serve, must outline the basic principles to be taught there. It must carefully supervise the schools to assure that these principles are taught. It must "see to it that nowhere are children left ignorant of them, that everywhere they should be spoken of with the respect which is due them."[12]

Within the schools the specific tasks of moral education must be accomplished by the teacher. According to Durkheim the teacher is the representative of the state. "Just as the priest is the interpreter of his god, the teacher is the interpreter of the great moral ideas of his time and his country."[13] Teachers must not subvert society by teaching their own personal values and beliefs, for to do so would reduce the nation to ". . . an incoherent multitude of little fragments in conflict with one another."[14] Teachers must be firmly committed to those beliefs and values central to society, for it is through the teacher's commitment to these central principles and the personal example set by the teacher that the child experiences and incorporates the moral order:

> Let him be attached to these ideas, let him feel all their grandeur, and the authority which is in them . . . cannot fail to be communicated to his person and to everything that emanates from him. Into an authority which flows from such an impersonal source there could enter no pride, no vanity, no pedantry. It is made up entirely of the respect which he has for his functions and . . . for his office. It is this respect which, through word and gesture, passes from him to the child.[15]

According to Durkheim, then, the primary function of education is to socialize new generations to overcome their egoism and to become productive members of society. Education contributes to the maintenance of the social system and the conservation of the national character. All children in a society must be exposed to it and therefore, to a point, education must be the same for all children in a society. Yet Durkheim also recognized that diversity is necessary. Because different occupational subgroups require different values and beliefs, children destined for these different groups need to have their own unique educational experiences. Nevertheless, some common educational core must remain; consequently, education is more uniform for young children, when the common principles are being taught, than for older ones.

It is easy to see the ideas of consensus theory in Durkheim's work on education. He emphasized the integration of society, the interdependence of its parts, the functions that are necessary for its survival, and the ways in which these functions are filled by different institutions. He stressed consensus of values and beliefs and their contribution to societal stability. At the same time, Durkheim spent little or no time dealing with possible conflicts between different groups. Who decides which values and beliefs should be taught? Are the interests of the "state" ever in conflict with the interests of the students? Through what mechanisms do we decide which children are destined for different occupations and therefore deserving of different types of education? Are teachers really the agents of the "state," or do they represent their students' families or the students themselves? These and many other important questions are not readily answered within Durkheim's theoretical framework.

### Talcott Parsons on the Classroom

Talcott Parsons was one of the most eminent theorists of the consensus school. Most of his work analyzed large social systems such as societies, but in his essay "The School Class as a Social System"[16] he applied the consensus mode of analysis to the classroom. The fact that his theories are applicable to social systems so large and so small highlights the very high level of abstraction of his basic concepts. Once again, the themes of structure-function, stability, integration, and consensus are illustrated.

The discussion begins with definitions of two major functions of the school class—socialization and selection. The socialization function is, of course, the one that Durkheim discussed. Parson's definition of it is quite similar to Durkheim's:

> The socialization function may be summed up as the development in individuals of the commitments and capacities which are essential prerequisites of their future role performance.[17]

In our discussion of Durkheim, we also referred to the future roles that students play in society. At that time, we mentioned the problem of deciding which students were destined for which particular societal roles. Parsons argued that in contemporary technological societies these decisions are made in the schools. It is the function of the educational system to "select" students for different occupational slots as well as to appropriately socialize those selected. The most important selection is between those who will go to college and those who will not. Although the allocation of students into separate academic and vocational programs may not formally occur until high school or even college, the process begins in a subtler form during the elementary school years. For example, some children are given higher grades, placed in "faster" reading groups, and encouraged to think about professional occupations. Those who are selected for college attendance will enter the more prestigious occupations and will rise to higher socioeconomic levels in society.

According to Parsons, the basis upon which schools allocate students into college-going and noncollege-going categories is achievement. Schools reward children with high grades and encouragement on the basis of what they are willing and able to accomplish. In the early school grades, this accomplishment is measured in both moral and intellectual terms. Children must show that they can behave properly, be cooperative, obey the teacher, be punctual, and so on. In the higher grades, the accomplishment is increasingly measured in intellectual terms. It is then not sufficient to try hard; one must also succeed in mastering the material.

Parsons' belief that schools reward children on the basis of achievement was central to his larger view of the integration of educational and economic systems in modern societies. Parsons argued that in modern societies people must be allocated to occupational slots according to their ability to perform adequately in those slots. Expertise is essential, as is making maximal use of whatever talent exists in the population. In less complex societies allocation to occupational and other positions could be (and usually is) based on criteria other than achievement. For example, such ascribed characteristics as a child's family background, race, ethnicity, or sex might determine what his or her adult role would be. Industrialization, however, requires allocation on the basis of achievement.

Parsons believed that there is general agreement throughout our society that allocation should be on the basis of achievement. Because of this agreement or consensus, teachers, administrators, parents, and the public at large understand what is being done in the schools and are basically supportive of them. One of the first socialization tasks of the school is to teach children that they will be evaluated on the basis of achievement so that students, too, can share in this basic consensus. Only then can we assure that the classroom itself will be stable and well integrated.

When children first arrive at school, they have not necessarily learned that achieved rather than ascribed characteristics are the proper bases for most societal rewards. In their own families, each child is valued as an individual and loved regardless of how well he or she compares to other children. Although the teacher is somewhat of a mother surrogate in the early school years, she or he is more objective about the child. The teacher remains affectively neutral, or uninvolved emotionally; treats all children alike according to uniform or universalistic criteria; and interacts with them only in terms of their respective roles as teacher and student. Gradually, the children internalize the values represented by this behavior.

Within the school class, some children will more completely fulfill the teacher's moral and intellectual requirements than others, and these will be rewarded accordingly. The unequal distribution of rewards in the classroom is potentially disruptive, but because the children quickly internalize the belief that achievement merits reward, the only remaining problem is to assure them all that the context within which that achievement is being measured is fair. In other words, they must believe that they all have an equal chance of doing well and that only differences in ability and motivation explain differences in their achievement. Certain mechanisms help ensure that this is the case. For example, children are generally age-segregated so that none is advantaged or disadvantaged by being substantially older or younger than the others. Children tend also to be sent to neighborhood schools, which results in some degree of homogeneity of such other ascribed characteristics as socioeconomic status, race, and ethnicity. Also, within the classroom, students are given common tasks and systematically evaluated by one lone, and therefore indisputable, authority: the teacher. Finally, friendship groups that grow up among students and various nonacademic activities that are valued by a student's peers provide alternative sources of reward. Those who do not do well academically can receive approval and support through participation in sports, extracurricular activities, or social events.

In summary, Parsons stressed the functional interdependence of educational and other societal institutions. He believed that two of the basic functions of education are socialization and selection. Through these two processes, the schools provide society with individuals well qualified for the roles they will fulfill. Allocation to these roles is on the basis of achievement and merit. Schools also both promote value consensus and depend upon it for their smooth operation.

As we shall see, Parsons' theory does not account for the considerable amount of controversy that surrounds educational goals and methods in contemporary society. He does not adequately deal with the abundant accumulation of empirical data that suggest that ascriptive and not simply achieved characteristics have a major impact on just how the educational system will allocate any particular individual. His analysis of the internal consensus of the classroom does not adequately account for the factionalization, hostility, and even occasional violence we see there.

### Conflict Theorists

Whereas consensus theorists focus on functional integration, core values, and social stability, conflict theorists focus on the coercive nature of society and the pervasiveness of social change. To the conflict theorist, power struggle is the main dynamic of social life. On the one hand, societies are held together by powerful social groups that coerce cooperation from the less powerful; on the other hand, societies are perpetually changing and in danger of disintegration because power struggles can result in new elite groups replacing the old.

Conflict theorists view social systems as divided into dominant and subordinate groups. The relationship between these groups is exploitative, with the dominant group taking all or most of society's valuables for itself. The dominant group also imposes its own values and world view on its subordinates. The subordinates are, however, a constant threat to the stability of the system, and the dominant group must be always on guard. As part of its effort to retain control, the dominant group might create social myths which legitimize its own position, co-opt potentially threatening members of the subordinate groups, "buy off" the opposition, or use physical force. In any case, the system cannot last forever. Violence may eventually erupt and the system might be destroyed. In time, however, a new social order will emerge.

The key concepts here are conflict, change, and coercion.[18]

*Conflict.* Consensus theorists emphasize integration and the complementary character of various parts of the social structure, but conflict theorists emphasize that social institutions and groups usually work at cross-purposes to each other. The goals and programs of one group are often at odds with the goals and programs of another. Certainly, the interests of those in power are sharply incompatible with the interests of those who are subordinate. Conflict, then, is pervasive, as each group struggles for dominance. Sometimes this conflict is relatively muted, but it is often open and violent.

*Change.* The continuous power struggles between groups result in a state of constant flux. Periods of relative calm and stability clearly occur, but they are interspersed by periods of rapid change and upheaval. Placid periods may be times when the opposing forces are gathering strength for the next battle, the calm before the storm. When the storm breaks, riot, rebellion, and revolution may result.

*Coercion.* Whenever, in the course of this panorama of struggle and change, any one particular group consolidates sufficient power, it will create a period of temporary stability and social order by coercing the less powerful into cooperation. This coercion will not be based solely on the use of force, however. Instead, the dominant group will propagandize and indoctrinate the oppressed in an effort to convince them that their oppression is legitimate. For example, a myth of the divine right of kings might be promulgated to legitimize an oppressive monarchy. Subjects who believe in this myth will be less likely to rebel against their royal oppressor because they believe his or her reign is the will of God. The powerful may also use their resources in a positive way as rewards for desired behavior. This can still be considered coercive as the phrase, "I'll make him an offer he can't refuse," implies.

Nevertheless, force—either positive or negative—and propaganda are never completely successful. There is always remaining resistance to oppression, and this resistance, combined with other inevitable changes in society, ultimately lead to social upheaval and disintegration. In time, however, a new cohesive order rises to replace the old.

### Samuel Bowles: A Conflict Perspective on Contemporary American Education

The writings of Samuel Bowles[19] provide a clear example of the application of the conflict model to contemporary educational institutions, especially those in the United States. The themes of conflict, change, and coercion appear throughout.

The heart of Bowles' argument is that the rise of public education in the United States occurred along with, and as a consequence of, advancing capitalism. Capitalism, he argues, requires a skilled and disciplined labor force, one which cannot be adequately socialized by the traditional institutions of family and church.

In precapitalist economies, skills are generally passed from parents to children under informal conditions—in the home, the field, or the shop. Capitalism increases the rate of technological change, however, and the skills required from one generation of workers may be radically different from those required from the next. Furthermore, capitalism requires literacy, mathematical and other technical knowledge that may not be possessed by the parental generation and may not be easily taught in an informal manner.

Capitalism also weakens the family and the church and makes each less effective as an agency of socialization. It increases the geographical mobility of workers' families, and thus weakens ties to the extended family. It sends children and parents out of the home and into different parts of the labor market, and thus weakens the nuclear family. It promotes secular beliefs in rational planning and decision making, and thus weakens the church. Social order is threatened as these institutions change and lose influence. Yet the old institutions are not suitable to the needs of the emerging capitalist elites.

At the same time, capitalism creates conditions that are potentially self-destructive. Workers are "thrown together in oppressive factories and the isolation which . . . helped to maintain quiescence in earlier, widely dispersed peasant populations . . . [breaks] down."[20] Inequalities of wealth become more apparent and are less easily justified by doctrines such as that of the divine origins of social rank.

In the United States, an additional threat was posed by the massive waves of immigrants that arrived in the late nineteenth and early twentieth centuries. These immigrants, with their diversity of languages, values, dress, and behavior seemed to threaten the orderliness and discipline of the workplace. It was feared that they would become criminals, political agitators, or burdens to the economy. A crisis seemed at hand.

The solution to all of these problems was offered by a system of mass education. Compulsory public schooling could accomplish several important goals, all in service to the capitalist class. First, mass education could supply workers with the cognitive, intellectual, and technical skills required by the capitalist economy. Secondly, it could supply workers who had already learned the values and behavior conducive to productive labor. Children could be taught punctuality, discipline, deference to authority, and acceptance of responsibility for their work. The social relations of the school (the relationship between teacher and students, for example) could replicate the social relations of the workplace and ease the transition from the family to the world of work.

Third, the schools could teach loyalty to the state and obedience to the law. This loyalty could be achieved by convincing children that the system was benevolent and just.

The schools, then, could provide the capitalist economy with a ready, willing, and able supply of workers, while at the same time assimilating foreign and potentially disruptive groups within the population. Bowles argues that it was for these reasons that a system of mass education was finally established in the United States.

Bowles takes his analysis one step further, however. He argues that our system of mass education not only supplies skilled and committed workers, but it also actually legitimizes existing inequalities in the social division of labor by suggesting that these inequalities are based on merit rather than on coercion. For example, the educational system appears to be open to all and to reward people on the basis of ability and willingness to work. Children are taught that they all have an equal chance of proving their worth, of receiving prestigious educational credentials, and of going on to positions of affluence and power in the larger society. However, Bowles argues that this is a myth. In fact, the educational system rewards children differentially on the basis of their class origins. Children from elite families become the elite of the next generation. Children of the poor remain poor. Consequently, the social division of labor is reproduced in each generation. Furthermore, because the system gives the appearance of openness and promotes this ideological myth, children believe that those in the dominant class are there because they deserve to be and that those who are poor are poor because they are lazy or uneducable. This effectively blinds most people to the oppressive nature of the system.

Bowles' analysis, then, points to the conflicting interests of various societal groups and the ways in which those in power can use such social institutions as the schools to justify and maintain an essentially coercive and exploitative system. Bowles' analysis does less well in explaining evidence that schools do permit upward mobility or in accounting for efforts to reform schools in the interests of greater social equality. When he does deal with these issues, however, Bowles argues that they are merely subtle mechanisms to maintain the system and not meaningful avenues to equality. Finally, Bowles' approach may blur important differences between social systems: They are all oppressive. Yet we know that educational institutions vary from society to society and, in each particular case, the balance of their contribution to societal inequality versus equality falls at a different point along a continuum. The bold outlines and stark contrasts Bowles draws between the oppressed and the oppressors may blind us to significant comparative variations.

### Willard Waller on Conflict in the Classroom

Willard Waller's *The Sociology of Teaching*[21] was first published in 1932 and has become a classic in the field. There are many reasons for its continuing acclaim, one of which is its description of the school as a social system in which stability is constantly endangered by both internal and external forces. The themes of conflict, change, and coercion are evident throughout.

Waller describes the school as

> . . . a despotism in a state of perilous equilibrium . . . . a despotism threatened from within and exposed to regulation and interference from without. It is a despotism capable of being overturned in a moment, exposed to the instant loss of its stability and its prestige. It is a despotism demanded by the community of parents. . . . It is a despotism resting upon children. . . .[22]

Clearly, Waller sees the school as a coercive institution. At the top are the teachers, given their authority by the community outside the school. At the bottom are the children, relatively (but not totally) helpless under their yoke. Here, the interests of the teachers are in unavoidable and universal conflict with the interests of the children. The teacher is the taskmaster, attempting to make the students learn the formal curriculum. The students are subordinate to them, but are much less interested in schoolbooks than in their classmates and informal activities. The teacher, then, must coerce the students into obedience and learning:

> The teacher-pupil relationship is a form of institutionalized dominance and subordination. The teacher and pupil confront each other in the school with an original conflict of desires, and however much that conflict may be reduced in amount, or however much it may be hidden, it still remains. The teacher represents the adult group, ever the enemy of the spontaneous life of children. The teacher represents the formal curriculum, and his interest is in imposing that curriculum upon the children. . . . The teacher represents the established social order in the school, and his interest is maintaining that order. . . .[23]

Note that Waller sees the age difference between students and teachers as one source of their perpetual conflict. Waller stresses that children have a culture of their own, one that develops primarily in the playgroup and is passed on from one generation to the next. Children, he points out, see the world differently from adults, they value different things, and prefer different types of activities. Adults, however, have power over children and try to force them to accept adult values and perspectives.

The teacher, then, is faced with a difficult and continuous struggle to maintain discipline and promote learning. Waller describes the major mechanisms of social control available to teachers, in descending order of efficacy, as: commands, punishments, management, shows of temper, and emotional appeals. Grades and examinations are, of course, important mechanisms of coercion. However, none of these methods is completely effective. Some "set the students and teachers at one another's throats."[24] Others result in long-enduring feuds between certain students and their teachers. At any time classroom order can collapse, with the teacher losing all control. Inevitably, however, if the teacher is to remain a teacher, he or she must reestablish order and maintain it. The teacher must win!

Waller points out that the coerciveness of this system is resented by both students and teachers, but none can escape it. However, students will subvert the teacher's rules, minimize the importance of academic success, and divert their enthusiasm and energy to other pursuits. In particular, students will turn to extracurricular activities and informal social relationships for alternative sources of reward and satisfaction.

In summary, Waller sees coercion rather than value consensus as the basis of classroom order. He believes that the interests of teachers and students conflict and that they engage in perpetual power struggles. At any time, classroom order can collapse, but it will be reestablished. Children, at least, have no hope of winning.

### Cautions Regarding the Use of Grand Theories

The aim of this brief review of conflict and consensus theories as applied to education has been to illustrate the crucial importance of organizing conceptual frameworks in sociological work. Of course, no set of concepts is sufficient in itself to illuminate and organize all the complexities of social life. Sociology simply has not come that far yet. As it stands, the best one can do is to carry a large conceptual tool kit. Then it will be possible to pick out those concepts that are particularly useful for the task at hand.

Theory by itself has some clear limitations, though. First, there is the problem that each explanation taken by itself seems persuasive. Durkheim and Parsons, Bowles and Waller may all sound convincing. There is no way in which theory, devoid of research, can tell us which alternative is best. Nor can it answer more specific questions about social life, such as "What percentage of students in this class have internalized values similar to the teacher's and what percentage have not?" Secondly, such grand abstract theories as we have been discussing can easily shade over into simple ideological rhetoric. Such rhetoric is characterized by rigid beliefs, oversimplification, the absence of self-skepticism, and a resistance to questioning. The conflict framework can deteriorate into an intellectual legitimization of revolutionary change, and the consensus theory can become a reactionary defense of the status quo.

As ideology, both conflict and consensus theory become sterile and monotonous. Adherents of each perspective talk past each other, neither hearing the other. Yet, dialogues between sociologists using diverse theoretical models constructively and with a willingness to test their ideas empirically can be useful indeed. We hope to illuminate some of the potentials of such a dialogue in the chapters that follow, although the contrasts between conflict and consensus theories are more relevant to some of the issues we will be discussing than to others.

Through the remainder of this book, however, we will emphasize the importance of empirical research as a check on theoretical speculation and as a contribution to theory building. The process of hypothesis testing is chastening. The usual case is that the data are complex, subject to different interpretations, and unreflective of clear-cut differences. There is a tentativeness, a desire for further evidence, and a recognition of complexities that grow out of a commitment to research.

This is not to say that sociologists should not have ideological positions or that their research much in some way be totally "value-free." Values enter research in any of a myriad of ways, from the choice of topics to be studied, through the formulation of hypotheses, the methodology adopted, to the final interpretation of the data. But a clear description of the research procedure and the publication of results permit each of us to assess the validity and reliability of the findings. The credibility of the research will rest, to a great extent, on our confidence that the values of the researcher have not led to more of a distortion of reality than an illumination of it.

## RESEARCH IN THE SOCIOLOGY OF EDUCATION

In recent years, there has been increased commitment to empirical research among sociologists interested in education. Conrad's review of the research literature in Educational Sociology during the decade of 1940 to 1950 showed that many writers used anecdotal stories and moral exhortations to buttress their arguments rather than rigorous and systematic research: " . . . only a fraction (of the studies) used standard tests, interviews, or observation, and almost no study was reported which used experimental techniques."[25]

The last three decades have brought a dramatic rise in research standards, however. Few pieces are not published that do not have at least some kind of empirical reference or documentation. Carefully reported field observations, large-scale surveys of national samples, and experimental designs are common. Statistical techniques for the analysis of complex and subtle relationships among numerous interacting variables have also been developed and permeate the literature.

Nevertheless, there is still room for improvement, particularly in tying the growing body of empirical findings back into theoretical paradigms so that general principles of social life can be established. A glut of discrete findings, with no organizing framework, can be as useless as the untested speculations of the "armchair" theorist.

## SOCIAL POLICY AND THE SOCIOLOGY OF EDUCATION

In some recent periods, sociologists have had increased opportunities to participate in the formation and implementation of national policies in education, law enforcement, welfare, the mass media, and so on. They have been invited to serve on commissions established by both government agencies and private foundations. They have served as fact finders and have formulated policy alternatives on the bases of their research and sociological expertise. Especially during the decade of the 1960s and its War on Poverty, federal funds were provided to sociologists to support experimental and demonstration projects through which new social programs were established. Federal financing has also been available for work on social indicators or the development of measures of social change. Additionally, sociologists have been called upon to evaluate continuing social programs, to assess their effectiveness and make recommendations for their continuation, modification, or termination.

In response to these opportunities, many sociologists have oriented their research more directly toward issues of policy concern. Policy-oriented research tends to concentrate on several particular themes.[26] One central theme of policy research is *goal clarification*, or sensitization to what our objectives and priorities actually are. Cross-cultural and historical analyses are particularly useful here because they highlight the wide range of goals that might be chosen and the variety of structures that might be used to accomplish them. A second major theme of policy research is its emphasis on large-scale *social trends* and on predicting how such trends might alter our institutions and our needs. Developing social indicators is an important example of this kind of policy research. Third, there is an orientation toward *institution building* in policy research. Policy-oriented researchers are often more interested in evaluating and reconstructing societal institutions than in contributing to the elaboration of abstract theoretical models. There is an *activist* or *moral* component to the researcher's work, a desire to improve social life. At times, there is even an optimism about social reform that is reminiscent of the faith of the Progressivists we mentioned earlier.

The deemphasis on grand theory, which is characteristic of policy research, is compatible with the needs of policymakers. Those responsible for policy development and implementation must be interested in research that deals with variables over which they have some control, rather than more abstract and intractable ones. Discussing the relative importance of value consensus or coercion for the maintenance of social order may be exciting to the sociologist, but it is of little use to the politician or the administrator. Policymakers work within a framework of what is possible for them to do, and their concerns are therefore more mundane than those of the professional social theorist. On the other hand, the unique contribution of the social scientist can be to enlighten the policymaker so that everyday problems can be seen in a larger context, as examples of more general phenomena and as products of a complex of social factors.

Research with a policy orientation has certain clear advantages and pitfalls. Chief among the advantages are the opportunity to exert some influence on national policy, and the excitement that comes from dealing with important and controversial issues. It is an opportunity, also, to be active rather than merely contemplative and to test one's ideas in real life. But there are also several problems inherent in policy research. First, there are the difficulties of producing high-quality research under the perennial constraints of too little time, money, and freedom. Government funding is unpredictable to say the least, and regulation of what questions the researcher may ask or who can be watched is often a problem. Secondly, there is the pressure to come up with politically acceptable results. A Republican administration may not want to hear that increased spending on social services is necessary. A Democratic administration might not want to be told to strengthen big business in the interest of a stronger economy. A third and related difficulty is that policy research is only one of many inputs into policy decisions. Particularly when the results of the research are incompatible with the interests of those who commissioned the research, sociologists may find themselves ignored or at least relatively neglected when final decisions are actually formulated. Finally, policy researchers cannot even be certain that their research will be made generally available. Many research reports have been "buried" in the file and have not surfaced again. Results relevant to many individuals, and especially to those who were the subjects of a study, may be kept from them by decision makers.

For these and other reasons, there is a certain ambivalence toward policy research among professional sociologists. We would, however, prefer to see it encouraged. Particularly in the field of education, sociology has a great deal to contribute to policy decisions. We hope this text will illuminate at least some of these potential contributions.

## THE SOCIOLOGY OF EDUCATION: FOR WHOM?

Many students who take this course are skeptical as to its practical usefulness and interest. Some of the reasons for this skepticism are traceable to the historical differences in the development of the fields of education and sociology we spoke of earlier. We hope that by now all of you have had your imaginations stirred and that you already believe the Sociology of Education has something to offer the sociologist, the educator, the liberal arts student, and the future citizen.

For the sociologist, the Sociology of Education offers a basic understanding of some of the processes through which culture is transmitted from one generation to the next, how social order is maintained, and how societies change. For the educator, the Sociology of Education offers a "set of concepts that will allow him (or her) to take account in . . . decision-making of organizational, cultural, and interpersonal factors . . ."[27] For the liberal arts student who does not intend to become either an educator or a sociologist, the Sociology of Education contributes to the development of a "sociologist imagination." As an amateur sociologist one can employ the analytical skills acquired here for fun, for the simple pleasure of translating what may appear to be individual troubles and experiences into social problems and group phenomena, or for utilization in planning social action programs. For the future citizen and potential parent, the Sociology of Education offers some understanding of the relationship between educational policy and the economic, political, and social life of the nation.

We have all been students; many of us have been or will be teachers or school administrators. All of us are citizens, and many are already voters. Our lives and our futures are inextricably entwined with education. We should do our best to understand it.

## NOTES

[1]Judson T. Landis, "The Sociology Curriculum and Teacher Training," *American Sociological Review*, 12 (February, 1947), pp. 113–16.

[2]For a more detailed discussion of the divergence between the disciplines of education and sociology see Donald A. Hansen, "The Uncomfortable Relation of Sociology and Education," in *On Education: Sociological Perspectives*, eds. Donald A. Hansen and Joel E. Gerstl (New York: John Wiley and Sons, Inc., 1967), pp. 3–35.

[3]Gene F. Sommers and Richard L. Hough, *Educational Sociologists Survey of the American Sociological Association Section on the Sociology of Education* (n.p.: Center of Applied Sociology, 1970), p. 25.

[4]We are indebted to our late friend and mentor, David Street, for these insights.

[5]National Commission on Excellence in Education, *A Nation at Risk* (Washington, D.C.: U.S. Department of Education, 1983); Study Group on the Condition of Excellence in American Higher Education, *Involvement in Learning: Realizing the Potential of American Higher Education* (National Institute of Education: Washington, D.C., 1984).

[6]This discussion relies heavily upon that of Ralf Dahrendorf, *Class and Class Conflict in Industrial Society* (Stanford, Calif.: Stanford University Press, 1959), p. 161ff.

[7]Emile Durkheim, *The Division of Labor in Society*, trans. George Simpson (Glencoe, Ill.: The Free Press, 1960).

[8]Emile Durkheim, *Education and Sociology*, trans. Sherwood D. Fox (Glencoe, Ill.: The Free Press, 1956), p. 72.

[9]Ibid., p. 81.

[10]Ibid., p. 68.

[11]Emile Durkheim, *Moral Education*, trans. Everett K. Wilson and Herman Schaurer (New York: The Free Press, 1961).

[12]Durkheim, *Education and Sociology*, p. 81.

[13]Ibid., p. 89.

[14]Ibid., p. 79.

[15]Ibid., p. 89.

[16]Talcott Parsons, "The School System," *Harvard Educational Review*, 29 (Fall 1959).

[17]Ibid., p. 297.

[18]The following discussion draws heavily from Dahrendorf, *Class and Class Conflict in Industrial Society*, p. 162ff.

[19]Samuel Bowles, "Unequal Education and the Reproduction of the Social Division of Labor," in *Schooling in a Corporate Society*, ed. Martin Carnoy (New York: David McKay, Inc., 1972), pp. 36–64. See Samuel Bowles and Herbert Gintis, *Schooling in Capitalist America: Educational Reform and the Contradictions of Economic Life* (New York: Basic Books, 1976) for a more thorough discussion.

[20]Bowles, "Unequal Education," p. 41.

[21]Willard Waller, *The Sociology of Teaching* (New York: Russell and Russell, 1961). We should note that most sociologists probably would not identify Waller as a conflict theorist. Still, the themes of the conflict perspective appear quite clearly in his analysis of classroom dynamics, as shall presently be illustrated.

[22]Waller, *The Sociology of Teaching*, p. 10.

[23]Ibid., pp. 195–96.

[24]Ibid., p. 365.

[25]Orville G. Brim, Jr., *Sociology and the Field of Education* (New York: Russell Sage Foundation, 1958), p. 10. Brim was referring to the conclusions of Richard Conrad, "A Systematic Analysis of Current Researches in the Sociology of Education," *American Sociological Review*, 17 (1952), pp. 350–55.

[26]Harold D. Lasswell, "The Policy Orientation," in *The Policy Sciences: Recent Developments in Scope and Method*, eds. Daniel Lerner and Harold D. Lasswell (Stanford, Calif.: Stanford University Press, 1951), pp. 3–15.

[27]Neal Gross, "Some Contributions of Sociology to the Field of Education," *Harvard Educational Review*, 29 (Fall, 1959), p. 87.

# CHAPTER TWO
# THE FUNCTIONS AND USES OF EDUCATIONAL INSTITUTIONS: COMPARATIVE PERSPECTIVES

In most modern societies, educational institutions are considered key instruments of social purpose. Governments formulate explicit educational policies and finance educational institutions on the assumption that education is necessary for both order and progress. On the one hand, education is expected to maintain hallowed traditions: respect for authority, obedience to the law, patriotism, and the like. On the other hand, education is expected to promote political, economic, and social development.

This much seems clear enough. However, the task of enumerating and empirically validating a specific list of educational functions and uses for any given society is a difficult one. Official goals and statements of purpose are often ignored or contradicted in everyday practice, and cannot be assumed to reflect the practical operation of the system. Furthermore, official programs generally have unanticipated and sometimes undesired consequences. How can we be certain to include all of the hidden effects of education, and how can we assess which educational effects are intentional and which accidental?

An analysis of a society's values might be helpful in guiding us to its central educational goals; but it is often unclear which values should be used. In pluralistic societies, the values of various subgroups may diverge dramatically, and no one group may be sufficiently powerful to control the shape of education in any stable way. For example, in the United States urban white ethnic groups are among those that approve the inclusion of prayers and other religious observances in the schools. Other groups support the constitutional requirement of a strict separation of church and state. These latter groups can cite numerous court rulings in their favor. Nevertheless, the struggle between these two opposing camps is far from over. Conservative local, state, and national politicians regularly advocate school prayer. President Ronald Reagan even suggested that a constitutional amendment should be adopted, if necessary, to make prayer in school possible. At times, one group achieves sufficient influence to introduce religious elements into some schools; state laws are introduced that permit some forms of religious observances in the schools, or administrators are persuaded to add a prayer to the daily classroom routine. Then the opposing groups must muster their forces and go to court again. At any one time or place the educational system might reflect the goals and values of only one of these two groups, but neither set of values can be ignored.

Educational systems differ in the extent to which they accommodate wide ranges of values within society. Our own educational system is relatively decentralized, permitting more responsiveness to local pressure groups than systems that are totally administered at a national level. Nevertheless, it is always difficult to determine which group's values and goals are most influential in shaping the educational process at any given time and place. Another problem in isolating the functions and uses of educational systems in modern societies is the rapidity of social change. Educational systems are shaped by large-scale social trends such as urbanization, industrialization, and professionalization. We will be discussing these trends and their influence on education later in this book, but for now let us simply say that the functions and uses of education alter as societies go through economic, political, and social developments such as these.

The difficulties inherent in the search for educational functions and uses are not, however, insurmountable. Some preliminary steps can be taken. An important first step is to sensitize ourselves to the wide range of possible variations in the functions and uses of education. A partial list and discussion follows in the next section. This list was derived, in part, from an analysis of variations in educational systems through time and in different societies. In this chapter, we will present brief sketches of some of these systems for you. Particularly, we will describe education in the U.S.S.R, China, and Africa. These sketches cannot give a total comprehension of what education is and has been like in these diverse parts of the world, but it can give at least some basic feel for the variety of possibilities that exist. Later in this book, we will be talking primarily about the United States. It is hoped that these cross-cultural illustrations will help you put the American experience in better perspective.

## CONTRIBUTIONS OF EDUCATION TO SOCIAL STABILITY AND CHANGE

Educational institutions are generally considered to be highly conservative. This is because cultural reproduction is one of the primary effects of formal systems of education.[1] Schools are always at least partially responsible for the transfer from one generation to the next of society's beliefs, values, sentiments, knowledge, and patterns of behavior. This process of socialization is conservative in that it perpetuates current cultural patterns and discourages deviation from them.

At the same time, however, educational institutions can and do contribute to social change. At minimum, schools are required to modify the content of their curricula so that they reflect new scientific and technological advances. Changing norms and beliefs might also be incorporated so that each succeeding generation learns something new and different.

Broadly speaking, then, education can be used for both conservative and dynamic purposes. Let us turn to each of these in greater detail.

### Education as a Conservative Institution

Because cultures are not inborn, it is necessary that they be taught to each new generation. In small, preindustrial settings, or "folk societies," this task can be accomplished through the simple means of including the young in adult activities so that they may observe, imitate, and learn through doing. In these ways children acquire the language, values, world view, and skills of their culture. Under circumstances such as these, all adults are teachers, and there are few, if any, special places or times when learning is formally supposed to occur.[2] From the beginning, the tasks children are asked to learn are considered important for their own and society's survival and so there are no questions of "relevance" or "motivation." Everything that is learned is useful and tied directly to daily life. But this is possible only as long as a culture is relatively undifferentiated and static. With modernization, culture becomes more complex and differentiated. Social change is rapid. The forces of change discussed by Durkheim and Bowles (described in Chapter 1) make the transmission of culture from each generation to the next more problematic. Institutionalized schooling becomes necessary for *cultural reproduction*.

Basic to the process of cultural reproduction is teaching youth to love and revere the established and traditional institutions of society. These usually include the family, religion, the government, and the general economic system. The early years of education are particularly important in developing these attachments, because early loyalties to these basic institutions are likely to persist. These attachments are formed before the child is capable of rational evaluation and criticism.

Schools present children with highly idealized pictures of their social institutions. They encourage the expression of allegiance through colorful rituals, oaths, songs, drama, and dance. In the United States, even kindergarten-aged children are generally required to salute the flag each day and to sing patriotic songs. If you have ever asked a young child to explain the meaning of such terms as "allegiance" or "indivisible" or "under God," you are aware that this pledge has emotional, but not cognitive, meaning for this age group.

In the process of learning reverence for established institutions, children also learn the traditional values upon which these institutions are built. It is during childhood that individuals are most susceptible to *value socialization.*[3] It is because we all recognize the importance of this early socialization that there are perennial struggles over which values should be taught in the schools. There is also considerable anxiety about the influence of teachers as models for children's values and character. Willard Waller has referred to American schools, especially those in rural areas, as "museums of virtue."[4] By this he meant that communities often want their schools and their teachers to teach the "old time virtues," or those values which they believe are central to the "American Way of Life," even when they know that most people do not actually live up to these values on a daily basis. In the United States, some of these central values include commitments to hard work, rugged individualism, private property, God, the traditional family, democracy, equality, law and order, and an active, practical orientation to life.

Schools make an explicit effort to teach these values, and plan curriculum and pedagogical techniques with them in mind. A school teacher in the Soviet Union may well ask the class "Which row can sit the straightest?" while an American counterpart may ask "Which student can sit the straightest?" The Soviet teacher encourages solidarity and conformity within groups by promoting competition between them. The American teacher promotes individualism and competitiveness by comparing each child to all of the others.

As schools inculcate values and loyalty to society's traditional institutions, they also serve as mechanisms of *social control.* You may recall from Chapter 1 that Durkheim saw individual egoism as a threat to social order and that he believed the schools could reduce this threat through moral education. As we pointed out, individuals who internalize society's values will be self-policing and supportive of the social order.

The school also functions as a mechanism of social control in the ways that Bowles described. If we believe that our traditional institutions are both legitimate and just, we will usually ignore evidence to the contrary, or suggest that there are only minor problems that can be worked out without radical change.

The school is used to maintain social control in a rather direct sense as well. Schools function as custodial institutions for the nation's young. In the United States, education is compulsory five days a week, ten months of the year. School attendance keeps children off the streets and, relatively speaking, out of trouble for much of the time. Children are confined, in groups, to special buildings in which they can be closely supervised and kept constructively busy. Extracurricular activities extend this supervision into after school hours and drain off youthful energy into acceptable channels. The schools also monitor children's personality development and behavior to make certain they are not tending toward destructive or criminal patterns. Referrals are sometimes made to counselors, social workers, and psychologists when behavior becomes too deviant or threatening. The importance of the use of schools for direct control over the young is highlighted by the efforts communities make each summer to find alternative ways of keeping "kids off the streets" when school is out. Jobs, supervised recreation, and summer camp programs are among the common school substitutes communities support.

Another way in which educational institutions promote social order and control is through the *assimilation* of subgroups whose values differ from those of the dominant group. We mentioned in Chapter 1 that many Americans supported the establishment of compulsory mass education out of fear for the potential disruptiveness of foreign immigrants. Schools in the United States were explicitly expected to strip immigrant children of their traditional cultures and inculcate American values and behaviors. From the perspective of the immigrants, American education meant radical change rather than cultural reproduction. This change was not always welcomed, of course, and it often had destructive effects on family life and individual self-concepts. We classify this educational effect as conservative, however, because although it means change for one group, it also means assured stability for those groups already dominant in the society. Whenever schooling is made compulsory and universal in a pluralistic society, assimilation is likely to be one of its central effects.

It has often been argued, of course, that schools can and should be used to *maintain subgroup traditions*, and thereby strengthen cultural pluralism.[5] In the United States, some programs in black, Puerto Rican, Indian, and other ethnic studies have been offered with this purpose in mind. Currently, instruction is being given in native languages, especially Spanish, in a number of schools, and there has been considerable debate whether dialects, such as black English, should be used as well. The impacts of such programs are not yet clear. Proponents argue that they can improve the self-esteem of minority groups, increase group solidarity, and enhance achievement. Opponents argue that they merely accentuate group differences, arouse intergroup hostility, and retard the full integration of subgroups into the "mainstream" of American life. Whatever the merits of the case, it is certainly true that the emphasis in American schools has been on assimilation, even when some efforts to respect and maintain subgroup traditions were attempted. The contemporary use of standardized textbooks and instructional materials and the centralization of teacher training, certification, and placement virtually assures that this will be the case even when some recognition of minority cultures is given in language, history, or other areas of study.

Schools, then, develop citizens for the state, ready to support its values and institutions. Even when schools seem to stress teaching purely cognitive skills, the broader goal of providing citizens is at work. For example, it is often argued that an informed and well-educated public is necessary for intelligent voting in a democratically oriented nation, and that the long-term preservation of public influence over political decisions requires a literate and assertive population.

Futhermore, all modern societies, democratic or not, require an educated workforce. Maintenance of high levels of technical and economic productivity demands literate workers and an adequate supply of individuals trained in highly complex technical and professional fields. The *training and development of competent workers* is, then, another primary function of the schools. As we shall see later, the effects of education on workers can increase pressures for social change as well as serve to stabilize traditional institutions. For now, however, we will stress the conservative aspects of this function.

First, schools can be used to assure an adequate number of workers in specialized but critical areas. For example, governments may respond to a shortage of scientists by offering scholarships and other financial inducements to science majors, opening new scientific academies, expanding science programs in high schools and colleges, and so on. Industries in need of scientists might publicize the high pay and benefits scientists can receive by recruiting on college compuses. They might also encourage high schools and colleges to expand science courses by providing financial subsidies, equipment, consultants, and student aid. In these and other ways schools are routinely used to provide an adequate supply of trained workers.

Second, schools can be used to motivate workers to commit themselves to their careers and occupations. We have already mentioned the fact that schools teach obedience to authority, punctuality, responsibility for one's work, and so on. Schools also teach us to see our worth as human beings in terms of occupational success. Men, particularly, are taught from an early age that failure in the labor market means failure as a person.

In all modern societies educational credentials are closely linked to occupational placement. One reason for this is that schools obviously teach the cognitive, technical, and vocational skills required for job performance. However, studies to be reviewed in Chapter 4 have shown that educational credentials and occupational activities are not always logically linked.[6] For example, jobs that involve only skilled labor may require a high school diploma, or jobs filled in the past by high school graduates may now require a college degree. Often, employers are aware that the skills required on the job have little overlap with the skills workers have acquired in their schools. Still, they persist in demanding seemingly unnecessary credentials. When asked, employers indicate that they believe that educational credentials represent more than just cognitive or technical skills: Educational credentials indicate that the individual has been successfully socialized in ways important to the employer. A diploma, then, indicates that an individual is at least minimally reliable. The graduate has managed to get to school on time, complete assignments, follow orders, stay out of trouble, and generally display the kinds of behavior desired by the employer. Employers use educational success as a measure of socialization to work-supportive attitudes and behaviors.

The link between educational credentials and occupational placement highlights another function that educational systems can fulfill, one which we mentioned in Chapter 1. Educational institutions play an important role in the *selection and allocation* of individuals for various positions in society. Contemporary systems of education in industrialized societies are usually based on universal compulsory primary education; that is, all the children of the society must receive at least a minimal education. But only some children are permitted to continue on to receive higher levels of training. This training becomes increasingly differentiated: first, into vocational, technical, and academic programs, and later into finer categories directed at more specific occupational slots. These slots bring with them differential pay, prestige, and power, so that allocation to occupational slots also means allocation to social strata or classes as well. As we indicated in Chapter 1, there is considerable controversy in the United States regarding the bases upon which this selection and allocation is made. Since we are now stressing the conservative functions of education, however, we will emphasize that schools often select and allocate in ways that reproduce social hierarchies in each succeeding generation.

One circumstance under which schools clearly *reproduce social hierarchies* is when the educational opportunities offered to various social strata are radically different from each other. For example, there may be no system of publicly supported education. Under this circumstance, only families that already have money can afford to send their children off to school, and only these children will qualify for high-status positions afterward. Or there may be publicly supported primary education, but only privately supported higher education, and so on. Historically, it has been common to limit formal education to the children of the elite, while keeping the masses illiterate. At other times, schooling has been more broadly available, but rigidly stratified. The children of the middle and working classes have sometimes received only technical-vocational training, whereas the children of the elite received a broad classical education. The classical curriculum was designed to prepare students for a lifestyle of leisure and authority; it was an education for "cultivation" rather than for practical expertise.[7]

It has also been common for schools to explicitly consider students' ascribed characteristics in admissions procedures. Throughout most of the first half of this century, racial, sexual, and social class quotas were explicitly used in the admissions procedures of many American colleges and universities. Even if certain characteristics, like being Jewish, did not totally destroy a student's chances for admission, possessing other characteristics (such as a father who was an alumnus) often gave other students the winning edge. Today many colleges still give preference to alumni children in the admissions process. Many also consider ascribed characteristics in their attempts to get a "balanced" or "well rounded" class.

Once admitted, ascribed characteristics often continue to affect students' experiences. For example, until late in the eighteenth century, students at Harvard were listed according to their father's positions.[8] Working-class youth in prestigious colleges often found their lives miserable. Their financial and social limitations kept them from sharing the leisurely and luxurious life of their affluent classmates. Poor and minority students still often complain about feeling alienated on some college campuses. Of course, diplomas from elite institutions are more prestigious than those from publicly supported institutions. They may carry considerably more weight in entrance into graduate or professional schools or in obtaining positions with elite national firms.

Finally, as we mentioned earlier, educational institutions can teach ideologies that *legitimize social inequalities* and support the dominant group. When this ideology stresses the openness of the system and the opportunities it offers everyone for upward mobility, the educational system might, in fact, permit a limited amount of such upward mobility. These few cases can be used as examples to the rest, as living proof that the system is, in fact, legitimate.

In summary, it is clear that the conservative functions and uses of education are numerous and widespread. They include cultural reproduction through the transmission of knowledge, values, attitudes, perceptions, and behavior patterns from one generation to the next. They include social control, through both socialization and direct supervision. They include the provision of patriotic citizens and the development of a competent and motivated workforce. Educational institutions also may be responsible for selecting and allocating individuals to occupational and other positions within the society. The mechanisms through which this selection and allocation occur can be used to assure the reproduction in each succeeding generation of existing social inequalities.

## Education and Social Change

Although education often functions to stablize and maintain the status quo, it can also promote social change and contribute to social unrest in a number of ways.

One of the important functions of education in contemporary societies is that of *cultural production*. By this we mean that colleges and universities, especially, are expected to be centers of research and development. Government agencies, private foundations, and large businesses invest vast sums of money in university-based research each year. Many university employees devote themselves entirely to research activities. Others, of course, teach and fulfill administrative responsibilities, but even these employees may be expected to engage in creative work. Professors may teach you what we know so far in each particular special area, but they are also expected to contribute to and expand that current body of information.

Along with doing research, professors write books and articles, create works of art, and design equipment. The phrase "publish or perish" refers to the expectation that faculty members will not only teach and do research but also that they will successfully disseminate their creative contributions beyond their own individual colleges and universities. In other words, these educational institutions perform the function of *cultural diffusion*[9] as well as cultural production. A similar function is performed when academics participate in the formulation of social policy. As we indicated in Chapter 1, researchers are often asked to indicate what applications the abstract ideas created in the academic world might have elsewhere in society.

Even high schools and primary schools are used for cultural diffusion. They diffuse not only new information but attitudes, values, and ways of viewing the world that may facilitate and encourage social change. When primary schools began teaching the "new math," they not only diffused knowledge about set theory but also introduced approaches to mathematical concepts that are basic to the widespread understanding and spread of computerization.

An important question to ask about cultural diffusion is: "Which culture is being diffused?" Clearly, not all new ideas get published, and not all new ideas get incorporated into public school curriculum. Conflict theorists might argue, for example, that in the United States only relatively conservative research projects are actually funded, and that teachers committed to radical ideas are often fired. And some groups will resist new ideas if they threaten cherished ideals. For example, religious fundamentalists in the United States resist the teaching of evolution and are currently resisting curricula that they feel will promote liberalization of attitudes toward drugs, sex, and other matters. Nevertheless, our cross-cultural comparisons will indicate that education has been used to diffuse radically new information and ideas, especially in societies undergoing rapid development.

For example, during periods of rapid industrialization and modernization, education has been used to teach new values (such as achievement, competition, and instrumental activism) and new habits (such as saving and punctuality) in order to facilitate economic development. The use of schools to teach a scientific belief system as opposed to a religious or magical one is also a common occurrence under modernization efforts. Actually, whenever there is an emphasis on scientific thinking, there is a tendency to undermine religious, magical, and heavily ideological belief systems. Science is built on principles of experimentation, objectivity, and critical evaluation, and requires the continuous questioning and testing of ideas. These orientations can undermine commitments to more traditional values and beliefs.

This effect of education on values and beliefs is actually another important way in which education can contribute to social change. Education can *promote the critical analysis of traditional institutions.* For example, Paulo Friere, a Brazilian educator, developed a method of teaching adult peasants to read that focused on the initial learning of politically important words, like *patron*, the Spanish word for wealthy landowner.[10] According to Friere, attention to highly significant politically oriented words dramatically increased the motivation to learn, and, at the same time, offered peasants an opportunity to develop a "critical consciousness." Their ability to analyze critically the economic order under which they lived was thereby enhanced.

In many countries, especially in the West, higher education, particularly, involves an intense and often critical analysis of institutions and values. Research suggests that one effect of higher education is to create a more skeptical attitude toward traditional institutions and liberalize social and political attitudes.[11] Even at the elementary or high school levels, education might have this effect. The diversity of views presented in American schools prompted at least one visiting Soviet educator to comment:

> It's obvious to me from reading your books that you Americans don't agree on a set of values to be transmitted to your children. Your books try to deal with every side of a question. Ours, admittedly, present only one side. It seems to me that you must create unimaginable confusion.[12]

There is still controversy about these diverse views in the United States.

Critics label as "secular humanism" any curriculum that seems to teach the relativity of human values and institutions. They see this as a threat to family and church.

In our previous section, we discussed the contributions that educational institutions can make to the maintenance of traditional social inequalities. In some cases, however, educational institutions have been responsible for the development of a new elite stratum. At other times, education has been used in an attempt to eliminate all elites and create a more equalitarian system. Education contributes to the creation of a new elite most often under conditions of rapid modernization. As more people are encouraged to acquire sophisticated technological and scientific skills, they may develop into a new educated elite. Their influence will grow because of the key role they must play in their country's development. Interestingly, the development of an educated stratum may occur more rapidly than the ability of a modernizing economic system to employ its members. In these cases, the educated group may be a source of social unrest and instability.

An excellent example of an attempt to use educational institutions to promote social equality exists in China. We will be discussing this example in detail in the next section of this chapter. However, in considerably less dramatic terms, many contemporary educational systems are designed to permit a certain amount of social mobility. In Chapter 8 we will focus on the interrelationships between social stratification and education in the United States. As we shall see, our system does permit large numbers of individuals born into diverse social class, racial, and ethnic groups to acquire a higher education and to rise into the upper middle-class.[13] In other words, educational institutions can be used to *alter or modify traditional socioeconomic hierarchies.*

Finally, it should be noted that universities throughout the world have often been centers for *rebellion and revolutionary ferment.* Students are often both idealistic and highly political. They tend, for many of the reasons we have already discussed, to be critical of the establishment. Perhaps because they are yet unfettered by either their own children or their own careers, they are also energetic, vocal, and willing to take risks. In this regard, it might be noted that some colleges and universities have actually institutionalized this critical stance and activist orientation. Departments and curricula have been developed with strong commitments to social change. Black Studies and Women Studies programs are excellent examples.[14]

In summary, educational institutions can clearly contribute to social change. Colleges and universities are centers of creative thought and discovery and all contemporary educational institutions disseminate new knowledge and values to younger generations. Because they disseminate new knowledge and attitudes, educational institutions can be used to prepare populations for modernization. In this process, educational institutions may be used to create new elite strata or promote greater social equality. They can both modify and transform traditional socioeconomic hierarchies. Finally, because education promotes critical attitudes and analysis, schools may contribute to skepticism toward traditional institutions and become bases of rebellion or revolution.

## COMPARATIVE PERSPECTIVES ON THE USES OF EDUCATION

We have discussed at some length the conservative and change-stimulating potentials of education. Now it is important to illustrate these more concretely. The wide range of actual goals and structures of educational institutions can be best seen through historical and cross-cultural comparisons. Thus, we now turn to brief sketches of the educational systems of China, the Union of Soviet Socialist Republics, and the African nations.

Educational systems of different countries can be compared on many dimensions—quality, quantity, internal structure and differentiation, goals, materials, resources, teaching techniques, effectiveness, curricula, mechanisms of social control, and so on. Because of limitations of current knowledge and space it is obvious that we cannot deal systematically with all of these dimensions of variation. Our goal is to illustrate the range of functions and uses of education, however, and so we have chosen materials that we believe highlight these issues best.

### Education in the Soviet Union

The Russian Tsars of the nineteenth century struggled to maintain a traditional feudal society in the face of rising pressures toward modernity. Yet, their educational policies permitted the development of a national system of education which, under Communist leadership, was eventually transformed into one of the strongest and most rigorous in the world.[15]

Education under the nineteenth-century Tsars was designed to indoctrinate students in the virtues of "Orthodoxy, Autocracy, and Nationalism."[16] There was a heavy emphasis on religion and patriotism throughout the curriculum. There was strict censorship of texts and lectures, prohibitions against study in foreign lands and the use of foreign teachers, insistence on the use of Russian for instructional purposes—even in areas in which this was not the native language—and abolition of all student and teacher organizations. Academic freedom was eradicated and secret police often disguised themselves as students in order to check on unorthodox ideas expressed by students or teachers.

These measures were designed to assure that students would be socialized to support the reign of the Tsars. Considerable efforts were made to insulate Russian youth from the intellectual ferment of other European countries, especially those which had experienced a revolution, and protest demonstrations by dissatisfied students or teachers were brutally repressed through the use of Cossack troops.

The system itself was highly stratified and clearly functioned to reproduce the Russian social hierarchy. The children of the aristocracy had their own exclusive and expensive private schools and tutors. Their education was classical in content and of generally high quality. The children of the middle classes received a more limited technical and vocational education. The children of the great masses of rural and urban poor remained unschooled and illiterate.

Superimposed on class inequalities were biases based on sex, religion, and region. Jews were discriminated against and generally denied access to higher education. Rural schools, especially in the southern and interior eastern areas, were of inferior quality.

Despite Tsarist efforts to use educational institutions to legitimize the traditional social order, Russian universities became centers of revolutionary thought, writing, and action. In the end, Tsarist repression failed. Many leaders of the Revolution of 1914 were students.

The creation of new educational institutions was a high priority of the Bolsheviks once they achieved power. In line with Marxist ideology, the new "unified labor school" was to be open to children of both sexes, all the social classes, and all religious groups. The previous system had been designed to maintain a rigidly stratified social order led by an aristocratic elite that despised common labor. The new schools were designed to level all social classes and to inculcate positive attitudes toward labor and laborers.

The schools were explicitly used as tools of the state. They were specifically employed to eradicate the previous social order, secularize the population, and develop commitment to collective rather than individualistic goals. A massive adult literacy program was launched, to help lay the foundation for industrialization and solidify loyalty to the new order.

Lenin's wife, Krupskaya, was a follower of the progressive American educator John Dewey. Under her influence, the new schools became permissive, child-centered, and closely tied to the problems of the community. At times these principles were institutionalized in an extreme form:

> Boundless freedom was given to the pupils. Those who won the revolution believed they could capture the young generation by freeing it from the harsh discipline from which they had to suffer and they rushed to the opposite extreme. The school was turned into a republic run by the students. They decided what and how to study. The authority of the teacher declined. He was only a guide and a comrade. Corporal punishment was forbidden. Examinations and marks were abolished, homework given up, textbooks despised.[17]

The oppression of the Russian classroom, like the oppression of the larger society, was to be abolished. The values and pedagogy of the new schools were to be consistent with the values of the new social order.

Nevertheless, the new permissiveness did not always extend from students to their teachers. There was considerable concern about the loyalties of teachers to the Bolshevik regime. Many teachers, of course, were representatives of the middle- and upper-middle classes, and it was feared that they might subvert the nation's youth. Consequently, students were encouraged to inform on their teachers, and sometimes even encouraged to inform on their parents. Not that everyone supported this idea. Pavlik Morozov, a young Pioneer and student of the period, testified in court against his father and was lynched by the townspeople in revenge. He was, however, later venerated as a revolutionary martyr by Soviet youth.

The Progressive period of Soviet education was short-lived. Industrialization required a skilled and disciplined workforce. Stalin soon directed a strengthening of the school curriculum (especially in the area of science), a return to the authority of the teacher, and a more rigorous system of student evaluation. By the onset of World War II the Russian school was heavily academic in orientation. Students spent twelve hours a day studying, and the earlier idea that students should spend time doing "productive labor" in the factories was abandoned.

The war created new problems, however. Among these was an acute labor shortage. As a result, students were again required to participate in factory and farm labor, and curriculum requirements were reduced. This policy was sometimes subverted in the schools, however. Despite the centralization of educational administration and the supervision of the Communist Party, school principals simply kept their brightest students in the classroom when the others were sent to the fields and the factories.[18]

### Contemporary Issues

Our knowledge of the detailed workings of Soviet education is limited by a general lack of published research and materials. Therefore, we must piece together our account from official documents, newspaper articles, and personal observations, some of which were made by trained social scientists.

Much has been written about the Soviet Union's commitment to early childhood education.[19] In major cities there is a wide network of public day-care facilities available to the children of working parents. These facilities are often located in the factories in which the children's parents work. Use of these facilities is, of course, optional. Approximately 85 percent of Soviet women work full-time during most of their childbearing years, and use of day-care facilities is certainly widespread. However, many Soviet parents do not make use of them. Instead, they prefer to leave their children in the care of a *babushka*, or elderly grandmother. Also, in some areas of the country—outside of major metropolitan areas—adequate facilities are much more difficult to find. As a result, only about one-third of all Soviet children have any experience in a public day-care center, nursery, or kindergarten before they enter school at the age of seven.

Once children enter school their days are long and busy. A few go off to boarding schools, but most stay home and attend local schools on a daily basis. There is apparently considerable controversy among teachers, parents, and school administrators over the amount of work demanded from students, beginning with the seven-year-olds in first grade. Even at this early age children are expected to do between two and three hours of homework each night. This amount increases through the grades to the point that children have little or no time for leisure. Educational reformers and parents have objected to this system as depriving youngsters of their childhood.

In 1973 a primary education of eight years was made compulsory throughout the Soviet Union. Compulsion was deemed necessary to keep rural youth from dropping out of school and to overcome the resistance of some ethnic groups to sending their daughters to school. Upon graduation from the eight-year school, students are encouraged to complete their secondary education with two or more years of general, academic, or vocational/technical education in a variety of institutional settings. Upon graduation the great majority enter the workforce. All those who complete their secondary education are eligible to pursue higher education, although relatively few actually do so.

Soviet institutions of higher education are state owned, supported, and managed with the explicit purpose of meeting the skill requirements of an advanced industrial society. Only one-quarter of secondary school graduates gain admission to these highly selective and narrowly specialized vocational institutes.[20] The numbers of students admitted are limited in accordance with employers' requests for trained personnel. In most, if not all, cases there are many applicants for each available place. Competition for training in certain popular specialties such as medicine, education, and the humanities is especially fierce.[21] The primary means of selection from among the surfeit of applicants is a rigorous entrance examination. The fortunate few who pass and are accepted receive high-quality training at state expense. No tuition is charged, and many students receive living expenses so that they may pursue their studies full time. Graduating students have no trouble gaining employment in their specialized fields.

Although in theory all Soviet citizens have equal access to higher education, there is evidence of sex, class, and religious bias. Although female students outperform males in school and on admissions tests, males are often admitted before them. Discriminatory admissions quotas arise because employers often specifically request *male* graduates. They consider this to be economically rational because the work careers of men are less likely to be disrupted by domestic and childrearing tasks.[22] Surveys indicate that students in the institutes are drawn disproportionately from well-educated, urban, professional families. They are advantaged not only by virtue of their relatively rich socialization experiences within the family but also by the extensive tutorial services that their parents can afford.[23] Finally, religious discrimination apparently enters into the selection process. In 1983 a dissident intellectual named Valery Senderov was sentenced to seven years in prison after releasing a study that showed that Jews applying for admittance to Moscow State University's mathematics department were given harder examinations and graded more harshly than other applicants.[24] As Dobson points out:

> Given the ideological insistence upon egalitarianism and the superiority of socialism over capitalism, the pattern of inequality in access to higher education continues to be a politically sensitive subject in the USSR.[25]

From nursery school on there is a heavy moralistic component in Soviet education, not only in curricular content but also in the structure of everyday school life. Infants share playpens so that they feel part of the collective from the start, and peer groups continue to be important throughout the educational process. Competitions are arranged between groups, not individuals, and teachers are trained to emphasize the precedence of group over individual needs.

Both Marxist ideology and Soviet educational psychology emphasize environmental determinism in human learning. The importance of group influences on achievement rather than genetic or individual personality characteristics are the focus of attention.[26] Classes are expected to advance at a relatively uniform rate, with the quicker students helping the slower ones. Older classes are often asked to "adopt" younger ones and help them adjust to school. Students who do not learn satisfactorily are seen as lazy and poorly motivated rather than less intelligent. It is the responsibility of the entire class to see that those students' work improves.

Many visitors to the Soviet Union have noted that this system produces young people who are exceptionally well behaved and socially responsible. But there are those who argue that the emphasis on conformity, group learning, and rote memorization is incompatible with the development of critical and independent thinking. These attributes seem necessary to continued economic development, especially in terms of developing scientific thinkers and technological innovators. Reformers have had some success in developing acceptable curricula, inspired by American high school science and math programs, which promote more critical approaches.

The difficult task is to confine this critical capacity to the sciences and not have it extend to areas of Marxist-Leninist ideology. Indeed, Jacoby recounts the story of an excellent urban school—Moscow Physical-Mathematical School 2—that attracted students from long distances because of its peculiarly stimulating intellectual environment.[27] Ultimately, it was closed because the students' "prove it" orientation extended too far. The contradictions between the goals of developing critical scientific thinking and uncritical acceptance of political dogma present a severe dilemma for the system. Students in Soviet institutions of higher education, like their counterparts throughout the world, mock the inefficiencies, pomposities, and hypocricies of government officials—and take considerable risks in so doing.[28] Communist Party officials appear to be nervous about college professors as well. During a meeting of the Communist Party's Central Committee in 1983, faculty members were warned to adhere strictly to ideological guidelines.

> Above all, the social sciences must be undeviatingly guided by revolutionary theory. There are truths which are not subject to revision, problems which were solved long ago and which brook no other solution.[29]

### Education in the People's Republic of China

The ancient Chinese established a national system of formal education approximately 4,000 years ago.[30] The schools were few in number and privately supported. Their curriculum was rigorous and designed to develop a small elite that could guide and control the masses. This elite was chosen on the basis of their ability to pass standard nation wide examinations that covered such widely variant skills as archery, horsemanship, musical ability, knowledge of Confucian teachings, public rituals, arithmetic, and calligraphy. Passage of the examinations qualified men for appointments as highly honored government officials called *mandarins*. Emperors—even dynasties—came and went, but these Chinese officials remained a stable characteristic of Chinese society.

Because the tests used to recruit officials were uniform and open to students from any social background, they have often been cited as the forerunners of modern civil service examinations and as channels of social mobility in an otherwise static society. Yet the system clearly favored the children of the elite. Only the wealthy could afford to establish schools, send their sons to be educated there, and pay the bribes examiners often expected before giving the students a passing grade. It has been estimated that only one or two percent of the aspirants passed the examinations each time they were given, and not all of those who passed actually received a government appointment. Once appointed, advancement in the hierarchy of public offices required even further study. This extremely selective system was successful in creating an educated elite whose chief service was to act as guardians of an elaborate and highly developed cultural tradition. Their rigid and esoteric education was not conducive to either practical competence or critical thinking, but the system survived until the nineteenth century. Then came decades of war, invasion, colonial exploitation, and revolution, during which the system finally collapsed.

In 1905 an Imperial edict abolished the traditional system of education and examinations. During the years that followed, there were continuing efforts to develop new, stable, and effective educational institutions. During the first four decades after the end of the old system, attempts were made by successive governments to expand educational opportunities, modernize and westernize the curriculum, and attack the problem of illiteracy among the masses. John Dewey and other prominent Western educators were brought in and consulted regarding educational development. Many students were sent abroad and returned with a modern commitment to technology, science, specialization, professionalism, and efficiency.

It was not until the success of the Communist Revolution in 1949, however, that political stability was once again achieved and new educational institutions successfully established. For the first eight years after the revolution, the Chinese attempted to transform education by using the modern Soviet system as a model. First, they worked to establish universal literacy and equal educational opportunity. They also used the schools as agencies of political socialization. Pupils were expected to be actively committed to socialist ideals and to guard against insidious tendencies toward selfishness, individualism, and elitism. The schools were supposed to graduate youth who were both "red and expert"— "inheritors of the revolution" who possessed the determination and skill to promote rapid industrialization.

Because the People's Republic of China is a poor agricultural nation with a severe shortage of qualified teachers, it was impossible to provide the highest quality education for all students. Thus, government officials decided to allocate a disproportionate amount of their limited resources for the creation of a special, high quality, "key school" system for the very best students. Because of its expense they also limited access to higher education, admitting only those who were able to pass rigorous entrance examinations. Although these measures were dissonant with their egalitarian values, the pragmatic decision was made to speed the creation of a scientific/technical community whose duty it was to create a higher standard of living for all by expediting the process of industrialization.

Over time, criticism of the new meritocratic educational system mounted and an anti-Soviet nationalism swept over China. During the Great Leap Forward (1957 to 1961), a number of egalitarian reforms were instituted, including the expansion of primary schooling in rural areas and the introduction of political and class criteria into the admissions processes. These new policies were designed to enhance educational opportunities, especially of the revolutionary, yet largely illiterate, agricultural workers. However, some of these egalitarian reforms had already been reversed when the Great Cultural Revolution began in 1966.

In large part the Great Cultural Revolution was a violent political-ideological struggle over educational policy as related to national development and perpetuation of the proletarian revolution. The leader of the Chinese Communist Revolution, Mao Tse-tung, felt that by following the Soviet example in constructing an educational system geared to modernization, the Chinese had begun to create a new elite of experts who, like the literati of old, considered themselves better than the less-educated masses. The Great Cultural Revolution was a means of humbling these "bourgeois intellectuals." It was directed toward diminution of the authority, pride, and prestige of the intellectuals and also toward a rekindling of their revolutionary commitment to serving all the people. During that decade Mao and his followers attempted to eradicate sharp distinctions between laborers and intellectuals, and between manual and mental work, which were deeply rooted in traditional Chinese culture. School teachers, professors, and educational administrators were primary targets of this intense governmental campaign to transform the stratification system.

The revolutionary conception of education promoted during the Great Cultural Revolution contrasted sharply with the conventional, meritocratic education that had evolved in the People's Republic of China. Whereas the conventional system promoted competition and achievement with the aim of rapid modernization, the new system stressed the centrality of revolutionary values: cooperation, social responsibility, and equality. Under the old system educators were often strict and authoritarian with their students and relied heavily upon rote memorization. The students were expected to be diligent, respectful, and docile. Under the revolutionary system teacher–student relationships changed radically. "Politics in charge" was the motto of the day. In practice this meant that politicians, local revolutionary committees, and youth gangs—the Red Guards—assumed direct power over educators and educational institutions. The Red Guards mounted a reign of terror, and the educators whom they accused of harboring Western and elitist values were persecuted, humiliated, beaten, tortured, and sometimes murdered. Teachers, professors, and administrators were forced to make public confessions of their ideological sins and were paraded through the streets in dunce caps. Libraries, laboratories, and equipment were destroyed. Foreign-language teachers were despised as promoters of alien ideas and values. In general, students were encouraged to criticize their teachers and rebel against pedagogical authority. Conventional curricula and standards were rejected as elitist. Grades were deemphasized and students were passed from grade to grade even if they did not learn their lessons. The traditional course of study emphasized theory and book learning in preparation for competitive entrance examinations. Mao favored practical, on-the-job training; thus, he encouraged work/study programs and the establishment of schools in factories. Mao also felt that the intelligentsia could learn a great deal from the masses; hence, educators and other professionals were required to spend a part of each year working in the fields alongside peasants and being instructed by them. Because Mao considered entrance examinations instruments of class domination, he actively encouraged students to cheat on them. One prospective student handed in a blank examination and on the back wrote a criticism of the test as unfair to those who had been working in the fields. When the incident was publicized, the student was quickly elevated to the status of national hero and admitted to an agricultural school. Ultimately the examination system was swept away by the revolutionary tide and replaced by decentralized admissions procedures that emphasized ideological commitment rather than technical expertise. As we noted previously, the conventional system included a variety of schools including the selective and favored "key schools," regular full-time schools, and irregular part-time work/study programs. During the Great Cultural Revolution this differentiation was criticized for institutionalizing class inequality. As a result the policy of concentrating scarce resources in support of education on the key schools was abandoned. To meet the goal of universal primary education and approach the goal of universal secondary education, courses of study were shortened and excess funds redistributed. Primary education was reduced from six to five years, secondary education reduced from six to four years, and higher education reduced from four or five years to one or two years. Part-time work/study was expanded greatly.

During the height of the Great Cultural Revolution, Chinese schools, colleges, and universities shut down for various lengths of time. Virtually all primary schools were closed for at least one year and many were closed for two or three. Colleges and universities ceased operation for even longer periods, from four to six years.

Chairman Mao died in 1976. Less than a year later the Great Cultural Revolution that he launched came to an abrupt end with the arrest and imprisonment of Mao's wife and her three close associates (the "gang of four") who had lead the mass movement after Mao's death.

### Contemporary Issues

It was not long before it became clear that the new leadership considered that the educational policies pursued during the previous decade had been disastrous. They quickly reversed most of the revolutionary changes.

Once again pragmatic considerations were given priority over ideological ones, and all efforts were directed toward facilitation of industrial development. In 1977 a new slogan was introduced: "Respect teachers, love students." It was part of a general effort to bolster the prestige and authority of educators. Discipline was reinstated along with regular examinations. Grades and high achievement were stressed. The proportion of time which a student was expected to be working in productive labor was reduced dramatically. The old three-tier system of elite key schools, regular full-day schools, and part-time work/study schools was reestablished. Within schools the practice of grouping students according to achievement was reinstituted. Governance of schools by revolutionary committees was replaced by more normal administration under Communist Party supervision. In higher education, scientists were given much greater autonomy, and research facilities were improved. Professors were encouraged to undertake foreign study in order to understand the state of the art in their fields. Entrance examinations were reintroduced, although other criteria were also to be taken into consideration. There has been a return to the conventional curriculum with its focus on basic theory. The decentralization encouraged during the Great Cultural Revolution has been halted and reversed, with the central government playing a larger role in coordinating curriculum and policy.

Not everything has been reversed, however. The shortening of the primary and secondary educational experiences has been maintained, along with the practice of sending urban youth to the countryside upon graduation. However, students who gain admission to scientific, technical, and foreign-language programs are exempted and allowed to continue their training without interruption.

Many serious problems remain. The People's Republic of China is still a poor country that lacks the resources to satisfy the educational aspirations of its citizens. Until all schools can be brought up to the calibre of the keypoint schools, inequalities in educational opportunities will exist. For those who reached college age during the Cultural Revolution, it is too late for catching up. Referred to as the "lost generation," these people are now considered too old to be offered precious spots in the newly reopened universities. Furthermore, the new leadership may have trouble providing both the financial support and political stability necessary for rapid scientific and technological development. A new scientific elite may turn its back on socialist ideals. It will be difficult as always for political authorities to attain the balance they desire between academic freedom and ideological commitment.

Present policies are criticized by some because they give priority to achievement and merit over equality. Mass discontent could arise again.

## African Educational Institutions

Although education in every African nation is unique to some extent, there are certain basic similarities among many African educational systems. These are based in broadly similar colonial experiences, widespread poverty, and the common desire to become economically, politically, and culturally independent. In the following discussion, no attempt is made to deal with the full complexities of education in the various African nations. Rather, we focus on a few basics that illustrate the range of potential functions and uses of education.

Before colonialization, education in most of Africa was informal and based on close daily interaction between adults and children. Some tribes maintained a complex system of elaborate rituals, which inducted youth into adulthood, but others relied solely on simple instruction, observation, and imitation.[31] Along with practical information and skills needed for daily survival, older generations taught younger ones complex belief systems and values. These tended to be religious and magical in their orientation rather than secular and scientific. Although there was considerable variation in the extent to which boys and girls were segregated by sex, the specific content of each child's informal education frequently depended on his or her gender, both in terms of specific skills and in access to key religious mysteries and symbols. Through ritual songs, dances, storytelling, emulation, and rites of passage, each new generation learned to play the adult roles of their culture. In these ways, a multitude of diverse and complex cultures were maintained for centuries.

Africans had only limited contact with European culture prior to the period of colonialization—that is, from 1880 to 1914. What contact had occurred was with traders, missionaries, and explorers. The period of colonialization brought many radical changes, however. European nations, using advanced weapons unfamiliar to most Africans, seized vast territories, established new political boundaries, and imposed European beliefs and social patterns on indigenous populations. Government officials, missionaries, and settlers legitimized their exploitation in terms of the doctrines of white supremacy and the "white man's burden." These doctrines proclaimed the superiority of European culture and the obligation of whites to bring "civilization" and Christianity to the "heathens." The costs of bringing this new civilization to Africa were to be paid by the indigenous populations supposedly benefiting from it.[32]

Europeans institutionalized formal schooling. Missionaries established schools to teach children the gospel and to save their souls. The colonial governments also established schools, however. These were modeled after schools in Europe. Their purpose was to develop a stratum of Africans who could help administer the colonies by filling lower level civil service posts as translators, clerks, and the like. It was also assumed that educated Africans would quite naturally respect the European conception of law and order. In other words, these schools were also a way to ensure continued European dominance through political socialization. Children would be taught to value European culture and to denigrate their own. They would also be taught that European dominance was right and appropriate.

At the same time, there was some fear about educating the indigenous population. Education has a way of raising expectations and promoting a critical attitude toward established institutions. Many European settlers preferred that African education be limited to technical, vocational, or agricultural skills. This would be directly helpful to settlers who needed help developing the land. Of course, settlers wanted a traditional academic education available for their own children and established schools for this purpose as well.

Africans, however, had something else in mind; they wanted access to the wealth and power of Western nations. They were interested in schools as channels of social mobility and avenues to material success. According to Anderson in his history of education in Kenya, *The Struggle for the School,* Africans resisted missionary schools until they taught reading and writing in addition to religion.[33] Furthermore, many rejected programs of technical and agricultural education because these were seen as dead-end occupations. Africans wanted what they correctly perceived to be the most prestigious form of education, the classical academic education of the European elite. Those Africans who were wealthy enough to do so sought out this education in private schools, often sending their children abroad to be educated in European colleges and universities.

One result of this effort to acquire a classical education was the creation of a new African elite that shared the world view and prejudices of European colonizers. People became alienated from their own traditions. They left the land, their kin, and their tribes to live in urban centers that were heavily westernized. They were introduced to new belief systems and political ideologies. Tribal loyalties often conflicted with aspirations for social mobility and acceptance into the European-dominated upper strata. In some countries, this educated stratum was not able to find jobs commensurate with their level of training and sophistication, resulting in even greater alienation and dissatisfaction. Neither were they willing to accept such crucial but poorly paid jobs as that of rural school teacher.[34]

Ashby has noted how strongly Africans identified with the traditions of elite European universities. Many insisted upon classical curricula, on studying Greek and Latin and European history rather than native languages and cultures. Many insisted upon hospital-oriented British medical education when an emphasis upon public health and preventative medicine would have been more relevant to the African situation. In their desire to maintain European standards in institutions of higher education, many were impractical and rigid. For example, they failed to lower admissions standards even when facilities were being only partly utilized.[35]

### Contemporary Issues

New African nations share certain basic problems with all developing nations. How can economic growth be maximized while maintaining or even enhancing national and cultural integrity? How can the fruits of Western knowledge and technology be enjoyed without economic and cultural dependence? How can educational institutions be restructured to achieve a maximal balance between change in terms of development and continuity in terms of language, tradition, and culture?

Until quite recently the conventional wisdom was that poor nations could develop most rapidly by emulating Western systems of education. Such schools, colleges, and universities, were seen as critical mechanisms of modernization: overcoming tradition, superstition, and mysticism. Only they could teach the new moral values and technical skills necessary for economic expansion. From this perspective the road to economic development clearly involved the expansion and reform of colonial educational institutions.

Critics have argued that such institutions have actually hindered the developments they desire.

> According to this view, the most important effect of most educational systems is to contribute to the enrichment of a small minority, the exploitation of a majority and the dependence of all upon international economic and academic standards and values. This situation, it is claimed, arises because countries have perpetuated school systems which, because they are hierarchical and exclusive, inevitably serve to create an elite while at the same time tying the majority to values which they can never attain and alienating them from their cultural and physical roots.[36]

Leaders in emerging nations are searching for new models for their educational institutions. They want schools that will foster nationalism and cultural independence, be practical rather than "ivory tower" institutions, and instill a respect for manual labor, national traditions, and new political institutions. Yet, at the same time, they want to have the schools make a contribution to economic growth. *The key dilemma is to develop new kinds of educational institutions that can successfully balance continuity and change.*

American institutions of higher education have been of some interest to these nations because they are considered more flexible, practical, and related to regional needs than British, French, and other previously colonial systems. Chinese institutions are also of interest in that they deliberately seek to dampen the thirst for more and more education, and through their political socialization efforts, seek to unify the country, boost nationalism, and create respect for manual labor. Just what form the new institutions will assume is not known, but it is clear that there is growing dissatisfaction with existing ones.

Since achieving independence, the expansion of educational opportunity has been the first item on the agenda of many new African nations. This concern for education reflects the desires and demands of the African people as well as the advice of many international experts on economic development. Let us take a relatively prosperous country—Kenya—for illustrative purposes. Kenya more than tripled its primary school enrollment in the years between 1970 and 1983. The total enrollment in 1970 was 1,427,589; in 1983, it was 4,323,822. Secondary schools almost quadrupled their enrollments during the same period. Still, many children do not complete the seven years of primary school, and less than one percent of the college age population is enrolled in higher education.[37] Because primary school graduates want to proceed to secondary schools and secondary school graduates want higher degrees, the internal pressure for continual expansion is tremendous. Almost a third of the national budget goes to education, drawing funds away from projects in agriculture, energy, transportation, health, military, and other areas.[38]

David Court and Dhanam Ghai have noted several severe problems that the government in Kenya is facing.[39] One difficulty stems from the fact that educational demand centers on a few expensive and prestigious schools. The many village self-help (Harambee) schools have low prestige and are considered inferior by many. However, they are cheaper and have a curriculum that is more practical in terms of local economic needs. The prestigious schools are modeled after the elite British schools and teach the abstract, liberal education courses that are considered the keys to the most desirable employment opportunities. However, the educational system has expanded more rapidly than the supply of jobs requiring academic skills. Many college graduates are unemployed. At the same time, some employers have increased their job qualifications so that many primary and even some secondary school graduates cannot find useful employment either. They have become adjusted to a Western urban life style and do not wish to return to the rural villages where jobs might be more available.

Another problem is that the examination system that is the basis of educational selection into high schools and colleges is inappropriate for local needs. Based on the British model, it tests skills that are largely irrelevant at Kenya's stage of economic development.

There is also considerable class bias in the Kenyan system. Children of those families that are politically and economically advantaged have benefited most from the expanded educational system, especially at the higher levels. Sexual and regional inequities also await reform. An urgent and basic problem derives from the fact that educational objectives are only stated in the most general terms. There is a desire that Kenya become culturally and economically independent to match the political independence recently achieved. But there is also the desire to have the most rapid economic growth possible.

The conflict between these aims is illustrated in such issues as whether English or Swahili should be the primary language of instruction. Swahili is the language of tradition, but English facilitates contact with the technologically advanced Western world.

## THE USES AND FUNCTIONS OF EDUCATION: CROSS-CULTURAL COMPARISONS

We hope that these three brief overviews of education in the Soviet Union, China, and Africa have illustrated the range of functions and uses that education can assume. In each case, it is clear that conflicts exist among some of these functions and uses. For example, using educational institutions to preserve cultural traditions may conflict with using them to promote economic development. Using education to promote socioeconomic equality may conflict with using them to maximize talent and develop a technologically sophisticated workforce. Using education to promote ideological purity may conflict with promoting science and creativity.

Each of the three societies we have discussed illustrates a different set of themes and historical development. Of these three cases, the Soviet Union has come the furthest in terms of modernization and industrialization. Its educational system is similar to our own in that it is universal, compulsory, and heavily meritocratic. The many educational changes that occurred in the Soviet Union since the revolution reflect responses to both ideological commitments and the realities of economic life. After the revolution, it was intended that the educational system would promote socioeconomic equality, and indeed, there is clearly more equality of opportunity now than in Tsarist times. Nevertheless, the Soviet educational system, like our own, has permitted the development of an intellectual elite that spurns manual labor and has a position of influence and material affluence relative to other workers in the system. One continuing problem for Soviet education is the conflict between its repressive political system and the critical orientation fostered by scientific thinking and quality higher education. This conflict is likely to continue for quite some time.

The case of the People's Republic of China also illustrates how an educational system was transformed in response to ideological commitments and a revolutionary restructuring of society. During the Cultural Revolution, the schools played a part in a social movement that aimed to assure socioeconomic equality throughout the society and to prevent the development of an intellectual elite. These ideological goals took precedence over economic goals. The prestige of the scholar was kept low relative to that of the worker. Ideological purity was rewarded above academic ability in the universities, and book learning was kept closely tied to practical pursuits. However, the present leadership has taken a more pragmatic stance and reversed many of these priorities in an effort to foster economic development.

Our review of the African case cannot do justice to the wide range of experiences the various nations and peoples there have had. It does, however, illustrate the effects on education of having the values of an alien and industrialized society imposed on a preindustrial one. In Africa, the educational system was used to replace indigenous cultures with European culture and to legitimize the dominance of the Europeans. To some extent, Europeans were successful. African elites emulated the educational patterns of their colonizers, although they did not accept a permanently subordinate position with regard to them. Presently, African nations are faced with the problem of developing educational systems that are suitable to modernization, but still capable of maintaining the cultural traditions and integrity of their nations. For the most part, these systems have a long way to go before becoming totally universal. The poverty of many of these nations plays an important part in retarding the development of their educational systems. Nevertheless, there is a strong commitment to education among the people and a belief that it is critical for further economic development.

In the chapters that follow, we will be focusing almost entirely on the educational system of the United States. Some of the themes discussed here will be reflected again in the American experience. Certainly, the ways in which education can serve both conservative and change-oriented purposes will again become apparent. This cross-cultural material will help you put the American experience in broader perspective.

## NOTES

[1]For a useful distinction between cultural reproduction through teaching and cultural production through research see A. Touraine, *The Academic System in American Society* (New York: McGraw-Hill Book Co., 1974), p. 115.

[2]Partial exceptions to this general rule are rituals, such as *rites de passage*, which are more formal, institutionalized activities during which important learning occurs.

[3]Frederick Elkin and Gerald Handel, *The Child and Society: The Process of Socialization* (Boston: Little, Brown and Company, 1972).

[4]Willard Waller, *The Sociology of Teaching* (New York: Russell and Russell, 1961), p. 34.

[5]David A. Goslin, *The School in Contemporary Society* (Glenview, Ill.: Scott, Foresman and Company, 1965), pp. 15–16. This illustrates the general difficulty in trying to draw a neat and clean distinction between conservative and change-producing functions and uses. Many would argue that a commitment to cultural pluralism in American schools would represent a radical change in policy given past assimilationist procedures. Still, in a fundamental sense *maintenance* of subgroup traditions is clearly a conservative function.

[6]For an introduction to this general area of concern see Ivar Berg, *Education and Jobs: The Great Training Robbery* (Boston: Beacon Press, 1971).

[7]Max Weber, *From Max Weber: Essays in Sociology*, edited and translated by H. H. Gerth and C. Wright Mills (New York: Oxford University Press, 1946), pp. 426–28.

[8]Paul Monroe, *Founding of the American Public School System* (New York: The MacMillan Company Press, 1940), p. 428.

[9]Logan Wilson, *The Academic Man* (New York: Oxford University Press, 1942), p. 3.

[10]Paulo Friere, *Education for Critical Consciousness* (New York: The Seabury Press, 1973).

[11]There is a large literature dealing with the effects of college attendance. Much of this is summarized in Kenneth A. Feldman and Theodore M. Newcomb, *The Impact of College Upon Students* (San Francisco: Jossey-Bass, 1969). A more recent and valuable addition to this literature is Herbert Hyman, Charles Wright, and John Reed, *The Enduring Effects of Education* (Chicago: The University of Chicago Press, 1975).

[12]Susan Jacoby, *Inside Soviet Schools* (New York: Hill and Wang, 1974), pp. 12–13.

[13]Some conflict theorists would argue that the limited amount of mobility allowed in the United States acts as a safety valve, preventing the build-up of revolutionary pressure and legitimizing the system. Thus, they would classify this as a conservative use of the schools.

[14]Ann Heiss, *An Inventory of Academic Innovation and Reform, (U.S.A.: The Carnegie Foundation for the Advancement of Teaching, 1973), pp. 86–95.*

[15]The following description of education in Tsarist Russia is drawn primarily from William H. K. Johnson, *Russia's Educational Heritage* (Pittsburgh: Carnegie Press, 1950) and Patrick L. Alston *Education and the State in Tsarist Russia* (Stanford, Calif.: Stanford University Press, 1969).

[16]Johnson, *Russia's Educational Heritage*, p. 96.

[17]Abraham Kreusler, "U.S.S.R.," in *Perspectives on World Education*, ed. Carlton E. Beck (Dubuque, Iowa: Wm. C. Brown Company, 1970), p. 117.

[18]Jacoby, *Inside Soviet Schools*, pp. 12–13.

[19]For a very positive assessment of Soviet early childhood education see Urie Bronfenbrenner, *Two Worlds of Childhood: U.S. and U.S.S.R.* (New York: Russell Sage Foundation, 1970). This discussion draws more from Jacoby's critical assessment, however.

[20]Richard E. Werstler and Wilma P. Werstler, "Soviet Education Today," *Phi Delta Kappan*, 62 (June, 1982), p. 212.

[21]Richard B. Dobson, "Educational Policies and Attainment," in *Women in Russia*, Dorothy Atkinson, Alexander Dallin, and Gail W. Lapidus, eds. (Stanford, Calif.: Stanford University Press, 1977), p. 284.

[22]Dobson, "Educational Policies and Attainment," pp. 286–87.

[23]Richard B. Dobson, "Social Status and Inequality of Access to Higher Education in the USSR," in *Power and Ideology in Education*, Jerome Karabel and A.H. Halsey, eds. (New York: Oxford University Press, 1977), p. 266.

[24]*The Chronicle of Higher Education* (March 9, 1983), p. 21.

[25]Dobson, "Social Status and Inequality of Access to Higher Education in the USSR," p. 266.

[26]John Vaizey, *Education in the Modern World* (New York: McGraw-Hill Book Co., 1967), p. 118.

[27]Jacoby, *Inside Soviet Schools*, pp. 197–200.

[28]Edmund J. King, *Other Schools and Ours: Comparative Studies for Today*, 4th ed. (London: Holt, Rinehart & Winston, 1973), pp. 334–36.

[29]*The Chronicle of Higher Education* (June 29, 1983), p. 1.

[30]Much of the following historical account is drawn from Stuart Fraser, "China," in Beck, pp. 124–51. See also R. F. Price, *Education in Communist China* (New York: Praeger, 1970).

[31]David G. Scanlon, *Traditions of African Education* (New York: Bureau of Publications, Teachers College, Columbia University, 1964), pp. 3–4.

[32]Much of the following historical account is drawn from John Anderson, *The Struggle for the School* (London: The Longman Group, Ltd., 1970).

[33]Anderson, *The Struggle for the School*, p. 16.

[34]Eric Ashby, *The African Universities and Western Tradition* (Cambridge: Harvard University Press, 1964), p. 41.

[35]Ibid., pp. 44–49, 53–70.

[36]David Court and Dharam P. Ghai, *Education, Society and Development: New Perspectives from Kenya* (Nairobi: Oxford University Press, 1974), p. 4.

[37]UNESCO, *Statistical Yearbook* (Belgium: UNESCO, 1985), pp. III-86, III-152, III-25.

[38]Court and Ghai, *Education, Society and Development*, pp. 1, 9.

[39]Ibid., pp. 13–21.

# CHAPTER THREE
# INDUSTRIALIZATION

Industrialization in the United States, as in other countries, brought with it basic changes in all aspects of life. Farming was replaced by manufacturing as the primary source of employment, and tertiary or white-collar occupations accounted for an ever-growing proportion of available jobs. The workplace changed in character, shifting away from the field and toward the factory and the office building. Factories and corporations multiplied and expanded.

These changes brought dramatic increases in productivity and affluence, especially for the middle and upper classes. They also brought rapid urbanization, the exploitation of labor, and the growth of unions. Education moved center stage to take on new roles in social, political, and economic affairs.

In this chapter, we will discuss the process of industrialization in the United States with an eye toward the interaction between economic and educational institutions. We will trace this interaction from the colonial period to the present, but we will focus our attention on the latter part of the nineteenth century and the beginning of the twentieth. These were turbulent years of urbanization, massive immigration, rapid growth in manufacturing, the progressive movement in politics and education, and the establishment of public school systems throughout the country. Obviously, we will not be able to say everything that would be relevant about this period, but we will touch upon the important highlights and emphasize several themes.

First, because we believe in the importance of a historical perspective, we will give a brief chronological overview of both industrialization and educational development in the United States. Our emphasis will be on the changing character of our economic institutions and their impact on educational goals, structure, and curriculum. Then we will go on to focus more explicitly on the role of educational institutions in the development of the labor force—the education-occupation nexus, as we call it. An analysis of the contributions that educational institutions make directly to technological development through research will follow. Finally, we will conclude with a look at educational systems as markets for industrial products and the impact of technology on the educational process. At the end of the chapter, we will discuss the implications of some of our findings for the formulation of social policy.

## HISTORICAL PERSPECTIVES ON EDUCATION AND ECONOMIC DEVELOPMENT IN THE UNITED STATES

Consensus and conflict theorists agree that a primary function of educational institutions is to prepare youth for productive employment. This involves developing not only technical skills but also moral values and attitudes. There is a broad correspondence between the needs of the economic sector for particular types of workers and the training and socialization experiences provided by the schools.

However, it is important to remember that economic development is a dynamic process. At one stage of development a large, relatively unskilled labor force would be most useful; at another stage, a highly differentiated and technologically sophisticated workforce would be more appropriate. If educational institutions are to supply a continuous stream of suitable workers to an economy moving through such stages, those educational institutions will also have to change and develop.

At any one time we can ask about the degree of correspondence between the educational and economic institutions of a society. This correspondence is likely to be greater at some moments than at others. Sociologists have usually emphasized the resistance of educational institutions to change and the lag between these institutions and the needs of the faster moving economic sector. We should remember, however, that educational institutions can sometimes outpace, rather than lag behind, economic development. This fact was referred to in Chapter 2 when we discussed developing African nations and the problem of training more sophisticated workers than their economies could yet employ. Sociologists have also speculated about the possibility that changes in educational institutions can lead to modifications in economic processes that might not otherwise have occurred. For example, education that encourages individualism, creativity, and assertiveness may produce workers who are dissatisfied with routine, dead-end jobs and who are more insistent on an active role in decisions affecting their worklives.

These issues will be discussed throughout our analysis of industrialization in the United States. In order to simplify our analysis, we shall divide American economic development into three distinct periods.[1] What we shall refer to as the *Pre-Industrial Period* extends for two centuries from the founding of the first colonial settlement in 1607 to the end of the War of 1812. The *Early Industrial Period* extends from that time for more than a century up until the New Deal era of the 1930s. Finally, the *Mature Industrial Period* extends from the Franklin Delano Roosevelt administrations to the present. It may be that we are now experiencing the initial phases of a fourth distinct period, one built on new computer and communication technologies.

## The Pre-Industrial Period

The earliest American settlements were primarily agricultural communities, with a small core of tradesmen, skilled craftspeople, and professionals.[2] Most were also religious settlements. Ministers were highly influential community leaders, and religious concerns played a prominent role in daily life. These societies were relatively undifferentiated, isolated, and self-sufficient. In time, however, the earlier settlements grew in size and density. Others were established up and down the eastern seaboard and gradually into the West. This expansion resulted in a more diverse and interdependent population.

Throughout this period, education was primarily a local responsibility, with each governmental unit passing its own laws more or less independently of the others. Eventually, the Tenth Amendment of the United States Constitution left the responsibility for education to the states. This reaffirmed the tradition of local control, although it permitted consolidation at the level of the state. Because of this tradition, however, the nature of our educational institutions varied considerably from one area to the next. We cannot detail all of this variation, but we will attempt to describe some of the most common patterns.

The educational concerns of the earliest settlers focused on two major issues. The first of these concerned religious duty and the necessity that each individual be able to read the Scriptures. This belief was particularly strong among the Puritans, who established the first school on this continent in 1630, just one decade after their arrival. The Bible and quotations from it were the basic instructional materials in this school. Schooling was also valued by the Puritans because it kept children constructively busy and safe from the Devil, their belief being that idleness led to temptation and sin. In 1647, the commitment of the Puritans to education led the Massachusetts Bay Colony to establish the first compulsory public educational system on these shores. The Old Deluder Satan Act, as it is called, required that all towns of fifty or more families establish a town school. Even before the passage of this law, however, over half of the towns of Massachusetts had already organized such a school. The preamble to the 1647 law makes the religious purpose of these schools clear by explicitly referring to "that old deluder, Satan" and his efforts "to keep men from the knowledge of the Scriptures . . . ."[3]

In other colonies, too, religion provided an impetus for the establishment of early schools. In the southern colonies, ministers were usually required to establish Sunday church schools as part of their regular duties. In Pennsylvania, responsibility for education was largely handed over to the various churches, freedom of religion being interpreted to mean freedom for each church to establish its own schools. Thus, the Quakers had their own system of schools, as did the Lutherans, the Moravians, and others. It was also common for teachers to be selected by local ministers or for them to be minister's assistants. Even when governmental authorities took responsibility for education, religious influence was strong because many colonies supported official churches. At the time of the ratification of the United States Constitution in 1789, and the agreement on a strict separation of church and state, five of the thirteen original colonies still had an official church.

The secularization of the curriculum of the schools was a slow process. The earliest texts, such as the *New England Primer*, were filled with references to Biblical stories and personalities. The later ones were less specifically religious, but still highly moralistic in character. Discussions of "good" and "bad" boys and girls, and the fate deserved by each, were popular textbook themes. In 1782, Noah Webster's *American Spelling Book* appeared and gradually replaced the popular *New England Primer* as the leading text. The *Spelling Book* was still sufficiently permeated by religion to contain such statements as "The Holy Bible is the book of God," "Good men obey the laws of God," and "God created the heavens and the earth in six days."[4] The concern for instilling obedience and compliant behavior is obvious.

If religion was one major motivation for the establishment of schools, vocational training and preparation for productive labor was another. Even before the Massachusetts Bay Colony passed its first compulsory education law in 1647, it had already passed, in 1642, a law requiring that all children not only be taught to read, but also that they be prepared for a trade or calling. The aim of this law was "the training up of children in learning and labor and other employments which may be profitable to the commonwealth."[5] Although this law did not specifically require that children be taught in schools, it did require that some vocational training occur. Similar laws were passed elsewhere, often empowering government officials to forcibly remove children from their parents if this training was not arranged. The most common form in which this vocational training occurred in the early colonies was apprenticeship.

Apprenticeship education consisted of placing children, both boys and girls, with a master for a period of approximately seven years. During this time, the children received training in the craft or occupation of the master. The master was responsible for housing, clothing, and feeding the apprentice during this period. In return, the apprentice was bound to work for the master without wage and to obey him as he or she would obey a parent. In time, most colonies also required that the apprentice be taught to read and write. Apprenticeship usually ended when a boy was twenty-one and a girl eighteen.

Initially, support for apprenticeship education was very strong in the colonies. This support seemed to derive from at least two sources. First, the apprenticeship laws were seen as a way of assuring the availability of an adequate number of skilled workers to provide the goods and services needed by a community. Second, they were seen as mechanisms that could minimize poverty and lighten the economic burden that unemployed individuals could be on their communities. In many cases, the apprenticeship laws pertained only to orphans and the children of the poor, those particularly likely to require community support. The large numbers of paupers, ex-prisoners, and debtors who arrived in the colonies as indentured servants were also a concern. The prosperous landowners in America wanted to assure that the children of these indigents would be trained for productive labor.

The children of wealthy families were usually not apprenticed, although apprenticeship was then an acceptable preparation for medicine and the law. More commonly, however, the children of the rich attended private schools and the boys then went on to college. In some colonies, the use of private tutors was also widespread. Teachers who came to America as indentured servants were sometimes hired to teach all the children of a particular family. The curriculum taught these children both in the private schools and at home was classical in content. Greek and Latin, philosophy, and history were among the subjects emphasized. Colleges continued this curriculum, providing an education for cultivation rather than for any vocation. What vocational training did occur centered on preparation for the ministry, and later on for law and medicine. Women were excluded from the colleges, and most other schools beyond the elementary level. Higher education for women was eventually provided in 1742 by Bethlehem Seminary, located at the Moravian settlement in Pennsylvania.

Even children who were eventually apprenticed, however, could receive additional education as well. Because of the common stipulation that apprentices had to be taught to read and write, special privately supported apprentice schools were established in some areas. Masters who did not want to bother instructing their apprentices in reading or writing would send them to these evening schools instead. Furthermore, many children received at least some education before entering apprenticeship.

Middle-class children usually attended private primary schools. In some communities, especially in New England, there were also town schools that all children were eligible to attend. These schools sometimes charged parents for their children's attendance, but the amount was kept small by contributions from the community at large.

The children of the poor had more varied experiences than their more fortunate neighbors. These children were much less likely to attend school at all, and if they did attend, often went to separate schools specifically established for the poor. Many of these children were needed at home for farm and household work and could not be spared to attend class. Others had no school available in their area. To serve the children of the poor, many churches established a network of Charity Schools, however. In addition, some communities established Pauper Schools. These were provided for children who were publicly declared paupers. In other cases, communities did not actually establish separate schools for the poor, but paid their tuition at private schools that were already available. In general, however, communities did not feel any great obligation to educate these children, and many went without any formal learning.

Black families constituted the bottom of the social hierarchies of the North and the South, and black children received less education than even the children of poor whites.[6] Prior to the Civil War, most Southern states made it illegal to teach a slave to read or to write. In North Carolina, it was even a criminal offense to give a slave any form of written material—book, pamphlet, or Bible. Some states even extended these laws to include free blacks and mulattoes. White Southerners openly expressed their fear that education would inevitably give rise to increased aspirations and discontent among the slaves.

Black children in other states were generally excluded from the public schools or sent to segregated schools when they were available. In 1787, for example, Boston blacks petitioned the legislature for schools since none were yet available for them.[7] In time, schools were established for blacks, but these were strictly segregated in the North as well as elsewhere. Often, these schools were denied their share of public funds for education, and private philanthropic support had to be secured.

In time, the apprenticeship system declined in popularity, and pressures for alternative types of vocational education increased. Apprenticeship was not well suited to the economic needs of the American Colonies. First, there was often a greater need for unskilled farm labor than there was for the craftsmen apprenticeship was geared to produce. This led to abuses in the system. Masters often used their apprentices to work their farms or perform other menial tasks. Only in the last year of the apprenticeship did they actually teach them the trade or craft they were supposed to be learning. Secondly, the burgeoning colonies offered enormous opportunities for success through free enterprise and personal ambition. Youngsters were impatient with their seven years of virtual servitude and not certain that the return for these years would be any greater than they could have assured on their own without them. The spirit of the Colonies and the frontier was one of freedom and experimentation, and was not really compatible with the restrictive, highly disciplined character of apprenticeship. Finally, America lacked a guild system. In Europe, it was the powerful guilds that used apprenticeship to carefully regulate entrance into their occupations, but America did not have the pressures of such an institutionalized system. By the late eighteenth and early nineteenth centuries, apprenticeship had already substantially declined.

As apprenticeship declined in popularity, the need for alternative methods of vocational training was felt by both business and aspiring employees. During the 1700s, a number of "private venture schools" were established in response to this need. These schools prepared students for occupations associated with commerce and transportation, two major sources of employment at the time. These occupations included bookkeeping, banking, and navigation. In 1751, Benjamin Franklin's Academy was opened and was soon followed by others. These academies were secondary schools that broadened the classical curriculum common at that time to include preparation for the "lower" occupations. By the early 1800s, there were over one hundred of these schools scattered throughout the nation. They were eventually replaced by the proliferation and transformation of public high schools during the nineteenth century.

Toward the end of the Pre-Industrial Period, the Colonies won their independence. New states were added one by one, and the territorial frontier expanded rapidly to the West. The War of 1812 served as a turning point after which no European power openly attempted to interfere with American economic and political development. In the developing cities of the Northeast, especially Boston, New York, and Philadelphia, industrial development was already underway. The first factories and spinning mills were built just prior to the turn of the century. These new workplaces rose to dominance during the next phase of development. As we shall see, their emergence was closely tied to the development of public education in the United States.

## The Early Industrial Period

The years from 1812 until the 1930s were turbulent ones. These were the years of major technological advances, rapid industrialization, urbanization, and massive immigration. The frontier was pushed to the West Coast, and the transcontinental railroad completed. Labor began flexing its political muscles and organized in favor of public educational reform and an end to child labor. During this period, the country endured the Civil War and Reconstruction, World War I, and the Great Depression.

### The Establishment of Compulsory Public Education

During the early phases of industrialization, great fortunes were accumulated by entrepreneurs as the factories, mines, mills, and new assembly lines produced goods in massive quantities for minimal cost. At the same time, though, the sweatshop conditions that had already developed during early industrialization in England were replicated here. Long hours and low wages were typical, and since there was a severe labor shortage, heavy reliance was placed upon child labor. In the new manufacturing industries, children as young as six worked eleven and twelve hours a day, from dawn to dusk, with only half-hour breaks for meals.

During this same period, labor was struggling to organize.[8] The rise of manufacturing concentrated workers in the cities. There, and in the factories, they became conscious of their common problems, and had opportunities to work together to solve them. Starting early in the nineteenth century, unions were formed to represent various occupational groups and to press for social change in their behalf. Shipwrights and carpenters were among the first to organize, but by 1830 a considerable number and variety of unions had been established. Soon these unions found a public voice through the press. The first issue of *The Working Man's Advocate*, a labor newspaper, was published in 1825. Labor unions also organized independent political parties and exerted considerable influence over established ones. Two issues that these labor unions focused on were the general inadequacies of public education and the exploitation of child laborers.

Labor leaders supported the spread of public education because they hoped it would weaken the class-stratified educational system in existence at that time. As we mentioned earlier, the children of the wealthy and middle classes attended private schools, while the children of the poor and much of the working class attended various types of charity and pauper schools, if they attended school at all. Even where systems of public schools did exist, they were usually thought of as charitable organizations and were attended only by those too poor to afford any alternative. Furthermore, the type of education necessary to prepare for the professions and other lucrative occupations was available only to the affluent.

The unions hoped that a public school system could be established which would provide comparable opportunities for the children of the working classes. They also believed that such an education was important for democratization and for assuring that they would have an equal voice in government and political decision making. Their fear was that the educational advantages held by the upper classes would give them a monopoly of both skill and influence.

The unions' educational proposals emphasized two issues. First, they wanted education financed through public funds, so that a low family income would no longer be an insurmountable educational handicap. Second, they wanted public schools that would appeal to a broad spectrum of the population. On the one hand, these schools would teach such academic subjects as reading, writing, mathematics, and science. On the other hand, they would teach such practical subjects as agriculture and would provide training in specific occupations. In this way, schools could replace the crumbling apprenticeship system as a mechanism for training youth for productive labor and, at the same time, prepare them to be literate and intelligent citizens. The unions emphasized that people from all social classes had potential for advanced learning and high status occupations. However they rejected the classical education of the elites as useless and maladaptive to industrialized society, even for the rich. The hope was, then, that the social classes might be drawn together in a school system that served a wide range of social, economic, and political needs.

As a result of union pressure, public school systems were established by the mid-nineteenth century in all of the major industrial centers where labor was organized. However, the spread of publicly supported education met opposition from many sources. There was considerable resistance to various proposals for raising funds to support public schools. All such proposals were costly to the middle and upper classes. In addition, they increased the role of government by giving government agencies the right to collect and distribute taxes, for example. There were also battles over how funds should be equitably distributed. Should small isolated communities with only a handful of families be as eligible as larger, densely populated areas for public money? Should private schools be equally eligible? It was customary until the twentieth century to share public funds with church schools, but this was often controversial. Gradually these issues were settled and systems of free public schools were established throughout the country.

Attendance at these new free schools was not often compulsory, however. Even when compulsory attendance laws were on the books, they were rarely enforced. First, there was a general feeling that such laws interfered with a family's freedom to control its own children. Second, many children worked, either on the farms or in the factories. The fact that child labor interfered with educational reform was not lost on the unions, of course. Unionists were one of the few groups to press for child labor laws early in the nineteenth century.

As we indicated earlier, the factory was an oppressive, and even dangerous, workplace. Yet opposition to child labor was not strong during this Early Industrial Period. Poor parents defended child labor as an economic necessity. Religious leaders defended it as a means of keeping youth from idleness and sin. Industrialists defended it in terms of the profit it generated and the free operation of the marketplace. This coalition of interests was so strong that it took more than a century before it was possible to get a constitutional federal law passed that restricted child labor. This law, the Fair Labor Standards Act, was passed in 1938. Before that time, however, the activities of labor unionists and others managed to get a number of local and state laws enacted.

One reason why labor unions opposed child labor was because the addition of children to the workforce lowered wages for adults. Industrialists supported child labor for the same reason: It gave them a larger and cheaper supply of workers. Attitudes changed, however, toward the latter part of the century, especially when massive waves of immigrants joined the labor pools of the big cities. The new laborers no longer came from northwestern Europe. They were Italians, Russians, Hungarians, Greeks, and so on. These immigrants brought with them new languages, customs, and values. Among these values was a greater commitment to communal enterprise rather than fierce individualistic competition. Business leaders and others viewed these groups with alarm. There were fears of increased crime, immorality, and pauperism. There was also concern that these immigrants would not adapt easily, or willingly, to the demands of the industrial workshop and that they might undermine economic progress or become a radical political force within the workers' unions.

But how could these diverse groups be assimilated? Was there any way that they could be "Americanized," enticed to surrender the customs, language, and values of their homeland and to adopt the Anglo-Saxon lifestyles of the American masses? And was there any way this could be done quickly? The best answer seemed to be the schools. The children of these immigrant groups could be "Americanized" in the schools. There, under the watchful eye of their teachers, they could learn the English language, be taught to dress and behave properly, and be inculcated with American values. A broad coalition of groups agreed on this solution: A massive public school system was needed. Progressive civic leaders and philanthropists saw public schools as a mechanism of social uplift and moral development, needed to counter the blight of the crowded inner cities where most immigrants lived. Industrialists now saw the schools as a mechanism to assure the continued stability of the economic order and the steady supply of willing and able workers. Immigrant communities, such as the Russian Jews, who had been discriminated against and excluded from educational opportunity in their homeland, saw the public schools as a mechanism of liberation and social mobility.

This is not to imply that there was no resistance or disillusionment with the public school proposals as they crystalized and were enacted. Union leaders, who had supported public schools all along, realized that these proposals would not lead to the kind of peaceful social reorganization they had envisioned. The social classes would still remain apart. These schools could only be seen as "an incidental device of social amelioriza-tion."[9] Still, they did represent some progress.

The immigrants also had some objections. The schools were severe in their efforts to erase all traces of foreign birth in their charges.[10] Children were mocked and embarrassed into accepting Americanization. Parents and children were pulled apart as the younger generation was encouraged to feel ashamed of and to reject their origins. Certainly the schools offered opportunity; but they offered it at a considerable price.

Throughout the nineteenth century, then, there was a steady spread of public school education and the proliferation of compulsory education laws. There were many loopholes in these laws at first, and a lack of coordi-nation among changes in the labor force, the communities, and the schools. As DeBoes described it:

> Employers, labor unions, welfare agencies, and school personnel had to learn to coordinate their efforts before carefully written laws could be consistently applied: child labor laws, work permits, welfare payments for dependent children, frequent school census reports, vocational schools and the like were needed.[11]

As public elementary schools proliferated, the demand for higher education also increased. In the second half of the century, public high schools were established with increasing frequency and secondary educa-tion became accessible to the middle and working classes to a much greater degree.

Martin Trow has referred to the forty years between 1870 and 1910 as a period of major transformation for the American secondary school.[12] At the beginning of this period, public high schools were few and far between. In 1870, there were approximately 500 in the entire country, and these were concentrated in the Northeast. Only 80,000 students were enrolled in high schools of all kinds, and only approximately 2 percent of all seventeen-year-olds were receiving high school diplomas. By 1910, over 10,000 public high schools were in existence. Over 1,000,000 students were enrolled in high schools and nearly 90 percent were in the public schools. Approximately 8.8 percent of all seventeen-year-olds were receiving a high school diploma.[13] However, it took until the New Deal of the 1930s before all the ingredients of our present system of universal compulsory publicly supported primary and secondary schools could be brought together and firmly established.

So far, we have focused on changes in the structure of education during this period. Let us turn now to an analysis of the changes in educational content and process that were accompanying these structural ones. As we shall see, the content of education shifted as schools were opened to the masses and in response to the needs of an industrializing economy.

### Changes in Educational Techniques, Philosophies, and Goals

From nearly the beginning of the Early Industrial Era until the Civil War, the Lancasterian system of education was popular, especially in urban areas.[14] Because the principle of public tax support was not firmly established, it was necessary that schools be as inexpensive and efficient as possible. The higher the costs parents had to assume, the fewer who could afford them. Of course, this interest in economy was also shared by communities and charitable organizations providing education for the poor. A variety of cost-cutting educational proposals were advanced that depended upon an extremely high pupil-teacher ratio and a rather mechanistic orientation toward learning. The most popular of these proposals was developed by Joseph Lancaster.

The Lancasterian system involved specifying every detail of classroom life. Careful attention was paid to architecture, acoustics, seating arrangements, grouping of pupils, and even such details as what to do with the students' hats: They were to be attached by strings to shirt collars, flipped off at the proper signal, and left resting on the students' backs.

In Lancasterian classrooms, one teacher was provided for every 400 to 500 students. This seemingly incredible ratio of teacher to students was possible because the system depended heavily upon the use of monitors, chosen from among the students themselves, for much of the instruction. There were monitors of reading and monitors of math, monitors of conduct, monitors of playgrounds, and monitors of slates. There were even monitors to supervise monitors. During most of the school day, students were divided into groups of ten, each supervised by a student who had already been taught the appropriate lesson by the teacher. These children usually assembled at the sides of the room, alongside large charts or blackboards which served each group. Costs were kept low by utilizing slates and sand tables, which could be erased and reused rather than paper, pencils, and books.

Most of the learning involved memorization of facts and figures by the students as they worked together in groups. Discipline was strict but depended on the use of rewards rather than corporal punishment.

In general, this system was viewed as a considerable advance beyond the smaller one-room school house typical of the day. There, one teacher usually dealt with as many as fifty to a hundred children. Without monitors or any systematic way of dividing up the classroom, teachers usually only managed to involve a small number of students in learning at any one time. The rest were left to learn independently, on their own. Under these conditions discipline was often a major problem. It was also difficult to systematically evaluate each student's work and to make certain that each progressed in an orderly manner from one level of work to the next.

By contrast, the Lancasterian school was highly disciplined and efficient. All children were actively involved in learning at the same time, albeit at some loss of individual responsibility. The curriculum was divided into minute segments that could be ordered in logical sequence; students could be tested on each unit and moved on. Attention was paid to the most minute detail of each student's behavior. For example, students were instructed that:

> While reading, as the eye rises to the top of the right hand page, the right hand is brought to the position seen in fig. 4, with the finger under the leaf, the hand is slid down to the lower corner, and retained there during the reading of the page . . . .[15]

The resemblance between the Lancaster classroom and the developing factories of the early nineteenth century is easy to envisage. The classroom, like the factory, often consisted of one large, undivided room. Only a small number of square feet were allotted to each student. The monitor's role was like that of factory supervisors. The work was exacting, repetitious, and boring. These similarities between the school and the workplace were not overlooked at the time, either:

> It was argued that the factory atmosphere of the Lancasterian system was ideal training for a developing industrial society. Movement from section to section and instruction in large numbers required orderliness and precise habits on the part of students . . . With large numbers of pupils, procedures of this nature required a high degree of organization. Training the child to be a cog in this type of machine was preparation for the routine of the industrial world.[16]

By the last half of the nineteenth century, the Lancasterian system was on the decline. In the beginning it had confined its teaching to reading, writing, and arithmetic, but as it expanded to include geography, history, and grammar, it was less successful. Graduating students were not only deficient in learning, but they seemed to have no motivation to learn. In addition, other forces were working to shape education. Among these was the increasing pressure to provide a broader curriculum, one that would include such practical subjects as applied science and industrial arts.

The pressure to incorporate a broader range of subjects into the curriculum of the expanding public elementary and high schools came from many diverse sources. These included educators, social theorists, industrialists, and labor union leaders. Not all of these groups shared the same motivations, of course.

Educators and social theorists were concerned primarily with the process of democratization. They argued that learning respect for manual labor should be an important part of each person's preparation for citizenship in a democratic industrialized society. Supporters of this viewpoint envisaged a system of education that struck a balance between mental and manual learning. They argued that the secondary education available at that time "separated the schools from their goal of training individuals for the existing social order and taught youths to think without teaching them to work."[17] Even worse, they added, schools often taught students to actively dislike manual labor.

Industrialists were concerned primarily with training the young for specific productive roles, in order to assure industry an adequate supply of workers. If this training could take place in the schools, the needs of industry would be met at public expense.

Union leaders were concerned primarily with increased opportunities for the children of workers and with maintaining their own political strength. At first, unions opposed vocational education. They believed that putting vocational training in the schools would weaken their ability to control entry into various occupations. In this sense, the old apprenticeship system seemed better for labor. But in time it was apparent to all that the apprenticeship system had totally broken down in the context of the new factories. Craftsmen, now working as employees themselves, had little incentive to teach the younger generation. Furthermore, many occupations were changing too rapidly for an apprenticeship system to keep up with them. Organized labor was finally won over by the notion that broad industrial training and a liberal arts curriculum would, in the long run, contribute to democratization and greater opportunities for workers' children.

By the mid-nineteenth century, there was considerable dissatisfaction with the traditional classical curriculum of most high schools and colleges. This curriculum gradually gave way to greater diversification. New professional programs were added in law, medicine, science, mathematics, and business. Requirements were reduced and a system of electives established. Even extracurricular activities were expanded and diversified. The first steps toward the professionalization of research in institutions of higher learning took place and the first graduate programs were established.

In 1862, the passage of the Morrill Act established the land-grant colleges and universities. These colleges were specifically commissioned "to promote the liberal and practical education of the industrial classes in the several pursuits and professions in life."[18] Thus, preparation for work in agriculture, engineering, teaching, and other vocations became increasingly incorporated into the curriculum of colleges and universities.

At the high school level, similar changes were taking place. First in private academies and then in public high schools, curriculum was broadened to include a wider range of liberal arts subjects and industrial training. In 1906, the National Society for the Promotion of Industrial Education was organized. Its aim was to obtain federal financing for industrial education programs. Such programs were extremely expensive since they involved the purchase of equipment, tools, and machinery. In 1917 the

Smith-Hughes Act was passed. This Act provided federal aid for vocational training in the public secondary schools.

> The Smith-Hughes Act symbolized for education the triumph of the industrial order and the modification of traditional secondary education to meet the needs of the new social-economic system.[19]

Yet, in some ways this seemingly progressive Act and the vocational education it produced were already lagging behind the rapid advances of the economic sector:

> The underlying principles and pedagogical methods were already outdated or on the brink of being useless for the new industrialism of the 1920s. Equipment, techniques, and instruction in the schools reflected the industrial and mechanical developments of the late nineteenth century rather than the innovations of the twentieth.[20]

The decreasing importance of the crafts as opposed to the newer manufacturing trades, rapid technological innovation, and the isolation of shop teachers from advances in the industrial plants meant that the schools lagged badly behind industrial needs.

Nevertheless, the high schools were permanently transformed. They had become places for the education of the masses. Whereas for decades past the majority of their students had gone on to colleges and universities, the majority now ended their education on completion of the high school program. High school no longer meant only preparation for higher learning; it meant terminal education and preparation for the labor market as well.

From that time onward, the American high school was characterized by a two-track orientation. Some students—and these were always disproportionately from the middle and upper classes—continued to pass through high schools on their way to colleges and universities. For these students, academic subjects were still provided. Others—and these were always disproportionately from the working and lower classes—terminated their education during the high school years or upon graduation. For these, vocational programs and industrial arts were developed. By the end of the Early Industrial Era, the comprehensive American high school had become firmly established throughout the United States.

The transformation of curriculum content and the opening up of educational opportunities to a growing segment of the population were not the only major changes to occur during this period. There was also, by the end of the Early Industrial Era, a transformation of educational method. This transformation was due largely to the work and influence of John Dewey. His work, and the influence that it gained, can also be seen as a response to the rapidly changing social, political, and economic climate of the times.

Dewey's first major publication, *The School and Society*, appeared in 1899, but Dewey's ideas were not widely adopted until after World War I.[21] Dewey's basic criticism of American education was that it had become divorced from the practical, daily experiences of the child.

At the turn of the century, American schools were detached from the daily lives of children in several important respects. First, they were detached in terms of the vocational training they both did and did not offer. As we indicated above, the last half of the nineteenth century saw a phenomenal growth in the number of public high schools and the development of terminal programs to accommodate the increasing numbers of students attending them. Particularly, high schools expanded their programs to include vocational courses. As we also indicated above, however, these courses lagged behind the needs and technological advances of the economic sector. American high schools did not really see themselves as equivalents of the technical and industrial schools that had already developed in Europe. Instead, they emphasized a general preparation for work and broad occupational training; not preparation for specific occupational slots. In this sense, they did not deal with the actual problems students faced outside the classroom when they tried to find employment.

Secondly, American schools denigrated popular culture and sought to purify and elevate students' tastes in art, music, literature, home decor, and so on. This tendency was especially evident in the schools' treatment of immigrants, which we discussed earlier. Fear that the entire country was "becoming debauched" by a "flood of imported barbarism"[22] characterized a school system that had become committed to uniformity of taste, aspirations, and sentiments. The realities of daily life as the children of the masses of working class families actually experienced it were not to be found within the classroom. The great heterogeneity of the population, the growing antagonisms between ethnic groups, and the diverse cultural heritages they represented were neither discussed nor acknowledged.

Third, American schools were detached from the daily lives of children in terms of the instructional methods through which subject matter was taught. Memorization was the most common technique. The authority of the lessons, whether learned from textbooks or the teacher's lectures, reigned supreme.

Dewey's critique of the educational system was based on his belief that learning is best when it grows from the student's direct experiences. The student interacts with the environment, encounters problems, asks questions, searches for solutions, and, in the process, learns. Dewey pointed out that this is the way people have learned throughout most of history and that only in recent years has the gap between knowledge and daily life become so great that young people see no relevance in the materials they learn at school. Memorization is tedious, he argued, and the curriculum content often unrelated to everyday needs.

Dewey advocated a closer relationship between the family, the community, and the school and a greater awareness of the home and neighborhood life of the child. In this way, subject matter could be presented so that it would have "a positive value and a real significance in the child's own life."[23] The school would no longer seem hostile and distant, but learning would be directed to the questions the child specifically asked about his or her own world.

Instruction, then, was to involve the active participation of children. Flexibility in terms of seating, movement around the classroom, and use of new instructional materials was encouraged. Teachers and textbooks would no longer be presented as the ultimate authority on what should be learned, but students' own initiative and interests would be respected. Dewey also advocated greater emphasis on group projects, building a sense of community within the school, and deemphasizing competition and individualism.

Dewey's progressivism had a profound and lasting effect on American education. However, the misapplication of his views has at times created excesses that have been criticized as undermining learning and promoting mindless conformity. Some have argued that the Progressive experiments of the twenties and thirties created the stereotypical organization man of the fifties: conforming, noncreative, and uncritical. Nevertheless, many of Dewey's ideas have been permanently incorporated into American educational practices.

In some respects, Dewey's work can be seen as a reaction to the mechanization of education and work that had accompanied industrialization in the United States. His theories clearly called for a humanization of the classroom. The schools, at least, could treat people as human beings rather than machines, and they could be used to overcome the alienation that seemed to be an inevitable concomitant of urban, industrial life. In other respects, though, Dewey's theory could be seen as a harbinger of economic changes in the offing. In time, the labor market would require workers who could get along easily and effectively with others, who could work together on group projects rather than in isolated parallel on the assembly line, and who could fill the ever-expanding demand for managers and administrators. It would also require workers who could solve practical problems in an economy that depended increasingly on continuous technological innovation and development. This is not to suggest that all of today's workers are permitted any great leeway for individual creativity and independence, but merely that there has been a shift away from the extreme forms of discipline and rigidity imposed earlier in our history. The growth of occupations in the areas of human services, management, and so on have also called for workers with greater interpersonal skills. Finally, reductions in the length of the work week and the working day, along with greater affluence for at least some major segments of the population, have meant that leisure activities are an important part of American life. Here, an ability to relate to others and to actively enjoy popular culture is central. Needless to add, perhaps, is the fact that leisure-time activity is in itself a major economic industry.

Though few would argue that the emergent structure of American educational institutions was perfect, it seems clear that the foundations of our present system were firmly in place by the end of this Early Industrial Period. Compulsory tax-supported primary and secondary schools had been established across the nation. They were not the radical engines of social transformation some had envisioned, but many believed that they provided major opportunities for individual improvement and social advancement. Private and parochial schools remained, but they no longer constituted a major part of the system. In addition, they were required to meet minimum state regulations and were being denied public funds. The principles of the neighborhood grade school and the common high school were firmly established. Public high schools were widely available and new programs for terminal students had been developed. The extreme separation of social classes in the schools was ameliorated, but the differentiation between terminal vocational programs and college preparatory programs in the high schools allowed some separation of the social classes to continue. Higher education remained primarily the prerogative of the wealthy, but relatively inexpensive and pragmatically oriented state colleges and universities were available and growing.

### The Mature Industrial Period

The pace of social change accelerated during the twentieth century. Technological advancement was especially rapid, as is most dramatically illustrated in the area of space exploration. The earlier volatile struggles between industry and labor were institutionalized in labor-management collective bargaining regulations, thus providing a new stability to the economy. Automation and bureaucratization reshaped American institutions. The character of the workforce changed with a dramatic expansion of white-collar relative to blue-collar occupations. Working conditions improved, and the pursuit of leisure became an issue for an increasingly broad spectrum of the population. Levels of educational attainment rose steadily. The symbolic center of the economy moved from the grimy mill to the gleaming corporate office building.

During this period, we endured World War II, the Cold War, the Korean War, and the Vietnam War. We experienced the civil rights movement, the antiwar protests, and demands for greater equality voiced by students, feminists, and a variety of cultural minorities.

In education this was a period of explosive growth. Part of this growth was due to the increasing proportion of the population that stayed in school for twelve or more years. But part of it was also due to a radical change in the American birth rate. After World War II, the birth rate soared to new heights, as the "baby boom" of the 1950s was created. These huge cohorts of children sent shock waves through the school systems of America. There was enormous pressure to expand facilities quickly and efficiently in order to accommodate the growing floods of students. This pressure was first felt in the elementary schools, then the junior and senior high schools, the colleges, and finally, the graduate and professional schools. As Figure 3–1 shows, the number of faculty members increased dramatically. The low birth rates that followed in the 1970s and early 1980s led to a period of retrenchment and reduction in force. Total elementary

**FIGURE 3–1.** Faculty in Educational Institutions.

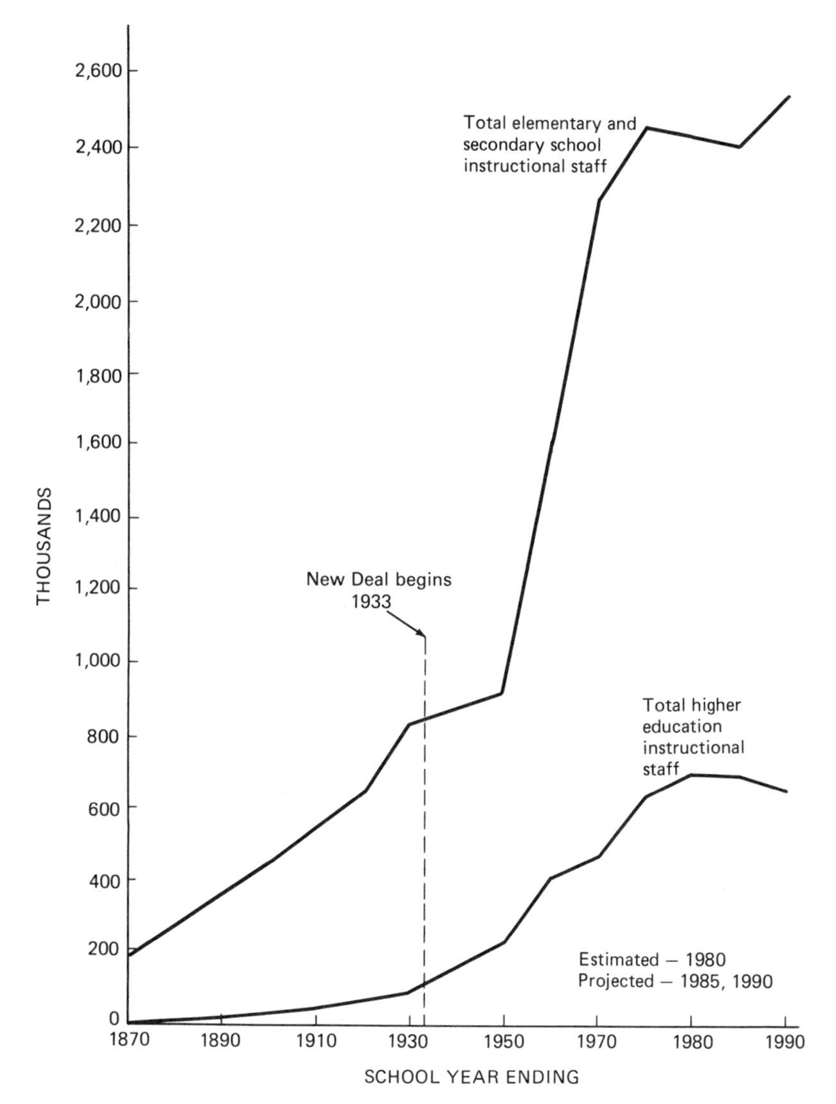


*Source:* Valena White Plisko, *The Condition of Education: 1984* (Washington, D.C.: Government Printing Office, 1984), pp. 32, 78.

and secondary school enrollment declined steadily between 1971 and 1983. Now the "baby boom" generation is having children and enrollment is increasing. Teacher shortages are a concern once again.[24] We will discuss the implications of these changes in more detail later.

The second element contributing to the explosive growth of education during this period was, as we suggested, the growing proportion of young people who stayed in school for twelve or more years. In 1940, only

49 percent of all eighteen year olds were high school graduates. By 1960, over 72 percent of all eighteen year olds were high school graduates, a percentage almost identical to today's. In 1960, 24 percent of high school graduates were enrolled in college. By 1970, it was 33 percent, almost identical to 1984 enrollment figures.[25] These enormous increases in the percentages of young people continuing their education through and beyond high school can be attributed to a variety of factors. One important factor has been the continued changes occurring in the labor market, with a marked increase in the demand for highly trained and educated workers:

> Between 1940 and 1950, the number of engineers in the country doubled; the number of research workers increased by 50 percent. Even more striking, between 1950 and 1960 the total labor force increased by only 8 percent; but the number of professional, technical, and kindred workers grew by 68 percent—and these, of course, are the occupations that call for at least some part of a college education.[26]

These trends were further bolstered by a general upgrading of educational credentials required for a wide variety of job categories, as we shall see later in this chapter.

In addition to the pressures exerted by the economic marketplace, the role of state and federal governments in encouraging college attendance must also be noted. There has been an increasing desire, on the part of federal officials especially, to develop a national educational policy in order to meet international economic, political, and military competition.[27] This interest took a sharp leap forward in the 1950s when the United States and the Soviet Union were in competition to be first into outer space. The Soviet Union shocked the United States by being the first country to send up a successful satellite—Sputnik I in 1957. A furor of educational debate followed and extensive revision of the American high school curriculum was demanded.[28] Greater emphasis was placed on training the intellectually superior child. More attention was paid to mathematics and science courses, and a general condemnation of the Progressive emphasis on life adjustment and experience rather than rigorous academic discipline and achievement occurred. The federal government made funds available for curriculum overhaul at the secondary school level and for the development of scientific programs at the college and graduate school levels as well. Also, a large number of scholarships and fellowships were provided to encourage students to specialize in these areas.

Aside from influencing the character of secondary education in the direction of more mathematics and science offerings, the general upsurge in governmental sponsorship of higher education contributed to the higher proportions of students remaining in school for long periods of time. The growing numbers of students going on to postsecondary education created what Trow has referred to as the "second transformation" of American secondary schools.[29] Previously the American secondary school had been transformed from an elite college preparatory institution to an institution serving masses of terminal students. Now, it was transformed again; this time from an institution serving primarily terminal students to one in which the majority were planning some kind of secondary education. Not that the terminal student disappeared, of course. High schools still had to accommodate the terminal student as well, but the increasing proportion of students with postsecondary educational plans created new kinds of problems for the schools. Among these were demands for curriculum reform, a need to upgrade teacher quality, and the problem of dealing with students who are motivated to acquire higher education but who lack the requisite ability.

Federal education policy took another direction in response to the Civil Rights protests of the 1960s. The federal government developed a variety of initiatives to enhance equality of educational opportunity including early childhood education, desegregation, and school nutrition programs. Then, when Ronald Reagan was elected president in 1980, the growth of federal education programs was curtailed in the name of a New Federalism. In accordance with the conservative philosophy of the Reagan administration, federal involvement, support, and regulation of education was reduced while state responsibility and control increased. However, the federal government has maintained its concern with educational quality, especially as it relates to international military and economic competition.

## THE EDUCATION-OCCUPATION NEXUS

### Education and Occupational Placement

The linkage between educational experiences and occupational placement has strengthened over time. Earlier in our history, when few individuals completed high school or went on to college, fortunes were made and lost without reference to a person's educational qualifications. Few jobs outside of the professions required educational credentials. Opportunities for ambitious, hard working individuals were numerous, first because of the expanding frontier and later because of explosive industrial growth. In addition, industry was less controlled by large impersonal bureaucracies, and possibilities for success as an independent entrepreneur were greater. Companies were smaller and more flexible. If you were hired as a mail dispatcher, but proved yourself clever and useful, you might some day move up to company president. Even the popular culture reflected an optimism about social mobility that is rarely matched today. Stories about Horatio Alger, the boy who was supposed to have made it from rags to riches through hard work, ambition, and often just plain luck, were told and retold.[30]

This is not to exaggerate the amount of mobility actually available to most people in the past. Few people ever really made it from poverty to wealth at any time in our history. The difference was, however, that being successful or not had very little to do with what amount of education you had acquired. Of course, having had a proper elite education might mark you as sufficiently cultivated to be a welcomed member of the upper class, but business success was possible without it, and money could buy a lot of influence and social acceptance.

Today, things are vastly different. The overwhelming majority of available jobs require some minimal level of education. Unemployment rates are notoriously high among high school dropouts, since even unskilled jobs often require a high school diploma. Jobs that promise the maintenance of a middle-class lifestyle often require a college diploma, and many require an advanced degree as well.

Many of these requirements are rigid and exist for entry-level jobs as well as for those with higher status. For example, if you want to become a senior executive of a large company you will have to acquire a college degree and perhaps even a master's degree in business before being hired—even as a junior executive or an assistant. You cannot usually accept a job as a high school-educated office clerk and hope to move up as you gain experience with the company. Americans work now in large bureaucratic organizations, be they businesses, hospitals, schools, or others. These large institutions are impersonal in the sense that they do not look at your unique strengths and weaknesses as an individual and adapt their job requirements to what you have to offer. Their formal job requirements are rarely modified or ignored. Even if an individual has personal influence, or "connections," he or she will usually have to meet these formal job requirements before being given the job. As Blau and Duncan have pointed out, the ability of a successful father to pass his own level of occupational success on to his son now rests primarily in his ability to provide that son with the appropriate educational opportunities.[31]

Another change that has occurred in the connection between education and occupational placement is a continuous escalation in the number of jobs requiring educational credentials and the level of educational credentials required. Ivar Berg has documented this rise in meticulous detail.[32]

The increased reliance on diplomas, degrees, and certificates has been associated with dramatic shifts in the American workforce during the last century. These changes are clearly evident in Figure 3–2. In 1880 most workers were employed in agriculture. Then for sixty years after the turn of the century industrial employment predominated. By 1960 the information sector of the economy was the largest, employing approximately forty percent of the workforce. Among the most important of the "information industries" are the following: computers, communications, entertainment, publishing, banking and credit, insurance, legal services, brokerage, advertising, research and development, and education. By 1980 sixty percent of all employed Americans were information workers.[33] The computerization of the economy is spreading so rapidly that by 1990 some knowledge of computers will be necessary in seventy percent of all jobs.[34] However, improved programming will almost certainly make future computers much easier to use, so it remains unclear just how sophisticated that knowledge of computers will have to be. Indeed, there is great uncertainty about the ideal curriculum and methods to train youth for productive work in the emerging information society. Yet the American public continues to rely ever more heavily upon educational credentials in occupational placement.

**FIGURE 3–2.** The Growth of Information Occupations, U.S. Work Force 1860–1980.

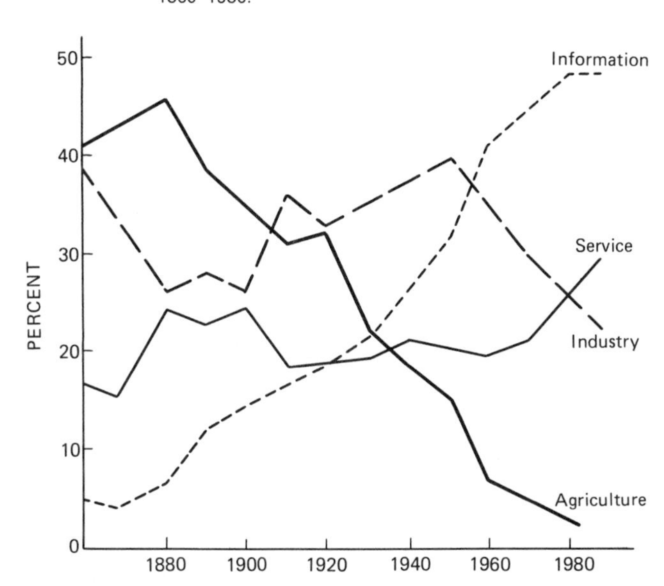


*Source:* M.U. Porat, *The Information Economy* (Washington, D.C.: Department of Commerce, Office of Telecommunications, 1977), p. 121.

## Human Capital Theory

For a long time it was simply assumed that educational requirements were being upgraded in a rational relationship to the increasing complexity of various jobs, a natural outcome of industrialization. Economists took this argument one step further. They suggested that increasing the general level of education of the workforce would contribute to increased worker productivity and therefore increase the gross national product. This concept, known as "human capital theory," treats investment in education in much the same way as investment in capital goods. The emphasis is on looking at the rate of return each type of investment will bring. To many economists, it appeared that investment in education brought a substantial return and this return justified public and private support of educational institutions. Although this reasoning has been extensively criticized, it remains very influential. In fact, as American scientific and technological dominance is being challenged in the international marketplace, policymakers are once again calling for increased investment in education. They argue that full development of our human resources is essential in order to increase productivity and maintain an edge in competition with Japan and other advanced industrial societies. In many respects American schools appear lax in comparison with those in other advanced industrial nations. American youths have fewer and shorter school days, spend fewer hours doing homework, and take far fewer courses in math and science.[35] Thus, in the hope of improving American competitiveness in world trade, politicians and board members across the nation have demanded more stringent curricular and graduation requirements.

Berg was one of the first sociologists to launch a critical attack on human capital theory.[36] He reviewed many of the technical problems involved in the economists' approach, but focused on the effect of this theory on employment. After gathering data from business managers and reanalyzing survey data collected by others, Berg concluded that employers had developed a blind faith in educational certificates. They had upgraded their educational requirements for job placement because of an unwarranted belief that more educated workers would be more productive, either individually or in terms of their overall effect on the economy. These employers had rarely actually compared the productivity of their more and less well educated workers. Berg concluded that:

> A search of the considerable literature on productivity, absenteeism, and turnover has yielded little concrete evidence of a positive relationship between workers' educational achievements and their performance records in many work settings in the private sector.[37]

Furthermore, Berg found that rates of job dissatisfaction and job turnover were often highest among the most well-educated workers. Approximately four out of five workers had jobs that did not actually utilize their capabilities. Training for a highly skilled, challenging job and then obtaining only a routine, unstimulating one led to frustrations and employment instability. Berg argued that employers would often do better by lowering rather than raising their job requirements. The actual skills necessary for successful job performance are often only loosely related to educational success.

This problem has been documented in other advanced industrial societies as well. James O'Toole suggested:

> A portentous social pattern is beginning to emerge in many industrialized nations. In socialist and capitalist economies alike, increasing numbers of highly qualified workers are unable to find jobs that require their skills and training. Thus, a large and growing number of individuals are forced to take jobs that can be performed just as adequately by workers who have far lower levels of educational attainment . . . . Where Marx had forecast that mass unemployment would become the salient characteristic of labor markets in advanced economies, it is now clear that underemployment—working at less than one's full productive capacity—is more accurately the hallmark of work in industrial societies.[38]

Although many industrial nations have successfully sought to expand educational opportunities, the boom in educational attainment has not been matched by a corresponding increase in the number of challenging jobs. Yet youths have raised their occupational aspirations, hoping for self-actualization rather than simply the traditional rewards of money and security. The picture becomes even gloomier when O'Toole looks closely at the demands of new jobs in the rapidly expanding service sector of the economy. He notes that many of these are dead-end jobs—lacking in security as well as opportunities for self-fulfillment. In line with these arguments, Berg is highly critical of government policies that encourage higher rates of college and graduate school enrollment and contribute to this rise in educational requirements. If so many workers are underemployed relative to their educational credentials, and if jobs can be successfully performed with less education, then it is foolish to continue to invest in education. According to Berg, the positive return hypothesized by the economists is not being realized.

## Education and Income

A second force encouraging the rise of educational credentialing is also related to human capital theory, but focuses on the return individual students can expect from their investments in education. The calculations involved in determining this kind of return are complex, and considerable disagreement still exists among economists regarding how this should be done. For example, return must be figured on the basis of how much money was invested in acquiring educational credentials. Clearly, tuition costs and book fees would be included here, but what about the costs incurred through forgoing income that otherwise might have been earned? While you are in school, you do not work, or at least you work less than you would if you were not in school. This lost income is considered a cost by some economists, but not by others. This latter group argues that the job opportunities available to high school graduates are so minimal that forgone income is not an important factor.

Estimates made during the 1960s placed the overall rate of return for investment in education at over 10 percent. In 1974, however, Mincer published an intricate analysis of 1960 census data that showed an even greater return.[39] By refining earlier models through the substitution of work experience for age as the individual moves through the life-cycle, Mincer concluded that years of schooling explained one-third, as opposed to the usual estimate of 7 percent, of the variation in the earnings of white, nonfarm males. Mincer suggested also that further refinement would bring this figure up to 60 percent.

However, Mincer's analysis deals only with white males. We know that the return on educational investment is considerably smaller for minority males, blacks, and all categories of women.[40] For example, in 1983 the median income of white males, aged 25 years and over, who were full-time year-round workers was $22,351 for those who had completed four years of high school, $30,339 for those who had completed four years of college, and $34,865 for those who had completed five or more years of postsecondary education.[41] Comparable black males earned $16,820, $24,123 and $29,468 respectively. Black males earned less than comparable white males at each level of education and therefore received a smaller return than whites for similar investments in education.

White females aged 25 years and over who were full-time year-round workers in 1983 had a median income of $13,787 if they had completed four years of high school, $18,452 if they had completed four years of college, and $22,877 if they had completed five or more years of postsecondary education. Comparable black females received $13,989, $18,543 and $22,837 respectively. Black females received more income than white females at two of the three educational levels. However, the differences between black and white women were much smaller than the differences between black and white men. Furthermore, within each racial group, women received very much lower incomes than comparable men, with the greatest differences occurring among whites. The highest return on education went to white males, who even as high school graduates made almost as much as white women with more than five years of postsecondary education.

Not all groups receive the same increment in salary for each additional investment in education. White males improve their income by 13 percent when they invest in education beyond college. Black males, though at a lower absolute level, improve their income by 22 percent.

Most analyses of returns on educational investments use data on middle-aged workers. A study of the wages of younger workers discovered a surprising fact. The study analyzed data on the early work experiences of 17,000 workers who were high school seniors in 1972. By 1979, seven years after high school, male college graduates did *not* earn as much as their peers who either did not attend college at all or went to two-year community colleges. The hourly wages of female college graduates, on the other hand, clearly were higher than those of their non-college peers. In the long run males as well as females profit from their college degrees because college graduates tend to have longer work lives, more frequent pay increases, superior fringe benefits, and less likelihood of unemployment. But in the first few years out of school, college does not have a substantial monetary payoff for men.[42]

Many factors explain differential rates of return on investment in education. Groups that are similar in education may still differ in other job-relevant ways, in intelligence or interpersonal skills, for example. However, patterns of discrimination have obviously played an important role. This discrimination includes differential opportunities offered to various socioeconomic groups as well as discrimination against minorities and women. Middle-class students get about twice as much return as working-class students on educational investment.[43] The dynamics involved here are not thoroughly understood, but it is clear that the lower adult incomes of some groups cannot be totally explained in terms of their lower levels of education. In spite of the influence of education on occupational placement, income is determined by many factors other than education.[44] We will return to these issues in Chapter 8.

One final note: Recent work has emphasized that the rates of return on higher education are strongly related to fluctuations in the job market. During the years from 1970 to 1975 the job market for college graduates as a group deteriorated. The professional and technical portion of the economy, into which most college graduates are placed, did not expand rapidly enough to absorb all the new graduates. The result was that many had to take jobs unrelated to their college majors, a situation that Mincer's research has shown dramatically reduces the payoffs of education.[45]

When students do enter occupations that are relevant to their majors and when the supply/demand ratio is favorable, college education can have a spectacular monetary payoff. For example, in the early 1980s industrial expansion produced a demand for computer scientists and engineers that far exceeded the supply of college graduates in those fields. As a result, beginning engineers and computer specialists were receiving starting salaries which were often twice as high as those received by college graduates who majored in liberal arts (fields where the supply of college graduates far exceeded the demand from employers).

Social scientists continue to debate the value of a college education.[46] Some feel that it is appropriate to define that value in strictly monetary terms. Others contend that any meaningful discussion of the issue must consider the contribution the college experience makes to such qualitative factors as personal growth and the development of artistic appreciation and intellectual insight. Despite the academic debate, most Americans continue to believe that education is worthwhile. As a result they are motivated to acquire as much education as possible, thereby contributing to the spiraling educational demands of employers.

### Seller's Credentialism

Some of the pressure to raise educational requirements for various job categories comes directly from workers and worker organizations. This is particularly true when occupational groups try to redefine themselves as professions. As we shall see in Chapter 6, professionalization is associated with having a body of esoteric knowledge and a lengthy socialization or educational experience. In attempting to establish their legitimacy as a professional group, the members of a particular occupation often argue that their members should be expected to have a college degree or even more advanced educational credentials. Rawlins and Ullman refer to the kinds of pressure exerted by occupational groups rather than by employers as "seller's credentialism."[47] A key element here involves the occupational group's interest in legal recognition and protective licensing laws. Such laws generally increase occupational prestige and automony as well as offer protection from encroachment by "charlatans" or "outsiders."

Sometimes the press for increased educational credentials reflects an interest in discriminating against certain groups who can be effectively excluded from the occupation as the credential requirements are raised. For example, Tractenberg has argued that the tests required for teaching and administrative positions in New York City's school system screen out otherwise qualified minority persons.[48] Certainly, any increase in the number of years of schooling required for an occupation tends to reduce the number of minority persons and women who can qualify.

## THE SCHOOL'S ROLE IN OCCUPATIONAL PLACEMENT

In a dynamic economy such as ours, marketplace demands are constantly changing. It cannot be assumed the schools, colleges and universities will produce a sufficient supply of students with appropriate vocational aspira-

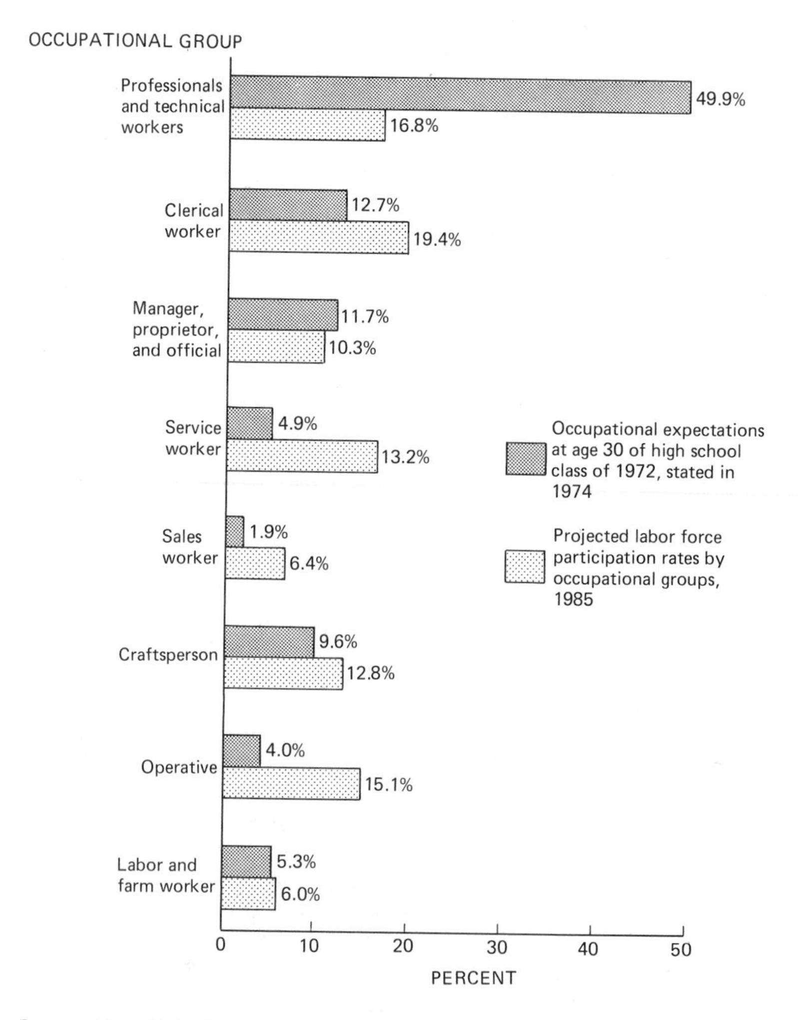


*Source:* Mary P. Golladay, *The Condition of Education: 1976 Edition* (Washington, D.C.: Government Printing Office, 1976), p. 123.

tions and skills to meet economic needs. In fact, as Figure 3–3 shows, the economy is not generating enough of the kinds of jobs to which students aspire. For example, whereas half of young adults questioned in 1974 about occupational aspirations indicated that they wished to be professionals or technical workers by age thirty, projections indicated that there would only be professional or technical positions for about 16.8 percent of them. Obviously many students are disappointed and will continue to be so. In 1980, a national sample of high school seniors showed a similar pattern of aspirations: over half said they would like to work in professional or technical fields.[49] In that same year, only 14.7 percent of the workforce were in those occupations.[50] Figure 3–3 also indicates an excess of jobs in other, less prestigious, occupations.

In an effort to help students make " . . . reasoned occupational decisions,"[51] the federal government has supported the development of career education programs. These programs use a variety of means including the systematic exposure of youth to a wide range of occupations, the development of specific job-related skills, encouraging work study experiences, and emphasizing the importance of an orderly process of occupational choice. In the process, students are to learn which jobs are most readily available and what rewards they can offer. Educational aspirations can then be adjusted accordingly. It is hoped that the fit between occupational aspirations and labor market demand would be improved and the numbers of overeducated workers reduced.

Critics of career education have argued that its goals are extremely vague, and perhaps, deceptive. For instance, Lazerson and Grubb argue that the real aim of such programs is to solve problems of unemployment, worker alienation, and overeducation by deceiving youth into believing that available work is intrinsically worthwhile rather than by sensitizing them to the ways in which workers are exploited and encouraging them to change the system.

This is a classic confrontation between consensus-oriented theorists and those utilizing a conflict perspective. One side professes a " . . . great abiding faith in (the American economic) system,"[52] while the other believes that all work in a capitalist system is degrading. As Lazerson and Grubb see it, career education is

> a politically safe reform evidently promising a great deal without threatening established economic and educational structures. That to us, precisely describes its limitations.[53]

There is considerable disagreement about the methods schools use to sort students into different programs and the processes through which students arrive at differential levels of educational and occupational attainment. We will look at these issues in greater detail in later chapters, but for now, let us at least indicate some of the principal mechanisms involved and some of the controversy that surrounds them.

Little is known about the internal dynamics of the elementary school class. Certainly, children at this stage are evaluated and graded by their teachers, and the child's academic record is initially established. As we indicated in Chapter 1, Parsons has suggested that the early evaluations that teachers make are based on judgments of the child's moral development as well as on his or her academic progress.[54] How well the child behaves is of critical importance, as is how well he or she meets the teacher's wide-ranging expectations.

There is some evidence that teachers may judge and evaluate children differently according to their ascribed characteristics. For example, children from minority groups or poor families may be judged deficient on the basis of ethnic and social class stereotypes. One study, by Ray Rist, showed that teachers sometimes group children according to their social class backgrounds and then proceed to encourage educational achievement in the high status groups and discourage it in the others.[55] Similar studies have been done on the effect of students' gender characteristics. Boys receive a disproportionate amount of teachers' attention, both positive and negative.[56] They are in trouble more often than girls, but they are also praised more often. In comparison, girls are often ignored, expected to be docile and cooperative, and not encouraged to any great heights of academic achievement.

There is also some evidence that educational and occupational attainment may be influenced by the content of elementary school textbooks and other instructional materials. In the past, they often reflected strong ethnic and class biases. Some of these have been modified. However, a number of studies have shown that these materials still reflect prevalent gender biases.[57] Women are rarely shown in work roles, for example, and when they are, these roles are limited to those of nurse, teacher, cafeteria worker and the like. The beginnings of educational and occupational allocation might be traceable to the early internalization of such messages on the part of students.

We will raise these points again later. However, it is important to note that there is no really definitive research that systematically links any of these kinds of early experiences with eventual educational or occupational attainment. The data are mostly qualitative and impressionistic, although they are often persuasive and insightful.

Somewhat more research is available on the allocation of older students into educational and occupational slots. This research has focused around several important themes. One group of researchers has approached educational and occupational allocation as a process of individual choice, looking at the factors that influence a student's aspirations, values, and motivations. By now, it has been firmly established that a person's ascribed characteristics, such as gender, ethnicity, and social class play an important part in his or her educational and occupational decision making. For example, working-class students are less likely than middle-class students to take academic programs in high school. These students' educational aspirations are also lower, and they seem to value education somewhat less. We will look at these relationships more carefully in Chapter 8.

Other researchers have looked at educational and occupational decision making as the product of institutional evaluation and allocation. Many of these have focused on the supposedly objective measurements—grades and tests—upon which students are placed in and selected for various programs. As we all know, decisions regarding which students will be admitted to high school courses, colleges, universities, and professional schools are made on the bases of grades and test scores. In addition, students get ideas about what they can reasonably aspire to as their academic records accumulate. If your college grades are low, and your college board scores mediocre, you will probably consider aspirations for medical school unrealistic.

As we shall see in later chapters, there are many reasons to doubt that these grades and tests accurately measure students' abilities, especially when the students involved belong to minority ethnic and racial groups. Nevertheless, since grades and tests are stressed in educational allocation, students worry about them and compete for them. Early in this century, college students were taught that grade-grubbing was crude and uncouth; the "gentleman's C" was held up as ideal.[58] The "C" was a respectable grade that could be achieved without working overly hard, competing with friends, or sacrificing a cultivated and relaxed style of life. The proliferation of graduate programs, the importance of these programs for occupational placement, the relative scarcity of places in the most prestigious institutions, and the consequent reliance on grades as a selection device have brought considerable change in this regard.

Another group of researchers has focused on guidance counselors and the kinds of advice they give and decisions they make. From this perspective the guidance counselor is seen as an agent of social differentiation. As Corwin has pointed out, in advanced industrial societies the question of occupational choice gradually leaves the home and shifts to the "experts" in the schools:

> The counselor is an intermediary between the adult world, the adolescent, and the family. He represents the adolescent's interest in a complex vocational world; and yet as a representative of adult society he is obliged, however reluctantly, to be cognizant of the interests of national defense and of the economy. Safeguarding these interests includes taking steps to assure that the growing demand for manpower is met, particularly in those areas of the economy which are most important to the nation's technological growth and the armaments race.[59]

A number of researchers have asked in detail about the kind of advice guidance counselors give to different types of students. Several studies have indicated that counselors sometimes advise students on the basis of the racial and sexual stereotypes generally prevalent throughout American society.[60] Students from minority groups, for example, might be discouraged from taking academic programs. Women may be counseled away from traditionally male fields such as engineering or chemistry.

Furthermore, when guidance counselors are responsible for allocating students to different high school programs, they may be similarly influenced by latent racial, sexual, or social class biases. One interesting study of this phenomenon was conducted by Cicourel and Kitsuse in Illinois.[61] They studied the process through which junior high school students were allocated into academic and nonacademic programs in their receiving high school. They discovered that the supposedly objective measures of class grades and achievement test scores used to make these decisions did not account for all of the placements that counselors made. Instead, the counselors' overall impression of the student as college-going material or not played an important part in the decision. The student's family background, his or her parents' aspirations, the student's dress and behavior all were influential. Consequently, some children were placed in academic tracks, in spite of lower grades and scores, mainly because they and their families were clearly middle-class, whereas other children were not put into these same tracks mainly because they and their families did not seem to be the type that was college-oriented. Rosenbaum found that children from middle class and upper-middle class families got more detailed explanations from counselors about the implications of tracking decisions than did working class children.[62] There was also some indication that counselors made efforts to dampen the "unrealistic" aspirations of disadvantaged children.

Of course, the high school counselor does face a difficult and complex job. As we underscored in Figure 3–3, many more young people aspire to high-level occupations than there are occupational places available. Similarly, more students probably aspire to a four-year college education than are capable of acquiring one. An important question, then, is what counselors should do about students' aspirations. Is it ever proper for them to "counsel down," or to try to lower the educational and occupational aspirations of young people? If so, how should they decide which students to deal with in this way?

One study relevant to this issue was conducted by Clark at several community colleges in California.[63] Clark argued that one of the important functions of community colleges is to "cool out" large numbers of students who aspire to a four-year college degree, but who do not have the ability to achieve one. These institutions have therefore established formal mechanisms through which they gradually redirect students' plans away from transferring to four-year programs and toward settling for the two-year vocational programs offered in the community colleges. The counselor's role is central to this process. It is the counselor's job to properly "interpret" the student's academic record, indicate the implications of the student's low grades and test scores, and help the student realize that transferring to a vocational program need not be interpreted as "failure."

Thus, as schools became increasingly differentiated and universal, their relevance for occupational placement was taken more seriously by educators, economists, government officials, students, and students' families. These changes created new organizational dilemmas for the schools. In particular, the processes by which students were moved through educational institutions became more complex. Decisions of selection and allocation had to be made more frequently and for larger numbers of students. Schools turned to grades, objective tests, and the office of the guidance counselor for help with these decisions.

## INSTRUCTIONAL TECHNOLOGY

Industrialization has affected the internal workings of the schools in other ways as well. As business people grew in influence, some sought to extend industrial techniques and principles to education. Many of their ideas were adopted, some experimentally, others on a more permanent basis. Others approached education primarily as a potential market for industrial goods and services. Manufacturers applied their technological expertise to the development of instructional materials. Potentially, at least, these materials could transform teaching methods and school organization.

Americans have long been believers in the value of technology. The assumption that new and better mechanical devices and organizational principles can keep productivity increasing indefinitely is widespread throughout American society. So is the belief that most problems can be solved in a rational and mechanistic way: The technological "fix," as it has been called, can take care of anything.

The rapid expansion of industry in the nineteenth and early twentieth centuries seemed to justify this faith in the efficacy of technology. Industrialists had the keys to success and affluence, and the influence of business leaders expanded. To many, it seemed reasonable that a wide range of social problems might be solved by the broad application of industrial principles, techniques, and products to American institutions.

In particular, these principles might be applied to the schools. Many analogies were drawn between the schools and industrial factories. For example, minimizing costs and maximizing efficiency were important in both. Thus, it was assumed that if industrial productivity could be increased dramatically through the introduction of new ways of organizing workers, these same methods could work in the schools. The intricate division of labor that characterized the new assembly line and the bureaucratic organization that characterized the corporation could be transposed into the classroom and the school. One result of efforts to apply these principles to the schools was described earlier. The Lancasterian schoolroom was based on a detailed division of learning material into small measurable units, the creation of a supervisory staff in the form of monitors, the systematic evaluation and promotion of students from one level to the next as their work was finished, and the creation of formal rules of procedure governing each minute aspect of classroom life. Other similar experiments were also instituted throughout the nineteenth century and into the twentieth.[64] Today we are more likely to hear about the application of cost accounting, systems analysis, computer technology and so on in the schools than about assembly line production, but the principle of applying business techniques to education remains the same.

To some extent, the "technological fix" has been applied successfully to the schools. Without increased specialization, bureaucratization, improved administrative techniques, and modern data processing equipment, the rapid twentieth-century expansion of our educational systems could not have taken place. Despite the nostalgia of many for a simpler and more personal school there is no evidence that the quality of education has actually suffered.[65] On the contrary, students have more and better materials, a greater variety of courses, increased freedom to choose among diverse educational alternatives, and a less authoritarian relationship with teachers and administrators. The little red school house was actually cold, barren, and disorganized. It was common to have schools shut down simply because teachers could not maintain order; corporal punishment was the standard method of discipline, and few subjects beyond elementary reading, writing, and arithmetic were generally offered.

Still, there are some important ways in which the school has remained impervious to technological advances and the application of business models to education. For example, the basic classroom unit of the school has remained fundamentally unchanged. The role structure consisting of one teacher to a room full of students is still with us, though the students are now homogeneous in terms of age. The teacher is still concerned with discipline, although the use of corporal punishment has diminished greatly, and the teacher's evaluation of students' work is still a major component of classroom life. Students are still expected to be obedient, punctual, and docile, rather than rebellious or even highly creative.

Teaching techniques still rely heavily on lectures, demonstrations, and drills. Blackboard and chalk, paper and pen remain the primary tools. A great variety of printed materials such as newspapers, workbooks, paperbacks, curricula guides and so on are available, of course, but their manner of utilization has not substantially changed. This mode of instruction has successfully resisted change for a long period of time. One reason is that the old ways have several advantages over the newer technologies. They are familiar, simple, and inexpensive.

## The Technological Dream

We may be witnessing the beginnings of a second industrial revolution that will transform the United States into an "information society." The development of communications and computer technology has been so swift that we have not had time to comprehend its impact fully. New information products have been developed including communications satellites, two-way interactive cable systems, optic scanners, videotape recorders, and laser videodiscs in addition to microcomputers. Individually and in combination, these inventions have the potential to fundamentally change the nature of education.

The amount of information that can be swiftly and cheaply accessed by students and teachers can be mind-boggling. For instance, in 1983 it was possible to store the information contained in 3,200 volumes on a single disc costing $20. Mass-storage devices were available that could store the equivalent of 200,000 volumes of information in one machine. In 1984 it was technologically feasible to store the entire contents of the Manhattan telephone directory in a unit the size of a postage stamp.[66] The rapid development of microprocessors has made it possible to miniaturize and drastically reduce the cost of computers at the same time that the range and scope of their capabilities was increased. Rolls-Royce automobiles could sell for $3.00 if it were possible for their manufacturer to improve cost efficiency as much as the microcomputer industry has done during the last decade.[67] It has been predicted that by the year 2000 or shortly thereafter computers will have replaced books as the primary means of delivering information to students.

Computers and related technologies may well transform the educational process. They can provide students with access to vast amounts of information from all parts of the world. When the computer replaces the classroom teacher as the primary source of information, the teacher's role will become that of coach and guide. The new knowledge machines could ease the teacher's recordkeeping duties and reduce the amount of time devoted to group, rather than individual, instruction. Computers are excellent and infinitely patient tutors that can be programmed to provide consistently positive feedback and an absorbing mix of work and play. Although to date most educational software has been little more than the electronic equivalent of flashcards, it can be much more liberating. Elementary-aged children can use computers to learn geometry while playing with the computer's graphics capabilities.[68] Music students can use it to compose and play back original pieces. Science students can use the computer as a tool to study the ways in which graphs of mathematical functions change as variables are changed, or to simulate laboratory experiments. When a laser videodisc is linked to a microcomputer, learning can be enhanced with still or motion pictures selected from among the 54,000 frames that can be sorted on each side of the videodisc. Using this technology, a biology student can analyze the process of cell division more carefully than has been possible in the past.[69] Indeed, through computer technology it may finally be possible to realize the educator's dream of a truly individualized adventure in learning—one that is determined by the student's curiosity and motivation and that challenges but does not overwhelm and discourage. Under such circumstances the traditional educational lockstep will be broken. Procedures regarding testing, grading, promotion, and graduation will have to be revised. The fact that microcomputers have become popular domestic consumer items opens the potential for vastly expanding learning outside the formal classroom. If it becomes common for students to learn at home using new technology, educators will be pressured to recognize and adapt to such learning.

But as usual there is a serious lag between technological and curricular development. The potential of the new technology will not be fully realized for some time to come. Certain characteristics of the educational marketplace, and of organizational and professional structure, impede technological diffusion.

### Educational Industries

The school market for supplies, audiovisual equipment, books, typewriters, television sets, and the like is big business to manufacturers. Publishers have long depended on textbooks as their bread and butter moneymakers. Manufacturers of other goods, such as computers, have sought to make increasing inroads in the education market.

From a strictly business point of view, the education market is enticing, but risky. Often the amount of money available for the purchase of supplies and equipment is limited. Koerner has suggested that many manufacturers overestimate the availability of funds because they concentrate on the enormous size of school budgets without recognizing that most money is spent on salaries and similar fixed costs.[70] In addition, the demand for new products is uncertain, while the cost of research and development is often high. Even the development of a prototype and the successful completion of a pilot project does not guarantee a smooth transition to large-scale acceptance and adoption. Furthermore, copyright laws have been increasingly inadequate to deal with the many ways in which materials can be pirated through the use of copiers and related types of machines. Up-to-date copyright legislation was not signed into law until 1976.

The school supply industry has also been highly fragmented. Sales representatives offer only a narrow range of products, and some are incompatible with each other or with those offered by other companies. As Oettinger describes it:

> Because technology now permits increasing interchangeability, not only in theory but also in practice, these diverse industries, hitherto in minimal competition with one another, find themselves in common markets. Their competition is characterized by a high degree of confusion and mutual incomprehension ensuing from their earlier isolation and their differing traditions. Torn between the desire to protect their traditional markets and the desire to move into hitherto inaccessible markets, they also scramble with their competitors for newly opening markets.[71]

From the perspective of the potential buyer, the array of overlapping and incompatible goods is confusing and discouraging. All these problems have been evident in the process of introducing microcomputers into the classroom. Educators have to choose from among a perplexing variety of hardware and software products as they attempt to develop "computer literacy" programs. Nevertheless, such programs are proliferating rapidly—critics say much too rapidly without sufficient thought, coordination, and planning.[72]

In addition, the suppliers of educational technology have often failed to communicate effectively with classroom teachers. Indeed, there has sometimes been a deliberate and conscious effort by developers to bypass teachers and to make their materials "teacher-proof." Such efforts are both insulting and threatening to teachers and contribute to their rejection of the new techniques and materials. In order for technological innovations to be adopted and used by schoolteachers, extensive in-service education programs are often required. Certainly this has been the case with regard to microcomputers. Developers have often been insensitive to the teachers' concerns, however, and have not benefited from the teachers' intimate knowledge about children and classroom life. Teachers are uniquely qualified to point out problems in materials and potential obstacles to their introduction into school routine. As Janowitz and Street have argued, many technological systems have a "built-in rigidity . . . which makes them unable to meet the varied demands of the public school systems." They are also too "elaborate and extensive" to adapt to "specific classroom needs."[73]

That is not always the case, however. The relatively unglamorous yet highly significant "paperback revolution" was brought about by technological advances in printing and binding. Those developments made it possible to cut unit costs significantly.[74] This stimulated highly competitive publishing and retailing businesses. Access to printed information increased, and local bookstores proliferated. A greater diversity of materials became available also, with increases in the publication of nonfiction, scientific, and highly specialized materials aimed at narrow markets. As a consequence, it is now easier for teachers to build individually tailored sets of materials for their courses. This technology does not, of course, require extensive alterations in the organization of the school or the classroom.

The information revolution based on new developments in the computer and communications industries promises to revolutionize the publishing industry once again. This second revolution should bring still greater access to information at even more greatly reduced costs. Instructional television is used widely and apparently successfully at both the elementary and higher education levels. *Sesame Street* and the *Electric Company* are examples of innovative and effective children's television programs. They were developed by the Children's Television Workshop, an organization composed of educational entrepreneurs, media experts, entertainers, and educational consultants. Working outside of the educational establishment, this group produced programs that used visually exciting television techniques and professional actors instead of the traditional (and relatively dull) real teacher lecturing to the television audience. Professional educators were consulted, however, and played a major role in program development. The programs have proved to be both fun for children to watch and effective in teaching them.[75] They have proven international successes and have been adapted to teach languages and values other than our own. At the college level, the British Open University has served as a successful model for providing quality instruction to nontraditional adult students. Gradually, standard practices are evolving to guide the development of new programs for serving learners at home.[76] At present the primary thrust is coordination and planning.[77]

## THE UNIVERSITY AND TECHNOLOGICAL DEVELOPMENT

Thus far we have discussed the relationship between education and industrialization primarily in terms of the impact of industrialization on educational structure and processes. As we mentioned in Chapter 2, however, educational institutions, especially at the college and university level, contribute to economic development. One mechanism through which this contribution is made involves the training and socialization of the workforce. We have already discussed the shifting nature of higher education as it adjusted to the needs of the economic sector for more professional and technical workers. A second mechanism through which institutions of higher education contribute to economic development was mentioned in Chapter 2. Colleges and universities are centers of scientific research, of cultural and technological production.

Clark Kerr has referred to the large, complex university, or multiversity, as a "knowledge factory."[78] Advanced industrial societies depend heavily on new ideas in order to maintain and increase productivity, and in many cases, industry and government rely upon the universities for these ideas. Faculty and staff at these institutions directly contribute toward economic development through their own research and publication. They also contribute, however, through their roles as teachers. It is their responsibility to train the next generation of researchers. Furthermore, in their role as consultants to industry, government, and the general public, professors apply their knowledge to a wide variety of areas and problems.

Because of the importance of research for economic progress, government, industry, and private foundations sponsor and encourage it. Financial support is provided in the form of grants for specific projects, and also in terms of the broad support given to universities. Research that is clearly useful for the solution of particular problems or for the development of improved technology is most widely supported. It has always been more difficult to find funding for so called "basic" research, in which the practical payoff is less assured.

Although the close working relationship between American universities and other institutions has been admired by other nations, it has sometimes been criticized at home. During the period of intense student protests during the 1960s, many students and faculty members criticized the influence of government, industry, and military interests on the universities. In particular, they attacked the reliance of universities on governmental support for research activities and graduate programs and the willingness of universities to conduct research for the military. In some cases, there were even restrictions on the rights of researchers to publish their results because of their military or political implications. As a result of these protests, many universities established rules to prohibit research that must be conducted in secret.

It also appears that the disenchantment of some Americans with science and technology has extended to the university. University research has spurred industrial advancement, but this has resulted in rapid increases in energy consumption, depletion of natural resources, and damage to the natural environment. Nonetheless, environmentalists in search of a solution to these problems have also turned to the university. Here they hope to develop new techniques that will be less environmentally destructive and to train future cadres of environmentally committed workers as agents of change. As has often happened in the history of the American university, special teaching programs—in this case ecological studies—have been established with the intention that they will contribute to the solution of a pressing social problem.

Consensus theorists are more likely than conflict theorists to be optimistic about the potential of university-based programs to contribute to the solution of major social problems. Conflict theorists would argue that such programs, sponsored as they typically are by established business and political interests, could only develop rather conservative proposals, which would not upset existing power relations. They would add as well that most major problems require basic and pervasive changes and cannot be satisfactorily handled by minor reform.

## SUMMARY, CONCLUSIONS, AND POLICY ISSUES

In this chapter we have seen that there has often been a broad correspondence between changes in the economy and developments in education. Early in our history education was available primarily for the wealthy and apprenticeship training was the mechanism through which skilled workers were provided. With industrialization came the need for a broad base of literate and disciplined workers. As business leaders began to appreciate the potential economic benefits of schooling, public education and compulsory school laws spread across the nation. Vocational training was incorporated into the high schools and colleges of the nation, and the land-grant colleges were specifically mandated to contribute to technological innovation and dissemination of information.

This is not to say that the correspondence between economic changes and developments in education was perfect or devoid of controversy. For example, legislation restricting child labor was enacted only after years of struggle between unions, philanthropic organizations, business leaders, and parents. The interests of many of these groups were in direct conflict with each other and their struggle to have their own interests predominate in the schools was a long one.

In addition, problems arose out of discrepancies between labor force requirements and educational outputs. Rising occupational aspirations have outstripped the availability of technical and professional jobs. This has increased the number of workers who are underemployed, at jobs below their abilities, interests, and qualifications.

It seems certain that the controversy over federal career education programs will not be settled soon. In the meantime, policy decisions have to be made and other relevant questions have to be raised. How serious is the problem of overeducation and underemployment? Under what, if any, circumstances should we discourage people from seeking high levels of education and prestigious occupations? If we should discourage them, how should we do this? Is it better to counsel people about their vocational prospects or to expand training opportunities and rewards in high demand fields, or to contract programs which prepare people for occupations with a glut of personnel? For example, is it better to cut back funding for graduate training in the humanities now that there is an oversupply of Ph.D.'s in that area, or should we only let prospective students know about these conditions and let them decide? Is it desirable for school counselors to be used to dampen the high occupational aspirations of some youth? Would such efforts increase conflict within the schools, demoralize and alienate large portions of the student body, or lead to further social class, racial, ethnic, or gender inequalities? We might even ask whether or not it is deceitful to encourage students to cooperate with our economic institutions as we now know them. Perhaps we should direct resources toward changing those institutions rather than adapting people to them. Perhaps we should concentrate on changing the workplace rather than the schools, increasing worker participation in decision making, striving to make routine jobs more challenging, and in other ways making ordinary jobs more attractive. Perhaps we need to be more radical even than that.

Questions can also be raised about the relationship between education and technological development discussed in this chapter. There have been innumerable ways in which technological development has made the restructuring of education and the introduction of new educational methods possible. For example, we mentioned the availability of more books and reading materials. On the other hand, many factors have inhibited the full realization of what technology has to offer. Inadequacies in the materials produced to date combined with the financial problems of local school districts, general resistances to new ideas, and the characteristics of teaching as a profession tend to inhibit innovation. To what extent should these inhibiting forces be seen as problems? As we pointed out, it is simplistic to equate innovation with improvement. Margaret Nelson and Sam Seiber put it this way:

> In view of the amount of fadism in educational change and the doubtful value of many widely accepted innovations, the sheer enumeration of adoptions might reflect only salesmanship or community pressures rather than enlightened educational reform. Consequently, the so-called barriers to innovation might actually be beneficial for American education.[79]

Nelson and Seiber base their position on their research in public schools. They asked a national panel of experts to judge the various innovations that had been adopted there. Many were judged to be of dubious value. Among these were programmed instruction, teaching machines, and television instruction.

Nelson and Seiber speculate that such costly, but poorly evaluated, technologies are adopted because of their publicity rather than educational value: " . . . the school administrator or trustee who can point to a tangible innovation that is readily comprehensible to the public may be viewed as reducing organizational vulnerability to local constituencies."[80] The political utility of educational innovations may therefore play an important part in their adaptation. In view of these facts, perhaps we should be skeptical about technological innovations in education. Certainly, the question of how many resources should go toward supporting these innovations rather than strengthening such traditional educational forces as teacher training is an important policy question.

Nevertheless, microcomputers have already been widely and quickly accepted. Their promise has been touted so widely and their price has been reduced so greatly, that they have proven virtually irresistible. By 1984, 82 percent of our elementary schools, 93 percent of our junior high schools, and 95 percent of our senior high schools were using microcomputers for instruction.[81] However, purchasing the machines does not guarantee their use, especially not their effective use.

At present, virtually all educators are in favor of "computer literacy" but there is little agreement on just what that entails. Computer programs are developing in a typically unplanned, uncoordinated, and uneven fashion.[82] As usual, the affluent suburban school districts are leading, and the poorer, inner-city districts are lagging behind. The equity issue is an important one. There is a real danger that unequal access to computers at home and at school will widen the gap between affluent and impoverished youth and that computer illiteracy will further diminish the life chances of minority youth. There is a gender equity issue also. Unless computer literacy for females is stressed, males may well dominate the computer rooms both within the school system and outside.[83]

It was not until 1983 that the federal government provided significant leadership by funding a national computer education center at Harvard University. It is hoped that the professors working in that group will develop reasonable standards and curricular guidelines. However, the pace of change in the field is so rapid that it will be extremely difficult for that group or any other to keep up with new developments.

There are also major personnel problems. In order to make effective use of computers, teachers will need a great deal of in-service training. That training will have to address both attitudinal and technical issues. But there is a severe shortage of trained computer experts in the schools, just as there is in private industry. Schools of education and computer science departments are not producing enough such experts to meet the demand.

Another important policy question raised by this chapter is whether or not we wish to continue to use education to promote further industrialization. There are those who would say, "No!" Ivan Illich, for example, argues that we must recognize the fact that there are limits to industrial growth and that it cannot continue forever.[84] Furthermore, he argues that the search for economic growth has resulted in oppressive social systems, the rapid utilization of dwindling natural resources, the production of huge amounts of waste and pollution, and the possible exacerbation of the already great international inequities in standards of living.

Most policymakers probably dismiss Illich as an alarmist. They continue to believe that standards of living can still be raised dramatically through further industrialization and that it is appropriate to strengthen our educational institutions in response to foreign economic competition and military threat. That line of reasoning is evident in the report of the National Commission on Excellence in Education, which states in part: "If an unfriendly foreign power had attempted to impose on America the mediocre educational performance that exists today, we might well have viewed it as an act of war."[85] As a result of this and several other influential reports issued in the 1980s, attention has been focused on weaknesses in the mathematics, science, and technological aspects of our educational institutions. There have been calls for improvements in both the quantity and quality of math/science education in elementary and secondary schools and for upgrading scientific/technological facilities in our colleges and universities. However, it is not clear where the money and personnel will come from to accomplish these improvements. Finances are tight and there is a severe shortage of qualified math/science/technology teachers and professors. We will gain more insight into the complexity of these problems in later chapters that deal with power and professionalism.

## *NOTES*

[1]We do this with the full recognition that any single periodization is bound to be less than totally satisfactory because of the complex nature of social change and the mixing of past, present, and future practices at any given time.

[2]The discussion of this period is based upon Forest Chester Ensign, *Compulsory School Attendance and Child Labor* (orig. pub. Iowa City, Iowa: The Athens Press, 1921 and republished New York: Arno Press and *The New York Times*, 1969), p. 33; Fred M. Hechinger

and Grace Hechinger, *Growing Up in America* (New York: McGraw-Hill Book Company, 1975); Paul Monroe, *Founding of the American Public School System* (New York: The Macmillan Company, 1940); Frederich Rudolph, *The American College and University: A History* (New York: Vintage Books, 1965), Chapter 1; Patrick J. Ryan, *Historical Foundations of Public Education in America* (Dubuque: Wm. C. Brown Company, 1965); Rena L. Vassar, *Social History of American Education* (Chicago: Rand McNally and Company, 1965); Rush Welter, *Popular Education and Democratic Thought in America* (New York: Columbia University Press, 1962), p. 45 ff.

[3]Monroe, *Founding of the American Public School System*, p. 110.

[4]Ryan, *Historical Foundations*, p. 204.

[5]Monroe, *Founding of the American Public School System*, p. 105.

[6]This part of our discussion is based on Stanley M. Elkins, *Slavery: A Problem in American Institutional and Intellectual Life*, 2 ed. (Chicago: The University of Chicago Press, 1968), pp. 52–80.

[7]Leon Litwack, "Education! Separate and Unequal," in Michael B. Katz (ed.) *Education in American History: Readings on the Social Issues* (New York: Praeger Publishers, 1973), pp. 253–66.

[8]Our discussion of this period draws heavily upon Monroe, *Founding of the American Public School system*, pp. 230–337; and Welter, *Popular Education and Democratic Thought in America*.

[9]Welter, *Popular Education*, p. 190.

[10]See Oscar Handlin, *The Uprooted* (New York: Grosset and Dunlap, 1951) and Hechinger and Hechinger, *Growing Up in America*.

[11]Peter P. DeBoes, "Compulsory Attendance," in *The Encyclopedia of Education* (New York: Crowell-Collier Educational Corporation, Macmillan Co. and The Free Press, 1971), p. 377.

[12]Martin Trow, "The Second Transformation of American Secondary Education," in *The School in Society*, eds. Sam D. Sieber and David E. Wilder (New York: The Free Press, 1973), pp. 45–61.

[13]U.S. Bureau of the Census, *Historical Statistics of the United States, Colonial Times to 1957*, Series H223–233 (Washington, D.C.: Government Printing Office, 1960), p. 207.

[14]Paul Saettler, *A History of Instructional Technology* (New York: McGraw-Hill Book Company, 1968), p. 27; and Monroe, *Founding of the American Public School System*, pp. 359–72.

[15]Monroe, *Founding of the American Public School System*, p. 367.

[16]Joel Spring, *Education and the Rise of the Corporate State* (Boston: Beacon Press, 1972), pp. 45–46.

[17]Vassar, *Social History*, p. 117.

[18]Ryan, *Historical Foundations*, p. 240.

[19]Vassar, *Social History*, p. 120.

[20]Ibid., p. 120.

[21]Our discussion of Dewey is based primarily on Oscar Handlin, "John Dewey's Contribution to Education," in *The American Experience in Education*, eds. John Barnard and David Burner (New York: New Viewpoints, A Division of Franklin Watts, Inc., 1975), pp. 200–40.

[22]Handlin, "John Dewey," p. 208.

[23]Ibid., p. 219.

[24]Valena White Plisko and Joyce D. Stern, *The Condition of Education 1985*, (Washington, D.C.: Government Printing Office, 1983), p. 3.

[25]U.S. Bureau of the Census, *Statistical Abstract of the United States* (Washington, D.C.: Government Printing Office, 1986), p. 149.

[26]Trow, "The Second Transformation," p. 50.

[27]Joel Spring, *The Sorting Machine* (New York: David McKay Company, 1976).

[28]Ibid., pp. 96–97.

[29]Trow, "The Second Transformation," pp. 50–51.

[30]Richard Wohl, "The Rags to Riches' Story: An Episode of Secular Idealism," in *Class, Status and Power: A Reader in Social Stratification*, eds. Reinhard Bendix and Seymour Martin Lipset (New York: The Free Press, 1965), pp. 388–95.

[31]Peter M. Blau and Otis Dudley Duncan, *The American Occupational Structure* (New York: John Wiley and Sons, 1967), p. 430.

[32]Ivar Berg, *Education and Jobs: The Great Training Robbery* (Boston: Beacon Press, 1971).

[33]Louis Robinson, "The Computer as an Enabling Instrument," in Russell Edgerton, ed., *Colleges Enter the Information Society*, (Washington, D.C. American Association for Higher Education), p. 5.

[34]James P. Johnson, "Can Computers Close the Equity Gap?," *Perspectives*, 14, 3 (Fall, 1982).

[35]"Mathematics and Science Education: Problems and Prospects," *Education Week* (July 27, 1983), p. 1.

[36]Berg, *Education and Jobs*.

[37]Ibid., p. 104.

[38]James O'Toole, "The Reserve Army of the Unemployed: I—The Role of Education," *Change*, 7 (May 1975), p. 67.

[39]Jacob Mincer, *Schooling, Experience and Earnings* (New York: Columbia University Press, 1974).

[40]Fred Hines, Luther Tweeten, and Martin Redfern, "Social and Private Rates of Return to Investment in Schooling," in *Woman in a Man-Made World*, eds. Nona Glazer-Malbin and Helen Youngelson Waehrer (Chicago: Rand McNally and Co., 1972), pp. 228–34.

[41]These and the following data are all taken from U.S. Department of Commerce *Current Population Reports*, Series P-60, No. 146, "Money Income of Households, Families, and Persons in the United States: 1983," (Washington, D.C.: Government Printing Office, 1985), pp. 158–165. The data presented here represent income rather than earnings. Comparable data on earnings were not available. The effect of using income instead of earnings is probably modest, however. Since we are using only full-time, year-round workers, income from unemployment, pensions, Social Security, and the like should be minimal. Data show that few people have substantial income from other sources, such as investments. Furthermore, such income is at least partially related to earnings and the ability to save enough money to invest, so it might be reasonably included in a measure of return on educational investment anyway. Note, also, that those with low levels of education are more likely to be unemployed, but this effect is not included in statistics on full-time year-round workers.

[42]National Center for Education Statistics, *Does College Pay? Wage Rates Before and After Leaving School* (Washington, D.C.: Government Printing Office, 1982).

[43]Christopher Jencks, Marshall Smith, Henry Acland, Mary Jo Bane, David Cohen, Herbert Gintis, Barbara Heyns, and Stephan Michelson, *Inequality: A Reassessment of the Effect of Family and Schooling in America* (New York: Basic Books, 1972), p. 223.

[44]Ibid., 176–246.

[45]Richard B. Freeman found that highly qualified blacks have not been affected in this way, according to the Carnegie Commission, *Sponsored Research of the Carnegie Commission on Higher Education* (New York: McGraw-Hill Book Company, 1975), pp. 178–79.

[46]See, for example, Richard B. Freeman and Herbert J. Hollomon, "The Declining Value of College Going," *Change*, 7 (September 1975), pp. 24–31; David R. Witmer, "Is the Value of College Going Really Declining?," *Change*, 8 (December, 1976), 46–47, 60–61; and Howard R. Bowen, *Investment in Learning: The Individual and Social Value of American Higher Education* (San Francisco: Jossey-Bass, 1977).

[47]V. Lane Rawlins and Lloyd Ullman, "The Utilization of College Trained Manpower in the United States," in *Higher Education and the Labor Market*, Margaret S. Gordon, ed. (New York: McGraw-Hill Book Company, 1974).

[48]Paul L. Tractenberg, *Testing the Teacher* (New York: Agathon Press, 1973), pp. 223–27.

[49]William B. Fetters, George H. Brown, and Jeffrey A. Owings, *High School Seniors: A Comparative Study of the Classes of 1972 and 1980* (Washington, D.C.: Government Printing Office, 1984), pp. 30–32.

[50]U.S. Bureau of the Census, *Statistical Abstracts of the United States* (Washington, D.C.: Government Printing Office, 1986), p. 400.

[51]Kenneth B. Hoyt, "Correspondence," *Harvard Educational Review*, 46 (November, 1976), pp. 650–56.

[52]Hoyt, "Correspondence," p. 652.

[53]W. Norton Grub and Marvin Lazerson, "A Response to Our Critics," *Harvard Educational Review*, 46 (November, 1976), pp. 662–67.

[54]Talcott Parsons, "The School Class as a Social System: Some of Its Functions in American Society," *Harvard Educational Review*, 29, 4 (Fall, 1959), pp. 297–318.

[55]Ray C. Rist, "Student Social Class and Teacher Expectations: The Self-Fulfilling Prophecy in Ghetto Education," *Harvard Educational Review*, 40 (1970), pp. 411–51.

[56]Pauline S. Sears and David H. Feldman, "Teacher Interactions with Boys and Girls," in Judith Stacey, Susan Béreaud, and Joan Daniels (eds.), *And Jill Came Tumbling After: Sexism in American Education* (New York: Dell Publishing Co., 1974), pp. 147–58.

[57]Women on Words and Images, "Look Jane Look. See Sex Stereotypes," in Stacey and others, *And Jill Came Tumbling After: Sexism in American Education* pp. 159–77.

[58]John S. Brubacher and Willis Rudy, *Higher Education in Transition* (New York: Harper & Row, 1958), p. 272.

[59]Ronald G. Corwin, *A Sociology of Education: Emerging Patterns of Class, Status and Power in the Public Schools* (New York: Appleton-Century-Croft, 1965). p. 192.

[60]See, for example, John J. Pietrofesa and Nancy K. Schlossberg, "Counselor Bias and the Female Occupational Role," in Nona Glazer-Malbin and Helen Youngelson Waehrer, *Women in a Man-Made World* (Chicago: Rand McNally and Co., 1972), pp. 219–21.

[61]Aaron V. Cicourel and John I. Kitsuse, *The Educational Decision-Makers (Indianapolis: Bobbs-Merrill, 1963).*

[62]James E. Rosenbaum, *Making Inequality: The Hidden Curriculum of High School Tracking* (New York: John Wiley & Sons, 1976).

[63]Burton R. Clark, "The Cooling Out Function in Higher Education," *American Journal of Sociology*, 65 (May, 1960), pp. 569–76.

[64]Monroe, *Founding of the American Public School System*, pp. 338–89.

[65]Between 1963 and 1980 the scores of high school students on a number of standardized tests declined steadily. Although it has been suggested that these declines reflected new deficiencies in the schools, there is no hard evidence to support this interpretation. Alternative explanations suggest that inadequacies in the tests, changes in the characteristics of students taking the tests, or alterations in curriculum may have been involved. Our own point is that there is more evidence to suggest that educational quality has improved over the last two or three centuries than there is evidence to suggest that it has declined.

[66]Robinson, "Computer as an Enabling Instrument," p. 7.

[67]Harold G. Shane, "The Silicon Age of Education," *Phi Delta Kappan* (January, 1982), p. 303.

[68]Seymour Papert, *Mindstorms* (New York: Basic Books, 1980).

[69]Francis D. Fisher, "Teaching, Scholarship and the Computer," *American Association for Higher Education Bulletin* (November, 1982), p. 4.

[70]James Koerner, "Educational Technology," in *Readings in Education 75/76* (Guilford: The Dushkin Publishing Group, Inc., 1974), pp. 158–61.

[71]Anthony G. Oettinger and Nikki Zipol, "Will Information Technologies Help Learning?" in *Content and Context: Essays on College Education*, ed. Carl Kaysen (New York: McGraw-Hill Book Company, 1973).

[72]Edward Fiske, "Computer Education: Update '83," *Popular Computing*, 2 (August, 1983), p. 86.

[73]Morris Janowitz and David Street, "The Social Organization of Education," in *The New Media and Education*, eds. Peter Rossi and Bruce Biddle (Chicago: Aldine Publishing Co., 1966), p. 226.

[74]Ibid., p. 240.

[75]R. Beanton, "How Effective is Sesame Street?," *The Reading Teacher*, 25 (May, 1972), pp. 804–805.

[76]Charles E. Feasley, *Serving Learners at a Distance* (Washington, D.C.: Association for the Study of Higher Education, 1983).

[77]Fiske, "Computer Education: Update '83," p. 86.

[78]Clark Kerr, *The Uses of the University* (New York: Torchbooks, Harper & Row, 1966).

[79]Margaret Nelson and Sam D. Seiber, "Innovations in Urban Secondary Schools," *School Review*, 84 (February, 1976), pp. 213–63.

[80]Ibid., p. 214.

[81]United States Bureau of the Census, *Statistical Abstracts 1986* (Washington, D.C.: Government Printing Office, 1986), p. 144.

[82]Fiske, "Computer Education: Update '83," p. 83.

[83]Linda Wyrick Winkle and Walter M. Mathews, "Computer Equity Comes of Age," *Phi Delta Kappan*, 63 (January 1982), p. 314; James P. Johnson, "Can Computers Close the Equity Gap?," *Perspectives*, 14 (Fall, 1982), p. 20.

[84]Ivan Illich, *Deschooling Society* (New York: Harper & Row, 1971).

[85]The National Commission on Excellence in Education: *A Nation At Risk: The Imperative for Educational Reform* (Washington, D.C.: Government Printing Office, 1983).

# CHAPTER FOUR BUREAUCRATIZATION

As societies modernize, ever-greater efforts are made to maximize the efficient accomplishment of goals through rational processes such as research and planning. Max Weber argued that the organizational form most compatible with these developments is the bureaucracy.[1] In industrial societies such as ours, bureaucracies are everywhere. The major governmental, military, economic, religious, and even recreational institutions are highly bureaucratized. Attempts to rationalize the educational process have been commonplace throughout this century. Thus, it is not surprising that our schools, colleges, and universities display certain bureaucratic characteristics. However, recent research suggests that the core processes of teaching and learning are *not* greatly constrained by bureaucratic rules and regulations. As a first step in understanding how this may be so, it is important to clarify just what a bureaucracy is.

## BUREAUCRACY AS AN IDEAL TYPE

Weber used a sociological tool known as the "ideal type" to describe the key elements in any bureaucratic organization. An "ideal type" is a conceptual rather than an empirical construct. It describes an "idea" rather than something that actually exists. For example, Weber's description of the "ideal typical" bureaucracy emphasizes that formal rules govern all important decision making within such organizations. It ignores the fact that in real, everyday bureaucracies rules are often violated. We even have an adage that reflects our belief that rules *should* be ignored, at least at times: "Rules are made to be broken," we say, and then proceed to do just that.

Ideal types can be very useful, though. They help systematize the analysis of social structures and provide standards against which real life, operating social systems can be compared. In this chapter we will compare American educational institutions at different points in time with Weber's ideal typical bureaucracy. There have been many analyses and reinterpretations of Weber's original description of bureaucratic organizations. Our approach will be relatively simple and straightforward. We will begin by delineating the key elements of this ideal type: goals, division of labor, hierarchy of authority, offices, and written rules.[2] After each aspect of the ideal type is introduced, we will summarize conclusions drawn from empirical studies of organizations. The research findings underscore the fact that deviations from the ideal type are common.

### Goals

Weber considered bureaucracies the most efficient means of organizing people to accomplish specified ends. According to his model, efficiency demands that the purposes of any given organization be limited in number, unambiguous, and explicitly set forth in a legal statute or organizational charter. Administrators are expected to work as disinterested experts toward the accomplishment of these established goals.

Contemporary sociological theory and research on complex organizations deemphasize the importance of official goals in orienting the behavior of officials in public bureaucracies. In reality, public service organizations typically have multiple, ambiguous, and even contradictory goals. Often certain goals are ignored, resented, and contested, not only by individual employees but also by important groups within the organization. Finally, goals are now seen as dynamic, rather than static. They are often displaced or redefined in response to internal and/or external pressure.

### The Functional Division of Labor

Complex tasks can be accomplished efficiently through a division of labor. The idea is to split a complicated task into its relatively simple and manageable parts. Then specific personnel are assigned to each part of the overall task. Specialization of roles promotes expertise.

The more highly differentiated the division of labor, the narrower the task of each individual worker, thereby making that worker more expert in his or her particular task. Each individual learns only a very limited number of responses, and repetition of these same actions over and over again makes performance automatic, accurate, and dependable. If the jobs are defined narrowly enough, they may be so simple that little or no individual judgment is needed. This idea of narrow specialization contrasts sharply with the traditional concept of the worker as a craftsman—a person who is responsible for completing an entire product from beginning to end.

Specialization can be, and often is, carried to such extremes that jobs become dull and monotonous. They lack challenge, seem unrelated to the larger goals of the organization, and deprive workers of opportunities for creativity. The costs of extreme specialization are often alienation and demoralization among workers. For example, workers on assembly line jobs often have high rates of absenteeism and dissatisfaction because of the monotony of their work. Nevertheless, the prevalence of such practices reflects a continued belief in their contribution to overall organizational efficiency.

### The Hierarchy of Authority

If an organization relies on a highly differentiated division of labor, it must also establish a way of efficiently coordinating all the discrete units of work. Each task must be performed in relation to all the others: No one person can suddenly decide to do his or her job differently, and each will have to work at a pace that is compatible with the others.

In bureaucratic organizations this problem of coordinating tasks is solved through a hierarchy of authority. Supervisory personnel are responsible for organizing, coordinating, monitoring, and evaluating the work of a specific group of employees. The hierarchy of authority is like a pyramid. At the bottom are large numbers of people. At each step upward there are fewer, and at the top there is one individual or a very small group of individuals who have authority over all the rest.

Ideally, every person in a bureaucracy knows or can easily find out who is the boss, what channels should be used to accomplish a given task, and what the relationship of one person's work is to that of another occupying a different position within the organization. However, many studies have shown that the formal lines of authority in an organization do not always coincide with the actual informal authority exerted in day-to-day operations.[3] Some individuals, by virtue of personal talents, charisma, or access to key pieces of information, exert much more influence than their official positions in the organization would indicate. Interestingly, these informal lines of authority often contribute to the efficiency of an organization. Perhaps you have come across a department secretary at school who knows more about what's going on than the department chairperson. When the secretary is out sick, things may grind to a screeching halt.

The hierarchy of authority in organizations employing professionals is often relatively loose and attenuated. Doctors and lawyers, for example, value autonomy and may therefore resent administrative regulations, supervision, and evaluation.

Although a hierarchy of authority is important for coordination, it can impede organizational efficiency as well as facilitate it. Communication in bureaucratic organizations is predominantly in a downward direction. Those in charge give directives to those below. Theoretically, of course, communication can and should go in both directions. If supervisors are to coordinate the activities of their subordinates, they have to know what work is being done and what problems exist at each level in the structure. Subordinates often restrict or distort the information they communicate upwards, however.

Think again of your school experiences. How often have you been willing to tell your teachers that their lectures are unintelligible or that the books they assigned are too difficult. The distance between supervisors and subordinates and the power supervisors have to dismiss or punish unsatisfactory subordinates can impede an organization's ability to operate at maximum efficiency.

### The Definition of Staff Roles as Offices

When we say that some individuals in a bureaucracy have authority over others, we mean this in a very special way. It is not the authority that a king has over his subjects or that a parent has over a child. Rather, it is authority that is formally defined and clearly circumscribed. It is limited to areas that are relevant to the work of the bureaucracy. Your boss can tell you to work faster, but not that you must exercise every morning before reporting to the office.

In addition to being formally defined and highly circumscribed, authority in bureaucratic organizations resides in the offices of the organization rather than in the people who occupy those offices. For example, if your boss quits, he or she no longer has any right to give you orders. On the contrary, you are expected to immediately transfer your obedience to whoever is hired in your boss's place. You obey the office or the rank, not the particular individual who is occupying it at the time, and you obey because you are getting paid to do so.

On the other hand, you also obey your boss because he or she possesses a certain amount of expertise. Positions in bureaucratic organizations are assigned on the basis of expertise. You are given a job because of what you can do rather than because of who you are. As your experience and expertise increase, you are promoted up the organizational hierarchy. Thus, in theory at least, supervisors know more than the people they supervise, and this serves to legitimize their authority.

Of course, we all know that real bureaucracies do not always work this way. Many factors other than expertise determine who will be hired for a job and who will be promoted. Because they have become expert in their narrowly specialized job, subordinates often know more than their supervisors about the particular job they are doing. This can lead to conflict. For example, college professors commonly bristle when nonacademic administrators issue regulations that constrain their teaching or research activities.

### Operation According to Rules of Procedure

We mentioned that authority within bureaucratic organizations is legally defined and narrowly circumscribed. The specific positions that exist within a bureaucratic organization and the rights and obligations belonging to each are clearly specified, as are the set of rules and regulations upon which all organizational decisions are supposed to be based.

Many organizations have books that clearly specify what rules and regulations must be followed under a variety of conditions and circumstances. Your college catalogue or student handbook are good examples.

According to Weber's theory, if everyone acted in accordance with the rules, coordination and efficiency would be maximized. Thus, bureaucrats are concerned with mechanisms of control, rewards for conformity, and punishments for deviance.

Actually, however, individuals in large-scale organizations routinely violate formal rules and comply with informal norms instead. These unwritten rules can supplement, contradict, or evade the formal norms. Critics of Weber argue that informal norms often make for a more humane organization, and several studies have shown that they can actually contribute to organizational efficiency rather than detract from it.[4]

Organizations sometimes develop so many complex rules of procedure that processes are slowed to a virtual halt. You have all had experiences with "bureaucratic red tape." Just think of your first few weeks at college, when you always seemed to have waited on the wrong line or appeared at the wrong office. As time passed, you "learned the ropes," and by now you are probably an expert on all the formal rules and informal ways of getting around them.

One reason why rules may undermine organizational efficiency is the tendency for them to "displace" the original goals of the organization. Rules originally established for some rational purpose become rigidly enforced, even when they no longer serve their original purpose. They become ends in themselves, rather than means to an end. In fact, one major criticism of bureaucratic organizations is that they are difficult to change. They encourage conformity to rules rather than creativity and innovation.

There is another important characteristic of rules in bureaucratic organizations: They are supposed to be applied objectively, to all relevant cases, without regard to the individual workers or clients involved at any particular time. In other words, each person is to be treated alike, according to the rules. In this sense, bureaucratic organizations are impersonal and universalistic. The rules apply whether you are a likeable person or not, whether your skin is black or white, or whether or not you are a relative of the boss. Personal prejudices are put aside and emotional involvements avoided.

Again, we know that real organizations do not operate this way. To some extent, however, bureaucratic organizations are criticized whether or not they follow such guidelines. For example, bureaucratic organizations are criticized when they allow prejudices to influence decisions. We decry the fact that some people have "pull" or that some people are not hired because of their ethnicity or gender. On the other hand, bureaucratic organizations are also criticized for being too impersonal and universalistic. Service organizations, such as hospitals and welfare agencies, for example, are accused of treating people like "cases" and having no compassion for individual suffering.[5]

We also know, of course, that people in bureaucratic settings develop feelings of friendship, as well as hostility, toward one another. Friendships among workers have been found to play an important role in both worker satisfaction and productivity. Although affective involvements can work to the detriment of organizational efficiency, they can also contribute positively to productivity and goal accomplishment. Friendships can enhance morale, lead to mutually supportive and helpful behavior, and increase output.

## EDUCATION AND BUREAUCRATIZATION: A HISTORICAL OVERVIEW

Now that we have the key elements of Weber's model in mind, let us use them to assess the changes that have occurred in our educational institutions over time.[6] Most sociologists agree that schools have become increasingly bureaucratized, although there are important ways in which they have not. There is some controversy, however, over the forces that have contributed to this bureaucratization and the implications of this pattern of development. Consensus theorists stress the compatibility of bureaucratically organized education with industrialization and the core values of American society. Conflict theorists stress that bureaucratization of the schools represents the triumph of middle-class business interests over the interests of the working masses.

These two perspectives taken together help us distinguish several major forces that contributed to the rise of bureaucratization in education. Among these were dramatic increases in the size and heterogeneity of the school-going population, the powerful position of business leaders during early industrialization, the subsequent applications of principles of scientific management to education, educational reformers, and the progressive movement of the early twentieth century. As we look at the ways in which schools have changed over time, we will point out the influences each of these forces had on the process.

### The Pre-Industrial Period

A variety of schools existed during the Pre-Industrial Period, but most were small and relatively undifferentiated internally. One teacher or master was generally in charge. He or she was responsible not only for instruction but also for keeping the schoolroom clean, arranging for supplies, keeping whatever meager records were necessary, dealing with townspeople, and even starting the schoolroom fire each morning. In some cases, such as in the larger Latin Grammar schools and the academies, more than one teacher might be employed or a single teacher might have assistants, but this did not occur until the eighteenth century and was restricted mainly to secondary-level education.

One teacher covered all the subject areas included in the curriculum. For the most part, however, few subjects were taught in each school. At the elementary level, most schools taught only reading and the catechism, with a little writing or arithmetic sometimes included. At the secondary-school level, most schools taught only a classical curriculum. These—the Latin Grammar schools—concentrated on grammar, rhetoric, and logic. Latin and Greek were the languages taught, although some also included English. One master was responsible for all instruction. A more diverse curriculum was taught in the academies. You may recall from Chapter 3 that these schools included such subjects as history, geography, commerce, and mechanics. Schools usually served children of rather diverse ages, and admission and graduation depended more on skill and school experience than age.

Schools were located in diverse settings throughout this period and were not always formally differentiated from other institutions in terms of physical space. Many met in the master's home. This was particularly true for the Dame Schools and for the earliest of the New England town schools. Later, each town constructed a special building to house the school in a central location. As the population in the colonies grew and dispersed over a larger geographical area, centrally located schools became less practical. Children could not travel long distances on foot, especially during the winter months. In New England, this problem was solved in several different ways. One involved moving the school from place to place during the course of the calendar year. The "moving school" often met in farmhouses located in various parts of the community. These were often called "kitchen schools," because that's where they met; though sometimes an extra room was added on for the school. Eventually, these evolved into separate schools for each area or district, and local schoolhouses were constructed.

Throughout this period, schools served rather homogeneous groups of children, except in terms of age. Some elementary schools of this period served both boys and girls, but many did not. The sexes were often segregated by restricting girls to attendance during only certain months of the year, usually the summer, or having them attend outside of regular school hours. For example, girls would be taught either very early in the morning or quite late in the afternoon. Secondary schools that received public funds were generally for boys only. Private schools for girls were available at both the elementary and secondary levels, however.

Many schools of this period served only one religious group and virtually all were restricted to white students. As we mentioned in Chapter 3, they were also relatively homogeneous in terms of socioeconomic status. Especially outside New England, poor and working-class children either did not attend school or went to a variety of pauper or charity schools. Ascriptive, rather than achieved, characteristics thus played an important part in determining whether or not a child attended school and what type of school he or she attended.

During most of this period, both legislative and administrative responsibility for publicly financed schools rested with local communities. As early as the mid-seventeenth century, however, special committees were generally chosen to take charge of school affairs. These committees were often elected on a yearly basis by all eligible town voters. As the population grew and dispersed, it became customary to have each part of the community represented on this committee. As multiple schools were set up to service the expanding population, however, the tasks of these committees became increasingly complex. Eventually, when district schools were established, each local area selected its own school committee.

These committees made all administrative decisions regarding the local school. They hired and fired teachers, set salaries, arranged for the maintenance of the schoolhouse, and so on. Other schools, both in New England and elsewhere, were run by ecclesiastical societies belonging to various local churches or by boards of voluntary trustees interested in the establishment of private schools and academies. In all cases, however, the authority exercised by these bodies was broad and arbitrary.

Teachers themselves represented a rather diverse population. For the most part, there were no formal mechanisms through which they were licensed. However, in at least some communities prospective teachers in public and private schools had to prove their qualifications to selected town officials. At the secondary-school level, ministers were often the only individuals sufficiently knowledgeable in the classical curriculum to make this kind of evaluation of a prospective teacher. We will discuss teachers in more detail in Chapter 6. The important point for now is that there were few if any formal requirements for establishing oneself in this occupation.

The teacher's authority over students, like the town's authority over the teachers, was broad and often arbitrarily exercised. Teachers were concerned with the moral character and after-school behavior of their students, as townspeople were concerned with the character and after-school behavior of their teachers. In the classroom itself, each teacher was left to devise his or her own individual method of maintaining order. Corporal punishment was widely practiced. On the other hand, students sometimes rebelled and even fought their teachers physically. If the teacher could not maintain discipline, he or she might be dismissed or the school might be closed down permanently.

If we summarize this broad overview of the schools of the Pre-Industrial Period, it is clear that they were not highly bureaucratized institutions. Although there was considerable variation from one to the other, each school was relatively undifferentiated internally. The roles within each school were usually restricted to two: teacher and student. There were no clearly delineated administrative posts, clerical staff, janitorial services, or other division of labor such as is seen in the modern school. There were few formal rules to govern how schools were run and few regulations affecting teacher training or qualifications. All students within a school were taught the same subjects, and these tended to be few in number. The students themselves tended to be a rather homogeneous lot, certainly in terms of race, religion, and gender. They were not, however, differentiated by age. What differentiation did exist tended to be between schools rather than within them. All of this was to change in the Early Industrial Period.

Before we go on to this next period, however, a word must be said about the many children of the eighteenth and nineteenth centuries who did not attend school, or who attended only briefly. As we indicated in Chapter 3, many of these children were apprenticed. Although some legal restrictions applied to apprenticeship training, the authority of the master over an apprentice extended to every aspect of the youngster's life. The apprentice learned by working alongside the master, and little if any formal instruction took place. Both lived as well as worked together. This form of education was, of course, the least bureaucratized of all. It existed primarily in a one-to-one, personal relationship between master and apprentice rather than in an organization formally established for the purposes of education.

## The Early Industrial Period

Numerous far-reaching changes occurred in the structure of education during this period. By the end of it, the basic structure of the contemporary American school was clearly and firmly established.

As we indicated in Chapter 3, this period—from 1812 to 1930—was a time of enormous growth in the number of students attending first elementary-level schools, and then high schools, across the country. This growth was attributable to several important factors. First, free public schools were gradually established throughout the nation. Financial arrangements for supporting these schools were formalized in local and state laws, and the stigma previously attached to attending them gradually faded. Second, compulsory school attendance laws were enacted and, by the end of the period, strictly enforced. Third, the population itself grew considerably as increasingly large waves of immigrants came to America's shores. Many of these immigrants settled in urban areas rather than moving directly onto farms. Some were immigrants from urban areas themselves, but many simply settled where job opportunities seemed greatest. The rapid expansion of industry during this period provided these jobs and attracted not only immigrants but also American citizens who migrated from rural communities into the cities. This was particularly true of the latter part of this period and meant that city schools in particular experienced a phenomenal growth in school-going population. It was here that the pressures for bureaucratization were first experienced.

At the same time that schools were receiving larger numbers of students, they were also receiving more diverse students. Not only did immigrants add to school diversity, but the general strengthening of public schools and the weakening of private ones did as well. As public funds were withdrawn from church-sponsored schools, for example, these became less viable financially, forcing many parents to send their children to public schools instead. The public schools began serving children from different religious groups and even different social classes. The poor and the working classes were more likely to send their children to school now that attendance was both free and required. Middle-class families were more likely to send their children to the same schools now that private schools were more expensive and they were being taxed to pay for the public schools whether or not their children attended them.

The school-going population also became more heterogeneous in other ways. With the spread of secondary school education, children of a wider variety of ages were found in the public schools. More students were staying longer. Also, schools were more often serving girls as well as boys and blacks as well as whites. Though these children were not always served in the same classroom or the same school, they were eventually accepted as part of the school-aged population for which government had some responsibility. Thus, schools had to be established that served these children, either separately or together.

The impact on the schools of this sheer increase in size and heterogeneity cannot be overestimated. There seemed to be no way for schools to handle these numbers and variations of students without more formal organization and regulation. Still, the particular solutions found to these problems resulted from other forces that were influential at the same time. For example, industrial expansion and the increasing power of business leaders were important. The success of industrialists in effectively and profitably organizing many complex and diverse businesses provided a model for those looking for solutions to educational problems. Industry seemed to have solved the problems of complexity and scale through bureaucratization, and this solution was potentially applicable to the schools as well. As we shall see, the use of industrial models in education reached a peak during the early twentieth century when the stress on efficiency in school organization reached some rather strange heights of absurdity.

Industry affected the schools in another ways. As we shall see, the administrative machinery for overseeing education became increasingly complex during this period. The number and influence of school boards grew. Business leaders were greatly overrepresented on these boards and were directly responsible for educational policy decisions and for hiring the personnel who would be responsible for educational administration.

The writings and activities of educators, both abroad and in the United States also influenced the development of schools during this period. In the United States, the work and ideas of such men as Horace Mann and Henry Barnard had a major impact on the bureaucratization of schools and the professionalization of teachers, especially during the 1840s and 1850s. These men promoted the standardization of curriculum, establishment of licensing procedures and training programs for teachers, and the development of mechanisms to assure efficient supervision and administration in the schools. Their purpose was to raise the quality of education and to assure the placement of teachers according to merit rather than political influence.

We will now take a more specific look at the increasing bureaucratization of the schools during this period; most particularly at the internal differentiation of schools, the elaboration of administrative and supervisory positions, the increasing importance of expertise and objective criteria in the hiring of school personnel, and the institutionalization of formal rules of procedure governing broad areas of educational life. To do this, we will return again to four of the basic elements of Weber's model of bureaucracy.

### The Functional Division of Labor

As we mentioned earlier, schools during the Pre-Industrial Period were really one-room classrooms with one teacher and a number of students, all treated more or less alike. The introduction of Lancasterian schools brought with it a system of differentiating students within the same class. In such classrooms, students were grouped according to their mastery of minute pieces of information and moved from group to group as they were ready for new material. This method of classification was impractical because it was based on such discrete bits of material, but the idea of classifying and grading students caught on rapidly during this period. By the end of the nineteenth century, dividing students into grades as we now do was fully implemented. Initially, schools were graded by simply combining into one building several separate schools that already existed in a community. These may have served somewhat different age groups and taught different sets of subjects. Later, new schools were established with grading planned from the first. Eventually, schools came to house several distinct grades and teach a wide variety of subjects. Each grade was taught by a separate teacher, but eventually certain subjects in each grade were taught by specialist teachers as well. Often, these specialists moved among the several schools of a district, teaching in each for one day at a time. For example, Katz cites evidence that in 1876 the Boston School District had the following specialists: general supervisor of drawing, special instructor in drawing, vocal and physical culture specialist, military drill specialist, high school French and German teachers, and a sewing specialist for the grammar school.[7] None of these instructors had been present in that district in 1850.

Children in these newly graded schools were classified increasingly by age. In part this age-grading was a simple solution to the problem of how to divide students up into reasonably manageable units of roughly comparable interests and abilities. However age-grading was also encouraged by developments in educational theory and psychology that stressed the unique developmental stages, problems, and potentials of children at different ages, as well as the benefits of having them associate with their age-peers. As we shall see later, age-grading also facilitated socialization to universalistic norms of behavior and evaluation.

By the end of the Early Industrial Period, children were age-graded and expected to move from one level to the next in an orderly progression. Many of the subjects studied in school were also differentiated by level, and here as well, students were expected to move from one level to the next smoothly and easily.

Of course, dividing students by age and offering a variety of subjects also resulted in the differentiation of teaching staff. Not only were there certain specialists for each school, but teachers—especially at the secondary school level—began teaching a smaller number of subjects. The classical curriculum was modified and a greater variety of courses offered. High schools instituted courses for terminal students, and students were given more freedom to choose which subjects they wished to study. At the same time, teachers became more narrowly specialized in one subject or another.

The first schools to acquire what we now think of as a "faculty," or several teachers of different subjects all teaching in the same school, were the academies. As you recall, these were the first schools to offer a really diverse curriculum.

### The Development of a Hierarchy of Authority

As the schools became more differentiated internally through the institutionalization of grading and subject matter specialization, they also developed a hierarchy of authority. Staff positions were differentiated vertically, with some teachers gaining authority over others. Katz reports that the following ranks existed in the Boston schools of 1876: master, submaster, principal, assistant-principal, teacher assistant, and usher.[8] Clearly, not all of these positions belonged to teachers. Some were primarily administrators, fulfilling a newly evolved set of distinct responsibilities in the schools. Early on, however, principals were master teachers, and not solely administrators.

In addition to the differentiation of an authority structure inside the schools, changes occurred in the relationship between schools and their communities. During the first half of the Early Industrial Period the district school predominated. These schools were run almost entirely by locally elected committees. The responsibility for education was vested in the smallest possible political unit. Some of these districts were exceedingly small, having as few as five or six children to educate. The specific responsibilities of district school committees were few, although their authority was broad. Usually, the elected officials were supposed to visit the local school at least once a year, keep track of expenses, and hire and fire the teacher. However, many committees did not fulfill their responsibilities, even when these were legally mandated. For example, a survey conducted in the mid-nineteenth century in Massachusetts revealed that out of three hundred towns about two hundred and fifty did not comply with the law requiring a visit to the local schools.[9] One reason for this neglect was that school committees were generally made up of volunteers; the members received no pay. As the tasks they were required to undertake grew in complexity, the difficulty of assuring that volunteers would take the time and effort to comply increased.

District schools were also impractical because of their small size. The growing acceptance of age-grading and the impossibility of instituting it when only a handful of students were involved gave impetus to the consolidation of district schools into larger units called Union Schools.

Meanwhile, as the number of schools, teachers, and students proliferated, the task of coordinating the schools became increasingly complex. Now that students were going on to high schools in greater number, more coordination was necessary to assure that students coming from a variety of elementary schools were sufficiently and uniformly prepared for the high school curriculum. Now that larger sums of money were being spent, budgeting became another complex task to be coordinated at state and local levels.

Mechanisms to cope with these complexities included the establishment of state level offices with responsibility for education. In 1812, New York State was the first to acquire a State Superintendent of Schools. Other states assigned responsibility to the State Treasurer. In time, however, most states established a State Board of Education along with a highly differentiated structure of administrative officers. State Boards appointed supervisors for counties and towns, and increased their responsibilities. The duties of the State Boards and their superintendents included examining and selecting textbooks, distributing educational funds, determining the length of the school term, preparing and examining teachers, supervising curriculum content, and overseeing the physical conditions of the school plant. Under these systems, administrative officers were always paid.

Of course, there was some resistance to this centralization of power and decision making. Resistance came mostly from local communities who resented relinquishing their own authority over their schools. However, by the end of the Early Industrial Period a complex system of supervision and centralization had been well entrenched in America's schools.

### The Definition of Staff Roles as Offices

During the Pre-Industrial Period few regulations existed regarding teacher qualifications. By the twentieth century, however, each state had a system for assessing the qualifications of individuals and for licensing them for teaching positions. The development of these systems was greatly encouraged by educational leaders and social reformers who were appalled by the frequency with which school positions were used as patronage jobs by local politicians. Increasingly, expertise, as measured by schooling and examinations, became the standard through which teachers met formalized requirements. At the same time, many states established a system of normal schools, or teachers colleges, for the training of school personnel. These will be discussed in Chapter 6.

The heightened emphasis on expertise in teaching also extended to administrative posts, and qualifications for these positions were also made increasingly objective over time. Around the turn of the century, great emphasis was placed on the administrator's managerial skills and the ability to run schools according to the principles of efficiency prevalent in industry at that time. The influence of business leaders on the boards that often selected the top administrators meant that those who were most likely to comply with these ideas were favored.[10] Even teachers were expected to become experts in the efficient management of their classrooms.

Callahan has documented the absurdities that often resulted from this definition of educational expertise.[11] Superintendents were urged to compute the unit cost of every conceivable activity in their schools, so that, for example, the cost per pupil of a history lesson in one school could be compared to the cost per unit of a similar lesson in another school. Subjects that turned out to be particularly expensive stood in dire danger of being dropped. Even within the classroom, complex computations of each student's progress and performance were recorded so that the efficiency of the teacher could be assessed.

In 1913, Franklin Bobbitt, an instructor in educational administration at the University of Chicago, published his ideas in the *Twelfth Yearbook of the National Society for the Study of Education.* They were typical of the period and very influential. After emphasizing the supreme importance of supervisors for the establishment of clear organizational goals and the coordination of efforts to attain those goals, he indicated that two important principles must always be followed. First, "Definite qualitative and quantitative standards must be determined for the product."[12] Second, "Where the material . . . passes through a number of progressive stages on its way . . . to the ultimate product, definite qualitative and quantitative standards must be determined for . . . each of these stages."[13]

What did this amount to for the classroom? Bobbit explained:

> The ability to add at a speed of 65 combinations per minute, with an accuracy of 94 percent is as definite a specification as can be set up for any aspect of the work of the steel plant . . . [the teacher] if asked whether his eighth grade pupils could add at the rate of 65 combinations per minute with an accuracy of 94 percent, could not answer the question . . . He needs a measuring scale that will serve him in measuring his product. . . . [14]

Consequently, Bobbitt and others recommended and helped develop a number of scales designed to measure such information. A teacher's efficiency could then be measured. A teacher who fell short of the standard would be "unmistakably shown to be a weak teacher." Further, this information would allow teachers to know the progress each student was making and allow superintendents to know which principals were running the most efficient schools. Thus, Bobbitt supported the development of scales to cover "every desirable educational product whether tangible or intangible."[15]

Many scales and tests were developed. In 1916, an item in the *American School Board Journal* reported that a system had been established at Bay City, Michigan, that adopted modern factory systems to the classroom. A group of substitute teachers were hired for the sole purpose of testing students and keeping records. At the time of the report, some fifty thousand tests had been given![16]

The point of much of this was that teachers, as well as administrators, could be evaluated "scientifically." If they lacked sufficient expertise and skill, they could be fired, with their inadequacies clearly documented. Furthermore, knowledge about the principles of "scientific management" became the basic component of an administrator's training. As Callahan points out, "the 'profession' of school administration was in 1910 in its formative stage, just being developed,"[17] and, as Callahan sees it, the expertise administrators were pressured to acquire produced administrators who were often anti-intellectual and not knowledgeable about either education or the social sciences. "As the business-industrial values and procedures spread into the thinking and acting of educators, countless educational decisions were made on economic or on noneducational grounds."[18]

### Operation According to Rules of Procedure

It is probably fairly obvious by now that these educational developments resulted in increasing standardization of procedures both within and between schools. The importance of coordinating the many diverse units involved and the stress on measurement and efficiency led naturally to the proliferation of formal rules of procedure. Teachers and administrators were increasingly required to keep detailed records of all their activities and their results.

Laws were promulgated to regulate employment processes, the placement of students, the distribution of funds, and so on. Administrative decisions were made at increasingly centralized levels and passed down the multilayered authority structure to principals and teachers.

For example, rules were developed covering the choice and provision of classroom books. During the first part of the nineteenth century, students provided their own textbooks. This had two frequent consequences. First, poor children often had no books. Second, each student in a class often had a different book from the others. In other words, a teacher was often faced with the task of teaching a geography lesson to ten children, each of whom was looking at a different text. By the end of the Early Industrial Period, regulations providing for centralized selection and distribution of texts had been introduced in virtually all schools across the country.

### Summary

It is clear that the Early Industrial Period was one of rapid bureaucratization of the schools. Katz has argued that this bureaucratization was essentially complete, in its modern form, by as early as 1880. During these years, authority over educational affairs was increasingly centralized and a complex hierarchy of authority developed. Roles within educational systems and within schools themselves were differentiated along numerous dimensions, such as teacher and administrator, staff specialist, and clerical aide. All educational decision making became increasingly regulated by formal rules of procedure. Standardization increased throughout the system, in order to facilitate coordination and make objective evaluations of accomplishment possible. The placement of teachers and administrators became increasingly controlled by formal testing procedures and credentialing processes. The emphasis on "expertise" and training increased steadily.

## CONFLICT AND CONSENSUS PERSPECTIVES ON BUREAUCRATIZATION

As you probably suspect by now, conflict and consensus theorists offer rather different interpretations of the processes of bureaucratization that we have just described. In particular, they disagree about the impact that bureaucratization has had on the opportunities available to various groups within American society.

Consensus theorists believe that bureaucratization led to an expansion of opportunities for the vast majority of citizens. With bureaucratization came universalistic criteria of evaluation, promotion, and selection. For example, it became increasingly difficult to award teacher or administrative positions on the basis of political beliefs, racial characteristics, or social class origin. Standardized tests and educational credentials were used instead. Similarly, in the classroom, children could not be arbitrarily denied access to educational programs, deprived of books, given failing grades, or shunted into inferior programs. Instead, educational decisions had to be made on the basis of written records, including students' scores on standardized intelligence and achievement tests, and accounts of classroom performance.

Furthermore, bureaucratization meant that the classes and schools attended by one group of children were similar to those attended by other groups. For example, it became possible for students to transfer from one public school to another, even if these schools were located at opposite ends of the country, and find that they fit in easily and quickly. Similarly, students from a variety of elementary and middle schools could attend the same high school, and all find themselves about equally prepared.

Even more fundamentally, perhaps, bureaucratization, with its centralization of power and proliferation of regulations governing education, meant that universal free compulsory public school education could finally be achieved. Procedures for raising funds for education, assuring the availability of adequate space, and policing attendance became institutionalized. This assured that all children would be provided with at least a minimal level of education, no matter how poor or how distant from an urban center they were.

Consensus theorists emphasize, then, the compatibility of bureaucratization with the values of a democratic society. Bureaucratization in education has made schooling available to a wide spectrum of our society's children. All children now go to school, regardless of race, ethnicity, gender, or socioeconomic status. In school, they are judged by universalistic criteria. If they are intelligent and hard working, they are rewarded by high grades, access to higher education, and ultimately, prestigious and lucrative occupations. Indeed, as consensus theorists point out, many of the educators and social reformers who helped bureaucratize the school did so with these goals in mind: educating all citizens for active participation in a democratic society and giving all equal access to societal rewards. Labor unions worked strenuously for the spread of educational opportunity for the same reasons. Thus, there was general agreement that bureaucratization was the best alternative for educational development, given the basic values of our society.

At the same time, of course, bureaucratization was compatible with industrialization and was supported, eventually, by business interests as well as labor. According to consensus theorists, bureaucratization rewards merit and therefore permits a more complete development of the nation's talent: It makes certain that people are placed in the jobs they are most capable of fulfilling. This is important because economic development requires an ever-increasing number of technologically sophisticated and professional workers. Bureaucratization of the schools also meant that children would learn the values and behavior patterns compatible with an industrialized economy. For example, they learn to be evaluated and to evaluate others in terms of universalistic criteria.

A somewhat different set of arguments is offered by conflict theorists. Rather than emphasizing the compatibility of bureaucratization with the realization of democratic goals, they point to the ways in which bureaucratization has limited rather than expanded equality of opportunity, especially for the children of the poor and working classes.

In surveying the history of bureaucratization of education, conflict theorists emphasize that bureaucratization was not as universally supported as consensus theorists imply. For one thing, bureaucratization removed a considerable amount of power over educational processes from local communities and the families whose children attended the schools. These communities and families often fought the centralization of power as antidemocratic. So did some church leaders and industrialists, at least early in the process. As a matter of fact, even working class and poor families often opposed the spread of compulsory school laws and did not take advantage of expanding educational facilities.[19]

Furthermore, bureaucratization was supported as much by racist elitist values as it was by democratic ones. As we indicated earlier, support for bureaucratization increased with the arrival of large waves of immigrants, and also with the growing numbers of urban poor. The children of these groups were viewed as a threat to the stability and purity of the American way of life. Their parents were seen as incompetent and ignorant, and it was argued that children should be removed from their influence as early as possible. As Katz points out, the concern of those reforming the schools through bureaucratization was often described in terms of promoting a neutral or classless education, they were clearly fearful "of the cultural divisiveness inherent in the increasing religious and ethnic diversity of American life."[20]

The impetus behind their reforms was to homogenize American culture and to impose on our increasingly diverse population the values of the dominant middle class. Katz quotes the task of education, as it was described to the Boston School Committee, to illustrate:

> . . . taking children at random from a great city, undisciplined, uninstructed, often with inveterate forwardness and obstinacy, and with the inherited stupidity of centuries of ignorant ancestors; forming them from animals into intellectual beings; and, so far as a school can do it, from intellectual beings into spiritual beings; giving to many their first appreciation of what is wise, what is true, what is lovely, and what is pure. . . .[21]

The school, then, would instill "cleanliness, delicacy, refinement, good temper, gentleness, kindness, justice, and truth" in the masses.[22]

We already indicated that bureaucratization of the schools was supported by business interests and on this point conflict and consensus theorists agree. However, conflict theorists point out that bureaucratization of the schools serves business interests because it trains workers in the skills needed for productivity and inculcates them with values that are compatible with their future positions in that economy.[23] Most workers, for example, are taught to be compliant, docile, and obedient. They are taught the importance of time and punctuality and hard work.[24] They may even be taught to be more cooperative with management and not to cause trouble in the workplace. For example, Katz points out that during the mid-nineteenth century, industrialists often viewed the educated worker as more diligent and acquiescent and less likely to act impulsively and passionately.[25]

There is another way in which bureaucratization serves the interests of the wealthier classes, according to conflict theorists. Whereas bureaucratization gives the semblance of equality, and therefore legitimizes the way in which societal rewards are distributed, it is in fact subtly biased against the poor and working classes. The middle- and upper-middle classes gained more from the bureaucratization of the schools than others because they retained control of the schools and were able to define the criteria upon which achievement was judged. For example, IQ tests have been used to "objectively" place children in different educational programs, although these tests do not accurately measure the abilities of poor children and those from minority groups. We will talk about some of the many ways in which the schools are biased against certain groups of children in other chapters. For now, however, we will simply emphasize that conflict theorists view the bureaucratization of schools as a process that has facilitated the perpetuation of inequalities based on class, race, ethnicity, and gender.[26]

## BUREAUCRATIZATION IN THE MATURE INDUSTRIAL PERIOD: THE CONTEMPORARY STRUCTURE OF THE SCHOOL

As we indicated earlier, the contemporary bureaucratic nature of our schools was well established by the end of the Early Industrial Period. The years since that time have shown some shifts toward further bureaucratization and some efforts to check or even reverse these shifts. In areas such as the rural Midwest, for example, the trend toward the consolidation of school districts has continued, and with it, centralization of control and standardization. In other areas, such as New York City, efforts have been made to decentralize an educational structure that is seen as unwieldly and unresponsive to local needs. There, as well as in other places, a renewed interest in community control of the schools has been evident for several years now.

In the nation as a whole there have been shifts in the role of state and especially federal government in educational decision making. The judiciary branch of government, in particular, has played a major role in affecting policies regarding desegregation, busing, funding, and affirmative action. Although these policies are still highly controversial and in a state of flux, the growing willingness of judicial bodies to mandate educational change represents a further increase in the centralization of power, the proliferation of formal rules and regulations governing educational decisions, and the further standardization of procedures from one school to the next.

In general, increases in bureaucratization are associated with increases in organizational size and complexity. American school systems have grown dramatically since the New Deal. Many factors have contributed to this growth: dramatic increases in school-age populations; the concentration of population in urban areas; and increased rates of enrollment, attendance, and graduation. In addition, the size of school systems has been augmented by the consolidation of many small school districts into larger districts that are intended to be more economical, efficient, and comprehensive. Consolidation has proceeded rapidly. The number of operating school districts in the United States dropped from 94,926 in 1947 to only 15,538 in 1980—an 84 percent decrease in only thirty-three years![27]

The complexity of educational systems has increased not only because of these increases in scale, however. The broadened conception of the school's role has contributed importantly to this trend. No longer is the school concerned only with teaching children basic skills. It is now expected to promote the development of the whole child. This means having staff members who are concerned with physical, psychological, social, and emotional, as well as intellectual, growth. As the schools have attempted to do more things for more students, there has been increased demand for bureaucratic coordination of so much diverse activity.

Many of these changes will be discussed in later chapters of this book. Now, however, we will focus more narrowly on the contemporary school as a bureaucratic organization. As we do, we will discuss the implications of the school's organizational structure for its day-to-day operations.

## Goals

Americans have a deep and abiding faith in schooling. Politicians, educational leaders, and ordinary citizens often profess their shared belief that our educational institutions can reduce, if not eliminate, ignorance and illiteracy. They also seem to believe that schools, colleges, and universities can contribute to the solution of many other serious social problems including poverty, economic stagnation, military weakness, nuclear war, alcohol and drug abuse, teenage pregnancy, unsafe driving, moral decay, ethnocentrism, and prejudice. Formal education has become modern society's panacea.

Many of our educational goals are at least potentially contradictory. For example, schools are expected to inculcate respect for traditional values and institutions at the same time that they are promoting critical thinking and creativity; promote assimilation of new immigrants yet help maintain subgroup traditions; provide safe, custodial care for students while promoting individualism, freedom, and self-expression; encourage students to be competitive with one another most of the time and yet be able to support others and to cooperate at other times; support high achievement and professional aspirations while also helping solve the problem of labor shortages in certain low-prestige occupations; emphasize both cognitive and socioemotional growth; uphold rigorous standards while showing sensitivity to the special needs of each and every child.

Not only are many goals and associated programs potentially contradictory but they are also often controversial and hotly contested by influential groups within the school system and the community. For example, teachers in any given district or school may be crosspressured by supporters and opponents of sex education, values clarification, bilingual or bicultural education, or gifted and talented programs. Thus, the curriculum at any given time represents the outcome of an ongoing struggle to shape the content of American education.

In case this list of multiple, vague, conflicting, and contested goals seems abstract, academic, and divorced from reality, it may be useful to reproduce the official goal statement of an actual New Jersey school district.

> Learn how to be a good citizen.
> Learn how to respect and get along with people who act and dress differently.
> Learn about and try to understand changes taking place in the world.
> Develop skills in reading, writing, etc.
> Understand and practice democratic ideals and ideas.
> Learn how to examine and use information.
> Understand and practice the skills of family living.
> Learn how to respect and get along with the people with whom we work and live.
> Develop skills to enter a specific field of work.
> Learn how to be a good manager of money, property, and resources.
> Develop a desire for learning now and in the future.
> Learn how to use leisure time.
> Practice and understand ideas of health and safety.
> Appreciate culture and beauty in the world.
> Gain information needed to make job selections.
> Develop pride in work and a feeling of self-worth.
> Develop good character and self-respect.
> Gain a general education.

Note that these goals, like those of other school systems, are vague, sweeping, lack priority, and are highly idealistic, one might even say utopian.[28] Given the heavy and direct dependence of public school systems upon local taxpayers, it is easy to understand why such goal statements are adopted. They make for good public relations but they do not represent serious attempts to provide concrete direction for the district's educational enterprise. In fact, it has been suggested that such goals can actually impede effective administration.

> There is a disposition by officials to express every aspect of the educational process in its ideal form; that is, to speak of what ought to happen rather than

> what is likely to happen. This obsessive preoccupation with goals makes it more difficult to communicate about the reality of processes instrumental to the goals.[29]

A sharp distinction must be drawn between such official, consensual, goals and the operative goals of the teaching staffs of different schools.[30] Operational goals are embodied in actual operating policies and practice. Such goals are much narrower and more pragmatic than official goals. When official goals are unbounded and unrealistic, administrators and teachers enjoy considerable discretion to construct distinctive goal priorities for their particular schools and classrooms. The freedom is not total, however. Standard operating procedures generally represent the outcomes of bargaining among power blocs within an organization.[31] Obviously there may be considerable disjunction between official and operative goals. For that reason, operational goals are not formalized or written down. In fact, they are often deliberately hidden from superiors or outsiders.

Still, there are certain tentative statements that can be made about the shared perceptions, values, and norms that help faculty deal with unbounded expectations. Teachers often feel that an uninformed public makes unfair, indeed impossible, demands upon them. Therefore, it becomes legitimate for faculty members to establish their own more reasonable priorities. It has been suggested that the operational priorities of most American schools consist of the following: respect for traditional values and institutions over critical social analysis; order over freedom; assimilation over maintenance of ethnic diversity; competition over cooperation; and cognitive growth over social-emotional maturation. Teaching staffs no doubt recognize that many outsiders will disagree with these priorities. That is one reason why teachers so often ask parents, board members, and even administrators to "Leave it to us, the ones who are most familiar with student needs." Lortie has suggested that teachers may become extremely cautious when faced with the necessity of making potentially controversial decisions without official guidelines.[32] After all, they are open to criticism from individual parents and special-interest groups who can argue that alternative priorities are not being followed. Under such circumstances conservative informal norms often emerge, such as: "Don't rock the boat"; "Keep it quiet. What the public doesn't know won't hurt them"; and "Avoid discussing controversial topics."

## The Functional Division of Labor

At the beginning of this chapter we indicated that bureaucratization involves the development of an increasingly complex division of labor. In bureaucratic organizations, the tasks necessary to accomplish the goals of the organization are broken down into smaller units, each assigned to a particular set of individuals as their primary responsibility.

Contemporary school systems in the United States are clearly characterized by a complex division of labor. Central to this division is the separation of administrative and teaching responsibilities. Although teachers still have administrative responsibilities in their individual classrooms, administrative authority within schools and school systems rests with individuals who are usually not actively involved in teaching. These individuals include, at the top, superintendents of schools, and, at the bottom, assistant school principals.

Administrators are responsible for such diverse tasks as hiring, assigning, and firing teachers, scheduling classes, coordinating the diverse activities of their schools, evaluating school personnel, representing the schools to outside groups, and putting the policy decisions of boards of education into practice. Administrators are often required to have experience as classroom teachers, but their training and qualifications are different from those of the typical teacher. Special examinations must be passed and educational credentials attained for most of these positions.

The functional division of labor in the schools is further enhanced by a proliferation of support specialists, both professional and nonprofessional, in the schools. Here we can include such individuals as clerical and secretarial workers, janitors and maintenance personnel, school nurses, speech therapists, guidance counselors, psychologists, learning-disability specialists, teacher's aides, cafeteria workers, and even security guards. These specialists proliferated as the goals of the schools expanded into areas of social and emotional development and as students became more numerous and diverse.

Even among teachers as a general category there is now considerable specialization and diversification. For example, teachers are differentiated according to the age of the students they teach. As you recall, one way in which schools coped with spiraling enrollment was by dividing students according to age. Teachers are now trained specifically for these age categories. A teacher who meets the formal educational requirements for early childhood is not thereby qualified to teach at the junior high school level, for example. The vast majority of teachers are clearly identifiable as specialists in early childhood, elementary school, junior high or middle school, senior high school, or college-level education.

Furthermore, teachers are differentiated according to the subjects they teach. The older the children being taught, the greater this subject matter differentiation generally is. Thus, in the elementary school, the same teacher may instruct in reading, arithmetic, social studies, and science. This would be unheard of at the high school level, and by the time we reach the college level, specialization is so great that one professor of English may be qualified to teach a course on Shakespeare, but not one on James Joyce. Usually there is also a clear division between faculty qualified to teach undergraduates and those qualified to teach at the graduate level.

Furthermore, teachers are differentiated according to the special needs and abilities of the children they teach. Some teachers work only with exceptional children: the physically handicapped, or the retarded, for example. Others work only with gifted children.

The types of specialization that have not developed in the schools are perhaps as interesting and important as the types that have. For example, there has been virtually no differentiation of teachers on the basis of their ability or experience. Of course, teachers do get paid differently, at least according to experience, but they do not perform different duties. The job of a rather incompetent and inexperienced newcomer is essentially the same as the job of an outstanding teacher with thirty years' experience. Organized schoolteachers have *resisted* differentiation within their ranks based on experience and ability. For example, teachers' unions have long opposed proposals to designate a few outstanding teachers as "master teachers." Teachers appointed to this prestigious new rank would receive extra pay and reduced teaching loads in exchange for their help in improving the instructional practices of their colleagues. Quite understandably, union leaders consider such proposals highly divisive.

At one time in our history, before the sharp division between administration and teaching that currently exists, a teacher could be promoted to the rank of master teacher and given some degree of authority over others. These master teachers taught as well as fulfilled administrative responsibilities such as supervising others. Now, however, there are few ways in which teachers can get a promotion without giving up the classroom. Department heads at the senior high school level usually continue to teach, of course, but because the number of positions is so much smaller than the number of teachers who would be eligible only a small number can advance in this way. A major exception to this characteristic of teaching is found at the college and university level. At these levels teachers can be promoted through a series of ranks, including instructor, lecturer, assistant professor, associate professor, full professor, and sometimes distinguished professor, and still continue as teachers. For teachers at other levels, however, promotion, or a "vertical" career up the hierarchy of authority, is impossible without becoming an administrator. We will look at some of the consequences of this fact for schools and teachers later on.

### The Hierarchy of Authority

The organizational chart presented in Figure 4–1 summarizes the hierarchy of authority that characterizes contemporary large-city school districts. At the top of the hierarchy is the board of education. Members of these boards are responsible for the formulation of educational policy and the selection of the superintendent who will be administrative head of the school district.[33] Their more specific duties generally include at least some responsibility for raising local funds for education, deciding how school funds should be spent, accounting to state officials for the expenditure of funds, advising school personnel on the interests of the community, reporting on the operation of the districts' schools to higher authorities, and, in general, making policy decisions affecting the local schools.

The vast majority of school boards are elected. However, in a few cases, they are appointed by a local mayor, city council, or some other governmental unit. Board members serve on a voluntary basis, and the fact that board members are lay men and women, rather than professional educators, is of central importance. Their role is to represent the general public in school affairs.

The superintendent of schools is the administrative head of the local school district and is responsible for the daily operation of the schools in compliance with the policy decisions of the board. Unlike the members of the board, the superintendent is a professional educator. The superinten-

**FIGURE 4–1.** Allocation of Major Responsibilities and Authority.

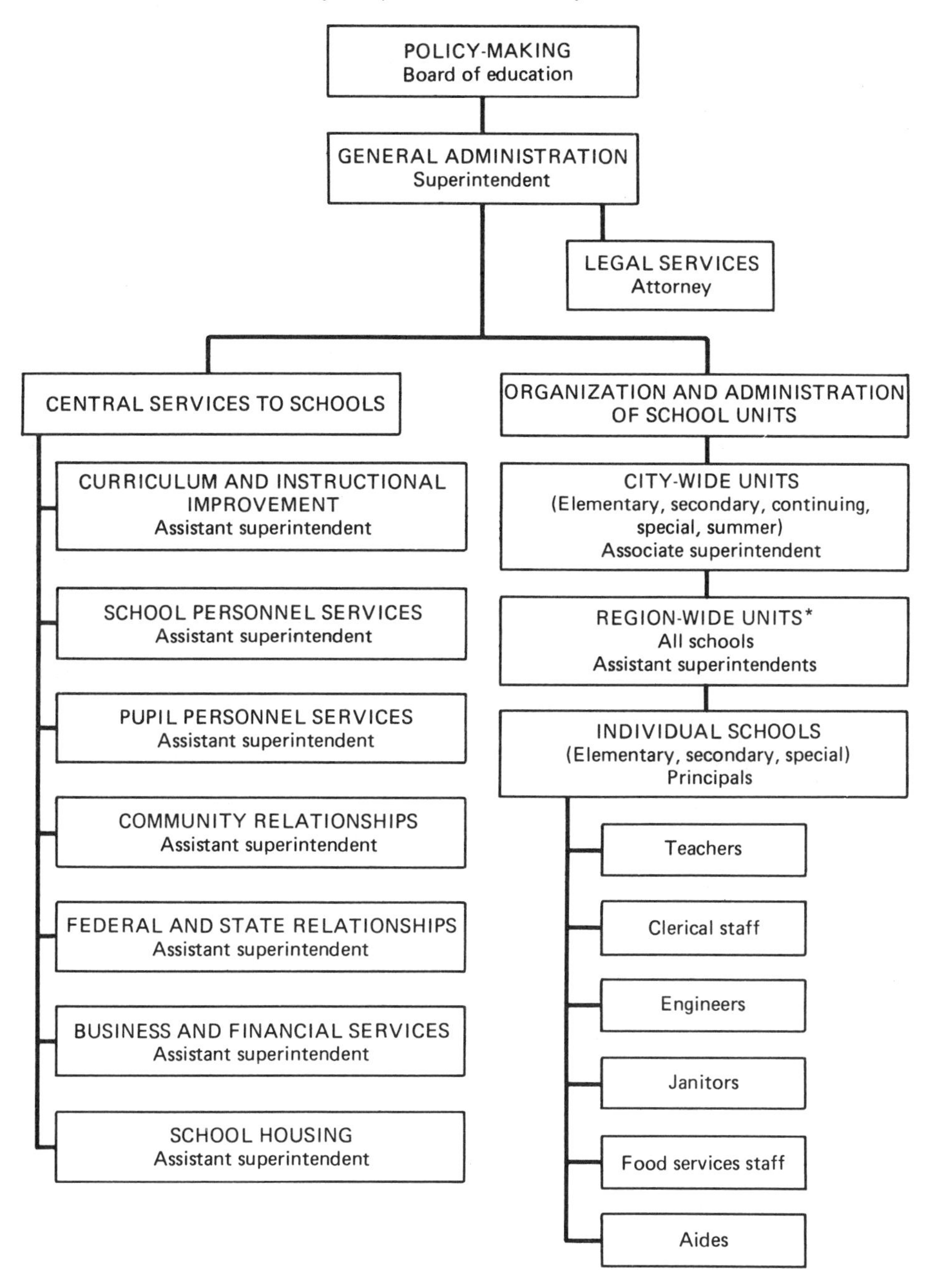


*Source:* Samuel Miller Brownell, "Superintendents of Large-City School Systems," in *Encyclopedia of Education*, 8 (New York: MacMillan and Free Press, 1971), 557.

* Some large-city school systems are not on a regional basis but have assistant superintendents in charge of elementary schools, of high schools, and of special schools

dent has a staff of support personnel, which varies in size with the school district involved. This staff may include a number of assistant superintendents—specialists in such areas as curriculum development—and clerical workers.

Directly under the superintendent and the superintendent's assistants, but at the administrative head of each particular school, is the principal. Each principal has a staff that may include one or several assistants, specialists, and clerical workers. Also under the principal's authority are the teachers, other professional personnel (such as the school librarian or nurse), and the nonprofessional workers in the school. At the bottom of the organization are the students.

Each school district operates within a larger organizational framework—the state system of education. Laws affecting education are spelled out either in the constitution of each state or in separate legislation passed at the state level. These laws generally determine the size and composition of the school districts, procedures for electing local school boards, procedures through which schools may be financed, minimum qualifications for district superintendents, principals, and teachers, and a host of other important issues. Each state has a structure for administering these laws and for making other policy decisions. There is always some kind of state level board of education, which is often appointed by the Governor, and an administrative head in the form of a State Superintendent or Chancellor of Education. A staff, in the form of a Department of Education, is usually provided. The powers of these offices vary from state to state, but they generally include planning and implementing state policy, and supervising and policing local school districts in the state.

### School Board–Superintendent Relationships

Educational policy is supposed to be formulated by local school boards and carried out by the chief administrator—the school superintendent—hired by these boards. The superintendent is an employee who serves at the pleasure of the board and who may, therefore, be dismissed when the board members decide his or her performance is unsatisfactory. In theory, a clear and mutually understood division of labor exists between the board and the superintendent—the board formulates policy and the superintendent makes certain it is implemented.

In practice, however, the situation is considerably more complex. The distinction between policy initiation and implementation breaks down in the daily operation of the schools. Superintendents can both initiate and sabotage policy through manipulating administrative procedures. Furthermore, a number of studies of superintendent—school board relationships have shown that superintendents frequently emerge as more powerful than the boards that employ them.[34] We will look at the detailed reasons for this in Chapter 7, but several of these reasons are directly tied to the bureaucratic nature of educational institutions. The proliferation of complex state and federal regulations, for example, gives superintendents the edge. As professionals whose full-time job involves mastering these regulations, they have a decided advantage over lay board members who are usually part-time, temporary volunteers. It is easy for a superintendent to overwhelm board members with details and to win them over by emphasizing his or her expertise and desire to serve. In many cases board members do not have to be persuaded. They have confidence in the superintendent and give that individual a great deal of latitude in running the district.

### Superintendents and their Subordinates

The ability of superintendents to observe, supervise, and evaluate their subordinates directly varies with the size and complexity of the school district. In small districts with only a few schools, the chief school administrator can, if he or she chooses to, keep relatively close track on the school principals and staff members. But in big-city schools, the physical and organizational distance between the central office and the individual schools grows and direct, tight control is impossible.

Even in small school districts superintendents minimize their use of formal, bureaucratic prerogatives to direct the activities of their professional assistants, principals, and teachers. They prefer to treat these individuals as trusted and respected colleagues, rather than as subordinates. Thus, superintendents generally rely more heavily upon friendly persuasion and advice than on official written directives to influence activities in the schools and classrooms.[35] This informal, relatively loose administrative style is advantageous in that it permits a great deal of initiative and flexibility at the operating levels of the system. However, it also permits duplication and uncoordinated effort.

In his three years of participant observation research on the school board of Eastmoreland (a small, five-school district), Robert Parelius found that articulation of programs between schools was a constant problem. The principals of the three neighborhood elementary schools acted as if they were feudal lords and the school was their independent fiefdom. Over time each neighborhood school developed its own distinctive normative structure. The three schools varied widely in procedures for screening and sorting new students, grouping for instruction, emphasis on individualized learning, and responsiveness to parental requests. When the students from all three schools came together in the single middle school, the problems engendered by lack of coordination became starkly evident. A single dramatic example will suffice. One of the elementary schools downplayed age-grading—emphasizing individualized instruction and continuous progress, especially in mathematics. By the end of the fifth grade many students in that school were working a year or more above their grade level. Another elementary school was much more traditional in its approach and tried to keep its best students working at grade level. As a result, the incoming sixth-grade class in the middle school had an unusually broad range of mathematical accomplishment. Nonetheless, each and every sixth grader was given exactly the same sixth-grade mathematics book regardless of whether the student entered below, at, or above grade level in mathematics achievement. Naturally, the parents of children who were below grade and those who had accelerated were extremely dissatisfied.

One might expect that school boards would adopt clear and detailed policies and procedures in order to ensure greater uniformity of educational practice among schools. They could then hold the superintendent responsible for seeing that those policies and procedures were successfully implemented. But board members seldom attempt to exert effective control in that way. Board policies tend to be broad and general, allowing plenty of room for educators to exercise professional discretion. In fact, educators within a given district are often unclear about what the board policies actually are. In a major study of 103 school districts, Deal and Celotti[36] found that there was little agreement between superintendents and principals about district policies. They also found little agreement between principals and teachers regarding policies within their own schools.

Teachers and principals who are used to great autonomy may resist their superintendent's efforts to tighten control. As a first step toward improving curricular articulation between schools in the Eastmoreland school district, the superintendent encouraged the teachers to develop charts that would define the "scope and sequence" of the district's curriculum. Many teachers apparently resented this task and devoted little time or effort to it. Consequently, the final charts were of little value. In fact, they were so worthless that the superintendent never even arranged to have them formally presented and explained to the board. The "scope and sequence" initiative degenerated into a futile ritual, a fiasco.

### Principal–Teacher Relationships

The principal is a middle manager. He or she is, on the one hand, a part of the administrative hierarchy, and as such is expected to implement directives from the board and central office. Principals are also responsible for observing, supervising, and evaluating teachers within that particular school. To the extent that the principal performs the role of *field administrator* and enforces unpopular dictates from above, he or she threatens the classroom teacher's traditional autonomy. Teachers understandably resent and resist such "outside interference." On the other hand, the principal is expected to act as the school's *relatively autonomous instructional leader*. Effective leadership (as well as the smooth operation of the school on a routine basis) requires the teacher's trust and cooperation. As part of their continuing effort to maintain good interpersonal relationships with staff members, principals often prefer to interact with teachers as senior colleagues rather than as administrative superiors. They prefer to suggest and persuade rather than issue orders.

Principals have broad, but not entirely unlimited, discretion in running their schools. Some state, district, and contractual guidelines are quite explicit, and strict adherence to them is demanded. For example, principals are not free to hire uncertified teachers, establish very large special-education classes, stop taking and reporting attendance, or demand that teachers work an extra hour each school day.

However, in a great many matters the principals can exercise their own judgment. The principal makes decisions regarding teaching assignments, scheduling, school activities, discipline, classroom procedures, and a host of other school matters. Principals, through their recommendations and evaluations, also have considerable influence over which teachers are hired and which nontenured teachers are dismissed rather than given tenure.

Because the principal makes so many decisions and controls many resources, he or she has many opportunities to reward cooperative teachers and punish troublemakers. For example, principals can assign teachers to more or less desirable classrooms, facilitate or hinder their requests for class materials, and give them a disproportionate number of "difficult" or "desirable" students.

There is little evidence that principals feel hemmed in by board policies. In fact, as we noted earlier, Deal and Celotti found that principals and superintendents typically cannot even agree about what the district policies actually are.[37] Parelius found that in Eastmoreland, principals and certain board members wanted policies to be written in vague and general terms so that they might be subject to quite disparate interpretations. It is not uncommon for principals to ignore, evade, or actively resist orders from the central office. And they tend to interpret instructions in the way that is most palatable for their staff. Some principals even establish their own ad hoc school policies with the full knowledge that these contradict official districtwide positions.

The larger and more complex the district is, the more difficult it is to achieve administrative coordination. David Rogers found that the central administration of the New York City school board often had to deal with rebellious and uncooperative assistant superintendents and principals.

> Field superintendents and principals often reinterpret directives to mean that they should do what they can to implement them in the light of their own superior knowledge of local conditions. Such reinterpretations could be anything from "passive sabotage" (as in Open Enrollment, when Negro and Puerto Rican parents were not informed of transfer opportunities) to more active efforts (such as telling parents at the end of the school year of the many costs and hardships involved in bussing their children out of the district or local school). If the directive was on a relatively noncontroversial matter, it might simply be filed away and disregarded.
>
> The fragmentation comes about as a result of the elaborate vertical and horizontal differentiation of the system dividing it up into a series of separate power centers. . . . Administrative studies of the system indicate that the divisions were often insulated from one another and tended to approach routine staffing, curriculum, and budgetary questions from the perspective of their own specialist logics. They functioned as separate baronies that just happened to be part of a larger structure.[38]

The ability of the superintendent to exercise effective authority is also influenced by the procedures through which subordinate administrators are selected and dismissed. In some cases, subordinates are firmly entrenched in the bureaucracy and are protected by tenure and tradition from attacks by the superintendent. In other circumstances, superintendents recruit their own staff, often negotiating this right when they accept their position. It is probably true, however, that turnover among superintendents is much greater than it is among their administrative underlings. The superintendent, as a convenient public symbol of the educational system, can be a scapegoat when dissatisfaction with local schools becomes vociferous.

It is important to remember, though, that the superintendent's authority over both staff and principals does not rest solely in his or her bureaucratic rights to supervise, direct, evaluate, hire, and fire them. Some of this authority may rest in the superintendent's expertise and the respect that underlings have for his or her advice and guidance. Some of this authority may also rest in loyalty to the superintendent as an individual.

Principals do not spend much time observing, evaluating, and providing feedback to their teachers.[39] There are several reasons for this. First, teaching is usually a private performance that takes place behind closed doors. The cellular structure of the typical school, with each classroom being a self-contained unit walled off from others, presents a clear architectural barrier. Bidwell believes this "structural looseness" helps account for the fact that teachers enjoy much more autonomy than typical bureaucrats.[40] Then there are certain contractual constraints. Virtually all collective-bargaining agreements between teachers' unions and school boards have clauses that severely restrict the principal's access to the classroom for evaluational purposes. The rationale for such clauses is that teachers, like other professionals, perform highly skilled tasks that would be disrupted by frequent administrative visitations. Informal norms also constrain the principal. Teachers consider the privacy of the classroom analogous to the privacy of the home. Courtesy then demands that this private territory not be invaded arbitrarily, without prior notice. The absence of clear consensus regarding excellence in teaching also inhibits evaluation activities. When teachers were asked what criteria administrators used to evaluate them, half the teachers included in one major study reported that they had no idea whatsoever.[41] They felt that such administrative judgments were arbitrary and capricious, as likely to focus on the bulletin board's color scheme as the quality of the lesson plan. Evaluations are even more difficult when the principal is not an expert in the particular subject being taught, or, as is very frequently the case, when the principal is a relatively young, inexperienced male and the teacher is a highly experienced female. Finally, time constraints severely limit the principal's supervisory activities. When researchers have shadowed or followed in the footsteps of principals, they have found principals so inundated by diverse management activities that the principals simply had very little time for direct observation and instructional leadership.[42]

One other aspect of the principal–teacher relationship should be mentioned. Although teachers tend to accept the authority of the principal, they also expect certain actions from the principal. Specifically, they expect the principal to back them up when parents or students challenge the teacher's authority. If they accept the duties associated with their positions as teachers, they also claim the right to be protected and supported by the principal. A principal may reprimand a teacher in private, but never in public in front of those challenging the teacher's authority. If the principal fails to fulfill this obligation, the teachers may strike back individually or collectively by simply ignoring orders or requesting transfers from the school. Becker concludes that "both parties to the conflict have at their disposal effective means of controlling the other's behavior, so that the ordinary situation is one of compromise if there is a dispute at all, with sanctions being used only when agreed-on boundaries are overstepped.[43]

### Teacher–Student Relationships

This discussion will be limited to a consideration of some ways in which teacher–student relationships are affected by virtue of the fact that they occur within a bureaucratic setting. Other aspects, specifically those relating to the socialization or teaching functions of the school and the schools as people-processing organizations will be discussed in the next chapter.

The activities of the teacher in the classroom are constrained in several ways by the bureaucratic nature of the school. For example, the coordination of classroom activities that permits students to move from grade to grade and teacher to teacher smoothly requires that standard units of materials be covered in each class. All students in the first grade must make approximately the same progress in reading, writing, social adjustment, and so on, so that the second-grade teacher knows where to begin and can cope with children drawn from a diverse group of first-grade teachers. Similarly, textbooks and other instructional materials may be chosen by committees of teachers, principals, or members of the superintendent's staff to assure further standardization and facilitate coordination.

In addition, the physical space of the school must be carefully scheduled and allocated. Not all classes can use limited outside facilities at the same time. Neither can all use the library, auditorium, or laboratory. Thus, teachers cannot allow bored or fidgety classes to take a recess or enjoy a change of scene anytime they feel it would be beneficial. Other rules and regulations such as those regarding the requisitioning of supplies, arrangements for field trips and other special activities, the consumption of food in school, and the use of facilities beyond normal hours also constrain classroom activity and consume the teacher's time and energy.

It is also the teacher's responsibility to instruct students in the rules relevant to their behavior in a bureaucratic setting. They are taught that they must line up at a particular spot, move with the bell, refrain from talking during fire drills, and, in general, obey all those in authority over them. They are also taught that they will be evaluated on the basis of their behavior and achievements, according to universalistic criteria, or criteria applied equally to all. In the next chapter, we will look more thoroughly—and skeptically—at these processes and their implications. After all, students are neither passive nor powerless, though schools may sometimes try hard to render them that way, and teachers are neither totally objective nor emotionally detached.

### The Definition of Staff Roles as Offices

According to Weber's model of the ideal-typical bureaucracy, authority rests in the office that an individual holds. This authority is highly circumscribed and restricted to areas relevant to the efficient operation of the organization. It is distributed to specific individuals on the basis of their expertise and according to objective standards of evaluation. Schools deviate from this model in at least three major respects.

First, as our discussion of the hierarchy of authority in American education indicated, legally based authority, or the authority of office, is just one of several bases upon which school personnel influence and control each other. Although formal authority in school systems is obviously vested in the offices that individuals hold rather than in the individuals themselves, their ability to influence others effectively necessitates additional types of authority, based on expertise, colleagial relationships, or personal characteristics.

Furthermore, informal networks of authority occur that may be unresponsive or in opposition to the formal networks. In some systems, principals may be able to exercise authority that is not "formally" theirs; in others, particular teachers, school board members, or even students might be important forces to be reckoned with. In this respect, schools have been found to be like all other real, as opposed to ideal-typical bureaucracies—no organization operates exclusively on the basis of legally assigned authority of office.

Schools are unique in some of the other ways in which they deviate from Weber's model. For example, the authority exercised in at least some levels of the educational hierarchy has been unusually broad, extending considerably beyond what would normally be considered relevant for the efficient functioning of the organization. This is particularly true regarding authority exerted by the schools over their students. As you know, schools routinely institute regulations governing students' personal appearance. Although the specific content of these regulations varies over time, they usually cover such issues as what hair and clothing styles are acceptable for each sex and for various types of school activities. Thus, girls might be permitted shoulder-length hair, but boys might be limited to hair cut above the collar line; girls might be forbidden to wear dresses higher than two inches above the knee, and boys might be forbidden to wear jeans, at least to special assemblies. Schools may also have regulations against smoking, or even carrying cigarettes anywhere on school grounds, kissing or hand-holding, or a host of other activities considered perfectly legal and socially acceptable in other social contexts. Such regulations have often been tested in court, with angry parents and students claiming that their civil rights have been abridged. Results have been mixed, however, and school officials sometimes enforce such rules with penalties as harsh as mandatory suspension.

Schools also exert broad authority over students in their efforts to oversee their social, emotional, and physical development. Schools can insist that students receive various forms of counseling or therapy, require them to hear lectures about hygiene, sexual reproduction, and marital life, and otherwise expose them to a broad range of socialization experiences seemingly irrelevant to academic competence. This broad authority of the schools has also been challenged in the courts, again with mixed results.

A third way in which staff roles within school systems differ from Weber's ideal-typical model is in the procedures through which they are filled. According to Weber's model, individuals must be hired to fulfill staff roles on the basis of expertise. However, many other factors play a major part in the selection, appointment, and promotion of teachers and administrators.

Considerable evidence exists to support the fact that ascribed characteristics such as race, ethnicity, and gender are important determinants of placement in school systems throughout the country. The vast majority of black teachers, for example, are hired to teach in predominantly black schools, and although many black children have white teachers and school principals, relatively few white children have black teachers and black principals.[44] Furthermore, any analysis of the racial, ethnic, and gender characteristics of school administrators throughout the United States will reveal that minority groups and women are grossly underrepresented among administrative ranks, and that the higher the ranks involved, the greater this underrepresentation becomes.[45] Interestingly, this was not always the case, at least for all the currently underrepresented groups. Women have lost ground as principals over the last few decades.[46] In many areas, so have blacks. This is because as some schools were integrated, black principals lost their jobs to whites.[47]

A study conducted by Gross, Mason, and McEachern on superintendents revealed some of the dynamics of school hiring and promotion procedures.[48] They describe hiring and promotions decisions as a dilemma for the superintendents. Virtually all of the 105 superintendents interviewed felt that the merit of the candidate should be the sole criterion for such decisions.

> This professional requirement may, however, be incompatible with the expectation of influential individuals in the community and with the interests of local organizations. A local politician or school board member whose word carries great weight at city hall or with the town finance committee may ask the superintendent for the "slight" favor of recommending a friend or relative for the local elementary principalship vacancy. . . . Some school board members may feel that since their position requires an expenditure of a great deal of time and energy without remuneration, their preferences among job applicants should be given special consideration by the school executive in his recommendations. Such situations may result in difficult dilemmas for the superintendents. By conforming to his professional obligation he may endanger his new school building program or his next budget request. By not yielding to the unprofessional expectations of school board members and key influentials in the community he may be endangering his own position.[49]

In this difficult situation 85 percent claimed to have resisted pressures for special favors, 10 percent admitted giving in to them, and 5 percent said they had managed some sort of compromise. Obviously any successful interference with the formal hiring process represents a major departure from the bureaucratic norm of universalism.

### Operation According to Rules of Procedure

Bureaucracies are characterized by extensive sets of formally specified rules and regulations, and schools certainly seem to fit this description rather well. As a matter of fact, critics of the schools have often argued that there are simply too many rules for schools to accomplish their goals efficiently and creatively. As we indicated earlier, rules have a tendency to become ends in themselves, and to be reinforced long after they have lost their original utility. Furthermore, rules can stifle creativity and innovation by blocking efforts to institute new procedures and methods. The red tape that has to be surmounted in order to get a program going might discourage efforts even before they are begun.

Some critics have argued that schools are particularly restrictive when it comes to regulating student behavior. According to Charles Silberman, "The most important characteristic schools share in common is a preoccupation with order and control.[50] Silberman and others feel that schools are almost obsessed with controlling students' speech, movement, thoughts, and even eliminatory functions! Rules specify which staircases students can use, when students may go to the bathroom, when and where they may eat, and when and what kind of physical exercise they must take during school hours.

Other critics have focused on the restrictiveness of rules governing teachers. As professionals, teachers might be expected to have final say in how they will go about practicing their profession. As we have already seen, though, teachers are not free to choose their own books, deviate from the standard curriculum, or radically depart from the educational procedures generally accepted in their school. Conformity rather than creativity in the classroom is rewarded.

Of course, it is important to remember that rules can free people from the arbitrary whims of superiors, eliminate gross instances of discrimination, and contribute to efficiency. Furthermore, not all schools are as steeped in formal regulations as some. Schools show considerable variation in terms of the rules governing student behavior, and this variation is probably linked to the social class, ethnic, and racial characteristics of the students involved. Schools serving middle-class white students are likely to be more permissive than those serving poor blacks, for example.

Some critics have even suggested that the schools suffer from an excessive looseness regarding rules rather than an oppressive rigidity.[51] In this regard the earlier discussion of "structural looseness," "field rebellion," and the relatively "primitive" nature of school organization is relevant. This is true because one of the most important functions of the rules is to define the authority structure. The following quote describing the operation of the New York City School system illustrates these points:

> The New York City school system suffers from a disease common to many public school systems, namely "under-control." It uses primitive procedures for budgeting, auditing, data processing, and evaluation. The information it produces is often not used by top policy makers and administrators. The result is that the system has functioned largely along traditionalistic lines, so

> that decisions are shaped not so much by administrative and technical expertise as through the informal friendships, cliques, and influence that constitute the internal and external politics of the system.[52]

From this perspective the school system is not run as a "tight ship," with the result being a resistance to new policies, favoritism, and discrimination. Adherence to informal norms in opposition to the formal norms, then, is seen as a major cause for the failures of the schools.

Research has also indicated that the formal rules often define roles in such a way that duties are overly extensive, conflicting, incomplete and/or ambiguous. The conflicts inherent in the principal's duties as head teacher and as administrative chief of a complex organization have already been noted. There simply is not time enough for the principal to fully meet these large and conflicting demands. The ambiguities regarding the division of labor between the school boards and superintendents have also been noted. The resultant struggle for consensus regarding spheres of authority and autonomy often results in bad feelings. This problem of overstepping the bounds of one's position and thereby invading another's sphere of concern and activity is quite general. It can be observed in counselor–teacher, teacher–student, and family–school relationships, for example. Fred E. Katz has argued that the formal rules of schools serve to define spheres of autonomy as well as responsibility.[53] This is clearly true to some extent; the point being made here, however, is that the rules for educational organizations are often not adequate to accomplish this goal.

## BUREAUCRACY IN HIGHER EDUCATION

Like the public schools, colleges and universities have become increasingly bureaucratized over time. Beginning as small groups of students studying under a handful of teachers, they have experienced dramatic increases in size and complexity, until today single institutions serve thousands of students and employ hundreds of faculty, administrators, and support personnel.

All of the basic elements of Weber's bureaucratic model can be found in these massive institutions: formal goals, a functional division of labor, a hierarchy of authority, staff roles defined as offices and many, many rules of procedure. Nevertheless, there are important ways in which colleges and universities deviate from Weber's model, and which set them apart from other educational institutions. We will discuss many of these deviations in future chapters.

### Increases in Size and Complexity

We noted earlier that bureaucratization generally accompanies increases in organizational size and complexity. Although our colleges and universities increased in size and complexity rather steadily from the time they were established, expansion accelerated rapidly during this century.

In 1953, approximately 5.3 percent of colleges and universities in the United States enrolled five thousand students or more. By 1963, this figure was up to 13 percent. By 1981, it was up to 22 percent.[54] As the number of large institutions increased, the percentage of all students enrolled in these institutions also increased. In 1981, more than half of all college and university students were attending institutions with 10,000 or more students.[55]

Even these rather impressive figures tend to understate the growth in scale experienced by institutions of higher learning in recent years, however. This is because they do not reflect the extent to which individual public colleges and universities are now treated as parts of complex city or statewide systems of higher education. As one recent study commission put it, "In the past, the term 'college' or 'university' referred to a particular institution. Now it refers to a far-flung system of campuses, each with a standardized name."[56] For example, in 1970, the State University of New York had sixty-five campuses and 314,000 students, and the City University of New York had eleven campuses with 123,000 students.[57]

Complexity in higher education has also been increased because of broadening of services over time. The central activity in most institutions is teaching, primarily undergraduate teaching. In order to provide instruction for large numbers of students, institutions find it necessary to have officials in charge of admissions, registration, payment of fees, financial aid, scheduling of classes and final examinations, the library, the bookstore, recording grades and computation of grade point averages, and academic counseling. All this, of course, in addition to the work of professors who do the actual teaching.

Typically, colleges and universities provide students with a number of other services as well, including housing, a multiplicity of extracurricular activities, transportation, police protection, psychological and vocational counseling, medical care, and recreational opportunities. More personnel are required to perform these tasks.

But universities and many colleges are expected to produce scholarly research in addition to providing instruction. Accomplishment of this goal necessitates the hiring of staff whose job it is to do just that. Professors are chiefly responsible for research. Some do it exclusively, although most do at least some teaching. But they often require secretaries, laboratory and research assistants, and computer aides in their work. They may also wish to have their own separate research institutes and facilities. Officials work to provide researchers with these needs because institutional prestige, and frequently fiscal well-being as well, are closely tied to research productivity. Institutions receive a percentage of all grant money awarded to their faculty to cover overhead and other expenses.

For the benefit of the faculty, special administrators publicize grant opportunities, handle the financial arrangements associated with research grants, lobby for increased governmental appropriations for research and development, and solicit funds in support of research from private foundations. In addition, university presses often publish research results.

This list of activities must also be extended to include maintenance of the physical plant, providing service to the general community, and the multitudinous tasks involved in handling the relationships between the university and its external environment. Important elements of the external environment include alumni; federal, state, and local politicians; major business and industrial firms; and voluntary organizations. We cannot discuss all of these tasks here, but their variety and magnitude are obvious.

## The Evolution of the Bureaucracy

The administrative structure that handles these complex tasks expanded with the colleges and universities, but the basic rudiments of this structure were established during the last half of the nineteenth century.[58] It was during this period that college presidents first began appointing assistants to help manage their institutions. At first, these assistants were recruited from among the faculty and were appointed as vice-presidents, librarians, bursars, and registrars. By 1900, these positions evolved from part-time assistants to full-time administrative offices. In time, each of these major offices was served by a staff of assistants and clerical personnel. Individuals trained in business management, librarianship, data processing, and so on increasingly replaced those trained only in academic subjects. At the same time, special positions were created to deal with student affairs. Deans were appointed to these posts, which eventually developed into modern divisions of student personnel services.

To coordinate the increasing specialization and diversification among the faculty, departments were created and individual professors were elected or appointed to serve as department chairpersons. Secretaries and clerical assistants were added to departments as they grew in size and as their tasks multiplied.

Today, the typical student confronts a morass of bureaucratic officials and complex regulations each day he or she attends school. The process of registration provides a good illustration. A *specific administrative officer*, the registrar, has responsibility for overseeing the whole operation. The officer is at the middle level of the larger administrative *hierarchy*. Above the registrar may be the various deans and their assistants, the president and the chancellor, and below him or her are a number of assistants, secretaries, clerks, and other support personnel. The process of registration is conducted in accordance with highly specific *rules* that give detailed instructions on the completion of forms, who must approve them, where and when they must be filed. In many institutions much of the previously onerous, routine, and boring work done by clerks is now computerized and done quickly and efficiently. The computer compiles and prints class rosters, filling the classes on an entirely *impersonal basis*, usually "first come, first served." Pleas to the registrar for special consideration on the basis of personal needs, desires, personality characteristics, kinship ties, or other ascribed factors will have little success.

It is not just at the individual college or university level that bureaucratic constraints have multiplied, though. The trend toward linking of colleges and universities into larger networks or systems has resulted in the burgeoning of bureaucracy at higher levels as well. Centralization of decision making in these large systems seems to be increasing at a rapid pace. Now that the great period of expansion created by the "baby boom" of the fifties is over, there is a mood of consolidation and fiscal tightening on many campuses. Firmer control over these large multimillion dollar institutions is being recommended by politicians as well as by many state-level administrators and educators. As a result:

> There are now statewide requirements for admissions and degrees, administratively convenient classifications of study such as "lower division" and "upper division," rules which detail operations for all teaching departments, and centralized procedures for deciding a host of nonacademic issues from parking to the selection of new furniture. . . . The solidarity and cohesion of the individual campus is threatened by the new multicampus framework. The constituent members of the campus community—students, faculties, administrators, trustees—are encouraged to organize themselves "horizontally" across the system and bargain at the state level for their special interests. . . . The arena in which decisions have to be made is thus greatly enlarged. Decisions taken on one campus . . . have repercussions elsewhere. Each campus is finding it harder to work out its own problems by itself.[59]

### Limitations of the Bureaucratic Model as Applied to Higher Education

Bureaucratization may be increasing in colleges and universities, but there are important ways in which these institutions are not highly bureaucratized. At present, the management systems of most colleges and universities are quite primitive, at least in comparison with those of private industries. There are few offices of institutional research on college and university campuses, and administrators must often make their decisions with only limited statistical information about their institutions.[60]

Furthermore, the structural looseness we noted with regard to public schools is even more extreme in colleges and universities. Classroom autonomy is bolstered by a strong tradition of academic freedom and, more concretely, by strong and prestigious professional associations, such as the American Association of University Professors. College and university instructors usually choose their own texts and design their own courses with little or no supervision. Supervision, when it exists, is usually by fellow professors, who approve admitting courses into the curriculum after reviewing descriptions of their general content.

Perhaps the most central impediment to total bureaucratization and the development of a clear hierarchy of authority in higher education is the fact that faculty members view themselves as competent professionals. Professionals, in all fields, expect autonomy in making decisions relevant to their areas of expertise. Consequently, they often come into conflict with administrators when they work in bureaucratic organizations. Professionals both resent and resist rules and regulations formulated by anyone other than their professional peers.

On college campuses, faculty often retain considerable authority over hiring, promotion, and dismissal procedures involving instructional staff as well as over the development of curriculum. Any efforts on the part of the administration to regulate these procedures is met with considerable hostility. In recent years, for example, many faculty members have objected to the establishment of affirmative action regulations affecting the procedures through which they may lawfully recruit new members.[61] Traditionally, faculty members at many institutions were recruited informally, through information and recommendations passed on by colleagues at other institutions. Knowing the right person and being in that person's favor was critical for obtaining a position. This system, known among many who object to it as the "old boy network," tended to exclude women and minorities, who had few contacts with influential professors at key universities. Consequently, affirmative action regulations generally require that job openings be widely advertised in professional journals and newspapers and that all applicants be given equal consideration along with those whose names might have been forwarded by personal friends. Many faculty members have resisted this system, insisting that it interferes with their professional prerogatives and forces them to account too thoroughly for their decisions. Resistance to the proliferation of bureaucratic forms that must be filled out as part of these procedures has also been great.

As we shall see, the power of the faculty relative to that of the administration varies with a variety of institutional characteristics as well as with the characteristics of the faculty itself. Whatever the situation, however, the presence of this core of professionals performing the central work of the institution represents a challenge to the authority of the administrative hierarchy. The fact that senior faculty members are often protected by tenure and cannot be dismissed except for rather serious neglect of their responsibilities also furthers their independence from administrative authority.

Faculty members may also hold values that are incompatible with bureaucratic procedures. For example, professors might be opposed to grading or to the particular ways in which students are supposed to be graded. We know of at least one prestigious professor who objects to grading Master's examinations when the student's identity remains anonymous. The idea behind this rule is to promote universalistic treatment, to assure that all students are judged according to the same criteria. But this professor argues that he must treat each student's achievements in relation to his or her past accomplishments. Obviously, he cannot provide this individualized evaluation without knowing which student is involved.

More common, perhaps, is the general uneasiness of professors with the application of business management techniques to education. The administrator's goal of efficient and economical operations is not always compatible with the faculty's conceptualization of quality education. We shall look at all of these issues more closly in Chapters 6 and 7.

## SUMMARY, CONCLUSIONS, AND POLICY ISSUES

In this chapter we looked at schools and school systems as complex organizations. It is clear from our discussion that schools at the primary, secondary, college, and university levels have all experienced a process of bureaucratization as they have grown in size and complexity. We noted, particularly, the increasingly fine division of labor, the proliferation of administrative positions, the growing reliance on rules and regulations, and the emphasis on expertise, universalistic criteria of evaluation, and impersonality that now characterize all of these institutions.

To date, bureaucratization appears to have had mixed consequences, however. On the one hand, the merits of bureaucratization are rather obvious. Bureaucratization has facilitated the development of free, compulsory public school systems throughout the country. These bureaucratic systems provide diverse services for students from virtually all social backgrounds and classes, offering a wide range of both academic and vocationally oriented courses. To the extent that the bureaucratic ideals of judgment on the basis of universalistic criteria, merit, and impersonal considerations have been successfully institutionalized, the opportunities for those students who were traditionally locked out of educational institutions on the basis of race, sex, or other ascribed characteristics have been improved. Furthermore, to the extent that bureaucratization has increased the effectiveness and efficiency of schooling, the public has gotten a better bargain for its tax dollars.

Naturally, there are many critics who feel that the schools are still biased and/or quite inefficient. Nonetheless, it seems likely that without bureaucratization, educational institutions would be less widespread, less equitable, and less effective than they presently are.

On the other hand, it does appear that educational bureaucracies, as they have developed, display several negative characteristics. Educational institutions are often rigid and resistant to change. Bureaucratic procedures interfere with organizational responsiveness and adaptability. Big-city school systems, especially, are often characterized as aloof, powerful, and unresponsive to the differing priorities of local communities. Furthermore, overspecialization produces bureaucrats who lose sight of larger organizational goals and become preoccupied with protecting their own limited interests. And the multiplicity of rules, the morass of red tape, associated with bureaucratization discourages individual spontaneity.

There are several different criticisms and, consequently, several different kinds of policy proposals, that have been set forth by critics of contemporary educational bureaucracies. We shall deal with three of them here. First, there are those who feel that the system's major weaknesses stem from the fact that it is not yet sufficiently bureaucratized. Such individuals suggest changes aimed at running each school, college, and university as a "tight ship." Then there are those who feel that bureaucratization has gone too far and that other forces within the schools should be strengthened. They suggest changes that, though not eliminating bureaucracy, put a greater emphasis on increasing professionalism. Finally, there are those who are fundamentally hostile to bureaucratic organizations and who advocate less formalized, smaller, and more intimate educational arrangements. We shall comment briefly on each of these policy positions.

In the body of this chapter we noted that there is a good deal of structural looseness in schools, colleges, and universities. Many reasons exist for this. The traditions of academic freedom, tenure arrangements, and demands for professional autonomy stand out as being especially important. The situation is compounded, however, by the "primitive" management and communications arrangements presently in existence. Some social scientists and many state and local politicians have proposed that more up-to-date management and budgetary techniques be instituted, that tenure be eliminated, and that teachers and professors be even more constrained by bureaucratic procedures than is presently the case.[62] Thus, the position of these critics is that bureaucratization has not yet proceeded far enough in the educational realm.

Others feel that it would be a sad mistake to continue to pursue further bureaucratization as the solution to our current problems. For example, Janowitz[63] feels that in the past educators have attempted to cope with emergent problems by adding new specialists to the staff of the school bureaucracy. Thus, the central staff of big city school systems has grown as experts in curriculum development, public relations, security, and other areas have been added one after another. As the functions performed by the central staff have expanded, the roles of local administrators and teachers have narrowed. Consequently, central officials have tended to treat principals and teachers as mere cogs within a great, centrally directed machine. The professional training, aspirations, and expectations of these personnel have been slighted as the central office has sent down orders from above.

This treatment has sometimes caused resentment and active resistence, particularly on the part of teachers. As Corwin points out, teacher militancy is more likely to arise in highly bureaucratized schools than in others.[64] However, teachers have more rather than less decision-making authority over their classrooms in these large hierarchical schools. Corwin interprets this seeming contradiction as indicating that teachers' aspirations for professional autonomy are "fanned by modest advances" and this leads to further militancy.[65] Thus, it is not bureaucratization *per se* that leads to conflict between administrators and teachers, but only "attempts . . . to apply close supervision, standardization, tight rules, and centralized decision-making in faculties that are attempting to increase their professional status".[66] The teachers' definition of themselves as professionals and their desire for professional autonomy are determining factors.

Janowitz argues that roles within large school systems should be redefined so as to afford principals and teachers greater professional autonomy.[67] According to his plan, policy-making and long-term planning would remain the functions of the school board, superintendent, and central district officers. However, administrative control would be decentralized, allowing local administrators, teachers, and professors greater autonomy and room to adapt, within basic policy guidelines, to local conditions. Principals would once again assume the role of principal teacher, rather than administrative specialist, and teachers would be chosen not only on the basis of their subject matter skills, but also on their ability to relate to students. Furthermore, teachers would be encouraged to become coordinators not only of classroom learning materials but also of community resources that might be brought into play in order to help the child. Teacher trainees would be encouraged to acquaint themselves with community organizations and social service agencies through participation in volunteer tutorial and other programs. Further, there would be extensive use of subprofessionals and volunteers drawn from local communities. This would prove helpful as another bridge between the school and the community. The overall thrust of his argument is that by expanding roles, rather than narrowing them, teachers and local administrators would become more effective and would gain both professional autonomy and respect. A decade later, such major studies as Goodlad's *A Place Called School* are calling for similar changes.[68] Decentralization of authority to local schools, principals, and teachers is recommended.

Finally, there are many critics whose distrust of bureaucracies and professionals runs so deep that they have given up all hope for the creative reform of large-scale public education systems. Robert J. Havighurst has contended that these critics ". . . tend to be anarchists, that is, they do not like rules and institutions set up by society to regulate the conduct and development of its members.[69] These critics propose a wide variety of alternatives ranging from greater experimentation in the public schools and the establishment of schools that are free from all or most rules and regulations, to the complete abolition of all schools or the "deschooling" of American society. We will review some of these proposals in our final chapter. As we shall see, all of them share a negative attitude toward bureaucratization and a positive stress on freedom, creativity, and spontaneity.

## NOTES

[1]Max Weber, *The Theory of Social and Economic Organization,* ed. Talcott Parsons, trans. A.M. Henderson and Talcott Parsons (Glencoe, Ill.: The Free Press, 1947).

[2]The last four of these elements were used in Charles E. Bidwell, "The School as a Formal Organization," in *Handbook of Organizations,* ed. James G. March (Chicago: Rand McNally and Company, 1965), pp. 972–1022.

[3]See Peter M. Blau and W. Richard Scott, *Formal Organizations* (San Francisco: Chandler Publishing Company, 1962) for an overview of these and related issues discussed below.

[4]Blau and Scott, *Formal Organizations,* pp. 89–115.

[5]See Blau and Scott, *Formal Organizations,* for an extended analysis of the problems unique to service organizations.

[6]Much of the historical review in this chapter is based on R. Freeman Butts and Lawrence A. Cremin, *A History of Education in American Culture* (New York: Holt, Rinehart & Co., 1953) and Paul Monroe, *Founding of the American Public School System* (New York: The MacMillan Co., 1940).

[7]Michael Katz, *Class, Bureaucracy, and the Schools: The Illusion of Educational Change in America* (New York: Praeger Publishers, 1971), p. 61.

[8]Katz, *Class, Bureaucracy, and the Schools*, pp. 62–63.

[9]Paul Monroe, *Founding of the American Public School System*, pp. 248–49.

[10]Raymond E. Callahan, *Education and the Cult of Efficiency* (Chicago: The University of Chicago Press, 1962), p. 7

[11]Callahan, *Education and the Cult of Efficiency.*

[12]Franklin Bobbitt, "The Supervision of City Schools: Some General Principles of Management Applied to the Problems of City-School Systems," in *Twelfth Yearbook of the National Society for the Study of Education, Part I*, (Bloomington, Ill., 1913), p. 11, as cited in Callahan, *Education and the Cult of Efficiency*, p. 81.

[13]Bobbitt, p. 11, as cited in Callahan, *Education and the Cult of Efficiency*, p. 81.

[14]Bobbitt, pp. 11–15, as cited in Callahan, *Education and the Cult of Efficiency*, p. 81.

[15]Bobbitt, as cited in Callahan, *Education and the Cult of Efficiency*, p. 84.

[16]"Efficiency in the Classroom," *American School Board Journal*, LII (August, 1916), p. 54, as cited in Callahan, *Education and the Cult of Efficiency*, p. 103.

[17]Callahan, *Education and the Cult of Efficiency*, p. 245.

[18]Ibid., p. 247.

[19]A major reason for this was that the poor needed their children's wages in order to survive. Compulsory school attendance was, for them, an economic hardship.

[20]Katz, *Class, Bureaucracy, and the Schools*, p. 39.

[21]Ibid., p. 40.

[22]Ibid., p. 31.

[23]See Samuel Bowles and Herbert Gintis, *Schooling in Capitalist America: Educational Reform and the Contradictions of Economic Life* (New York: Basic Books, 1976) for an overview of this position.

[24]Katz, *Class, Bureaucracy, and the Schools*, p. 32.

[25]Ibid., p. 33.

[26]Ibid., p. 54.

[27]Roald F. Campbell, Luvern L. Cunningham, and Roderick F. McPhee, *The Organization and Control of American Schools* (Columbus, Ohio: Charles E. Merrill, 1965), p. 94; Valena White Plisko, *The Condition of Education, 1983 Edition* (Washington, D.C.: Government Printing Office, 1983), p. 29.

[28]Howard S. Becker, "Personal Change in Adult Life," *Sociometry*, 27, 1 (1964), pp. 40–53; Seymour Bernard Sarason, *The Culture of the School and the Problem of Change* (Boston: Allyn & Bacon, 1971).

[29]Richard L. Warren, "Context and Isolation: The Teaching Experience in an Elementary School," *Human Organization*, 34, 2 (1975), pp. 139–48.

[30]Charles Perrow, *Organizational Analysis: A Sociological View* (Belmont, Calif.: Wadsworth, 1970); L.B. Mohr and others, "Administrative Structure, Effectiveness and Efficiency: A Prospectus for Research on Organizational Aspects of Education" (Washington, D.C.: National Institute of Education, mimeo, 1975).

[31]R.M. Cyert and J.G. March, *A Behavioral Theory of the Firm* (Englewood Cliffs, N.J.: Prentice-Hall, 1963); Michael Radnor, "Administration and Management in Educational Organizations: A Discussion of Issues and Proposal for a Research Program for the National Institute of Education. (Watsonville, Calif.: mimeo, 1974).

[32]Dan C. Lortie, "The Teacher's Shame: Anger and the Normative Commitments of Classroom Teachers," *School Review*, 75 (1967), pp. 155–71.

[33]In a small number of districts, the superintendent is an elected official. Because the overwhelming majority of superintendents are appointed, most research focuses on these cases. Aside from occasional comments, we will confine our discussion to superintendents appointed by their board of education.

[34]For a good discussion of the variables affecting the power of superintendents and their boards, see L. Harmon Zeigler and M. Kent Jennings, with G. Wayne Peak, *Governing*

*American Schools: Political Interaction in Local School Districts* (North Scituate, Mass.: Duxbury Press, 1974) and Norman D. Kerr (pseudonym), "The School Board as an Agency of Legitimation" in *Governing Education: A Reader on Politics, Power, and Public School Policy*, ed. Alan Rosenthal (Garden City, New York: Anchor Books, Doubleday & Company, 1969), pp. 137–72.

[35]R. O. Carlson, *Executive Succession and Organizational Change* (Chicago: University of Chicago, Midwest Administration Center, 1962), pp. 30–38, as cited in Bidwell, *The School as a Formal Organization*, p. 1004.

[36]Terence E. Deal and Lynn D. Celotti, "How Much Influence Do (and Can) Educational Administrators Have on Classrooms?," *Phi Delta Kappan*, 61, 7 (March, 1980), pp. 471–73.

[37]Ibid., p. 472.

[38]David Rogers, *110 Livingston Street: Politics and Bureaucracy in the New York City School System* (New York: Vintage Books, 1969), pp. 299–301.

[39]Robert Dreeben, *The Nature of Teaching: Schools and the Work of Teachers* (Glenview, Ill.: Scott, Foresman and Company, 1970), pp. 57–75.

[40]Charles Bidwell, "The School as a Formal Organization," in *Handbook of Organizations*, ed. James G. March (Chicago: Rand McNally and Company, 1965), p. 976.

[41]Sanford Dornbusch, "A Theory of Evaluation Applied to Schools." Speech delivered to the Sociological Research Association, New York City, September 1, 1976.

[42]Van Cleve Morris, Robert L. Crowson, Emanuel Hurwitz, Jr., and Cynthia Porter-Guthrie, "The Urban School Principal: Middle Manager in the Educational Bureaucracy," *Phi Delta Kappan*, (June, 1982), pp. 689–92.

[43]Howard S. Becker, "The Teacher in the Authority System of the Public School," *Journal of Educational Sociology*, 27, (November, 1953). pp. 128–41.

[44]James S. Coleman, Ernest Q. Campbell, Carol J. Hobson, James McPartland, Alexander M. Mood, Frederic D. Weenfeld, and Robert L. York, *Equality of Educational Opportunity* (Washington, D.C.: Government Printing Office, 1966), pp. 3, 15–16, 126–30.

[45]In 1975, the *New York Times*, "Women in Classrooms, Not the Principal's Office," July 13, 1975, section 4, p. 7, reported that 80 percent of elementary school principals, 98 percent of high school principals, and 99 percent of superintendents were men. See also U.S. Equal Employment Opportunity Commission, *Minorities and Women in Public Elementary and Secondary Schools* (Washington, D.C.: Government Printing Office, 1981), p. 3.

[46]The percentage of female elementary principals was 55 percent in 1923, 38 percent in 1958, and 19.6 percent in 1973, according to Gretchen Niedermayer and Vicki W. Kramer, "Women in Administrative Positions in Public Education," (Philadelphia: Recruitment Leadership and Training Institute, 1974), p. 2.

[47]U.S. Commission on Civil Rights, *Twenty Years After Brown: Equality of Educational Opportunity* (Washington, D.C.: Government Printing Office, 1975), pp. 69–70.

[48]Neal Gross, Ward S. Mason, and Alexander W. McEachern, *Explorations in Role Analysis: Studies of the School Superintendency Role* (New York: John Wiley & Sons, Inc., 1958), pp. 258–267.

[49]Ibid., p. 259.

[50]Charles E. Silberman, *Crisis in the Classroom*, (New York: Vintage Books, 1967), p. 22.

[51]Rogers, *110 Livingston Street*, p. 343.

[52]Ibid., p. 343.

[53]Fred E. Katz, "The School as a Complex Organization," *Harvard Educational Review*, 34, (Summer, 1964), pp. 428–55.

[54]U.S. Department of Health, Education and Welfare: *Biennial Survey of Education in the U.S.: 1952–1954*, Chapter 4, Section I (Washington, D.C.: Government Printing Office, 1959), p. 12: U.S.D.H.E.W. *Digest of Educational Statistics* (Washington, D.C.: Government Printing Office, 1964), p. 93; U.S.D.H.E.W. *Digest of Educational Statistics* (Washington, D.C.: Government Printing Office, 1975), p. 90; W. Vance Grant and Thomas D. Snyder, *Digest of Education Statistics, 1983–84* (Washington, D.C.: Government Printing Office, 1984), p. 104.

[55]Ibid., p. 105.

[56]Frank Newman, *Report on Higher Education* (Washington, D.C.: Government Printing Office, 1971), p. 23.

[57]Ibid., p. 23.

[58]This account of the bureaucratization of higher education is based on E. D. Duryea, "Evolution of University Organization," in *The University as an Organization*, ed. James A. Perkins, (New York: McGraw-Hill Book Company, 1973), pp. 15–37.

[59]Newman, *Report on Higher Education*, p. 25.

[60]Barry M. Richman and Richard N. Farmer, *Leadership, Goals, and Power in Higher Education* (San Francisco: Jossey-Bass, 1974).

[61]See Richard A. Lester, *Antibias Regulation of Universities: Faculty Problems and their Solutions* (New York: McGraw-Hill Book Company, 1974), and Phyllis Zatlin Boring, "Antibias Regulation of Universities: A Biased View?," *American Association of University Professors Bulletin*, 61 (October, 1975), pp. 252–55, for an overview of these issues.

[62]For example, with regard to higher education, see Richman and Farmer, *Leadership, Goals, and Power in Higher Education*, and Robert M. O'Neil, "Tenure under Attack," pp. 178–99 in Bardwell L. Smith and others, *The Tenure Debate* (San Francisco: Jossey-Bass, 1973).

[63]Morris Janowitz, *Institution Building in Urban Education* (Chicago: The University of Chicago Press, 1971). Similar proposals are made by David Rogers, *110 Livingston Street: Politics and Bureaucracy in the New York City School System* (New York: Vintage Books, 1969), pp. 299–301.

[64]Ronald G. Corwin, *Education in Crisis: A Sociological Analysis of Schools and Universities in Transition* (New York: John Wiley & Sons, 1974), p. 255.

[65]Ibid., p. 255.

[66]Ibid., p. 256.

[67]Janowitz, *Institution Building in Urban Education*, pp. 41–60.

[68]John I. Goodlad, *A Place Called School* (New York: McGraw-Hill, 1984), pp. 271-320.

[69]Robert J. Havighurst, "Requirements for a Valid 'New Criticism'," pp. 210–22 in *Pygmalion or Frankenstein? Alternative Schooling in American Education*, eds. John C. Carr, Jean Dresden Grambs, and E. G. Campbell, (Reading, Mass.: Addison-Wesley, 1977), p. 212.

# CHAPTER FIVE THE ORGANIZATION OF STUDENT LIFE

Teachers and administrators organize student lives in a variety of important ways, but experienced educators understand that students also influence one another. Indeed, student groups and cultures have a far greater impact on the educational process than is generally acknowledged. This chapter describes not only the bureaucratic processing of students, but also the ways in which students themselves help shape their education.

## SCHOOLS AS PEOPLE-PROCESSING ORGANIZATIONS

Schools belong to a general category of organizations whose central tasks involve the processing of people rather than material objects.[1] Hospitals, social work agencies, prisons, and job-training centers are other examples of this type of organization. All of these organizations have several characteristics in common and share certain problems that are linked to these characteristics.

One problem faced by all of these organizations is that people who are centrally involved in the internal workings of the organization are there on only a temporary basis. Students graduate; patients die or get better; and prisoners complete their sentences. Because these individuals move in and out of the organization while staff members remain relatively stable, the question of how much authority should be granted to the transients is always a sensitive one. For example, should students or patients, or even prisoners, be given a voice in setting policies that will be in effect for many years after those particular individuals leave? Can members of an organization be expected to exercise authority responsibly and with sufficient commitment when they will be in that organization only temporarily? How much influence should these transients have when the values and objectives of one group may vary from those of others who follow them?

A second example of problems faced by people-processing organizations involves the differences between people and other types of raw materials. The materials with which most organizations work are passive and easily standardized. General Motors arranges the delivery of necessary parts and goes to work putting them together into automobiles. However, people are neither passive nor available in uniform lots. They can resist or even sabotage the work of an organization and they can have diverse characteristics, which makes processing them difficult or even impossible.

People-processing organizations must always be concerned with obtaining the cooperation of those they are processing. In some cases this is easy. Most hospital patients willingly comply with hospital regulations and procedures without special efforts on the part of the organization involved. Most prisoners require added inducements, however. Coercion, in the form of lengthened terms or confinement to punishment cells, and rewards, in the form of time off for good behavior, are some of the tactics that prisons must use to assure inmate cooperation. In schools, students are motivated by grades, praise, and interesting assignments as well as by threats that they will be kept after school, given additional punitive work, reported to their parents, or even suspended. In both cases, organizational resources must be used to assure the cooperation of those being processed.

People-processing organizations must also be concerned that those being processed do not usurp control over the organization, exert undue influence on the organizations' staff, or otherwise divert the goals and procedures of the organization. For example, it is important that teachers do not lose "control" of their class. When this happens, teachers are no longer able to assure that their students will comply with the rules of the school or that they will master the appropriate curriculum materials, and hence, the smooth operation of the organization will be disrupted.

The lack of uniformity among people who must be processed also leads to numerous specific problems. For example, an unusually heterogeneous group of people might mean that an organization has to develop different procedures for handling different types. This might place a great burden on both the financial and other resources of the organization. It might also create problems in treating all groups equitably, dealing with charges of discriminatory practices, or remaining innovative enough to adapt to the needs of diverse and changing populations.

Of course, people-processing organizations differ from one another in several important respects. Some are considerably more concerned with changing the people they process than are others. Hasenfeld has pointed out that diagnostic clinics, job placement offices, credit bureaus, and juvenile courts process people, but do not try to change them.[2] In these organizations, classifying, labeling, and allocating individuals to other institutions is the primary task. At the other extreme, prisons, mental health clinics, and hospitals are centrally concerned with changing the people that they process. Even among these people-changing organizations, though, there are clear and important differences. Some are designed to rehabilitate or radically alter their clients; others are designed to restore people to a previous existing state of well-being; and still others are designed to take individuals a few steps further in a process of development already started somewhere else. We would put the school in this last category of organizations. Schools are designed to further the socialization processes begun in the family. They assume, for the most part, that what they teach is consistent with what the student has learned earlier at home or in other educational institutions. When it is not, the organization may be unprepared for the resultant problems.

There is another important way in which people-processing organizations differ from one another. Organizations vary in the degree to which they process people as individuals or as groups. As Wheeler has pointed out, schools are excellent examples of organizations that process people in batches, or *collectivities*.[3] Students enter school as part of a class and move together through the organization in an orderly fashion. Relatively few students are either left back or skipped ahead. In addition, each class is just one of a series of similar classes, some of which are a year or two ahead in the process and others a bit behind. This means that each class can look forward to see what is coming next, as well as look back to see where it has been. We will discuss some of the implications of this collective and serial method of processing students in the latter parts of this chapter.

Now that we have an initial overview of the characteristics of people-processing organizations, we will turn more specifically to the ways in which schools process students. We will look at recruitment and selection; screening, and sorting; teaching the student role; monitoring; termination and certification. For each set of processes, we will look at the organizational constraints that affect educational decisions and outcomes for the school and for the students.

## Recruitment and Selection

Three major facts shape recruitment and selection processes in the public schools. First, school attendance is compulsory. Children throughout most of the United States must be enrolled in school between the ages of six and sixteen. Individual families or their children cannot decide to withdraw from school if they are dissatisfied or uninterested in what is happening there.[4]

Second, the public schools have a near monopoly on elementary and secondary education. Public schools are entirely supported by taxes and are therefore "free" in the sense that no child who lives within the district must pay tuition. Private schools, on the other hand, receive limited public funds and are, therefore, relatively expensive and beyond the means of most families. The overwhelming majority, 89 percent, of American students attend public schools.[5]

Many of those who choose private schools select schools that teach religious or other values they hold dear or that reflect their own educational philosophies more completely than do the public schools.

When large numbers of parents exercise such choices the effect on local public schools can be substantial. For example, the public schools may find themselves with a disproportionately large percentage of the community's "problem" children because these are the children private schools are free to reject. The public schools might also find the heterogeneity of their student body drastically reduced as most children from a particular ethnic or social class background are withdrawn. A study done several years ago in a community with a low-cost Catholic school system described such effects:

> Under these conditions, the public schools may become dumping grounds for the less gifted and "problem" Catholic children. This had actually occurred in the . . . neighborhood of "Bay City" where the public school contains a handful of Protestant children and the problem children whom the . . . parochial school either would not accept or expelled. Among the general population, and more significantly among the teachers in "Bay City," this school is reputed to be the worst in the system. In some neighborhoods in our large metropolitan areas, the public schools have as their constituencies children from the two extremes of the class system, those from the fairly high non-Catholic groups and those from the lowest rungs of the occupational ladder.[6]

Under these conditions, public schools might lose in other ways as well. Parents who send their children to private schools may be less likely to support raising taxes to improve the public schools.

Individual schools within the public school system enjoy a monopoly over the students within their attendance zones. School boards establish attendance zones for district schools. Parents who reside within the boundaries of such zones are generally required to enroll their children in the school serving their area.

Of course, parents often do exercise some limited choice by deciding where their family will live. Parents are free to settle in a city, a suburb, or a rural community. They can choose a location in terms of the reputation of its local schools. They can even move into small homogeneous communities in which the schools are particularly likely to reflect their own values. Of course, the amount of choice parents have in selecting a residence is related to their financial status. As always, the wealthy have more options than the poor.

The third major factor affecting public school selection and recruitment is that these schools are compelled to accept all eligible children within their jurisdiction. Public schools have little control over the number or characteristics of these eligible students. Except for a few relatively extreme cases, all children living in a school district must be accepted. Public schools can neither refuse to admit nor summarily dismiss students who are unmotivated. Consequently schools have sometimes been lumped together with state mental hospitals, reformatories, and prisons as organizations in which neither the organization nor its clients have much control over who enters and who does not.[7]

However, school boards do have some means of manipulating the social characteristics of student bodies. Historically, boards have often gerrymandered school attendance zones, closed old schools and built new ones, and used bussing in efforts to promote class and racial segregation. In recent years, courts have ordered that these same measures be used to promote desegregation.

We have identified three major factors which shape the recruitment and selection processes in schools. These are compulsory attendance, public school monopoly, and compulsory acceptance of eligible students by public school officials. These factors have important implications for the organization and operation of schools.

One implication is that schools are greatly affected by changes in the sheer number of students available in a community. Schools cannot normally recruit children from outside their district to increase their enrollment or turn away students if there are too many. Of course, the number and cost of local private schools is a factor that affects the availability of students. Another major factor is demographic change resulting from migration in or out of a community or from shifts in a community's birth rate. A school district can find itself short of children because its surrounding community has "aged." Younger couples may have moved out of the community to seek jobs or opportunities elsewhere. Those who remain may be older families whose children are already grown. Consequently, the school may find itself with too many teachers or other resources and too few students. Or a school may find itself suddenly overwhelmed by children if there has been a recent influx of young families to the surrounding area. This can occur if large industries open local divisions in an area or if major new housing developments are constructed.

In the past, waves of immigrants from abroad and mass migrations from rural areas within the United States have had these kinds of effects. However, some of the greatest impacts on the schools have been caused by changes in the birth rate. The rapid rise in the birth rate that occurred after World War II, producing the baby boom of the 1950s, created havoc in the nation's schools. First, elementary schools, then high schools, and finally colleges and universities felt the impact of these swelled ranks of young people. Schools went on double and triple sessions to accommodate them all. Extensive campaigns to recruit and train teachers were inaugurated. Massive new building projects were initiated. Now these "babies" have passed out of the schools and into adulthood. The cohorts following the baby boom were small, producing a "birth dearth" which, in turn, caused school systems across the country to retrench—to close school buildings and reduce the teaching force. Now that the "baby boomers" are childbearing adults, their large numbers are again resulting in a rise in the number of school children. New schools must again be built and a teacher shortage is developing.

Another important implication of the school's inability to control admissions is related to a point we made earlier: People-processing organizations have special problems because their clients may be very diverse and may resist the organization's efforts to process them. Many people-processing organizations deal with these problems through highly selective admissions procedures. By limiting their admissions only to certain types of individuals, the organizations can concentrate their resources on a narrow range of procedures that are appropriate for these homogeneous clients. By limiting their admissions only to those who are willing to cooperate with the organization, they can avoid having to devote organizational resources to problems of control. The clients are selected according to their motivation to facilitate the work of the organization. They will also have the values, talents and other characteristics best suited to the organization's goals and methods. Some private schools are highly selective as are a few prestigious colleges and universities. Harvard, for example, is in the enviable position of being able to pick and choose from among a pool of highly qualified applicants. However, the great majority of American colleges and universities are nonselective.[8] Community colleges are generally required by law to accept all high school graduates no matter how meager their academic accomplishments. And many colleges are so financially hard-pressed and so threatened by declining enrollments that they cannot afford to be selective. They need students to fill classrooms and dormitories and to provide, through tuition payments, funds to meet operating expenses. Nonselective colleges and universities face many of the same motivational and remedial problems which confront public schools.

Public schools are nonselective institutions which must admit children of widely varying attitudes, levels of ability, and experiences. They must take children from diverse backgrounds and a wide variety of preferred lifestyles. They must also take many students who are not particularly happy about being in school. Classroom teachers are often given the demanding (if not impossible) task of motivating and challenging each student within classes that are so heterogeneous as to contain students who are gifted, average, retarded, physically handicapped, cooperative, bored, and disruptive. The fact that school is compulsory means that many students are in school reluctantly and that motivation and control must therefore be central issues in the school's daily operation. Student cooperation is not automatic. Neither are students necessarily sympathetic to the goals and methods of their teachers. Nor do students always have the intellectual or other skills that school personnel consider necessary for successful processing.

From the point of view of the school, then, this great heterogeneity of the student body represents a sizable challenge. How can one organization develop methods that will be effective for this great variety of clients? How can resources be equitably distributed so that the needs of all types of students are met? How can schools produce a standard product, from one grade to the next or one level to the next, when the raw recruits with which they begin are so diverse?

In part, this great diversity among students is one major reason why schools have not become as highly bureaucratized as they otherwise might have. Teachers simply cannot treat all children identically when they are, in fact, so very different from each other. No one teaching method, curriculum, or evaluative technique is going to be appropriate for all children, or even for all children of a particular age. Some flexibility must remain so that adaptations to the needs of individual children can be made.

## Screening and Sorting

The student body of the typical American school is much too large and heterogeneous to be taught as a single group. In order to increase educational efficiency and effectiveness, students must be divided into smaller, more homogeneous, and manageable learning units. Chronological age is the primary basis upon which students are differentiated. Age-grading is nearly universal and exerts a profound impact on the organization, curriculum, and even extracurriculum of virtually all American public schools. Within each age-grade, however, there is still considerable allocation of students to different programs, classes, and learning groups. The processes of screening and sorting students begins upon entrance and continues throughout the school career.

Boys and girls entering kindergarten or first grade are screened to determine appropriate class placements. Initial assessments are made of entering students' speech, hearing, visual acuity, motor coordination, emotional maturity, attention span, and reading readiness. New students are also routinely screened for mental retardation and various specific learning disabilities such as dyslexia and hyperkinesis. Such screening procedures have been developed on the theory that early identification of learning problems facilitates their remediation. When the screening process works correctly, students with special needs are provided with the kinds of educational experiences necessary to maximize their potential.

However, American public schools are institutions of mass education and as such deal most adequately with the normal or average student. Exceptional students have often been misidentified, inappropriately labeled, segregated, and stigmatized. In the recent past, the standard operating procedure of American schools was to place students with a wide variety of learning disabilities together, in their own separate special-education classes apart from "normal students." Those classes were often misused as "dumping grounds" by teachers eager to remove hostile and nonconforming students from their classes.[9] Although the screening procedures established by school districts were often elaborate, they were still flawed. Children were often inaccurately classified.[10] Minority students, especially males, were greatly overrepresented among the classified students. Suspicions grew that many of the classification procedures were racially biased as well as unreliable.[11]

These concerns gave impetus to the enactment by Congress in 1975 of Public Law 94-142, the Education of all Handicapped Children Act. A major provision of that law is that, whenever possible, children classified as handicapped must be educated within the "least restrictive" environment possible, which is usually interpreted to mean the regular classroom. This process, commonly known as *mainstreaming*, promises to bring about an overall improvement in education of handicapped youth. However, ordinary classroom teachers are usually unfamiliar with learning handicaps and appropriate means of dealing with them. Ideally special education teachers would work with the regular staff on behalf of mainstreamed students. But close consultative relationships between classroom teachers and specialists are rare. Teachers are often reluctant to ask advice from outside experts, perhaps because they are reluctant to admit that they do not know what to do or perhaps because the teacher sees the specialist as a transient expert who is insufficiently familiar with the classroom and school.[12]

Federal statutes attempt to ensure that the educational needs of handicapped children are met, but no such laws protect intellectually precocious or "gifted" students. Research indicates that exceptionally able students also need special educational experiences in order to fulfill their intellectual potentials.[13] Such students are often bored by the slow pace of the normal curriculum, and many actually drop out before finishing high school. Gifted students thrive when they are stimulated by understanding teachers and challenged by peers of equal ability. Julian Stanley of Johns Hopkins University has shown that under optimally individualized conditions, exceptionally able junior high school students can master a whole year's work in science or mathematics in only a few weeks of concentrated study during the summer. But in many, if not most, public schools conditions are far from optimal for such students. Rigid, age-graded curricula deny opportunities for acceleration, and already overworked teachers are unable or unwilling to provide such students with enrichment opportunities. It has been estimated that no more than half of America's gifted children have been identified and placed appropriately.[14] As with handicapped students, many educators are concerned that identification procedures may be unreliable and biased, and that gifted students will be segregated, labeled, and stigmatized. A mathematically gifted student once told the authors of this text that his peers called him "genius." We said that was fine, that it was a compliment. His reply was "Not the way *they* say it."

All elementary school students, not just the exceptional ones, are screened and sorted. Students' academic ability, behavior, gender, race, and ethnicity are all considered by at least some schools as they assign students to classes.

Two major types of ability grouping are employed at the elementary school level. *Tracking, or cross-class grouping,* involves sorting children into relatively homogeneous, fast, average, and slow classes. In 1971 Findlay and Bryan reported that some use of this type of grouping was made at the elementary school level in approximately one out of four American school districts.[15] This practice is apparently less common today. However, the second method, *ability grouping within classes,* is routinely used in heterogeneous elementary level classes.[16] There are diverse levels of student ability and achievement within such classes, but teachers form relatively homogeneous instructional subgroups. They usually establish three groups for reading and three for mathematics.[17] Teachers strongly support the practice of ability grouping, presumably because they believe it makes both teaching and learning easier.[18] Teachers often form ability groups even in tracked classes, if they feel that the range of student ability or achievement is sufficient.

Tracking, or cross-class grouping, is much more widespread at the middle school and high school level than it is at the elementary level. Goodlad's 1983 study found all thirteen of the senior high schools sampled to be tracked in English/language arts, mathematics, social studies, and science.[19] The curriculum of American schools generally becomes differentiated by ninth grade. In addition to placing students of similar academic achievement together, some schools also track students into different programs entirely. Less academically able students often take vocational track courses that are designed to prepare them for full-time employment immediately upon graduation from high school. The best students are usually in the college track, studying those subjects that are required for admission to colleges and universities. The remaining students are in the general track which, depending on the specific courses included, may or may not prepare them for college.

Sociologists and other social scientists have studied both ability grouping within classes and tracking extensively. Their concerns have focused on several critical issues. First, how accurately can schools assess students' academic abilities and accomplishments? Minority students and students from poor families are found to be disproportionately represented in vocational tracks and slow ability groups. Is this because of bias in the tests used to evaluate and classify students? Secondly, does ability grouping really meet the learning needs of all students or are some children given greater educational advantages by being placed in one group or another? Thirdly, what is the impact of ability grouping on children's self-esteem? The research evidence regarding these and related questions will be reviewed in Chapter 8.

## Teaching the Student Role

One of the first tasks faced by the schools with each incoming group of children is teaching them the student role. Children learn what norms are associated with their new position: what rules they must obey and how they should interact both with teachers and others students. There are at least three points to keep in mind about this process.

First, from the point of view of the school as an organization, success in teaching the student role is essential for smooth and efficient daily operations. The school could not function if children did not learn to arrive on time, go to their proper classrooms each day, remain quiet when the teacher is talking, and generally cooperate with the directives of teachers and administrators. The more successful the school is in teaching the student role, the fewer resources—such as time and personnel—have to be allocated to keeping students under control.

Second, the exact content of the student role is linked to other characteristics of the school, such as its bureaucratic structure and the value that it places on achievement. Obviously, it would not be important for students to arrive on time if schools were relatively informal learning centers to which children could go voluntarily whenever they were interested in learning something. On the other hand, if this were the case, then developing curiosity and self-initiative might be important components of the student role. The content of the student role cannot be divorced from the context within which that role exists.

Third, the content of the student role is in itself an important part of what the child learns in school, and something that carries over into other roles the student will be expected to fulfill in the future. Eisenstadt,[20] Parsons,[21] and others have pointed out that in contemporary societies school serves as a transition between the particularism of the family and the universalism and impersonality of most other institutions. In the family, the child is valued as a total person, and loved unconditionally. In most other contemporary institutions, however, individuals interact with each other in terms of relatively narrow role relationships rather than as whole human beings. Each person is treated like every other person playing the same role, and each must prove worthwhile through his or her behavior and achievements.

The school is the first major institution within which people experience this kind of interaction. The earliest years of school are more like the family than the later ones. Kindergarten teachers are, in general, more willing to display affection and more tolerant of personal idiosyncracies among students. As the student moves into higher grades, however, the classroom and the school itself become increasingly bureaucratic in atmosphere. By the time a student is ready for graduation, he or she has learned all the role components necessary for successful participation in similarly structured organizations.

Of course, not all theorists who stress the importance of the student role for future role behavior sound quite so sanguine about this process. As we shall see, other theorists have stressed the negative attributes of the student role, pointing out that students are socialized to be passive and conforming. Such students may easily fit into large bureaucratic workplaces, but they will be incapable of creativity, social criticism or rebellion.

Now let us turn to the specific content of the student role and to the relationship between this content and the school as an organization. Dreeben has isolated four elements that he considers central to the student role. These are independence, achievement, universalism and specificity.[22]

The norm of independence prescribes that some tasks ought to be accomplished without help from others. Students must learn that teachers, peers, and even parents cannot be legitimately expected to help them every time they find a task unpleasant or difficult. Students must learn to do the best they can by themselves. According to Dreeben, this norm is encouraged for several reasons. Given the large classes with which most teachers are faced, it is necessary that students learn to do as much as they can without assistance from the teacher. This norm may be difficult for some children to learn at first because they are used to a one-to-one relationship with their parents and siblings. However, independence is widely valued among adults, and most parents can be expected to encourage their children in this direction. An additional reason for promoting independence is that it facilitates evaluation and grading. When children receive considerable help from others, it may be difficult to get an accurate assessment of their abilities or how much work they are actually completing.

The norm of achievement specifies that students will be evaluated in terms of their achievements and rewarded differentially according to how well they do. It also includes the dictate that all students ought to work hard and try to master classroom materials to the best of their ability.

The norm of universalism specifies that all students are to be treated alike and judged according to the same standards and criteria. No student can expect special treatment on the basis of ascribed characteristics or informal connections they may have with school personnel. All students must accept the fact that rewards will be distributed in the classroom according to merit alone. Dreeben points out that there are several characteristics of the contemporary school that facilitate the internalization of this norm. One of these is the fact that children are age-graded. Another is the fact that they tend to be relatively homogeneous in terms of family background and other ascribed characteristics. This means that children can accept the idea that they are all starting off approximately equal in terms of their potential to do well in school. Any differences in achievement can then be legitimately attributed to differences in ability and motivation and, therefore, are deserving of reward.

The norm of specificity prescribes that students and teachers will interact with each other only in terms of segmental role relationships. The large number of students in each classroom makes more intimate relationships between students and teachers difficult to establish. In addition, the large number of students in each class and school limits intimate relationships among students as well. The higher the grade level of the students, the more often they will interact with classmates as impersonal fellow role occupants rather than as friends.

Dreeben's analysis of the student role is relatively positive in tone. Dreeben, like Parsons, stresses the compatibility between this role and the future roles students will play in the larger society. Dreeben does not raise questions about many ways in which schools violate the norms he attributes to them, however. Neither does he discuss the costs, to children and society, involved in learning the student role. He ignores many negative aspects of this role highlighted by others, such as Jules Henry.

Henry has analyzed the student role from a critical perspective and has argued that a key component of that role is "giving the teacher what she wants."[23] In concrete terms this means being docile, compliant, and keenly attentive to the teacher. Henry believes that academic success derives chiefly from the ability of a child to comply with this norm. According to Henry, teachers give off signals that indicate what the correct response to each question is. Students quickly learn to pick up on these signals and respond in the appropriate way. Henry illustrates with an example:

> The children have been shown movies of birds. The first film ended with a picture of a baby bluebird.
>
> *Teacher*: Did the last bird ever look like he would be blue?

> The children did not seem to understand the slant of the question, and answered somewhat hesitantly: Yes.
> *Teacher*: I think he looked more like a robin, didn't he?
> *Children, in chorus*: Yes.[24]

In trying to understand just why grade-school students should be so interested in pleasing the teacher by giving the "right" answers, Henry does not make reference to the formal mechanisms of social control, the testing-grading-certifying system. Rather, he observes that the classroom is an anxious place for students. It is a place in which the student performs in front of both the teacher and fellow students, the teacher's agreement or disagreement is visible to all, and one is subject to the criticism or even ridicule of fellow students if a "dumb" answer is given. Thus, the urge to please the teacher is very strong.

Some additional insights into how the student role is learned have been offered by Harry Gracey. Gracey studied socialization in the kindergarten classroom and concluded that "The unique job of the kindergarten in the educational division of labor seems . . . to be teaching children the student role.[25] As Gracey describes it, the key element in the student role is obedience to school rules. The routines and rituals of the kindergarten are unimaginative and highly structured, but children must learn to master them. Gracey describes the major activities of a kindergarten he observed: hanging coats and sweaters outside the classroom; sitting on the floor in a semicircle while the teacher takes attendance; assigning students to monitor duties; "serious time," recitation of the Lord's Prayer; flag salute and singing a patriotic song; sharing time or show-and-tell, divided into separate periods for boys and girls; a brief open discussion about a zoo trip that ends in confusion; imitations of animal movements accompanied by music; calisthenics done in table groups; worktime in which a picture is drawn; free play; clean up; snack time; rest time; singing, and an end-of-the-day ritual. During much of the routine the children seem to have a very good time although the situation is highly structured and minimizes spontaneity and creativity. Being quietly obedient has been important throughout.

Of course, we do not know how typical Gracey's kindergarten is. Gracey found the atmosphere sufficiently oppressive to title his work "Kindergarten as Academic Boot Camp." However, others might argue that the children were learning important lessons about self-discipline and group life.

Philip Jackson has also analyzed the early school years and, like Gracey, has focused on the seemingly endless rules and regulations governing school life.[26] Jackson has argued that what children learn most in the first years of school is to be patient and wait their turn, to be punctual, and to obey the rules. Jackson has referred to this learning as the "hidden curriculum." This

> . . . other curriculum might be described as unofficial or perhaps even hidden, because to date it has received scant attention from educators. This

> hidden curriculum can also be represented by three R's, but not the familiar ones of reading, 'riting, and 'rithmetic. It is, instead, the curriculum of rules, regulations, and routines, of things teachers and students must learn if they are to make their way with minimum pain in the social institution called *the school*.[27]

Jackson emphasizes the arbitrary character of the rules, regulations, and routines, and how they are often used to break up ongoing activities that may be successfully absorbing the students' interest. Children must learn to regulate their activities according to the clock or the bells. They must learn to put up with disruptions, delays, and distractions. Unquestioning acceptance of these annoyances is a sign of a good student, one who has mastered the student role.

There are also norms that specify how a good student should interact with fellow students. It is desirable that she or he get along with others, but that sociability be kept within bounds. Generally the ideal student is quiet and nondisruptive, a good citizen. But citizenship within the classroom does not imply that a student should feel responsible for helping peers who learn more slowly. Rather, the ideal student will pursue his or her own achievements, patiently waiting if necessary for others to keep up. As we noted in Chapter 2, this individualistic and competitive orientation stands in sharp contrast to practices in China and the Soviet Union, which emphasize collectivism and cooperation.

Many critics of the student role fear that students learn this role all too well and that this role permanently damages their development. Paul Goodman,[28] Edgar Friedenberg,[29] Charles Silberman,[30] and others have worried that students learn to go through life striving to please authorities, and ignoring or suppressing their own interests along the way. Friedenberg has also stressed the political orientations learned at the high school level. He has argued that high school students are denied many basic human rights and privileges. They have little or no influence over school policies and few, if any, ways of appealing the arbitrarily exercised authority of school personnel. Consequently, school not only makes students into overly compliant adults, but is also teaches them that the democratic ideals discussed in their classrooms have little relationship to the way people actually live. Such students can have very little understanding of what democratic government really means and very little ability to defend democratic processes as adults.

A study by Buford Rhea in two major high schools in the Boston area adds empirical support to some of Friedenberg's points.[31] Rhea found that, in general, students recognized but did not resent their subordinate and passive position in their schools. Instead, they accepted powerlessness willingly, pointing out that the school was providing them with a good education and that they would not have the ability to share power with school personnel wisely. Of course, Rhea's findings might not be replicated in schools that are obviously not providing a good education for their students, but the point is interesting nonetheless. Do schools socialize young people to accept passively the decisions of those in authority and to perceive themselves as less wise and capable than those who are in charge?

You may have noticed that thus far our discussion of the student role has included few references to learning to be creative, experiencing joy in intellectual accomplishment, expanding aesthetic appreciation, or developing enthusiasm for learning. As you have probably guessed by now, most analyses of the student role suggest that very little of what goes on in school encourages children in these directions. As a matter of fact, several observations and studies have described the ways in which schools discourage this type of development. Given the problems of coping with large numbers of students and the pressures toward producing standardized results, teachers often find highly creative children problems rather than assets.[32] Spontaneity and unusual responses to classroom assignments can disrupt routines, require extra time and attention, and challenge the teacher's sense of control. Teachers, in general, seem to appreciate bright children, but the bright child who refuses to conform either behaviorally or intellectually is labeled a "troublemaker." The slow child who refuses to conform may be an even greater problem.

Those youngsters who successfully internalize the student role can probably expect to get through school with a minimum of difficulty. They will respect their teachers, obey the rules, and always try their best. It is probably safe to say, however, that this is only one way of mastering the student role. In spite of all we have said so far, students are not totally passive in the school environment. They can manipulate teachers, provide each other with social support, undermine or reinforce various school norms, and otherwise make their presence felt by school personnel. As you recall from our discussion of people-processing organizations, people always represent a dynamic force, or at least a dynamic potential. The second half of this chapter will focus on the ways in which students react to and help create the student role.

### Monitoring

All people-processing organizations have means through which they monitor, or keep track of, the people that are being processed. These monitoring procedures can serve any of a number of divergent purposes.

First, monitoring can be used for the purpose of determining whether or not the organization is meeting its goals. This type of monitoring is conducted at several levels in the schools. At the classroom level, individual teachers may use students' test grades and classroom performance as indications of how well they are meeting their teaching goals. At the school level, principals may use the performance of students in different classes as indications of the success of various teachers as well as the effectiveness of the school in general. At the district or state level, superintendents may compare the performances of students at different schools; and at the state or even national level, the performance of school districts, states, and regions may be compared with one another to determine the relative effectiveness of each.

In recent years, the growing concern for educational quality and fiscal accountability has resulted in increased demands for monitoring. Traditionally, the local school board served as the major monitoring agency, of the school but county and state boards have now become more involved. Teachers, principals and superintendents must spend increasing amounts of time preparing reports regarding students (i.e., enrollments, racial and national origins, daily attendance, truancy, dropouts, acts of violence, suspensions, acquisition of minimum basic skills, and achievement test scores) and fiscal affairs. Public officials scrutinize these reports in order to determine whether or not the schools are conforming to official guidelines.

Some states regularly collect standardized test scores for the purposes of monitoring educational effectiveness. Procedures of this type are often met with considerable resistance, however. Critics argue that standardized tests do not accurately reflect learning, that scores on standardized tests are not good measures of school effectiveness, and that test scores can be used invidiously to justify discrimination against certain groups of students, teachers, or schools. Nevertheless, using standardized tests to measure school outcomes continues to be popular. Often test scores are compared with those obtained at other times in order to assess trends in school effectiveness. You may have read about the decline in SAT scores that began in the 1960's and continued until the early 1980's. Scores on other standardized reading and mathematics tests declined at the same time and there has been considerable debate about the meaning of these declines in terms of school effectiveness and reform.[33] It is difficult to tell whether or not these declines represented real changes in how much was being learned or whether they reflected shifts in the types of skills being learned, changes in the characteristics of the students taking the tests, or problems in the tests themselves. It is equally difficult to understand why these scores now appear to be on the rise.[34]

The last several years have witnessed an increasing interest in developing systematic methods of monitoring educational processes however. Programs have been developed to help teachers analyze their curriculum goals in terms of minute units of skills. The progress of individual students can then be assessed for each particular unit, giving a detailed picture of how each student, class, or school is progressing. Some of these programs are computer based and permit data to be fed into centralized terminals that provide information about how any particular class or school compares with others that are using the same goals at the same time. These types of programs are open to the same criticisms as those using traditional standardized tests: Are the measures reliable? Do they really reflect all the important types of learning that occur in the classrooms and can student performance be interpreted as a measure of teacher effectiveness when students vary so much from class to class? Furthermore, most of these programs rely on the teacher to judge whether each individual student has met a particular goal or not. Considering the stake that the teacher might have in showing that his or her pupils are progressing smoothly, the reliability of these measures is open to additional questions as well.

Monitoring of this type is clearly a mechanism of control as well as a means of self-assessment. It can be used to sanction people for poor performance as well as to improve procedures or encourage innovation. The simple knowledge among school personnel that data of this type are being collected can affect performance and motivation. However, it is not clear that such effects are always in a positive direction. Morale can be negatively affected, and teachers may sometimes be encouraged to teach only those skills they know will be tested rather than to be concerned with a broader educational experience for their students.

Furthermore, the likelihood that monitoring procedures will result in major educational reform is probably not very great. As we have suggested earlier, schools, like many other bureaucratic organizations, are relatively resistant to innovation. Add to this the chronic lack of monetary and other school resources, the general paucity of information regarding what types of reforms would be most effective, and disagreements among parents, educators, and community representatives about educational goals and it is not surprising that little change has resulted from information gathered through monitoring procedures.

Monitoring is also used for other purposes, however. For example, monitoring is used for the purpose of evaluating students so that decisions regarding their future within the schools can be made. Here the monitoring procedures are viewed not as measures of the organization's success but as measures of the student's potential to succeed under different types of organizational experiences. This type of monitoring is necessary to the extent that the school is differentiated and that a variety of alternative treatments are available for students. In other words, if the classroom, the school, or the larger school system sorts students into different groups according to their interests, motivations, or abilities, then procedures must be developed through which this sorting takes place. Usually, decisions regarding student allocation are made on the basis of information gathered through monitoring procedures. Students' grades, scores on standardized tests, and evaluations by teachers and counselors all play a part in these decisions. The same information that can be used to assess the effectiveness of the school is, in this case, used to assess the talent, interests, and motivation of students.

These decisions can be viewed from a number of perspectives. In one sense, the schools are deciding that different types of students can be more effectively processed in one program or another and that their treatment in the organization must be geared to their ability and other characteristics. In another sense, the schools are using these decisions to reward or punish students for their school-related behavior. Placement in various programs or tracks may bring with it different amounts of prestige, as well as different educational experiences, affecting both short-term and long-run opportunities. In other words, these decisions can be seen as mechanisms of control and so can the monitoring procedures upon which they are based.

Grades are clearly used for control purposes, as every student knows. High grades bring status and approval, not only from the school but also from friends and family. Low grades bring embarrassment and harassment. Grades are not simply a way of evaluating the student or a way of measuring the student's progress. They are rewards and punishments in themselves and are used to elicit cooperation from students who might otherwise be more resistant to organizational procedures.

In this regard, it is noteworthy that grades are given by teachers, the same people who are responsible for students' mastery of the curriculum and the same people who monitor students for evaluative purposes. These functions can be, and sometimes are, separated from one another. For example, when standardized tests are given and a student receives a score, the teacher affects that score only to the extent that he or she influenced the student's test performance. In some educational systems, outside examiners routinely come in to test students on their mastery of certain subject areas. In these cases, too, the teacher has no direct influence on the student's final grade, and the teacher cannot use this grade as a means of coercing cooperation. Many social scientists have criticized the way in which grades are used in the United States today. Schools have responded to this criticism by experimenting with eliminating grades, developing pass/fail grading systems, and using contract grading. Solid empirical analysis of such experiments is still generally lacking, however. In the second part of this chapter, we will discuss more completely the effects of grading on students and their learning experiences.

### Termination and Certification

All people-processing organizations have procedures through which the relationship between the organization and the people being processed can be formally terminated. However, organizations vary in the extent to which they, as compared to their clients or other outside agencies, have control over their own termination procedures. Organizations also vary in terms of the variety of termination procedures available to them and the degree to which their termination procedures involve certifying or labeling clients in some formal or systematic way.

As we indicated when we discussed admission and selection procedures, the public schools have few mechanisms through which they can influence the make-up of their student bodies. Schools are required by law to accept all eligible students. They are then required to keep these students until they either (1) successfully complete the school's course of study and are graduated; (2) voluntarily transfer to another school for which they are eligible; (3) "drop out" of school after reaching the legal age for doing so; or (4) are shown to be unfit to attend the school by virtue of physical, emotional, or behavioral problems. In this latter case, the school may ask students to voluntarily withdraw, but they can generally suspend or expel the student if voluntary withdrawal is not effected.

For each of these modes of termination, we can discuss the relative influence of the school as compared to students or outside agencies in initiating and shaping the relevant procedures. Let us look first at graduation. Graduation is unique among the several modes of termination in that it involves a positive certification by the school that the graduating student has successfully met all academic and other requirements specified by the school, school district, and state. However, this may or may not be the case. Because schools are restricted in their ability to terminate students in other ways, graduation may be used as a method of "getting rid" of students who would otherwise be a "burden" to the school for several additional years. Students who are behavior problems, as well as those who do not really have the skills to succeed in the conventional classroom or for whom no adequate educational resources exist, may simply be graduated. There have certainly been many cases in which barely literate students have been awarded a high school diploma. State and local school officials have attempted to remedy this situation by establishing "promotion gates." These new policies require that students in specified grades pass a standardized test in order to be promoted to the next school grade. In theory this form of monitoring puts an end to "social promotion" as a standard school procedure, forces schools to offer remedial help to failing students, and ensures that students in the higher grades will have at least minimal levels of competence. However, the results of research evaluating the impact of "merit promotion" on achievement are inconclusive.[35] One reason is the enormous variation in how schools meet the needs of low-achieving students. If students are simply retained in grade without receiving adequate instructional services, little gain can be expected. Schools must commit themselves to providing adequate learning climates, skilled teachers, and the resources necessary to succeed. Unless disadvantaged students are provided with very substantial extra help, they are likely to fail and ultimately drop-out in frustration.[36]

In spite of state regulations that set minimum graduation requirements, there are considerable variations from school to school in terms of policies for promotion, bases for grading, general standards for achievement, and requirements for a diploma. Yet the diploma itself is used by many agencies outside of the school as a requirement for admission. Some of these agencies can directly influence the graduation policies and requirements of the public schools by refusing to accept diplomas granted under some programs and giving special preference to those granted under others. For example, colleges and universities set minimum entrance requirements in terms of the number and types of courses students must complete before admission. They may also set requirements in terms of the grading system within which such courses must be evaluated. These requirements force high schools to adjust their academic diplomas, at least, to meet these standards. The public upheaval would be considerable if students in a particular school district discovered that their diplomas were being rejected by colleges and universities across the country.

Similarly, business and industry can influence requirements. In cases in which a major corporation hires a large number of graduates from a local vocational program, for example, it may be able to exert informal influence over that program's graduation requirements.

Voluntary accreditating organizations, such as the Middle States Association of Colleges and Secondary Schools or the New England Association of Schools and Colleges, also influence educational programs and graduation requirements. These organizations set standards for school facilities, faculty credentials, and other school characteristics, as well as course offerings and requirements for graduation. Only schools meeting these standards are officially "accredited" by these organizations.

Nevertheless, much variation in grading, promotion, and graduation policies remains. As we indicated in Chapter 2, American education is highly decentralized compared to education in many other parts of the world. It is difficult to know exactly what learning skills and motivation any particular diploma represents. One solution that employers and institutions of higher education use to get further information is to ask for recommendations from teachers and counselors and to interview perspective employees and students. This information then supplements the formal certification of the diploma. Another solution used by employers and institutions of higher education is to administer additional standardized tests. Many large corporations require prospective employees to take written examinations. So do most colleges and universities. Specialized organizations have even been established for the purpose of developing and administering such examinations. Most students are familiar with the Scholastic Aptitude Test, just one of a series of tests developed by the Educational Testing Service and used by colleges, universities, and professional schools to evaluate applicants. Because of the role of these tests in securing admission to these institutions, public schools must structure their curriculum with them in mind. Many schools even provide special courses strictly designed to prepare students for these tests. Almost all schools inform students about these tests and help them arrange to take them.

In addition to these formal procedures that help employers and other institutions evaluate school diplomas, informal mechanisms also play a role. Over time, schools acquire an informal reputation for being relatively easy or difficult. Many employers and institutions of higher education evaluate students' grades and diplomas in terms of these reputations. A student graduating from a high school with a reputation for being highly competitive and tough may be given preference over one graduating from a school known to promote any one who attends class regularly and does not cause any trouble.

Whatever the merit behind graduation in any particular case, however, the event is usually marked by an elaborate ritual known as the graduation ceremony. It is clearly the most important ceremonial event in the schools each year. It is marked by special attire, processionals, speeches, school songs, and other elaborate symbolic events. Proper recognition is given to those who have upheld the ideals of the school most successfully, and the graduating class is officially sent out into the world with the best wishes of their alma mater. In American society high school graduation is a major *rite de passage*, marking the transition into adulthood for those not going on to higher education.

The second way in which schools and students can terminate their relationship with each other is if students voluntarily transfer to other educational institutions. Transfer to other schools represents a major source of pupil turnover in American's public schools. America is a highly mobile society and each year approximately one in every five families moves.[37] Student turnover tends to be higher in some areas of the country and for some groups of children than for others. Poor inner-city children are particularly likely to change schools. This creates problems for both the students and the schools, although the degree to which schools have become standardized across large regions of the country eases the adjustments involved. Nevertheless, the schools must accept all students transferring into their district and allocate resources to deal with children transferring either in or out.

Earlier in this chapter, we discussed the issue of private schools and the options that parents sometimes have in sending their children to these rather than public schools. We also discussed the possible impact of these decisions on the schools and emphasized that public schools may, in some cases, be left with many children rejected by private institutions. However, it is also true that public schools can urge the parents of students with learning or adjustment problems to transfer them to private institutions, or even to public ones designed to cope with children with special needs. Schools can exert informal pressure on families to voluntarily transfer, even when the school can not legally require them to do so.

Urging students to voluntarily leave a school may, in some cases, represent an effort to terminate a student gently rather than through harsher means. For example, if a student could be expelled from a school for behavior problems, the school may try first to convince the student's family that he or she would benefit from the special care a school for disturbed children would be able to provide.

At the level of higher education, such efforts often revolve more around potential academic failures than behavioral or emotional problems. Students who look as if they will not be able to meet minimum grade requirements for remaining in school until graduation may be urged to voluntarily change schools or programs.

Clark's pioneering study of the "cooling-out" function as it operated in California's junior colleges was noted in Chapter 3.[38] Those two-year colleges were established with two goals in mind. One was to provide terminal two-year degrees for the vast majority of students who were not interested in a four-year program or who lacked the academic skills to complete one. The second goal was to provide an opportunity for a small minority of students to transfer into the state college system after two years of preparatory work. Students' expectations reversed these priorities, however. As it turned out, most students wanted the transfer program rather than the terminal degree.

The response of the colleges was to make systematic attempts to dissuade students from continuing in the transfer-oriented curriculum. These attempts centered on establishing an "objective" record that attested to the students' academic weaknesses and on redefining the terminal programs as intelligent career choices rather than as second-best. To do this, students were given pre-entrance tests and placed in remedial classes when necessary; they were told how long it would take before they could even begin to accumulate credits that would be transferable; counseling interviews were conducted prior to each semester to evaluate the students' progress or lack of progress; a special course was required that focused on having students come to grips with their vocational and ability test scores and to develop "realistic" occupational aspirations; a record consisting of the students' papers, grades, and test scores was accumulated; and notices of academic deficiency and probation status were sent out regularly. In short, the students were gradually eased out of the transfer program. On the one hand, their lack of ability was constantly set before them and, on the other, the benefits of the two-year programs were constantly reiterated. A more recent study of the City University of New York (CUNY) drew similar conclusions. Alba and Lavin concluded that students who attend two-year colleges are less likely than similar students attending four-year colleges to receive a bachelor's degree. However, the researchers were unable to document the specific mechanisms through which the community college students became discouraged from continuing with their schooling.[39]

The third type of termination we referred to earlier was "dropping out." This type of termination is most relevant to those students who are legally old enough to withdraw from school. Generally, dropping out is seen as failure, both on the part of the individual student involved as well as on the part of the educational system itself. Theoretically, schools are supposed to make every effort to retain students, or at minimum, to transfer them into other programs. However, schools may sometimes encourage dropping out to rid themselves of troublesome students. In its national survey, High School and Beyond, the National Center for Education Statistics studied the high school graduating class of 1982, first when the students were sophomores and again when they were seniors. The study found that 14.4 percent of the public school students had left high school without a diploma sometime after their sophomore year.[40]

High School and Beyond clearly showed that dropouts do not represent a cross-section of American public school students. Males were more likely than females to leave school early (14.6 percent versus 12.6 percent). Minority students dropped out more frequently than white students (white: 12.2 percent; black: 16.8 percent; Hispanic: 18.7 percent) and the poor dropped out more frequently than the middle class (lowest socioeconomic status: 22.3 percent; highest socioeconomic status: 7 percent). These data also show that there was a strong link between parents' and children's educational experiences. Almost 23 percent of students from homes in which the father had less than four years of high school dropped out. When fathers had completed college, the rate was only 6.8 percent. Students who were themselves doing poorly in school were also more likely than others to drop out. Only 3.7 percent of the sophomores who were in the highest test-score quarter dropped out compared to 24.8 percent in the lowest quarter.[41]

Studies of dropouts have shown that most have a record of school failure and that many have been "left back" or retained in grade at least once.[42] This means that they have fallen behind their age cohort and are older than their classmates. Dropouts also tend to have severe reading problems and to have found school unpleasant and discouraging. The majority have been discipline problems in their schools, although approximately one-fourth of the boys and half of the girls have not. Their delinquency rate is about eleven times that of nondropouts. About one-quarter of the parents of high school dropouts are apparently indifferent to their child's decision to drop out and about another one-quarter actually encourage it.

Monetary factors are often reported as an important reason for dropping out. The student's income may be needed at home or for self-support. Also, students report embarrassment at not being able to come to school properly clothed or not having enough money to join peers in recreational activities.

In spite of considerable propaganda to the contrary, having a high school diploma does not necessarily increase an individual's chances of getting a job or making a better salary. Particularly among young people living in depressed urban communities, and particularly among those who are also members of minority groups, unemployment rates may be as high for those who have graduated from high school as they are for those who have not.[43] Obviously, there is little monetary incentive for staying in school when this is the case.

Many of the factors that contribute to dropping out also contribute to the generally lower levels of academic attainment and achievement among students from working-class and economically disadvantaged homes as well as among those who are members of various minority groups. We will discuss these factors in Chapter 8. As we shall see, these factors include not only the schools themselves but also the experiences of young people in their homes and the larger society.

We have not yet discussed suspension and expulsion, two additional means through which students can be temporarily or permanently barred from school attendance. Surprisingly little research has been done on these processes. However, a few things can be said. First, students from economically disadvantaged families and students who belong to racial and ethnic minorities are disproportionately represented among those who are suspended or expelled from school.[44] Many people have charged that these groups of students are given harsher penalties for disciplinary offenses than are students from white middle-class families, so that they wind up being suspended for an offense when another student might simply be reprimanded or required to report to school early. There is at least some evidence that this is, indeed, the case.[45]

Second, in spite of the severe consequences that suspension or expulsion may have for the life of a child, these punishments have, for the most part, been meted out with little or no protection of the individual student's rights. In most cases, students have not been entitled to a fair hearing or an appeal. In recent years, such proceedings have been increasingly challenged in the courts. A clear trend in the direction of protecting the constitutional right of students from arbitrary and repressive school regulations is now discernible.

In the past, many courts repeatedly upheld suspensions for the violation or criticism of school rules. Students who wrote articles or made speeches critical of school personnel, facilities, or procedures were routinely suspended. There is even a case on record of an expulsion caused by a student's mother who criticized the teacher in front of the class. Students who violated dress and appearance codes were also routinely suspended.

In upholding these actions, the courts generally argued that a primary function of the schools was to teach discipline and good citizenship through obedience to the law.[46] Therefore, the content of the school rules was less relevant than the simple fact of failure to obey or respect authority on the part of the student. In addition, the courts often justified seemingly arbitrary rules on the basis of promoting uniformity among students. Diversity in dress, for example, was seen as divisive and threatening to the orderliness of the school as a whole.[47]

In recent years the courts have been more insistent that schools respect the students' right to expressions of individualism that are not a clear and direct threat to school order.

As one judge put it:

> The limits within which regulations can be made by the school are that there be some reasonable connection to school matters, deportment, discipline, etc., or to the health and safety of the students. . . . The Court has too high a regard for the school system . . . to think that they are aiming at uniformity or blind conformity as a means of achieving their stated goal in educating for responsible citizenship. . . .[48]

Courts have also become more sensitive to students' constitutional rights. In the famous *Tinker* case of 1968, the Supreme Court established the principle that students do not "shed their constitutional rights at the schoolhouse door."[49] In this case, students had been suspended for wearing black antiwar armbands to school. The Court ruled that the suspension violated the students' right of free speech.

There have also been changes regarding students' right to a hearing before they are suspended. In January 1974, the Supreme Court ruled that any student facing suspension for even a short amount of time "must be given oral or written notice of charges against him and, if he denies them, an explanation of the evidence the authorities have and an opportunity to present his version."[50] In this case, the Court also recognized the students' right to an education as a property interest.[51] In February 1975, the Supreme Court went a step further. In the case of *Wood v. Strickland*, students' right to sue school officials for damages if they believe they have been illegally disciplined was upheld. School officials could no longer protect themselves by pleading ignorance of the student's constitutional rights or showing that they had acted in good faith.[52]

School officials, naturally, have not welcomed these decisions. Many have claimed that the courts are making it difficult, if not impossible, for the schools to maintain adequate discipline. They argue that school personnel can no longer make disciplinary decisions quickly and decisively and that students are more contemptuous of school rules. Furthermore, now that there are questions regarding the liability of school officials for "illegal" procedures, there may be greater reluctance on the part of private citizens to serve on school boards or on the part of school personnel to make disciplinary decisions at all.

## STUDENT CULTURE AND YOUTH CULTURE

Thus far we have treated students as relatively passive agents undergoing school processing procedures with little autonomous involvement or resistance. We have all but ignored the fact that students, like all human beings, have their own sets of perspectives, values, and interests, which they bring with them when they enter the schools. On the basis of these characteristics and the common problems they face in the schools, students seek each other out, forming friendships and coalitions. Together, students react to and modify the school environment, shaping school life perhaps as much as they are shaped by it.

### Student Culture as a Response to the School Environment

Earlier in this chapter, we pointed out that students enter schools in groups, or classes, and that they pass through schools on a collective basis. This gives students ample opportunity to interact with one another, to discuss common problems, and to develop a degree of consensus regarding how these problem should be handled. The solutions that students develop to meet the common problems they face can result in modifications of the educational process as school personnel attempt to define and regulate it. These solutions are passed on from one class of students to the next so that they become part of the general folklore of students in each particular school or program.

In Chapter 1 we described Willard Waller's conceptualization of the student–teacher relationship. You may recall that Waller emphasized the conflicting interests of teachers and students and the methods by which students seek to undermine the teacher's authority or rebel against it. As Waller noted, most students will inevitably react negatively to academic pressures. Because studies, tests, and grades are bound to be relatively unpleasant in comparison with play and friendship, students tend to minimize the importance of studies and increase the importance of the peer group. Teachers, on the other hand, have an important stake in keeping students oriented toward academic work.

Waller refers to cheating, bluffing, flattery, and attempting to establish a personal relationship with the teacher as some of the methods students use to avoid doing class assignments and to acquire satisfactory grades. Of course, as Waller points out, teachers develop techniques of their own to cope with these tactics. The school environment becomes a product of both sets of participants and the interaction between them. In other words, the social order of the classroom and the school as a whole is *negotiated*.

When most children begin their schooling, they are quite naturally naive about testing and grading, never having experienced these processes before. They do not appreciate the importance of good report cards and high grade point averages. However, through a largely unresearched socialization process, most elementary school children eventually do come to understand the central place of grades in the scholastic value system. By the time teenagers reach high school they have acquired a "grade point average (GPA) perspective." This perspective guides their academic efforts.

According to the GPA perspective, a student's primary focus should be on getting the grades necessary to achieve the student's goals. Everything else about the learning process is secondary. The objective may be minimal (i.e., to pass the course) or ambitious (i.e., to be admitted to Yale), in either case getting the grade is central. Educators tend to see grades as a means of motivating students to achieve larger ends, such as learning, professional preparation, or intellectual development. However, from the students' GPA perspective, grades become ends in themselves, not means to more important ends.

Buford Rhea interviewed students in two of the top high schools in the Boston area about the importance of grades. As their comments below indicate, the students operated on the basis of the GPA perspective.

> Well, in East High you work for good grades so you can go to college. It's just—you know—everybody is obsessed with the fact, and I know even I [am].
>
> Your parents don't know what you know, and people don't know what you know, and the colleges don't know what you know, so if you're going to try for anything you're going for the grade. I mean the payoff. I mean, you may have the knowledge, but it's not going to do you any good. If you want to go someplace and you want to go to college or anyplace, you have to have the grades, anyway at least to graduate from high school.[53]

Jules Henry also discovered an extreme emphasis upon grades among "straight kids" at the high school level. He found that student norms legitimized cheating in order to get good grades. He also noted that some teachers were so naive about cheating that they failed to proctor examinations and thereby set up a situation in which students who did not join in on the cheating were actually penalized.[54]

The concept of the GPA perspective was first articulated by Howard Becker, Blanche Geer, and Everett C. Hughes in a study of the student culture at the University of Kansas where they spent two years doing fieldwork as participant observers. They interacted with students extensively in a broad range of social settings, including classes, dormitories, fraternity and sorority houses, and other formal and informal organizations. Their general goal was to "analyze the patterns of collective actions students develop in their academic work, under the major condition of a relationship of subjection or unilateral authority with the college faculty and administration."[55]

The GPA perspective grew out of the fact that within the Kansas system good grades were of critical importance. If a student's grades fell below a certain minimum, he or she was expelled from the University. In addition, a minimum grade point average was required for a variety of campus activities, such as running for office in the student government. Even fraternity and sorority life was affected by grade requirements. If the average grades of a particular fraternity or sorority fell below a certain point, the organization was barred from a variety of social and extracurricular activities.

Consequently, grades became an important element in judging both students and teachers. Students with high grades received more informal prestige than others, and "easy" teachers were sought out more often than those with a reputation for being tough graders. The GPA perspective permeated and guided a wide range of student decisions, such as course selection, time allocation, and the establishment of priorities. Students often pursued grades instead of their intellectual interests, avoiding courses in which the risk of getting a low grade was substantial.

In pursuit of grades certain common strategies were evident. These included pumping professors for detailed information about test questions and the material to be covered, seeking knowledge about and playing into the professors' prejudices and idiosyncracies, cramming just before tests, apple-polishing, avoiding all readings that were not strictly required, engaging in spirited disputes over the grading of tests, cheating, and simply giving up all hope when total failure seemed imminent. Formally organized living groups such as fraternities and sororities viewed scholarship seriously as it was one dimension upon which overall prestige was accorded. Thus, they institutionalized the pursuit of grades through the maintenance of test and paper files, the appointment of scholarshihp chairpersons and the requirement that study hours be strictly observed.

Becker, Hughes, and Geer also found some slight evidence for two other perspectives among undergraduates—a professional orientation and liberal arts orientation. In the first of these, students judged their academic experiences in terms of their relevance for prospective professional careers, rather than grades; whereas in the liberal arts perspective each student made decisions in terms of ". . . [opening] himself to new ideas, new emotion, and new ways of looking at the world."[56] But the investigators concluded that both of these perspectives were rare and supplemental, rather than alternative, to the GPA perspective.

Under the influence of the GPA perspective, students undermined the goals of the administration and the faculty. They did not maximize their intellectual development, although from the point of view of the administration and faculty this was the underlying purpose of the college system. Thus, they developed collective strategies that distorted and deviated from the ideals of the institution:

> The opportunity to deviate arises from the disjunction between those ideals and standards and the mechanisms that have been created and institutionalized to realize them, the disjunction, for instance, between a system of courses, credits, and grades and the conventional aims of a liberal education. By obeying the dictates of that system, students not only can but in a real sense must deviate from those aims. They deviate as well even from the aims implicit in the grade system, by adopting strategies designed to get grades rather than to acquire the knowledge grades supposedly represent. They deviate most, perhaps, by refusing to accept the premise that the student's major effort and first priority in college must go to academic work.[57]

Others have noted similar "deviations" at the graduate level. In their interaction with professors, students go through elaborate efforts to "psych out" and impress professors. Extreme competitiveness for grades is common, and some students feel that those who are most intellectually oriented are most likely to drop out.[58]

The research team of Hughes, Becker, and Geer first studied student culture at a medical school during the 1950s. Conditions at this school were ideal for the formation of a student culture, defined here as

> . . . a whole body of conceptions and images of problems and situations and of proper and justifiable solutions of them arrived at by the students; in part passed along from one generation of students to another, in part apparently rediscovered—or at least reinforced—by each succeeding generation as they pass through the same experiences.[59]

The environment was ideal for the formation of a student culture because the students were not only processed as a group, but all members of each class took the same courses, received the same assignments, and took all their tests together. They had extensive opportunities to interact with each other in their classroom, small laboratory groups, and living quarters. The students were also relatively isolated from external influences by virtue of their near total immersion in their studies. There was little time for other activities or for friends.

The academic problems faced by these students were overwhelming, at least initially. The amount of material to be learned was impossibly large and the pressures to receive acceptable grades were great. There was no way that they could do everything that their teachers seemed to demand, and yet there was no way they could determine which tasks should be assigned higher priority than others.

Out of their interaction and discussions of these problems, the students developed several perspectives upon which there was broad consensus. They concluded that it was indeed impossible to learn everything, and therefore decisions had to be made about what would be learned and what would not. They concluded that what should be learned was the material that they would be asked on tests and they agreed that the best teachers were those whose lectures closely coincided with test materials. The faculty, however, disparaged this type of teaching because it was viewed as spoon-feeding. The students also agreed that the only really important material for them to learn was that which would be directly relevant to their practice of medicine after graduation. The more esoteric or research-oriented concerns of the faculty were seen as a waste of time.

In line with these perspectives, the students developed certain shortcuts in laboratory procedures and clinical exercises. These shortcuts became normative among the students and were legitimized by the beliefs specified above. For example, third-year clinical students were formally required to turn in detailed and time-consuming summaries of all cases they treated. By the students' own definitions, however, most of this work was irrelevant to their future needs. Some cases were so routine they had seen several of them; others were so unusual that they would probably never see one again. So the students decided among themselves that they would turn in only a small number of reports and selected the cases to be written up according to their own normative preferences. The faculty apparently accepted this number of reports without much complaint, although they were not happy about it. Through mutual support and cooperative action, the students successfully modified their own educational program.

Another way students can influence their learning environment is through their freedom to "elect" certain classes and ignore others. In college and to a lesser extent in high school, students are often free to choose which courses they are going to take. Through careful selection of courses they are able to shape the content of their education to a significant degree. At least partly in response to students' demands for greater freedom in the 1960s, colleges and universities across the country reduced the number of required courses needed for graduation. Although many schools reintroduced greater constraints in the more conservative 1980s, students still exercise considerable free choice in designing their programs. When given the opportunity, many students opt to minimize their liberal arts courses and maximize what they perceive to be "vocationally relevant" courses.

Colleges and universities typically operate on the basis of an enrollment economy. That is, they allocate teaching positions on the basis of student demand. So when students turn away from history, philosophy, sociology, and other liberal arts courses, those departments shrink while business and computer science departments grow. Because the choices that students make can directly affect departmental operations and the careers of individual professors, the student, as consumer, has more power than is generally realized.

Parelius and Berlin described the reactions of historians within two colleges, one public and private, to sharply declining enrollments. The historians in Private College felt that they were in a desperate competition with other departments and divisions for good students.

> Ease up, I think, is the best way to say we've dealt with the enrollment problems. And it's a disease, because one department eases up and the other department says—"Oh-oh, they are getting enrollment. Now we'll ease up a little bit . . . .

These historians were demoralized by the compromises in professional standards that they felt they were forced to make. They pandered to the desires of their poorly prepared clientele by introducing "schlock" (attractive but intellectually weak) courses, lessening academic demands, spoonfeeding, and easy grading. Although the State College historians had experienced almost identical enrollment declines and staff cuts, they refused to compromise their tough standards. They were proud of their department's reputation for good teaching and tough grading. As compared to their Private College counterparts, the State College historians were less fearful about their futures and more cohesive in their colleagial relationships. Security and social support appear to be necessary if academic standards are to be maintained in the face of sharply declining enrollments and intradepartmental competition for students.[60]

David Riesman analyzed college student consumerism and its impact in some detail. Intercollegiate competition for student enrollments and accompanying tuition dollars has intensified as the size of college-entering cohorts has begun to shrink. As a result, many financially troubled independent institutions have been forced to cater to students by abandoning entrance, matriculation, and curriculum requirements.[61] Riesman emphasizes the fact that, "Students exercise . . . influence continuously: by the level of effort they are prepared to make; by their responsiveness to what interests them and their indifference or even disappearance when they are bored, as they so often claim to be."[62]

### Student Culture and the Extracurricular Life of the School

In the last section, we discussed student culture as a response to the academic organization and demands of the school, but student culture also evolves in the context of extracurricular programs and social activities. These programs and activities play an important part in shaping student values and behavior and have a variety of effects on students' educational experiences both in the classroom and out.

The formal extracurricular programs of schools vary with the age of the children involved, but most include such activities as service and hobby clubs, music and drama groups, social events such as trips and dances, and sports. These programs fulfill a variety of purposes. First, extracurricular activities can be used to channel youthful energy into approved directions. These activities are supervised by adults and kept generally "wholesome." Ideally, sex, drugs, and violence have no part in officially school-sponsored programs, so they provide safe leisure activities that keep students out of trouble during after-school hours. In addition, these activities can be used to deflect student discontents with the academic side of school life and channel their hostilities elsewhere. Students can let off steam and unwind by screaming at their rivals on the football field.

Second, extracurricular activities can be used to promote cohesion both within each particular school and between each school and its surrounding community. Whatever other disagreements students may have with each other or with school personnel, everyone is willing to go out and root for the home team. Sports teams, as well as other competitive groups, such as math teams, can become symbols of their entire school, giving everyone a sense of identification with and pride in their school. Similar effects occur with the surrounding community of the school. There is nothing quite like a championship basketball or football team to arouse a sense of unity among local citizens and, as many colleges and universities know all too well, there is nothing like a championship team to get alumni contributions pouring in to previously empty coffers.

Third, extracurricular activities can provide students with areas of achievement alternative to those offered by the classroom. For those students who are not interested in or capable of academic success, the extracurricular life of the school provides ways in which they, too, can gain prestige and feelings of accomplishment. Of course, for all students these activities offer an opportunity to develop a wider range of talents, to become "well-rounded," as the traditional description of ideal development would put it.

Fourth, extracurricular activities provide opportunities for students and faculty to interact with each other in less formal settings and in more heterogeneous groups. Students can interact with others who share their interests and talents rather than being restricted to those in the same class. From the point of view of the formation of student culture, such interaction facilitates the spread of group norms beyond individual classrooms or programs. Furthermore, the informal interaction between faculty and students that occurs during these activities helps establish personal and affective ties between these groups. Such ties then affect classroom interaction because they make it more difficult for teachers to adhere to universalistic norms and affective neutrality. The teacher's actions may be softened by appeals to personal ties, and the students know this.

Whatever the diverse functions of the extracurricular life of the school, many critics have argued that it detracts from the academic goals of the school and lowers student achievement. After all, the extracurricular activities often compete with classroom assignments for the time and energy of students. The most famous study of student culture at the high school level focused on this and other issues involving the extracurricular life of the school. This study was conducted by James Coleman and published in 1961 as *The Adolescent Society*.[63]

Coleman collected a range of information form questionnaires, files, and interviews at ten high schools in northern Illinois. The schools were chosen to maximize diversity in terms of size and community composition. Among the ten schools were ones from a prosperous farm town, an affluent suburb, a working-class suburb, and several other small towns and cities. An urban working-class parochial school for boys was also included. Coleman's analysis focused on the relative value students placed on academic, extracurricular, and social achievements, and how these values affected students' academic performance.

One way in which Coleman determined what the students' values were was by asking them how they would most like to be remembered by their classmates. They were given three choices: Boys could choose "brilliant student," "athletic star," or "most popular"; girls could choose "brilliant student," "leader in activities," or "most popular." The results were unambiguous and strikingly similar from school to school. The number-one choice among the boys at each school was to be remembered as an athletic star. The number-one choice among girls fluctuated between "leader in activities," and "most popular."

A similar pattern was revealed when the students were asked to indicate which items were important for a student's popularity. For boys, being an athlete was the factor most often listed first. For girls, being in the leading crowd and being a leader in activities headed the list.

When Coleman asked specifically about what it takes to become a member of the leading crowd at school, similar responses were obtained. For boys, having a good personality and reputation, being an athlete, and having good looks were most often cited. Having a car and good clothes were also important. For girls, a good personality, good looks, nice clothes, and a good reputation were the most frequently named.

These and other responses revealed that each student's popularity and peer group status seemed to depend primarily on his or her participation in the extracurricular life of the school. Other activities and achievements were of secondary importance. The effect of scholastic achievement on student popularity varied from school to school and with the sex of the student involved. For the most part, though, grades were not particularly important. In most schools, high grades alone, unaccompanied by achievement in other areas, could actually detract from a student's popularity, especially in the case of girls. On the other hand, when high grades were added to outstanding success in other areas, it could enhance popularity. The "all-around boy" who was an athlete as well as a scholar was more popular than the boy who was successful in athletics alone. Nevertheless, students who were actually members of the leading crowds seemed to have been even more anxious than others not to be remembered as brilliant students and even many of those named by others as best scholars were not anxious for the honor.

What was the effect of these values and behavior on actual academic achievement? Although Coleman's data are not definitive, they suggest that the degree to which students were willing to work for high grades was directly related to their perception of how much status and popularity those grades could bring, or conversely, how much status and popularity they might lose by having good grades. The impact was greatest on girls, for whom the negative sanctions for brilliant scholarship were keenly obvious. Coleman compared the IQ scores of best boy scholars and best girl scholars. He found that in spite of the fact that the average IQ of all boys was lower than that of all the girls, the average IQ of boys named as best scholars was *higher* than that of girls named as best scholars. Coleman concluded that if a girl

> . . . wants dates and popularity, she is constrained from working to her scholastic capacity. Consequently, many of the brightest girls manage to hide their intelligence, leaving somewhat less bright girls to be named as best scholars.[64]

Somewhat similar findings were revealed when Coleman compared the IQ scores of the students who made the best grades in each school. He found that the greater the importance of good grades for obtaining membership in a school's leading crowd, the higher the IQ scores of those who obtained the highest grades. Coleman concluded that "students with ability are led to achieve only when there are social rewards, primarily from their peers, for doing so." Nevertheless, the students in Coleman's study were obviously paying some attention to grades. Those students who were planning on a college education tended to keep their grades high enough to meet admission standards even if they did not maximize their full potential.

The importance of extracurricular success is noted in other studies of the values of high school students also. Wayne Gordon did an intensive study of one high school in which he had worked for a decade as a classroom teacher and guidance counselor.[65] His knowledge, gained from participation observation, was supplemented by questionnaires and structured interviews. Like Coleman, he found that the prestige of individual students was better predicted on the basis of participation in athletics, the school band, certain prestigious clubs, and other key social groups, than on the basis of academic excellence.

Jules Henry's case studies provide further evidence. Henry argues that ". . . the athletic complex is a natural pivot of social life, school politics, and the competitive sexual ritual, where a girl measures her success by the athletes she dates."[66]

Buford Rhea's study of top high schools in the Boston area also adds to our knowledge of these phenomena.[67] Rhea's respondents indicated that they participated in school-sponsored activities at least partially because they thought it would help them gain admission to prestigious colleges. They strove to build up dossiers indicating their commitment to "well-roundedness." Thus, peer group status is not the only reason students participate in extracurricular activities. At least among college-oriented students, the processing procedures of the colleges actually help shape high school extracurricular life.

Many important changes have swept the high schools and colleges of the United States since most of these studies were done. The use of drugs has greatly increased among young people, and sexual attitudes and behavior have become more permissive. During the late sixties and early seventies, a wave of political activism engulfed the schools. This activism began in the colleges but later filtered down to the high schools as well. The Antiwar Movement, the Civil Rights Movement, and the Women's Liberation Movement all had their effects. Presumably, the presently widespread conservatism and vocationalism among students has also had an impact. Although we cannot be certain about the ways in which these social and political events have shaped student subcultures, we can venture some guesses on the bases of some available studies of students' attitudes. For example, there is evidence that women are now entering college with higher educational and occupational aspirations, as well as more feminist attitudes toward adult sex roles. These attitudes are probably affecting their academic values, participation in extracurricular activities, and interactions with males.[68] Furthermore, women are now able to win popularity through athletic accomplishment in a way that was open only to men in the past. As a result of federal legislation, funding differentials between young girls' and boys' sports have narrowed, and girls' participation in athletics has increased. The outstanding success of the American women's team in the 1984 Summer Olympics has been attributed to greater support for women's athletics. Perhaps being a member of a team is now replacing cheering it as an important boost to a female's popularity.

Whatever changes have occurred in the specific content of student cultures, however, the basic principles underlined by the research we cited undoubtedly still hold true. As a group of individuals interacting with each other over a long period of time and faced with a common set of problems, students continue to develop their own group solutions to these problems and to modify their school environments as they do.

### Adult Values and Student Values: Congruence and Conflict

Much of our discussion thus far has focused on student culture and the ways in which it seems to undermine the goals of school personnel and other adults. Yet there are many indications that students' values are not all that different from those held by their parents and even their teachers. Student culture may be a response to the environment of the school, but it is also a product of the values to which students have been successfully socialized by the adults around them.

It is at least partially for this reason that Coleman and others have found that the specific content and emphasis of student cultures vary with the characteristics of the communities from which the students are drawn.[69] For example, Clark and Trow reported that students coming from working-class backgrounds are particularly likely to form subcultures valuing vocational goals, whereas middle-class students are more likely to enter subcultures valuing either fun or scholastic achievement.[70]

Furthermore, many studies that have explicitly compared the values of students and either parents or teachers have found more overlap than discrepancy between them.[71] Even students who on the surface appear to be rebellious or revolutionary may have values that are consistent with those of their parents.[72] Students also place a high value on their parents' approval.

One major study comparing student and teacher values was conducted by Raymond Eve.[73] Eve constructed questions presenting specific situations dealing with cheating, disruptive mischief, balancing sports and studies, fighting, selling and buying marijuana, partying versus studying, and the importance of buying a car as opposed to saving for college. Students and teachers filled out the questionnaire separately and anonymously.

The results indicated that the positions of teachers and students were essentially the same in that both groups: (1) felt it was right for a talented football player not to go out for football if he thought it would result in poor grades; (2) disapproved of both buying and selling marijuana; and (3) were neutral on the question of whether the student should spend money on a car despite parental desires that it be saved for college. But the teachers were more likely than students to disapprove of cheating, disruptive mischief, fighting, partying, and drinking. On all of these items except the one regarding mischief, student attitudes were disapproving, but less so than those of teachers. Even with regard to the mischief item, which dealt with bringing firecrackers into the school and setting them off, students were not strongly supportive. Male students were found to espouse more anti-adult attitudes than females, a finding supported by numerous informal observations. But contrary to common stereotypes, white students adhered less closely to the official school values and norms than did black students. Eve concludes:

> Taken as a whole, this study has provided evidence that although students do maintain a statistically distinct value system, this system is primarily conventional in its orientation and differs only to a relatively small degree from the value system of the adult world.[74]

Braddock replicated Eve's study using a national sample of high school students and came to the same conclusion.[75]

The similarities between youth and adult values has also been discussed by Bennett Berger.[76] Berger points out that the irresponsibility and hedonism sometimes described as the core values of youth are held in varying degrees by individuals at all life cycle stages, living a wide variety of lifestyles. Berger confirms, as well, that a large percentage—probably the majority of youth—accept their parents' values, achieve independence with parental support and encouragement, and can best be described as serious and responsible young adults from early in their school careers onward.

Clearly, the issue of divergence or overlap between student, youth, and adult values is not yet settled. For our purposes, though, it is enough to recognize that students bring values with them when they enter the schools, but that these values respond to the environment of the school, shaping that environment and being, in turn, shaped by it.

## SUMMARY, CONCLUSIONS, AND POLICY ISSUES

In this chapter, the school was analyzed as a people-processing organization. Five key steps in the processing of students were identified: recruitment and selection; evaluating, labeling, and classifying; teaching the student role; monitoring; and termination and certification. For each process, some of the diverse forces that shape school decision making were noted and the impact of these decisions on students was discussed.

In the second part of the chapter, some of the collective reactions that students have to the academic and extracurricular demands of school life were outlined. It was clear from our discussion that students are not merely passive agents of educational processing. They bring many values and abilities with them when they enter school, develop collective solutions to the problems they encounter there, and sometimes successfully modify their educational environment. Students also provide rewards for each other in the form of friendships, popularity, and status. These rewards are usually earned by achievement in the extracurricular and social life of the school rather than through academic success. Thus, students may divert some of their energies away from achieving academic goals and toward these other activities. Nevertheless, there is considerable evidence that most students do not radically deviate from their parents' values and pay sufficient attention to academic goals to realize the expectations they share with these important adults.

Virtually all aspects of student processing have come under criticism. Some people have criticized the near monopoly over recruitment that public schools now enjoy and have suggested that competition for students would encourage greater educational efficiency, variety, and quality. Proposals to generate this competition through voucher plans will be discussed in our concluding chapter. Others have focused their criticisms on the ways in which schools screen and sort students into different learning groups, charging that such procedures are discriminatory, detrimental to learning, overly competitive, and elitist. They suggest, instead, sensitivity to the needs and progress of each student as an individual, in the context of mutual support, equality, and respect. The official definition of the student role in the traditional classroom and the monitoring, termination, and certification processes of schools have also come under fire.

In Chapter 9 we will discuss many of these criticisms and the diverse proposals for school reform suggested in response to them. At this point, however, we will discuss only two. We will review proposals to alter current grading practices and proposals to alter existing definitions of the student role.

### Grading

Current grading practices have been widely criticized. Grades themselves have been characterized as being rigid, inaccurate, and incomplete means of conveying information; unrelated to fundamental aims of learning; poor predictors of later success in adult activities; and mechanisms of social control rather than motivators of learning.[77] Graders—such as teachers, professors, and teaching assistants—have been criticized as being ignorant of the basic principles of testing and measurement, uncertain as to their class objectives and the aims of their tests, careless in test construction and arbitrary and capricious in the actual assignment of grades.[78] One critic has offered the following examples as illustrations:

> After assigning quite high mid-term grades, an instructor declared that students were being coddled. Without any warning, term papers were graded very harshly. . . . The final was graded equally severely. Course grades for the class of over 40 included one A, and C, and a few D's; the rest were F's.
>
> Students in a senior course were assigned 15 journal articles. . . . The only examination question over this considerable volume of material asked students to match the articles' authors with the titles. Challenged by a colleague, the instructor argued he could assume that a student who could do this matching understood the material.
>
> A freshman who had maintained a C average on all his tests received a final grade of F. The instructor explained that the student had exhibited an improper spirit toward the subject matter and refused to alter the grade.[79]

Although these examples come from higher education, such practices certainly occur at all levels of education. At this point, we do not know how frequently they occur, however.

The proposals offered to alleviate these abuses have been numerous and diverse. They range from relatively minor adjustments in procedures to the total elimination of all grades and evaluations. Among the proposals that have attracted the most attention are contract grading and pass/fail and credit/no credit arrangements.

In contract grading the student and teacher agree on what quantity and quality of work will be necessary for a particular grade. The student is then left alone to do whatever level of work he or she chooses. When the student is finished, there can be no disagreement about the grade because the conditions for it have been clearly specified in the beginning.

In pass/fail arrangements, the student either passes the course or fails it; there is no other formal evaluation of his or her work. The assumption here is that students will be able to relax and concentrate on learning, decide how they will distribute their time among various subjects according to their own interests, and regard their teachers as mentors rather than judges. The credit/no credit arrangement is similar. However, even if the student does not work or does not master any of the material in a course, he or she is not punished by a failing grade. The student simply does not receive credit for the course. This means that the student cannot use the course toward a degree, but that there is no blemish on the student's record. Presumably, both the pass/fail and credit/no credit arrangements encourage students to experiment in a wider range of courses and levels of study, since they do not have to worry about keeping their grade point averages up. Unfortunately, there has not been sufficient evaluation of experiments with these arrangements to determine their precise effects.[80] However, one problem that some schools have encountered involved the reactions of other institutions to these arrangements.

Rutgers College experimented with a pass/fail system for all freshmen and discovered that graduate and professional schools were unhappy with it. The most competitive and prestigious of these institutions began counting a Pass as equivalent to a C. Needless to say, this was a great hardship on students whose other grades averaged close to an A. As a result, the college dropped this program and returned to its earlier grading system. Other institutions do not always run into this problem, however. If the percentage of the students' grades reported as pass/fail is small, the graduate schools may simply give somewhat greater weight to the student's score on the Graduate Record examination when evaluating them and not count the Pass as equivalent to some numerical grade.[81] During the 1980's many, but not all, colleges and universities returned to traditional grading practices. Currently, the Massachusetts Institute of Technology still gives freshmen pass/no record grades in all classes, and it is possible for students at Brown University to take *all* undergraduate courses on a pass/no credit basis.

Other proposals for changing grading systems include giving lengthy written evaluations to each student rather than a specific grade, having instructors send in grades but not revealing them to the students, having students grade themselves, and giving all students in a class the same grade depending on the class' general level of achievement.[82] Some have suggested, however, that any kind of evaluation is detrimental. Becker and his associates, who were dismayed by the GPA perspective they uncovered in their research, argued for this position.[83] Certainly, many teachers as well as students would favor this proposal. As Waller pointed out a long time ago, teachers get trapped by the grading system as much as students.[84] Many teachers find grading a distasteful task that interferes with their ability to relate to students in a supportive way and to concentrate their energies on teaching.

Conflict and consensus theorists approach the issue of grading from their own perspectives and tend to arrive at different policy proposals. Nathan Glazer, who works from a consenus model, emphasizes the utility of grades in assuring that the most capable individuals arrive at the most challenging social positions.[85] Competition among students for high grades and admission to institutions of higher education on the basis of these grades is therefore functional in matching ability to occupational placement. Conflict theorists disagree. From their perspective, the major effect of the grading system

> has been to maintain the existing socioeconomic class structure, smooth the way to socioeconomic advancement for those clearly possessing the desired special characteristics while systematically hindering and discouraging others. From the primary grades up . . . those culturally unattuned to the dominant social class have been discouraged, shunned, and labeled incompetent.[86]

As we shall see in Chapter 8, students from socioeconomically disadvantaged groups tend to get lower grades than those from the middle class. Conflict theorists interpret grades and the standards by which they are assigned as mechanisms to maintain the current social class system. The fact that grades in school do not seem to predict how well people do within their occupational groups once they get there is cited as additional evidence that grades have little to do with placing the most competent people in the most demanding jobs.

Whatever your view of the impact of grading on the allocation process, it seems clear that there is room for improvement in the ways students are tested and evaluated. Milton and Edgerly have pointed out that unless this improvement occurs soon, it is likely the courts will begin intervening in the process.[87] We already discussed the role of the courts in regulating suspension procedures. Milton and Edgerly believe that this is just part of an overall trend resulting from "an increased sophistication of students, a new regard for higher education as a social necessity and an individual right, the expansion of civil rights protections by public authority, and . . . the new age of majority . . ."[88] They predict that unless teachers—especially college professors—"begin to make drastic improvements in testing and grading practices, there will be intrusions on their autonomy from without. . . ."[89]

### Redefining the Student Role

James S. Coleman and others on the Panel of Youth of the President's Science Advisory Committee have presented a wide-ranging critique of contemporary secondary schooling that centers on the student role.[90] Their fundamental criticism focuses on the passivity, dependence, narrow cognitive orientation, and individualism fostered by the present system.

The passivity is evidenced by the general tendency of students to simply follow the orders of their instructors without question or rebellion. This encourages intellectual and emotional dependence rather than self-motivation, curiosity, and self-assurance. Students do not learn to manage their own affairs or to take responsibility for their own actions. Further, the schools focus on narrow cognitive goals and do not train students for active, instrumental leadership in occupationally relevant roles. They artificially segregate youth from adults and make learning occupational roles difficult. Thus, they do not really contribute to the many ways in which young people need to mature as they move into adulthood. Finally, schools foster intense individualism and competition between students, which hinders the development of responsible attitudes toward others and toward society as a whole.

To correct these problems, the authors of the report make a number of policy proposals. We will focus on those involving changes in school structure and the relationship between school and work. First, the authors propose that the long-term trend toward large comprehensive high schools be reversed. They propose, instead, much smaller schools in which students can play a more active role in school life and interact with adult teachers and administrators in a more informal way. As they see it:

> Youth in large schools are more often passive spectators of action, less often participants, more often followers, less often in leadership roles than youth in small schools.[91]

Furthermore, large schools tend to be impersonal and to segregate students into different age and ability groups. Little sense of common purpose or community is experienced by either students or teachers.

Second, the Panel proposes more specialized schools—such as schools of performing arts, science, journalism, broadcast media, and so on. These schools would have a clear sense of purpose and organizational identity. They would give students the experience of intensive involvement in some area of interest and would encourage a sense of sharing between students and teachers. In addition, these schools would draw students from wide geographical areas and therefore be more integrated in terms of the social class, racial, and ethnic characteristics of students.

Having a variety of schools to choose from would also give students an opportunity to exercise their judgment and to experience the consequences of their own decisions. It would also encourage schools to compete with one another for students, and perhaps lead to greater innovations in programming and curriculum.

Third, the Panel proposes that school and work be alternated with each other so that students can experience more interaction with adults and assume greater responsibilities. This could be done in any of several ways, but the Panel particularly recommends either allowing students to leave school for a semester or two at a time in order to work or arranging for half-time schooling and half-time employment. Both patterns, they feel, would facilitate the transition from school to work. Ironically, the Panel points out that child labor laws, considered at one time a major reform in the interests of youth, are now a hindrance to arrangements that could be beneficial. The older pattern of introducing youth to work at an early age apparently had some positive aspects to it.

Fourth, the Panel suggests that work organizations can be modified so that they take over some of the educational responsibilities now confined to the schools. Older or more knowledgeable workers could teach others, or organizations could make use of modern technological devices that would enable employees to spend a few hours each day in self-teaching activities.

Finally, the Panel proposes that schools become "agents for youth" by assuming responsibility for all aspects of growth and development. In this capacity, schools would make use of the community and its resources, using other institutions and settings as learning environments. Thus, the school would coordinate a large number of diverse activities for each student rather than concern itself only with the narrow provision of teaching services.

Through these proposals Coleman and his colleagues hope to interfere with the development of student and youth subcultures that hinder maturation and make passage into adult roles difficult. In particular, they hope to undercut the dependency, passivity, and irresponsibility of youth, which they see as a direct result of the current age-segregated, impersonal, and authoritarian nature of the schools.

These proposals are, of course, only one set of solutions to problems focusing on the student role in today's schools. We will look at others in Chapter 9. The proposals we discussed here are somewhat unusual, however, in that they focus heavily on the issue of youth cultures and their negative impact. As we indicated earlier in this chapter, there is considerable overlap between youth and adult values, and one might certainly ask if young people will learn substantially different values through closer interaction with adults than they do under current arrangements.

## *NOTES*

[1]Yesheskel Hasenfeld, "People-Processing Organizations: An Exchange Approach," *American Sociological Review*, 37 (June, 1972), pp. 256–63.

[2]Ibid., p. 256.

[3]Stanton Wheeler, "The Structure of Formally Organized Socialization Settings," in *Socialization After Childhood*, eds. Orville Brim, Jr. and Stanton Wheeler (New York: John Wiley & Sons, 1966), pp. 51–116.

[4]Some states do permit home schooling. But this alternative form of education is so burdensome for parents that it is rarely utilized.

[5]Valena White Plisko, ed., *The Condition of Education 1983* (Washington, D. C.: Government Printing Office 1983).

[6]Peter Rossi and Alice Rossi, "Some Effects of Parochial School Education in America," *Harvard Educational Review*, 27 (Summer, 1957), pp. 168–99.

[7]Richard O. Carlson, "Environmental Constraints and Organizational Consequences: The Public School and Its Clients," in *Behavioral Science and Educational Administration Yearbook, Part II*, ed. Daniel E. Griffiths (New York: National Society for the Study of Education, 1964).

[8]David Owen, *None of the Above: Behind the Myth of Scholastic Aptitude*, (Boston: Houghton Mifflin, 1985), pp. 230–32.

[9]Jane R. Mercer, "A Policy Statement on Assessment Procedures and the Rights of Children," *Harvard Educational Review* 44, (February, 1974); P. Schrag and D. Divoky, *The Myth of the Hyperactive Child and Other Means of Child Control* (New York: Pantheon, 1975); Seymour B. Sarason, *The Culture of the School and the Problem of Change* (Boston: Allyn & Bacon, 1982), pp. 235–45.

[10]Jane R. Mercer, *Labelling the Mentally Retarded* (Berkeley: University of California Press, 1973), p. 189; David Kirp, "Student Classification," *Harvard Educational Review*, 44, (February, 1974); Carl Milofsky, *Special Education: A Sociological Study of California Programs* (New York: Praeger, 1976); Sally Tomlinson, *A Sociology of Special Education* (London: Routledge & Kegan Paul, 1982), Chapter 7.

[11]Carl Milofsky, *Special Education*, p. 34.

[12]Sarason, *Culture of the School*, pp. 158–60.

[13]A. Harry Passow, ed., *The Gifted and Talented: Their Education and Development, 78th Yearbook of the National Society for the Study of Education*, Part 1 (Chicago: University of Chicago Press, 1979).

[14]Julian C. Stanley, "On Educating the Gifted," *Educational Researcher*, 9, (March, 1980), pp. 8–12.

[15]W. G. Findlay and M. M. Bryan, *Ability Grouping* (Athens, Ga.: Center for Educational Improvement, 1970).

[16]John I. Goodlad, *A Place Called School* (New York: McGraw-Hill, 1984), p. 141.

[17]Goodlad, *A Place Called School*, p. 141.

[18]National Education Association, *Ability Grouping* (Washington, D. C.: NEA, 1986).

[19]Goodlad, *A Place Called School*, p. 150.

[20]Samuel N. Eisenstadt, *From Generation to Generation: Age Groups and Social Structure* (Glencoe, Ill.: The Free Press, 1956).

[21]Talcott Parsons, "The School Class as a Social System: Some of Its Functions in American Society," *Harvard Educational Review*, 29 (Fall, 1959), pp. 297–318.

[22]Robert Dreeben, *On What Is Learned in Schools* (Reading, Mass.: Addison-Wesley, 1968).

[23]Jules Henry "Docility, or Giving Teacher What She Wants," *Journal of Social Issues*, 11, 2, (1955), pp. 33–41.

[24]Ibid., p. 34.

[25]Harry L. Gracey, "Learning the Student Role: Kindergarten as Academic Boot Camp," in *The Sociology of Education: A Sourcebook*, ed. Holger R. Stub (Homewood, Ill.: The Dorsey Press, 1975), pp. 82–95.

[26]Philip W. Jackson, "The Student's World," in *The Psychology of Open Teaching and Learning: An Inquiry Approach*, Melvin L. Silberman, Jerome S. Allender, and Jay M. Yanoff, eds. (Boston: Little, Brown, and Company, 1972), pp. 76–84.

[27]Ibid., p. 81.

[28]Paul Goodman, *Compulsory Mis-Education* (New York: Horizon Press, 1964).

[29]Edgar Z. Fiedenberg, *The Vanishing Adolescent* (Boston: Beacon Press, 1959).

[30]Charles E. Silberman, *Crisis in the Classroom* (New York: Vintage Books, 1970).

[31]Buford Rhea, "Institutional Paternalism in High School," *The Urban Review*, II (February, 1968), pp. 13–15.

[32]Jacob W. Getzels and Philip W. Jackson, *Creativity and Intelligence: Explorations with Gifted Students* (New York: John Wiley & Sons, 1962), p. 293.

[33]Gene Maeroff, "Educators Search for Cause of Lower Scores on S.A.T.," *New York Times* (October 27, 1976), p. 51 and Annegret Harnischfeger and David Wiley, "Achievement Test Scores Drop. So What?" *Educational Researcher*, 5 (March, 1976), pp. 5–12.

[34]Owen, *None of the Above: Behind the Myth of Scholastic Aptitude*, pp. xvii–xxi.

[35]David F. Labaree, "Setting the Standard: Alternative Policies for Student Promotion," *Harvard Educational Review*, 54 (February, 1984), pp. 67–87.

[36]Edward L. McDill, Gary Natriello, and Aaron M. Pallas, "Raising Standards and Retaining Students: The Impact of Reform Recommendations on Potential Dropouts," *Review of Educational Research*, 55 (Winter, 1985), p. 427.

[37]For example, see Current Housing Reports, Series H-150-73D, *Annual Housing Survey*, 1973, Part D, *Housing Characteristics of Recent Movers for the United States and Regions*, (Washington, D. C.: Government Printing Office, 1975), p. xvi.

[38]Burton R. Clark, "The Cooling-Out Function in Higher Education," *The American Journal of Sociology*, 65 (May, 1960), pp. 569–76.

[39]Richard D. Alba and David E. Lavin, "Community Colleges and Tracking in Higher Education," *Sociology of Education*, 54 (October, 1981), pp. 223–37.

[40]Valena White Plisko and Joyce D. Stern, eds., *The Condition of Education 1985* (Washington, D. C.: Government Printing Office, 1985), p. 201.

[41]Ibid., p. 208.

[42]Our discussion of dropouts draws heavily from Daniel Schreiber, "Drop-Out—Causes and Consequences," in *Encyclopedia of Educational Research*, ed. Robert L. Eble, (New York: The Macmillan Company, 1969), pp. 308–16.

[43]Bennett Harrison, "Education and Underemployment in the Urban Ghetto," in *Schooling in a Corporate Society: The Political Economy of Education of America*, 2nd ed., Martin Carnoy, ed. (New York: David McKay Company, Inc., 1975), pp. 133–60.

[44]David L. Martin, "Are Our Public Schools Really Ignoring the Very Children Who Need the Schools Most?" *The American School Board Journal*, 162 (April, 1975), pp. 52–57.

[45]This pattern was reported as early as 1949 in August B. Hollingshead, *Elmtown's Youth: The Impact of Social Classes on Adolescents* (New York: John Wiley & Sons, 1949), pp. 185–92 and reaffirmed recently in Martin, "Are Our Public Schools Really Ignoring the Very Children Who Need the Schools Most?"

[46]Richard L. Berkman, "Students in Court: Free Speech and the Functions of Schooling in America," *Education and the Legal System, Harvard Educational Review*, Reprint Series 6, 1971, pp. 35–63.

[47]Ibid. p. 63.

[48]*Myers* v. *Arcata Union High School District*, Unreported decision, quoted in ACLU, *Academic Freedom in the Secondary Schools*, rev'd Cal. Rptr. 68 (Ct. of App. 1969) as cited in Berkman, "Students in Court," p. 52.

[49]John P. DeCecco and Arlene K. Richards, "Civil War in the High Schools," *Readings in Education 76/77*, Annual Editions (Guilford, Conn.: Dushkin Publishing Group, 1976), pp. 91–96.

[50]Ibid., p. 95.

[51]Ibid., p. 95.

[52]Ibid., p. 95.

[53]Buford Rhea, "The Myth of Institutional Paternalism in High School," *The Urban Review*, 2 (February, 1968), pp. 13–14.

[54]Jules Henry, *Culture Against Man* (New York: Random House, 1963), p. 205.

[55]Howard S. Becker, Blanche Geer, and Everett C. Hughes, *Making the Grade: The Academic Side of College Life* (New York: John Wiley & Sons, 1968), p. 13.

[56]Ibid., p. 22.

[57]Ibid., p. 132.

[58]James Harvey, *The Student in Graduate School* (Washington, D. C.: American Association for Higher Education, 1972), and Ann M. Heiss, "Berkeley Doctoral Students Appraise their Academic Programs," *Educational Record*, 48 (1967), pp. 30–44, as cited in Harvey, *The Student in Graduate School*, p. 11.

[59]Everett C. Hughes, Howard S. Becker, and Blanche Geer, "Student Culture and Academic Effort," in *The American College: A Psychological and Social Interpretation of Higher Learning*, ed. Nevitt Sanford, (New York: John Wiley & Sons, 1962), p. 518.

[60]Robert J. Parelius and William Berlin, "Dynamics of Decline," *Change*, 16 (July/August, 1984), pp. 12–17.

[61]David Riesman, *On Higher Education: The Academic Enterprise in an Era of Rising Student Consumerism* (San Francisco: Jossey-Bass, 1980), p. 108.

[62]Ibid., p. 278.

[63]James S. Coleman, *The Adolescent Society: The Social Life of the Teenager and Its Impact on Education* (Glencoe, Ill.: The Free Press of Glencoe, 1963).

[64]Ibid., p. 255.

[65]C. Wayne Gordon, *The Social System of the High School*, (Glencoe, Ill.: The Free Press of Glencoe, 1957).

[66]Henry, *Culture Against Man*, p. 190.

[67]Rhea, "Institutional Paternalism."

[68]Ann P. Parelius, "Emerging Sex-Role Attitudes, Expectations, and Strains Among College Women," *Journal of Marriage and the Family*, 37 (February, 1975), pp. 146–53, and "Change and Stability in College Women's Orientations Toward Education, Family, and Work," *Social Problems*, 22 (February, 1975), pp. 420–32.

[69]Coleman, *Adolescent Society*, pp. 279–84, and Burton R. Clark and Martin Trow, "The Organizational Context," in *College Peer Groups: Problems and Prospects for Research*, eds. Theodore M. Newcomb and Everett K. Wilson (Chicago: Aldine, 1966), pp. 17–70.

[70]Clark and Trow, "The Organizational Context," p. 28.

[71]For an alternative view, see M. Kent Jennings and Richard G. Niemi, "The Transmission of Political Values from Parent to Child," *American Political Science Review*, 62 (March, 1968), pp. 169–84.

[72]Richard Flacks, "Young Intelligentsia in Revolt," *Trans-action*, 7 (June, 1970), pp. 49–55.

[73]Raymond A. Eve, "Adolescent Culture,' Convenient Myth or Reality? A Comparison of Students and their Teachers," *Sociology of Education*, 48 (Spring, 1975), pp. 152–67.

[74]Ibid., p. 165.

[75]Jomills Henry Braddock, "Academics and Athletics in American High Schools: Some Further Considerations of the Adolescent Subculture Hypothesis," Center for Social Organization of Schools, Report No. 275 (April, 1979).

[76]Bennett M. Berger, "On the Youthfulness of Youth Cultures," *Social Research*, 30 (Autumn, 1963), pp. 319–42.

[77]For catalogues of the criticisms of grading see Robert L. Thorndike, "Marks and Marking Systems" in *The Encyclopedia of Educational Research*, 4th ed., ed. Robert L. Eble (New York: Macmillan, 1969), pp. 759–66; Jonathan R. Warren, *College Grading Practices: An Overview* (Washington, D.C.: Eric Clearing House on Higher Education, 1971); and Howard Kirshenbaum, Sidney B. Simon, and Rodney W. Napier *Wad-Ja-Get?: The Grading Game in American Education* (New York: Hart Publishing Company, 1971).

[78]Ohmer Milton and John W. Edgerly, *The Testing and Grading of Students* (New Rochelle, N. Y.: Change Magazine and Educational Change, 1976).

[79]Ibid., pp. 13–15.

[80]Warren, *College Grading Practices*, p. 3.

[81]Ibid., p. 3.

[82]Kirschenbaum, Simon, and Napier, *Wad-Ja-Get?*, pp. 292–307.

[83]Becker, Geer, and Hughes, *Making the Grade*, (N. Y.: Russell and Russell, 1961), pp. 138–41.

[84]Waller, *The Sociology of Teaching*, p. 365.

[85]Nathan Glazer, *Remembering the Answers: Essays on Student Revolt* (New York: Basic Books, 1970), pp. 245–49.

[86]Warren, *College Grading Practices*, p. 9.

[87]Milton and Edgerly, *The Testing and Grading of Students*, pp. 50–52.

[88]Ibid., p. 50

[89]Ibid., p. 52.

[90]Panel on Youth of the President's Science Advisory Committee, James S. Coleman, Chairman, *Youth: Transition to Adulthood* (Chicago: University of Chicago Press, 1974).

[91]Ibid., p. 154.

# CHAPTER SIX
# PROFESSIONALIZATION

Most people think of teaching as a profession. Yet probably few have analyzed exactly what distinguishes professions from other occupations. Sociologists who have looked at this question extensively, disagree among themselves.[1] No one characteristic makes the critical difference. Still, there does seem to be a complex of factors that are associated with occupations normally regarded as professions. These characteristics include highly specialized and esoteric knowledge, extensive university-based training programs, considerable autonomy in making professional judgments, an ideology that stresses service and commitment rather than personal gain, and membership in nationwide organizations of fellow practitioners.

As you might suspect by now, conflict and consensus theorists view these characteristics somewhat differently. Consensus theorists emphasize the importance of esoteric knowledge, socialization to the profession, and service orientations. Conflict theorists focus on the power relations between various occupational groups, tend to debunk professional claims to specialized expertise and altruistic motivations, and stress the power of professional organizations to promote these legitimizing myths, control access into the occupation, and serve the self-interest of those who are already members.

From either perspective, however, occupations seem to fall on a continuum, with some more and some less professionalized than others. Each occupation is in a continuous state of flux, as it responds to changes in the society at large as well as to forces internal to the occupation itself. Some occupations become more professionalized over time; others become less.

In this chapter, we will be looking at teaching from this dynamic perspective. First, we will give a brief historical overview of teaching as it evolved until the early twentieth century. Then we will focus on contemporary issues relevant to the emergence of teaching as a profession. Throughout our discussion we will look at teachers in higher education as well as those in the public schools. As we shall see, the process of professionalization has been radically different for these two occupational groups.

## OCCUPATIONAL EMERGENCE AND GROWTH

### The Pre-Industrial Period

During most of the Pre-Industrial Period there was little that might be identified as a teaching profession.[2] Most people who assumed teaching responsibilities did so on a temporary basis to supplement their income or support themselves while they were in transition between other activities. Many teachers were ministerial students, physicians, indentured servants working off the price of their bond, or minister's assistants. Many others were full-time ministers who taught Bible reading and the catechism as part of their more general responsibilities.

There were rarely any specific qualifications required for teaching positions, and the credentials that teachers did possess varied widely from place to place and from one type of school to the other. The most rigorous standards of the period were upheld in the early New England schools, where the schoolmaster was more nearly a professional than elsewhere in the colonies. Those supported with public funds taught either in the regular town schools or the Latin Grammar schools. However, school hours were long, and schools were in session continuously throughout the year, except for occasional holidays.

Teachers in the Latin Grammar schools were highly respected, college-educated, and entitled to the honor of having "Mr." prefixed to their names at a time when ordinary citizens were called Goodman or Goodwife.[3] Their jobs were relatively permanent and well paid, and they were sometimes exempted from various taxes and military service. The Massachusetts Bay school law of 1647 required each town of one hundred families to support a Latin school, and although not all such towns readily complied, many went through considerable effort to acquire a satisfactory master. These masters were usually examined by the town's minister before being hired, since only he was sufficiently educated in the classics to judge the competence of the prospective teacher. By the turn of the century, Latin schoolmasters in Massachusetts had to obtain licenses from the ministers of two towns in addition to the one in which they intended to teach.[4] Latin schoolmasters in other colonies went through similar, but not as extensive, procedures. In all cases, Latin schoolmasters were male. They were also expected to be of upright character and members of the community's official church.

Although some Latin masters apparently made a career of their profession, most taught school on only a temporary basis. Some—and this was particularly true of the southern colonies—were actually missionaries sent by religious societies to propagate the faith. Others were divinity students from Harvard or Yale or minister's assistants waiting for their own ministry. Most of these teachers were well qualified and reputable. In addition, there were a number of teachers who were trained in Europe and who wandered from place to place in the colonies accepting teaching jobs on a short-term basis. Although many of these "taught with great power and influence," many others were of "questionable morals" and often ran afoul of the law.[5]

Teachers in the vernacular town schools were paid about half as much as the Latin School teachers and were not generally as well-educated. Nevertheless, their salary was considered to be adequate and many were graduates of colonial colleges. There was a chronic shortage of teachers during this early period, and this probably contributed to the high regard most communities had for those they managed to attract. As with the Latin schoolmasters, these teachers were all male and members of the community's church. They were usually hired by a committee of selectmen and sponsored by the local minister.

The least rigorous standards were probably applied to the teachers of private schools, and especially to the Dame schools. These schools were taught by local women in their own homes for young children who had not yet mastered the alphabet. Such mastery was necessary before a student could enter the town school. Many of these women could barely read themselves and did little more than babysit their charges. Their pay was exceedingly low. In time, these schools were incorporated into the local public schools, but conditions did not substantially improve for either teachers or students.

The position of teaching as an occupation deteriorated substantially in New England during the eighteenth century and came to resemble conditions in other areas throughout the colonies. As we explained in Chapter 3, the growth and dispersal of the population in the eighteenth century meant that many children could not walk to the one school generally located in the center of town. The solutions to this problem involved either having the school move from place to place every few months or to divide the school into different sessions. In the first instance, children who had previously been attending school all year now had access to school for only a few months, when the school was in their particular area. In the second, the school served older boys in the winter (because they were hardy enough to get there), and young children and girls in the summer (because they were not as necessary for planting and harvesting as were older boys).

These changes had an important impact on teaching as an occupation. At first, the regular full-time teacher simply moved with the school or taught both winter and summer sessions, but eventually different teachers were hired for each location and each session. These changes were solidified when local communities or districts were finally given control of their own schools and required to raise local money to support them. These districts were often small and short of funds. Consequently, they searched for the least expensive way to staff their local school. One place they began looking for schoolteachers was among women. Women were not permitted in either the Latin Grammar schools or the colleges and did not have the same formal educational credentials as men, but women were willing to work for a considerably lower wage. Few alternative occupations were open to them. Women were first hired to teach school during the summer months. At this time, most students were young or female, and people were used to having women teach such children in the Dame schools. In time, the economic advantages offered by female teachers led to a greater acceptance of them for older boys as well. The standard salary formula when female teachers were hired by the town schools was "Twelve months of school taught by a female be reckoned as equivalent to four and four-fifths months of a master's school."[6] By this time, teaching was no longer a year-round occupation; teachers were employed for only a few months each year. The salary, prestige, and job security of the teacher greatly diminished.

During most of the eighteenth century, the situation remained pretty much unchanged. Teachers were expected to know only enough to teach the few subjects that they would cover in class. They were also expected to be of good moral character and loyal to church and state. Given this, it was assumed that anyone could teach. There was no popular conception of teaching as either an art or a science. Teachers were under no obligation to stimulate, excite, or even interest their students in learning. In most classes, students were left to learn largely on their own and the teacher's role was limited to examining them to see if they had been successful. As we indicated earlier, teachers often had large numbers of students—especially in more populated areas—and few textbooks or teaching materials. Pay was low and job security nonexistent.

College teaching as an occupation emerged fairly early in the colonies. Harvard graduated its first class in 1642, and several other colleges quickly followed suit. These early colleges were founded primarily to train ministers for the colonies, although the provision of higher learning for others was also recognized as important. The earliest faculties consisted almost entirely of ministers. Many of these had churches of their own and taught students at home on a part-time basis. In time, however, the faculties were increasingly drawn from senior students and graduates of the colleges.

The faculties were generally small. Harvard opened with one teacher, and the charter it obtained in 1650 specified that its full faculty should consist of five tutors plus a president. Even so, beginning shortly after it received its charter and continuing throughout the seventeenth century, there were never more than three tutors employed at any one time. Most tutors left their posts quickly, serving as teachers only until they received pulpits of their own.[7]

Although some of the earliest faculty members seemed to have had a voice in college affairs, the pattern that soon emerged in the colonies was that of strong control by boards of trustees and college presidents. The small number of faculty, their high rate of turnover, their inexperience and youth contributed to this development. Many teachers were treated like "senior students helping . . . in discipline and instruction."[8] By the fifth and sixth decades of the seventeenth century instructors were often forbidden to reside outside the college, take pastorates, marry, or otherwise break rather complex sets of college regulations. They had no job security and could be dismissed at any time, although by the end of the century a few institutions required an administrative hearing before a faculty member was dismissed.

There were, however, a small number of faculty members who were treated differently. Beginning in the first half of the eighteenth century, but occurring with greater frequency in the second, colleges began adding "professors" to their faculty. Until this time, all faculty were of the same rank and taught pretty much the same subjects. Their tasks were divided not by subject matter, but by class. For example, one tutor would teach all subjects to the freshman class, and another would teach the seniors. But now colleges began receiving special endowments to establish "chairs" in such areas as Divinity, Mathematics, and Oriental Languages. The individuals chosen for these positions were older and more prominent than the regular faculty.[9] They were also accorded greater privileges. Professors were generally allowed to live off campus and marry. Their appointments were assumed to be permanent. Because of their greater prestige, autonomy, permanence, and expertise, these professors were the most professionalized group among college faculty.

### The Early Industrial Period

The nineteenth century witnessed a number of major changes in the nature of teaching as an occupation. These changes enhanced the professional stature of education generally, and of teaching more specifically.

The general context within which these changes occurred was discussed in several of our earlier chapters. You may recall that the nineteenth century was one of great educational debates and reforms. By the end of the century, adequate compulsory attendance laws had been enacted, mass public education had been firmly established, and a considerable amount of educational centralization and bureaucratization had occurred. Also by the end of this century, teaching had emerged as an occupation widely recognized as a profession, with a specialized body of expertise, formal training programs, and national organizations.

Among the several diverse factors that contributed to the professionalization of teaching during the Early Industrial Period was the influence of European educational ideas and techniques on American schools. During the early part of the nineteenth century, a number of prominent American educators traveled abroad to observe the educational systems of various European states. Some of these travelers were sent by their state legislatures; others went as private citizens. Most returned with a host of ideas about educational reform and published extensive reports and recommendations.

Soon American educators such as Henry Barnard and Horace Mann were developing their own ideas about educational reform, conducting surveys to evaluate local school systems in various states, and working for change. Almost uniformly, these educators called for improvements in teachers' skills, the establishment of normal schools for the training of teachers, and the upgrading of teachers' salaries and working conditions. They also discussed methods of teaching, the organization of school systems, and curriculum development.

The ideas of these educators affected American education by creating a climate of opinion sympathetic to educational reform.[10] Legislators, community leaders, and the public in general became increasingly willing to provide funds and resources for the realization of these proposals. The men and women advocating these ideas were appointed, in many cases, as superintendents of state school systems or similar posts and had an opportunity to work directly for these reforms. The spread of these ideas was also greatly facilitated by the proliferation of magazines and journals dealing with educational issues during this period.

A handful of these magazines were produced during the first quarter of the century, but from about 1825 onward their number multiplied rapidly.[11] The earliest magazines were aimed at public officials, clergy, and others who were interested in the operations of the schools. They covered a variety of topics, many concerning the need for mass public education. The later magazines and journals, such as the *Common School Journal of Massachusetts* started in 1838 by Horace Mann, Secretary of the Massachusetts Board of Education, were aimed at classroom teachers, with the hope of getting their support for educational reform and educating them regarding new classroom techniques and philosophy. Many of these journals were circulated free to teachers by state legislatures. One effect of these journals was to contribute to "the creation of a professional sentiment,"[12] or a feeling of identity among teachers. Another effect was to develop a sense of professional standards and concerns.

Many of the reforms advocated in these publications were only slowly realized. As we indicated in the last section, by the beginning of the nineteenth century the district school was a common feature of American education. While the development of the district schools provided for extensive local control over education, it also resulted in deteriorating conditions for teachers. The proliferation of local schools required that more teachers be hired, but provided fewer funds for hiring them. As Monroe points out:

> So far as the teaching was concerned the system reduced salaries to the lowest possible point, the competition always being toward the minimum; it failed to maintain any adequate standards of preparation or of attainment; it furnished little opportunity for improving school conditions; it made the lowest

> paid and hence the most poorly equipped teacher most sought after; it fostered frequent changes and short tenure of office and rendered desirable the earliest possible escape from the profession.[13]

Improvements in teachers' working conditions and salaries were slow in coming. As late as 1844, school budgets were so low that one Massachusetts school had only $5.60 for an entire year. Teachers were often paid less than one dollar per week. This was supplemented by "boarding around." Teachers were housed and fed by various families in the district, moving from one to the other on a regular basis. This custom "added materially to the discomfort and unattractiveness of the profession."[14]

In 1855, it was still possible to conclude that for many

> . . . schools a cheap teacher is almost invariably sought, and almost invariably a poor teacher is employed, a very poor teacher, or one quite inexperienced; and even the unprofitable services of these incompetent teachers must be speedily terminated. Few of these schools are kept more than four months in the year, the period required by law in order to be entitled to public money.[15]

These conditions existed until the end of the century in some parts of the United States, particularly in the Midwest and West. However, especially in the East, salaries took a substantial turn for the better after the Civil War.

Improvements in the training and preparation of teachers were also rather slow in developing. Until the nineteenth century, special teacher training programs were nonexistent and the belief was widespread that anyone who knew the basic material to be covered in class could teach. One of the first forms of teacher education was introduced early in the century in conjunction with the rise of Lancasterian monitorial schools in the cities. As was discussed in Chapter 3, the organization of these schools was extremely complex, involving several hundred students to each teacher and a system of student monitors. Mastery of this system required training, and the New York City school system began apprenticing boys for this purpose.[16] These boys were given special instruction for a few hours each morning, worked as monitors during the day, and were eventually certified as teachers. Other school systems just used older boys who had had experience as monitors in such schools. Here, then, were some rudimentary beginnings of teacher training. But the demise of the monitorial schools in the first half of the century put an end to it.

Another early type of teacher training emerged in a few private schools and academies. You may recall from Chapter 3 that these schools provided a broader and more vocationally oriented education than did the colleges and Latin Grammar schools of the day. Many of the academies saw teacher training as one of their purposes and established special departments for prospective teachers. In New York, the academies were a major source of public school teachers from approximately 1820 to 1850.[17] There, as in other states, public funds were eventually provided to subsidize the teacher training programs of the academies. However, they came under rather extensive criticism and were eventually replaced by normal schools. The criticism included the fact that the academies provided little in the way of methods training. Instead, students studied general academic subjects with a heavy emphasis on those they would eventually teach in the classroom. Teaching methods were briefly covered, usually in a few special lectures. The students had no supervised experience in teaching, and there was apparently little long-range commitment among students toward teaching as a career. Most were planning to teach only temporarily.

Many advocates of separate normal schools for the preparation of teachers were influenced by observations of schools in Prussia that had been established for this purpose. Agitation for such schools in the United States began as early as the turn of the century but became increasingly vocal during the twenties and thirties. Advocates of these ideas popularized them in the many educational magazines established during this period and worked toward these ends as members of legislative bodies and prominent educational administrators.

Central to the move towards normal schools was a new conception of the teacher's role in the classroom. Until this time, much learning involved the rote memorization of textbooks filled with questions and answers of an abstract and often uninteresting variety. Under the influence of such European educators as Johann Pestalozzi, a new conception of childhood and education began to emerge. From this point "education was conceived as a process of developing the child, through the enrichment of experience . . ."[18] This required a "new type of teacher, one instructed in psychology and trained in method."[19] Teaching came "to be based on certain psychological principles, not on superficial knowledge and crude craftsmanship of the individual teacher."[20]

The normal schools differed from the academies precisely in terms of their more rigorous attention to teaching methods and schoolroom organization. In time, many normal schools even added demonstration schools in which students could observe and even practice teaching as part of their curriculum.

Nevertheless, the normal schools were essentially equivalent to the academies and high schools in the academic level of their courses. The first normal school was established in Massachusetts in 1839 and their numbers multiplied until by 1900 each of the forty-five states then in the Union had established one.[21] However, these schools did not usually have any entrance requirements, the course of study was only one or two years, and a great many students never stayed to graduate. Standards were raised only gradually, in response to increasing concerns about teacher quality and also because of the greater availability of high school level education in most parts of the country. By 1900, Massachusetts required a high school diploma for entrance into its normal school, but other states lagged considerably behind.

As the standards for admission to normal schools were raised, their course of study was extended and their curriculum broadened. The conception that "teachers, like other professionals, had to be liberally educated,"[22] grew in popularity and, by the turn of the century, normal schools were transforming themselves into teachers' colleges. Normal schools continued to exist, but with decreasing frequency, well into the Mature Industrial Period.

In addition to the growth of normal schools and teachers' colleges, teacher training was advanced in the liberal arts colleges and universities across the country. Colleges and universities began offering courses in education around the middle of the nineteenth century. Many developed schools of education or departments of education. By 1900, over one-fourth of the colleges in the United States offered courses in education.

The expansion of college—and eventually, graduate level—courses in education was closely tied to two factors that should be kept in mind.[23] First, a body of expertise was developing that provided justification and legitimization for including these subject areas in liberal arts colleges and university settings. The history of education, educational philosophy, and educational psychology were among the earliest bodies of knowledge to gain acceptance. Second, states were increasingly taking over certification authority from local districts. The requirements for teaching licenses became more rigorous and increasingly included not only certain academic courses and a diploma from a recognized college or normal school, but also specific courses in education per se. These requirements pressured colleges to teach these courses when they might otherwise have been reluctant to do so.

In addition to improvements in teacher education through the development of special schools and courses, mechanisms to educate in-service teachers also developed during this period. The need for such training was considerable. As late as 1898 in Massachusetts, only 38.5 percent of the public school teachers had attended a normal school, and only one-third of these had completed the course there.[24] One mechanism that was developed to cope with this problem was the teachers' institute. First begun in the late 1930s, these institutes met for from two to eight weeks at a time and offered teachers courses in academic subjects taught in the public schools, as well as courses on methods. Their aim was to improve teachers' qualifications and enhance their competence. They also helped contribute to professional morale and to the sense that teachers did, indeed, represent a professional group.

Improvements in other aspects of teaching as an occupation were also slow in developing. Teachers remained poorly paid throughout this entire period, although salaries did rise gradually beginning after the Civil War. In spite of the chronic shortage of teachers due to the enormous expansion of public school education during this period, little was actually done to make the job more materially attractive. Starting around the turn of the century there was some increased discussion of such matters, but not much action. Generally, teachers could be arbitrarily dismissed from their posts by their board of education, received little if anything in the way of retirement or pension benefits, and were subjected to numerous restrictions in terms of their lives outside the classroom. For example, it was common to forbid teachers to smoke, dance, date, play cards, drink, or gamble.

Interestingly, teachers were not very vocal or organized in their objections to these conditions. Nevertheless, teachers became increasingly conscious of themselves as a professional group, and beginning in the first half of the nineteenth century they began forming local teachers associations. State organizations were formed, beginning in Alabama in 1840, with organizations in all but two states by 1900.[25] In 1857, the National Teachers Association was founded. This organization became the National Education Association in 1870 and represented a wide range of administrative and teaching groups. The NEA made substantial contributions to the growth of education as a profession primarily because it encouraged debate about new and controversial ideas in education and disseminated them among teachers and administrators. It did not have much effect on legislatures, however, and did not work to improve the working conditions of the classroom teacher.

In 1916, the American Federation of Teachers was formed. This group was organized by teachers who wanted to ally themselves more closely with labor. In their opinion, the NEA was too strongly dominated by administrators and "could not play a militant role for the improvement of American education."[26] The AFT affiliated itself with the American Federation of Labor. As we shall see, these organizations both became more militant and powerful in the Mature Industrial Period.

To summarize, the Early Industrial Period saw teaching make enormous strides in the direction of professionalization. Teachers became conscious of themselves as an occupational group, and teaching came to be defined as a career rather than a purely transitional pursuit. Teacher training was institutionalized in special schools and departments. The typical training period was lengthened into a four-year college level program and extended to include academic as well as methods and educational courses. A body of expertise relevant to the classroom developed and was recognized by the establishment of graduate departments of education. Teachers joined together in organizations to promote their own interests as well as to improve their own learning and competence. These changes were so great that Monroe described them as "the creation of a profession."[27] Instead, we would say that teachers came a long way in this direction, but that many changes still lay ahead.

### Teachers in Higher Education

As in public school teaching, teaching in higher education underwent a considerable transformation during the Early Industrial Period. Here, too, professionalization increased, but its specific dimensions were quite distinct from those that characterized teaching in the public schools.

One of the principle differences that developed between public school teachers and those working at the college level involved the basis of their expertise and the nature of their training. As we explained in the last section, public school teaching became increasingly professionalized as a body of knowledge specific to the task of teaching was developed and institutionalized in the normal schools. The public school teacher's expertise was rooted in knowledge about child development, classroom management, teaching skills, and so on. This was not the case for college faculty, for whom the old conception of teaching as something that anyone with sufficient academic expertise could successfully do prevailed. Professionalization came to be based not on specialized knowledge about teaching but on specialized knowledge in the individual disciplines that were taught.

This trend of emphasizing expertise in an individual discipline began with the introduction of special endowed chairs during the Early Industrial Period and was strengthened as greater proportions of the faculty at the major colleges were made up of such specialists.

The growth of specialization was also prompted by the great proliferation of scientific knowledge during this entire period. The college curriculum diversified, and it soon became impossible for any one person to teach more than one or two of the many subjects offered in depth. By the end of the Early Industrial Period the practice of dividing the college into departments—each specializing in a relatively narrow body of knowledge—was firmly established.

At the same time, the expansion of scientific knowledge and the growing research orientation of academic faculties contributed to the establishment of universities. In the last couple of decades of the nineteenth century, several major colleges developed graduate level programs, and such institutions as Johns Hopkins and Clark were founded primarily as graduate institutions. These institutions made it possible to increase the level of training obtained by college teachers. At the beginning of the Early Industrial Period few college teachers had more than a B.A. degree and those who had, had been educated abroad. By the end of the period, the Ph.D. was considered the appropriate degree for senior faculty members—at least at the more prestigious institutions.

The existence of the universities not only increased the length of training required for college teachers, but it also contributed to the research and discipline orientation of this training. The Ph.D. degree was granted on the basis of scholarship and research, and had nothing to do with specific training for the classroom.

The discipline orientation of college faculties was also enhanced by the development during this period of national, and even international, learned societies. These societies typically sponsored annual meetings at which the latest research and theory in the discipline was discussed, published journals to disseminate the best of these new materials, and became sources of job information and recruitment.

In time, many professors began orienting themselves more toward the national or international community of scholars in their discipline than toward their own individual colleges or universities. Earlier in this period, "the vision of a college professor as an independent expert with a mission transcending the college where he happened to teach was almost unknown,"[28] but this vision was soon to become pervasive, especially in the universities and the more prestigious colleges.

Throughout most of the Early Industrial Period, however, the working conditions of college faculty were far from what we would picture as appropriate for professionals. The vast majority did not have any protection from arbitrary dismissals, and even the custom of allowing hearings before dismissal was dropped. Faculty could be dismissed for innumerable reasons including expressing ideas that their board of trustees or college president found unacceptable. College presidents tended to be domineering, and there were many battles over who should control the shape of the curriculum, course content, choice of books, and so on. The faculty lost most of these battles, at least until the twentieth century.[29]

In 1913, six hundred college professors united to form the American Association of University Professors. The purpose of this organization was to serve the interests of the profession through collective action. The two major activities specifically mentioned at the time were the establishment of "general principles respecting the tenure of the professional office and the legitimate ground for the dismissal of professors" and to establish "a representative judicial committee to investigate and report in cases in which [academic] freedom is alleged to have been interfered with by the administrative authorities in any way. . . ."[30] The work of this organization in protecting the autonomy and independence of college faculty became increasingly vigorous and effective during the remainder of this period. It successfully won tenure and other protections for major segments of the academic community.

By the end of this Early Industrial Period teaching at the college and university level had become considerably more professionalized than it had been earlier. The period of training had been expanded from the three or four years required for a B.A. to the six, eight, or more required for an M.A. or Ph.D. The body of scientific knowledge, publications, and research that constituted the college and university professors' areas of expertise had greatly expanded and had been divided into a series of specialized academic disciplines. National and international societies of scholars, along with a national organization for the improvement of working conditions and the protection of academic freedom had been developed. Because professors controlled the awarding of Ph.D. degrees in their own disciplines, they were in firm control over entrance into their ranks. This control was enhanced by their growing influence over hiring, promotion, and dismissal procedures. Nevertheless, by the end of this period, many college and university faculty were not protected by tenure, dismissals for expressing unpopular political views were still possible, and salaries were low compared to other occupations requiring similar levels of educational investment.

## THE MATURE INDUSTRIAL PERIOD

The character of teaching as an occupation has continued to change over the last several decades. In this section, we will look at the nature of these changes and the current state of teaching as a contemporary occupation. Particularly, we will focus on recruitment and selection; expertise; training and socialization; career patterns and commitments; rewards and satisfaction; and professional organizations and unions.

## Recruitment and Selection

### Recruitment

Teaching is a highly visible vocation. Our system of compulsory schooling and mass higher education exposes everyone to teachers and the obvious facts about teaching as an occupation. From an early age we all spend many hours watching teachers work and interacting with them.

In 1975, Dan Lortie published a major study of teachers in America.[31] As part of his research, Lortie asked a sample of 94 teachers in the Boston area about the attractions of teaching as a career. He then compared his results to those of a national survey conducted by the National Education Association. Lortie found that one of the attractions teaching had for a number of people was that it enabled them to continue their association with the schools. The experiences they had had there, with particular areas of study, or with particularly inspirational teachers, pulled them back into the schools as adults. Many of these individuals decided to become teachers while they were still children and stayed with that choice permanently. As some of them put it, they "liked school" and wanted to work there. Schools, then, directly account for at least some of the recruitment of successive generations of teachers. By providing exposure to teaching as an occupation and by providing rewarding experiences to children they assure at least partial replacement of their teaching ranks.

Nevertheless, school-based experiences explain only a small portion of the many factors that contribute to individuals' decisions to enter teaching. Other major factors include the variety of attractions teaching offers, the ease with which people can enter teaching, and the limited range of alternative options opened to many individuals.

*Attractions.* When Lortie asked teachers what attracted them to their occupation, several types of rewards were mentioned with relatively high frequency, although no one reward was mentioned by a majority. Among those mentioned most frequently were the opportunity to be interpersonally involved with people and the opportunity to perform an important service for the community. Among the rewards mentioned relatively infrequently were material benefits and benefits derived from teachers' unusual work schedules.

The opportunity to be interpersonally involved with others was the attraction cited most frequently in Lortie's sample. From his own data and the National Education Association's data, Lortie concluded that this attraction had wide-based appeal. Men as well as women, elementary school as well as high school teachers, mentioned it often. Teaching seems to appeal to many who like to work with people (particularly youth), and unlike nursing or social work, it offers a unique opportunity to work with a wide range of young people who are healthy and generally free from serious problems. In a 1980 survey, almost 70 percent of all teachers mentioned the desire to work with young people as a major reason for their entering teaching.[32]

The opportunity to perform an important service for the community was mentioned by 17 percent of Lortie's sample and 28 percent of the National Education Association respondents, making it the second most frequent response among this latter group. Earlier in this chapter, we mentioned that some theorists consider a service orientation to be an important characteristic of professional occupations. Teaching does seem to have this characteristic. Certainly, the image of the dedicated teacher is a pervasive one in American culture. Lortie suggests that teachers may even be more idealistic than their responses on the attraction of service suggests. When asked about what factors they believe attract and hold *other* people to teaching, the teachers in Lortie's sample mentioned service two and a half times more frequently than when they were asked what attracted them. Lortie believes that people project their own motivations onto others, so that answers to this question actually reflect the teachers' *own* motivations. He feels that the teachers may have been inhibited about appearing too idealistic when talking about themselves. An alternative explanation of this finding might be that teachers themselves believe the popular image of the teacher as a dedicated person. They know that this image may not fit them as individuals, but they still believe that it fits a great many of their colleagues. In 1980, 40 percent of the teachers said that the significance of education in society was a major reason for their entering teaching.[33]

Material benefits were rarely mentioned. Only 6 percent of Lortie's sample mentioned factors such as salary or job security. By 1980, 21 percent mentioned job security, but salary was still rarely a factor.[34] One reason for this might be the fact that teaching does not compare favorably to alternative occupations, and especially professions, on salary. Lortie does not think this is the case, however. Rather, he believes that teachers are hesitant to appear materialistic; that because of their image of teaching as an occupation with dedicated personnel, they hesitate to stress the material benefits they derive from it. As evidence, Lortie returns again to the question about other people's motivations for remaining in teaching. A much higher percentage of respondents referred to material benefits on this question than on the question they answered about themselves.

A similar pattern was discovered regarding rewards derived from the "time compatibility" of teachers' work schedules. Time compatibility refers to the fact that teachers work relatively short hours and fewer days each year than most full-time workers. Also, their hours and vacations coincide with the school schedule of young children. Thus, teachers' working hours are compatible with many other kinds of activities and interests, and particularly with the tasks of raising a family. The fact that only 4 percent of Lortie's sample mentioned time compatibility as a major factor in their decision to enter teaching and only 14 percent mentioned it even as an attraction that teaching has in general is striking. Lortie brushes past this finding without really explaining it. He does show that when asked about other people's motivations, teachers mention time compatibility with greater frequency—44 percent of the time to be exact—but Lortie cannot account for this discrepancy. Perhaps, again, teachers are reluctant to appear concerned with selfish ends or practical considerations. Perhaps, also, the importance of this factor in teacher recruitment has been grossly exaggerated. Teachers frequently do school-related work at home, after the end of the formal work day, and many teachers work second jobs at night or during the summer months. For them, the image of the teacher as a person with unusual amounts of leisure or time flexibility does not fit. Still, the importance of time compatibility for parents who are assuming childcare responsibilities makes Lortie's finding something requiring further exploration.

In 1981, 22 percent mentioned the long summer vacation as a major attraction. For those over 30 years of age, the figure was 27 percent.[35] Two other factors mentioned frequently in the 1981 data were interest in a subject-matter field, mentioned by 44 percent of the teachers (66 percent of high school teachers) and influence of family, mentioned by 22 percent.[36]

*Ease of Entry into Teaching.* Although the formal requirements for teacher certification have increased considerably since World War II, in some ways it has actually become easier to become a teacher. Schools of education have never had stringent admissions standards, and during the 1970s, as the job market for teachers tightened and enrollment in teacher-training programs declined, the standards were relaxed even further. The standards were lowered in order to expand the number of trainees and thereby avoid layoffs of college faculty. The strategy may have saved some faculty positions, but it also exacerbated the oversupply of teachers. Because newly certified teachers were having difficulty finding employment, the education major became even less attractive to incoming students. Again, admissions standards were lowered. The surplus of teachers grew, but the quality of the pool diminished each year.[37]

Historical data indicate that American teachers have always gotten low scores on standardized tests of academic ability and achievement.[38] But in recent years the scores have gone from bad to worse. Whereas national averages on the SAT exam declined steeply during the 1970s, the scores of prospective teachers dropped even more sharply. In 1970 to 1971, verbal (472) and math (506) scores of freshman elementary education majors were somewhat above the national averages of 455 and 488, but by 1975 to 1976 their verbal scores had sunk to 14 points below and the math scores to 15 points below the national averages.[39] When these scores are ranked relative to those of students entering other majors, education students come out near the bottom.[40]

These data point to the inescapable conclusion that, on the average, our prospective teachers are relatively incompetent academically. Hence, it is not surprising to find that few of the courses that teacher trainees are required to take are intellectually demanding. Thus, rather poor students are routinely able to acquire teaching certificates during the four-year course of study leading to a B.A. degree.

One does not have to make an early and sustained commitment in order to enter teaching. It is possible to decide on teaching after first experimenting with other occupations or after having been out of the labor market for some time. Because the required courses are commonly offered at night and during the summer, it is comparatively easy for working people to prepare for teaching careers. In sum, preparation for teaching requires relatively modest expenditures of time, money, and effort.

The ease with which teaching can be entered can be thought of as a positive attraction in many cases, but it is best considered as a "facilitator."[41] Ease of entry makes it more likely that certain groups of people will choose teaching rather than something else, especially when they are faced with a variety of other constraints, but it does not represent a strong pull by the characteristics of the occupation itself. Ease of entry means that a more heterogeneous group can be successfully recruited to teaching. People from a variety of life-cycle stages and a variety of socioeconomic conditions can "make it" into teaching, when entry into other professions would be impossible.

*Restricted Alternatives.* When people make important decisions they usually consider the range of alternatives open to them and the relative costs and benefits of each. The same is true about decisions regarding occupations. Certainly, some people seem to drift into occupations almost without thinking about them, and others decide very early in life, before they can rationally weigh their choices, but most probably go through at least a cursory consideration of their options. Sometimes, final choices are made not so much in terms of the positive attractions of certain possibilities as in terms of the lack of available alternatives.

In Lortie's study, approximately three-quarters of the respondents had considered an alternative occupation before entering teaching. His data suggest that many decided on teaching because their alternative choices were not viable. Approximately one-third of the teachers in his sample said that "they had wanted to go into another line of work but were unable to do so because of external constraints."[42] For many of these, "teaching 'came close' to a primary, but blocked aspiration."[43] For example, an English teacher may have once hoped to act, but directs school plays instead.

Primary aspirations are blocked in many ways. One way is through parental opposition. Lortie found several teachers, primarily women, whose parents were opposed to careers in the theater, opera, and even nursing. As "dutiful daughters," their children gave up these aspirations and became teachers instead.

In many more cases, primary aspirations were blocked by socioeconomic factors. Financial obstacles were the most frequently mentioned blocks in Lortie's sample. People who preferred medicine, but who could not afford medical school, became biology teachers. People who wanted to go on for higher degrees, but could only afford the low fees at their local State Teachers College, wound up in the classroom, although they had no original desire to be there.

Sometimes, primary aspirations were blocked only indirectly. A number of female teachers apparently "settled" for teaching because their first preference was not compatible with plans to marry or raise a family.

One woman gave up a career in dietetics and another gave up plans for doctoral study to support husbands who were in school and to facilitate homemaking.

Apparently, no women in Lortie's sample reported giving up primary aspirations because of perceived discrimination against women in their preferred occupations. This is interesting in light of the generally accepted opinion that women have always entered teaching in large numbers because it was one of the few "respectable" middle-class occupations that would have them. When Lortie asked his respondents which alternative occupations they had considered, women rarely mentioned prestigious or highly lucrative professions. Instead, they referred to nursing, social work, library work, office positions, and the performing arts—all occupations that are traditionally open to females. It would appear, then, that these women were not "settling" for teaching simply because they were women. Still, there is considerable room for doubt. Women are socialized from an early age to have relatively low occupational ambitions, and to view occupations in sex-stereotyped terms. By the time they actually choose an occupation for themselves, they may not even consciously consider a wide range of possibilities. Or, perhaps, they briefly consider these possibilities but reject them because of perceived discrimination or because counselors, parents, or friends discourage them.[44] For these women, a choice between the typical list of acceptable semi-professional occupations is clearly a choice conditioned by restricted alternatives, even if they are not consciously aware of how these restrictions were imposed.

It is becoming increasingly apparent that the education profession used to benefit from the gender and racial discrimination practiced by other professions. Talented blacks and women often sought teaching positions as a means of social mobility and personal fulfillment. Now that these individuals have vastly improved opportunities to enter other professional fields, they are taking advantage of those opportunities. In recent years the number of blacks entering teaching has dropped dramatically, and the academic ability of white, female, first-year teachers has declined consistently.[45]

Unfortunately, data comparable to Lortie's are not available on college and university teachers. However, public school teaching and college or university teaching are sufficiently alike for us to expect that many of the same motivations affect both groups. Both are likely to be concerned with service, for example. On the other hand, higher education offers greater material rewards, prestige, autonomy, and intellectual satisfactions, and so we would expect that these latter factors would be mentioned as attractions more frequently by college faculty than by public school teachers. One study that is relevant to this point asked a national sample of thirty-three thousand graduate students about their reasons for attending graduate school.[46] Many, but not all, of these students were planning on an academic career. Their answers emphasized the importance of intellectual growth as a primary factor, and intrinsic interest in their special field as a secondary factor in their reasons for being in school. Increasing their earning power was much less important to these students than were intellectual pursuits.

Nevertheless, over 40 percent agreed that these material considerations were involved in their decision. By contrast, few of Lortie's respondents expressed any concern with either intellectual pursuits or financial rewards.

Now let us turn to the characteristics of those who enter teaching, keeping these motivations in mind as we do.

*Gender.* One of the most conspicuous facts about recruitment to teaching is the striking relationship between gender and careers in education. As you may recall from our historical discussions, teaching in colonial America was a male occupation, except for the Dame schools that served very young children and a few private schools for older girls. By 1855, however, women public school teachers were twice as common as men in all but one of the New England states. By 1900, women school teachers outnumbered men throughout the entire country. Today, approximately two out of every three school teachers are women.

There are, however, important gender-related differences in the placement and careers of school teachers. Whereas over 60 percent of all female teachers teach in the elementary grades, only one-fourth of all male teachers teach at this level. Whereas over one half of all males teach at the senior high school level, only 24 percent of the females teach at this level.[47] Consequently, 84 percent of all elementary school teachers are women, but only 43 percent of senior high school teachers.[48] Furthermore, males predominate as school administrators and superintendents. In 1975, 80 percent of all elementary school principals, 98 percent of all high school principals, and 99 percent of all school superintendents were male.[49] In 1981, 81 percent of all elementary school teachers and 95 percent of all high school teachers worked under a male principal.[50] Over 85 percent of all principals were male.[51] However, there has been a rapid increase in female enrollment in graduate programs in educational administration. So the old pattern of male monopoly may be changing.[52]

In institutions of higher education, only slightly over one quarter of all teachers are women.[53] Women tend to be more heavily concentrated in institutions with relatively low prestige and poor working conditions, such as community colleges.[54] In general, women comprise a higher percentage of the faculty in institutions oriented toward teaching rather than research. Within individual colleges and universities, women are clustered in departments that traditionally have had lower prestige and lower salaries, such as home economics, nursing, social work, library science, and education. They have been grossly underrepresented in the natural sciences, many of the social sciences, and business administration. In addition, women are disproportionately found in the lower, untenured academic ranks of instructor and lecturer, and are relatively unusual at the rank of full professor.[55] At all academic ranks, women tend to make less money than men.[56]

Few college presidents are women. Estimates vary from five percent to eleven percent.[57] The great majority of these are nuns heading small, church-related colleges. Women are also commonly entrusted with the leadership of nonsectarian women's colleges. Women have also been found to be grossly underrepresented as vice-presidents or top assistants to the president.[58]

There are several facts that help explain these patterns of employment. First, as we suggested earlier, women have had relatively few occupational alternatives open to them. Teaching, probably because it involved the care of children and was not viewed as intellectually taxing, was generally seen as "appropriate" for women, but careers in government, business, medicine, law, and the like were not. For many years it was virtually impossible for women to gain even the educational credentials necessary to enter many of these occupations, let alone be hired or establish a practice once they were educated.

Then, too, women have traditionally assumed the responsibility for child care in American families. The "time compatibility" factor, which we discussed earlier, made teaching an occupation that could be more easily combined with childrearing than most. Teaching also permitted relatively easy movement in and out of the labor market with different life-cycle stages. A teacher could work for a few years, stop to care for young children, and return again later without losing very much. Similarly, teaching has always permitted a high degree of geographical mobility. If a woman's husband changed jobs and location, she could follow and find another position without too much difficulty. Schools, of course, are everywhere.

Men, on the other hand, had a much greater variety of occupations from which to choose. Many of these were both more lucrative and prestigious than teaching, and offered greater opportunities for independence and leadership. As such, they were viewed as appropriately "masculine" in ways that teaching was not. In recent years, teaching—especially of young children—has been seen as a nurturing occupation and as such it was incompatible with the stereotyped image of the adult male. This image pictured a "real man" as competitive, aggressive, and unemotional rather than loving, giving, and supportive. Even today, when our views of appropriate gender roles are becoming more flexible, there is considerable stigma attached to the male who wants to teach kindergarten or first grade.

Furthermore, teaching is a "careerless" profession.[59] There is no career ladder to challenge and motivate exceptionally talented and ambitious teachers. The rank and responsibilities of beginning teachers are essentially identical to those of very experienced classroom teachers. This structure makes it relatively easy to move in and out of teaching, as women traditionally did when they dropped out for some years to care for their own young children and returned later when their childrearing responsibilities decreased. But the structure frustrates those who seek rapid advancement. The only way up is to move out of the classroom—to abandon teaching for an administrative (bureaucratic) career.[60] As administrators, they have the opportunity to earn promotions through a series of ranked positions, gaining prestige, responsibility, and salary as they rise.

Though both men and women are often interested in a "career," men are particularly socialized to be ambitious and to measure their success as adults by their success on the job. Research has indicated that men are more likely than women to enter teaching with the move into administration already in mind.[61] Male teachers acquire more education than female teachers and tend to concentrate their graduate courses more clearly around acquiring credentials for administrative posts.[62]

Women have generally been discouraged from becoming administrators, and they have often been denied on-the-job socialization experiences that would pave the way for such careers. Given the generally inhospitable, male administrative environment, it is not surprising that in the past many exceptional women who did become administrators had to be "pushed, cajoled, persuaded, and even driven to their managerial positions by male administrators."[63] We mentioned earlier that teaching does not require as great an investment in education and training as many professions. Traditionally, women have not been socialized to take their own career aspirations seriously. Rather, they have been urged to see their future activities as centering in the home and as supportive of and supplemental to their husband's. Consequently, women and their families may have been less willing to invest in career preparation and less worried about issues of promotions and material benefits. Teaching, which required only minimal investments, seemed ideal. Of course, these attitudes are changing, but they have been widespread for many generations.

Another important factor that explains the differential entry and career patterns of men and women in teaching is discrimination against women, both in admission to advanced educational programs and in selection for teaching and administrative posts. Women have been denied equal access to graduate education, discouraged from acquiring higher degrees, shut out of important information and communications networks, and generally viewed as less serious, less committed, and less capable.[64] Of course, men have also been discriminated against, particularly when it came to training or hiring for the kindergarten and early primary grades.

Many of the assumptions underlying this discrimination are now being challenged and, as we said in an earlier chapter, affirmative action legislation now makes discrimination on the basis of sex illegal in educational institutions receiving federal funds. Recently, too, some research has been directed at these assumptions. For example, Neal Gross and Anne Trask completed a study of 189 big-city school systems and focused on sex as a factor in administrative competence.[65] They were able to document that student achievement and teacher performance were higher on the average in elementary schools headed by women principals than in those headed by men.

Gross and Trask interpret the superiority of female administrators as the result of the greater amount of teaching experience women acquire before moving into administration. The women in their sample averaged about three times as much teaching experience as the men. One-third of the male principals, as compared to only 3 percent of the female principals, had no elementary teaching experience at all.[66]

*Social Class.* Teaching, at any level, is considered a solidly middle-class occupation. Yet many individuals who enter teaching are from working-class backgrounds. These individuals are upwardly mobile: Their parents worked in blue-collar occupations and, for the most part, did not have a college education. In 1981, over 70 percent of all teachers had fathers who had not attended college.[67]

Several characteristics of teaching as an occupation make it a convenient route to upward mobility. As we indicated before, teaching requires only a minimal economic investment compared to the more prestigious professional occupations. It is also highly visible. Whereas the exact route to executive status or partnership in a law firm may seem vague and uncertain to families who have not had a member graduate from college before, the route to teaching is more likely to appear both clear and manageable. Furthermore, teachers may be the only middle-class role models easily accessible to these families and their children. Identification with the teacher and the teacher's values may be strong. As Elliot put it:

> Teaching as a relatively uninstitutionalized profession has long been credited with a crucial intermediary position in social mobility, especially in the longer perspective of mobility over two or three generations. It seems likely that the first generation to achieve educational success in a family will be particularly liable to encapsulation within the education system itself. Such children lack the family connections or support to provide alternatives to the goals and values suggested by the educational institutions.[68]

Teaching may also appear to offer more security than other types of occupations. You do not have to depend on building up an individual practice, for example, or attracting clients. Hiring, especially in large city systems, is based primarily on educational credentials and scores on licensing examinations. Once one is hired and has passed a probationary period, there is the likelihood of tenure and a more or less guaranteed position for life.

The same general facts also seem true of higher education. Although entrance into college and university teaching is more difficult than entrance into public school teaching, there is still high visibility once the student has reached college, a heavy emphasis on merit, and considerable potential for job security. Furthermore, it has often been possible to finance one's own way through graduate school through fellowships and part-time jobs as a teaching or research assistant.

Approximately 24 percent of all American academicians come from families in which the father was engaged in a blue-collar occupation. This percentage has increased slightly over time, so that 18 percent of the faculty who are sixty years of age or older come from blue-collar families as compared to 25 percent of those in their thirties.[69]

Within both public school teaching and teaching in the colleges and universities, however, there are some additional patterns related to social-class background. As late as 1961, the social-class background of high school teachers was higher than that of elementary school teachers. This difference had virtually disappeared by 1971,[70] but in the colleges and universities social-class variations according to quality and type of institution continue to exist. Only 15 percent of the faculty in high-quality universities had fathers who were blue-collar workers. The percentage is 24 percent in low-quality universities, and 30 percent in low-quality colleges and junior colleges.[71] Thus, the massive expansion of higher education during the 1960s, and in particular, the growth and expansion of junior colleges, seems to have provided an avenue of upward mobility for faculty as well as students.

We do not know the precise reasons for these patterns. However, the higher the level at which an individual teaches, the greater the educational credentials usually required. As we shall see in Chapter 8, in addition to costing time and money, many other factors make these credentials more accessible to economically advantaged groups.

Men and women have not used teaching as a route to mobility with the same frequency. Male public school teachers have been more likely than female teachers to have fathers who were blue-collar workers.[72] These differences might be explained by the variety of alternatives available to and considered by each of these two groups. Women, whether they have been middle-class or not, have been limited in their choice of careers by both socialization and discrimination. Men, on the other hand, experience few limitations as a group, but, of course, do experience advantages and disadvantages linked to social class. Middle-class men are much more likely to consider and gain admittance to high-status professional and business positions than are working-class men, and, of course, the salary and security offered by teaching will look better to the son of a factory worker than the son of a physician. This is not to say that women are not affected by socioeconomic variables, but rather, that whatever their background, they have clustered in a small number of occupations with modest economic and status returns. Many of these—such as teaching—are acceptable to middle- and upper-middle-class families for their daughters, but not for their sons.

### Selection

During much of our history, the demand for teachers exceeded the supply. In recent years, this was particularly true of the decades of the 1950s and 1960s. During this period, the World War II "baby boom" cohorts passed through the schools, putting pressure first on elementary schools, then secondary schools, and finally, institutions of higher education. Institutional growth was rapid, and the demand for teachers was high. To meet this demand, active recruitment campaigns were initiated and many individuals were hired without full professional credentials. Because they were in great demand, qualified teachers and professors found it easy to move from one geographical area to another and from less to more attractive institutions. School systems, however, could not be too selective. It was difficult enough simply meeting basic needs.

In the 1970s, this situation began to change radically. Due primarily to a sharp drop in the birth rate, fewer new students began entering the elementary schools and the secondary schools. At the same time, greater numbers of individuals, prepared to enter teaching, were leaving the colleges and universities. Because the demand for teachers had been so great while the students of the fifties and sixties were in school, they grew up thinking that teaching offered guaranteed employment and security. Similarly, the colleges had geared up to producing large numbers of teachers and provided both space and encouragement. Figure 6–1 shows that a large surplus of schoolteachers developed during the first half of the 1970s and continued through 1982. However, the projections shown on the graph indicate that past surpluses will soon be transformed into increasingly large shortages. There were indications in 1984 that the decadelong decline in enrollment within teacher-education programs had bottomed out and perhaps was beginning to reverse itself.[73] If enrollments continue to pick up, the shortages will be less severe. The large reserve pool of certified teachers who are presently unemployed or working in other fields might also help fill developing vacancies. Even if a rough balance between supply and demand is achieved, it will not be across-the-board. The long-existent shortages in special education will continue, and the newly emerging shortages of math and science teachers are likely to become even more serious. Because mathematicians and scientists, especially computer scientists, can earn so much more by working in business or industry than as teachers, teachers are abandoning their classrooms, and it is increasingly difficult to recruit new teachers in those fields.

**FIGURE 6–1.** Estimated Supply of New Teacher Graduates and Estimated Total Demand for Additional Teachers.

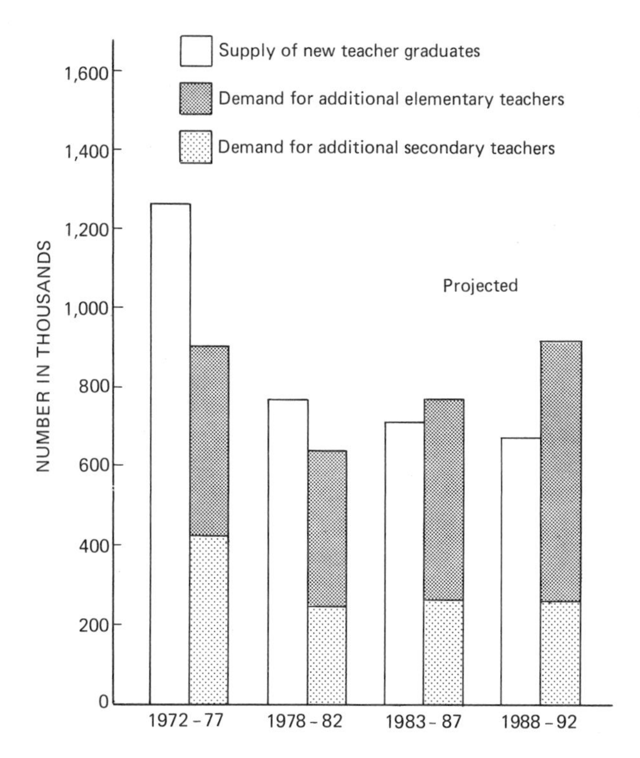


*Source:* Valena White Plisko, National Center for Education Statistics, *The Condition of Education: 1983* (Washington, D.C.: Government Printing Office, 1983), p. 37.

There is no evidence that school administrators took advantage of the "buyer's market" in order to upgrade their staffs in terms of academic ability. Quite to the contrary, the quality of the American teaching force, as measured by SAT scores, deteriorated during the period of surplus supply. Public concern over the poor quality of the teaching force grew to the point that state politicians and education officials finally stepped in. They demanded that prospective teachers pass competency tests in order to gain certification. In 1983, nine states had such testing programs in place and at least twenty-four others were either considering or actually planning competency examinations. Although such screening measures may well help to improve the quality of the teaching force, they have already raised a sensitive political/racial issue. Where teacher competency tests have been used, the results have varied with race. Significantly higher percentages of white teachers than black teachers have passed these tests. For example, in Florida in 1982, only 35 percent of the blacks who took the state certification test passed, whereas the overall success rate was 83 percent. States have threatened to revoke the accreditation of teacher-training programs if many of their graduates fail the certification tests. If they do so, many predominantly black institutions will be in serious trouble. Overall, the certification testing movement threatens to diminish the pool of minority group teachers dramatically.[74] Charges have been made that these tests are racially biased and that minority students receive inferior preparation for them. Questions have also been raised about the validity of these tests as measures of effective teaching.

The employment picture in higher education contrasts sharply with that at the lower levels. Since 1965 there has been a surfeit of prospective professors with newly granted doctoral degrees in hand. The surplus developed when graduate departments continued to expand even though undergraduate enrollments began to level off. The boom period of the 1960s is long past. At present many more American colleges and universities are retrenching rather than expanding. The predictions now are that the number of doctorates produced will remain relatively constant near 30,000 per year until the turn of the century. Between now and then there will be job openings for only one out of every three prospective professors.[75] Obviously the outlook is grim, especially in the near term. Colleges and universities have seized the opportunity provided by this supply glut to expand the number of part-time faculty positions. This move increases institutional flexibility and cuts costs, but it does little for those seeking traditional academic careers. In the longer term, the impending retirement of large cohorts of faculty initially hired to teach the baby-boomers provides a glimmer of hope. Also, once the larger cohorts of children now entering school reach college age, the demand for professors will increase.

Under these new circumstances it should be possible for institutions at all levels to upgrade their staffs through increasing selectivity. It will be possible for schools to take only those who have the desired credentials. We have already seen the beginning of this trend. In 1961, 15 percent of public school teachers did not even have a bachelor's degree; but by 1971, 97 percent had at least a bachelor's degree.[76] Ten years later, in 1981, the figure was 99.6 percent.[77] In the academic year 1960–61, 27.3 percent of all *entering* professors had Ph.D. degrees and another 18.4 percent had master's degrees. By 1969, 40 percent of *all* professors had Ph.Ds and another third had master's degrees.[78] By 1981, 61 percent had Ph.Ds and another third had master's degrees.[79]

As would be expected, the percentage of faculty with doctorates varies radically by type of institution, being above 72 percent for universities and 4-year colleges, and dropping to 15 percent at the junior college level.[80] One of the interesting unanswered questions raised in the current market situation is the extent to which the junior colleges will select research-oriented Ph.Ds as new faculty and what effect this would have on those institutions. Similarly, to what extent will high schools begin recruiting people who would previously have found employment in junior colleges and colleges? In any case, it is a safe bet that many institutions will seek to "upgrade" their faculty in the years before demand again increases at the college level. The "ease" with which people entered college teaching in the past has lessened. The educational investment has increased while opportunities for voluntary geographical mobility, rapid promotion through professorial ranks in institutions of higher education, and chances of obtaining tenure have declined.

## Expertise

In order for an occupation to be recognized as a profession, it is crucial that it have a strong base of expert knowledge. This knowledge should be widely recognized as complex, extensive, esoteric, and possessed only by fully trained members of the profession.

School teachers can claim professional recognition on the basis of at least two sets of expertise. One is their mastery of teaching methods and techniques of classroom management. The other is mastery over particular disciplinary specialties. At the college and university level, the ability to do significant scientific research, write, or create new works of art also serves as a basis for professional recognition.

### Teaching Methods

A broad spectrum of commentators on American education have argued that although there are courses and books dealing with teaching methods, the actual knowledge base upon which these depend is weak. Interest in teaching methods is a relatively recent development and, consequently, little systematic research has been done on teaching per se. Furthermore, attempts to integrate questions of classroom technique with more developed bodies of expertise, such as psychology or sociology, have not progressed very far. As Lortie puts it:

> The study of medicine and engineering is rooted in science; law and divinity can point to generations of scholars who have contributed to their development. Neither holds for education, for specialized study of the subject has a

> short history and an erratic connection with the mainstream of intellectual development in modern society.[81]

Furthermore, in the years during which educational technique has been the focus of academic attention, there has been little success in actually codifying the knowledge and experience gained by each generation of teachers. Again as Lortie points out:

> . . . there is no equivalent to the recording found in surgical cases, law cases, and physical models of engineering and architectural achievement. Such records, coupled with the commentaries and critiques of highly trained professors, allow new generations to pick up where earlier ones finished . . . the beginner in teaching must start afresh, largely uninformed about prior solutions and alternative approaches to recurring practical problems.[82]

As we shall see in the next section, teachers often find that their academic training does not prove helpful for solving classroom problems. Thus, teachers themselves do not always believe that they possess a "common technical culture."[83] Too much of their work seems to be based in their individualistic adjustments to the classroom rather than in a collective body of established traditions or scientifically validated principles.

The general public also tends to doubt the expertise of the typical teacher. Many parents feel that they know just as much—if not more—about children than teachers and that their opinions and advice about classroom life are just as valid. Studies of parents' attitudes and preferences regarding schools have also shown that many parents want teachers to concentrate on discipline, hard work, and the mastery of basic subjects rather than on making classes interesting, encouraging creativity, or being understanding and friendly toward students.[84] However, much of the literature on teaching that appeared during the 1970's stressed the importance of these latter concerns. Experiments with open classrooms, learning contracts, and the like, coupled with their frequent failure and disagreements among teachers regarding their effectiveness, probably discredited the teachers' "expertise" in the eyes of many parents.

Teachers at the college and university level do not usually make any claims to pedagogical expertise. In general, they do not take any training in teaching methods and often do no practice or supervised teaching before their first regular assignments. As we mentioned earlier, the idea that anyone who knows his or her subject area sufficiently is capable of teaching still prevails in academia. Interestingly, though, the last few years have showed a spurt of interest in teaching techniques. In sociology, for example, a professional journal is now devoted to the topic, as are special study groups in the American Sociological Association.[85] Efforts to develop methods for evaluating and improving teaching are being encouraged by several groups, and graduate departments are being urged to provide students with training in the classroom. We mentioned in the last section that colleges and universities can now be more selective in hiring because of the excess number of Ph.Ds. One direction this selectivity may take is toward a greater concern with the teaching ability of faculty members as well as greater concern with disciplinary expertise. We should point out, however, that at present there is probably even less systematic knowledge about teaching at the college and university level than at the public school level. It also seems very unlikely that college and university faculty will ever base their claims for professional recognition on mastery of teaching methods rather than on competence in their discipline.

### Disciplinary Specialties

Subject matter specialization is still rather rare in the elementary grades, in which the teachers generally introduce students to a broad variety of subjects. Specialization is much more pronounced in high schools, colleges, and universities. Among the faculty of the most prestigious colleges and universities, specialization has been carried to rather extreme lengths. As one old joke puts it, the university professor "learns more and more about less and less, until he finally knows everything about nothing!"

But there can be little doubt that specialization is conducive to the development of expertise and that expertise is central to the professional standing of an occupation. Advanced degrees—the Master of Arts for public school teachers and the Doctor of Philosophy for professors—are symbolic of mastery over complex bodies of theory and research. Those who hold such degrees probably believe that they, as individuals, are professionals even if some others in their occupation are not.

One way in which college and university faculty display their disciplinary expertise is by publishing their ideas and research in specialized professional journals and books. These publications show that their authors are familiar with the body of knowledge that makes up their special field and that they are creatively adding to it. Generally speaking, the more prestigious a particular college or university is, the more heavily faculty jobs and promotions will be tied to these publications rather than to teaching, broad-based scholarly activity without publication, administrative skill, or other kinds of contributions to the institution or the community. Certainly, the national and international reputations of individual academicians depend almost entirely on research and publications.

The research activities of college and university faculty can also be considered independent sources of professional status, representing skills that are somewhat distinct from mastery over the *content* of their discipline. Ben-David has pointed out that research was once considered either a pastime or a special calling for a charismatic few. By the twentieth century, however, "research became a professional service like law or medicine . . . a career in which it was justified, within the limits of professional ethics, to search for opportunities to work and to sell one's services under the best possible conditions."[86] As such, it was legitimate to seek out work—primarily in the form of research grants—from government, private foundations, and any other interested source.[87] Particularly after World War II, the amount of money available for these purposes skyrocketed.

The prestige and power of faculty who are successful at obtaining large research grants is greater than that of those who are not. Because their colleges and universities profit financially (and in other ways) from their success, faculties with large numbers of productive researchers can generally attain more autonomy from administrative control, higher salaries and benefits, and lighter teaching loads.[88] Many faculty members rarely publish or receive grants, however, and their status as professionals rests more heavily on their educational credentials, mastery of the content of their special field, and teaching. Their leverage in confrontations with administrators is decidedly less.

## Training and Socialization

### Public School Teachers

Perhaps the most devastating critics of present teacher-training practices are young teachers themselves. They describe many of their courses, especially those in methods, as being of the "Mickey Mouse" variety—easy and devoid of substance. They criticize these courses for not providing realistic preparation for teaching duties, claiming that they focus on uptopian goals impossible to achieve in the average classroom.[89]

Practice teaching is much more highly valued among education students than are their methods courses.[90] However, critics point out that practice teaching may be poorly supervised and of short duration. The student usually stands in for a regular classroom teacher, carrying out his or her policies and programs. There is little room for experimentation or actual leadership. The regular teacher has little incentive to supervise or instruct the novice, and may simply consider the time during which the student teaches as a free bonus. To the extent that the teacher does supervise, though, the student may learn bad habits as well as good. Students are not necessarily placed with the better teachers in a school.

Given all this, it is not surprising that beginning teachers experience considerable shock once they assume full classroom duties. They assume these duties all at once, in full measure, on their first day on the job. The task is more difficult than they had realized. There is no one in the room to help, and they know at once that they must sink or swim. Their ordeal is largely private, and much is learned simply through trial and error.[91]

Of course, beginners often turn to experienced teachers or administrators for help, but they use these sources only selectively, "adapting" other people's practices to their own "personal styles and situations."[92] Among Lortie's respondents, two-thirds emphasized that direct classroom experience was their major means of learning how to teach. Thirty-eight percent mentioned that other teachers were important, but interestingly, almost half of these were referring to former teachers rather than peers.[93] In other words, they had learned by observing and interacting with teachers while they were still students.

It is clear from these facts that teachers develop rather private and individualistic solutions to classroom problems.[94] As we discussed earlier, their expertise does not seem to derive from a shared body of principles applicable to the daily life of the classroom. Neither does their expertise seem to be based in a common set of practices developed through close contacts and communications among teachers. When teachers do learn from others, they pick and choose from many alternative models and add to these their own personal idiosyncracies. Their training does not produce a homogeneous group of technically expert practitioners.

### College and University Professors

Training to teach at the college or university level involves several years in a highly specialized graduate department. The student studies little beyond one particular discipline—taking courses, passing comprehensive examinations, writing a master's thesis, and perhaps finishing a dissertation. Ideally, the dissertation is a major piece of original research, and the Doctor of Philosophy is a research degree.

When asked to assess their graduate education, the vast majority of students express high levels of overall satisfaction.[95] Nevertheless, they also voice a considerable number of complaints. Among these complaints are the irrelevance of their programs for future employment, the lack of adequate training for both teaching and research, overspecialization, and pressures to conform.[96] Indeed, there are many aspects of the graduate student role that provide reason to complain. The experience is usually fraught with tension and anxiety. Competition among students may be fierce. Faculty sponsors may be highly critical and rarely available. The work load may be horrendous, and pressures to hurry up and finish may increase as the student ages beyond the typical point of entering the labor market. Lortie has referred to some of these experiences as a series of "shared ordeals."[97] Students turn to each other for support and understanding, and they develop a sense of solidarity and collegiality that molds their identification with their discipline and their preparation for it—something which, Lortie points out, is missing in the experiences of the public school teacher.

Some groups of graduate students may have greater "ordeals" than others. Several studies have suggested that faculty and male graduate students may be openly antagonistic to female students, refusing to take them seriously or to provide necessary intellectual support.[98] Charges of the sexual exploitation of female graduate students by male faculty have also been voiced frequently, and there is evidence that women have been discriminated against in admissions and financial aid.[99]

Graduate training usually does not include any instruction in teaching. However, a great many graduate students help support themselves by becoming teaching assistants. Teaching assistants often have full responsibility for undergraduate courses, although at other times they may merely assist regular faculty by grading examinations, advising students, and so on. They rarely receive much in the way of supervision, however, and formal instruction in how to teach is extremely rare. Teaching assistantships are usually awarded on the basis of a student's grades and general progress, and not on the basis of teaching ability.

To what extent does graduate training prepare students for their roles as college and university faculty? The answer is not simple. For one thing, there is a great deal of variation in professional role requirements from one academic institution to the next. A Carnegie Commission Report indicated that only 17 percent of the faculty at high-quality universities spent as many as 9 hours each week in the classroom; however, 79 percent of these had recent publications as proof of their research productivity. At the other extreme—in junior colleges—82 percent of the faculty spent at least 9 hours a week in the classroom, but only 14 percent had recent publications.[100]

In a more recent survey, faculty at 2-year colleges averaged six hours a week on research and scholarship and fifteen hours in the classroom. Faculty at 4-year colleges and universities averaged ten hours per week on research and scholarship and eleven hours in the classroom.[101] The educational background of these faculties varied accordingly. At the high-quality universities of the Carnegie Report, 59 percent of the faculty possessed a Ph.D.; at the junior colleges, only 5 percent had the Ph.D.[102] More recently, over 70 percent of faculty at 4-year colleges and universities have been shown to have the Ph.D., but only 15 percent of the faculty at 2-year colleges.[103]

Thus, there appears to have been a rough correspondence between graduate training and role requirements. Institutions that expected high research productivity required the Ph.D., a research-oriented degree. Institutions that expected large amounts of teaching required only a master's degree. Furthermore, there was evidence of a rough match between these institutions' role expectations and their faculty members' preferences. Individuals interested in research were much more likely to be affiliated with research-oriented institutions and individuals interested mainly in teaching were found primarily in the teaching-oriented institutions.[104]

We noted earlier that changes in the academic labor market will enable many junior colleges and teaching-oriented institutions to "upgrade" their staffs by hiring Ph.Ds. If this happens, a large number of "frustrated researchers" may emerge in these institutions. On the one hand, these colleges will have faculty members who have been trained to do research and want to do it. On the other hand, they will have heavy teaching loads and few institutional supports to facilitate this research. One graduate-student friend of ours recently described the "severe role discontinuity" she experienced after accepting employment at such a college. The college not only expected her to do a great deal of teaching, but intended to evaluate her primarily in terms of the numbers of students she attracted to her classes. The contrast between the values of her graduate instructors and those of her employer was nothing short of a "reality shock."

It may be that many future academics would be better served by a new degree program that trains and certifies them as teachers rather than researchers. Such a program might go beyond a master's degree by acquainting prospective professors with some of the new educational technology, new journals devoted to teaching, and new programs for work and study outside the classroom. At this point, however, it is research that brings maximum prestige and a secure sense of "professional" accomplishment—and we do not see change on the horizon.

## Career Patterns and Commitments

Professionals are expected to be strongly committed to lifelong careers in their chosen occupations. Ideally, their professional identifications are so strong that they rarely consider leaving their profession, except for compelling reasons. Most professional schools do not want casual students, and professional training for someone who may not actually practice a profession over a long period is generally seen as a waste.

### Professional Commitments among Public School Teachers

Commitment to schoolteaching is reflected in choices to enter the profession and to persevere in it. The data indicate that teaching is a low-commitment field. Perhaps as many as 20 percent of those who are certified to teach each year never actually become full-time teachers.[105] Large percentages of those who do enter leave within the first three years. One researcher found that 79 percent of males and 66 percent of females survived beyond the first year, but only 40 percent of males and 28 percent of females remained active after four years.[106] More recent data indicate that perseverence is increasing and that gender differentials have diminished. Mark and Anderson studied teacher survival rates in the St. Louis metropolitan area and found that 84 percent of the males and 81 percent of the females survived beyond the first year. Further, 65 percent of the males and 57 percent of the females survived after four years.[107]

Among men, aspirations for administrative careers in education are a major factor in the relatively low commitment to teaching.[108] Administration offers a "career" in ways that teaching does not. Higher salaries, promotions, prestige, and power are all much more available to the successful administrator than to the teacher.

Traditionally, aspirations for administrative careers have not been an important factor in lowering commitment among women. However, large percentages of women left teaching upon marriage or motherhood, and most admitted to putting their careers secondary to family considerations. Among women, then, those who never married showed the highest levels of commitment to their occupation, and stayed the longest.[109] The others varied their participation in the work force according to their life-cycle stages, dropping out when young children or a husband's career demanded it.

When commitment to teaching is measured by the number of hours worked each week, the differences among men, unmarried women, and married women are very small.[110] Secondary school teachers tend to work slightly longer each week than elementary school teachers, and men are concentrated at the secondary level. If level of teaching is taken into account, it is the unmarried woman who works the longest hours, with men and married women, in that order, coming next.[111] Men and women also spend their work-related hours differently. Women spend more time than men each week doing instructional tasks such as grading papers or writing lesson plans after school. Men spend more hours than women in compensated noninstructional activities, such as coaching sports.[112]

If commitment is measured in terms of personal funds spent on "professional growth activities," women come out on top. A higher percentage of female teachers report earning additional college credit, and females report spending more money than men on college expenses. This is a reversal of the earlier tendency, reported as late as 1976, for men to outspend women.[113] Overall, male teachers earn higher salaries than female teachers.[114] This means that female teachers are spending a higher percentage of their salary on continuing their education than are males.

There are strong indications that these patterns may be changing, especially in regard to women. For example, the 1971 survey of teachers by the National Education Association Research Division showed that the "percentage of women who have interrupted their careers for marriage or full-time homemaking had declined from 17 to 10 percent from 1966."[115] The 1981 NEA survey show this figure to have remained stabilized over the last decade.[116] This in spite of the fact that an increasing percentage of women teachers have been married over these years.[117] Indeed, research by Parelius on college women has shown that there is a real shift in the percentage who intend to remain in the labor market even if they marry and become mothers.[118] The uninterrupted career pattern has become increasingly common. Changes in the teaching labor market may have contributed to this trend. Because of the excess number of teachers over the last several years, it became increasingly difficult for women who dropped out of teaching to return. Now the demand for teachers is again on the rise. It remains to be seen whether or not changing attitudes toward careers for women will keep women in the workplace when they again have the flexibility to move in and out with ease.

*Burnout* is common among social-service professionals, including teachers. The teacher's lonely and stressful work often produces mental and physical exhaustion. Emotional detachment, irritability, lack of concern for student welfare, and diminished professional commitment are commonly noted symptoms of burnout.[119] There is no standard measure of burnout, but reluctance to teach again if given a second chance to choose a career is a reasonably good indicator. A nationwide survey of teachers conducted by the National Education Association in 1981 found that 36 percent of those sampled would "probably" or "certainly" not enter teaching again. This percentage has increased steadily from a low of 11 percent in 1961.[120] A 1982 survey of teachers in New York State asked, "If you had it to do all over again would you teach or go into another profession?" Forty-seven percent of the respondents indicated that they would go into another profession.[121] Although this may reflect expanded employment alternatives as well as dissatisfaction with teaching, burnout does appear to be a large and growing problem.

### Professional Commitments among College Professors

Very little information is available about the career commitments of college and university professors. The 1969 Carnegie Commission Survey of Faculty and Student Opinion asked faculty respondents to agree or disagree with the statement: "I tend to subordinate all aspects of my life to my work."[122] Less than half of the respondents agreed, either strongly or with reservations. Differences between men and women were relatively small: 45 percent of the men, as compared to 41 percent of the women, agreed. When marital status was considered, though, differences between the sexes were greatest among the married—with 44 percent of the men, but only 32 percent of the women, agreeing. These results suggest a somewhat lower level of commitment among married women, though it is important to remember that the majority of both sexes disagreed with the statement.

Graduate students were asked an identical question.[123] Overall, the women were about as likely to agree as the men. Women who were divorced or separated stood out as being exceptionally committed, more so than any other category; married women and divorced or separated men were the least committed.

Married women are also more likely than men or other women to drop out of graduate training.[124] It is always important to keep in mind, however, that men and women may be faced with different types of experiences and opportunities. Feldman did an extensive analysis of dedication among male and female graduate students.[125] He concluded that the ways in which women "appear" to be less dedicated than men are probably a result of differential treatment by faculty and resultant blows to the women's self-concepts and confidence. In addition, marriage seems to handicap the female graduate student, but stabilize and benefit the male; divorce seems to have a positive, freeing effect on female students, though, at least in terms of dedication and success in career preparation.[126]

The overwhelming majority of both men and women who complete the Ph.D. enter the labor market and stay there. For example, Centra's study of 3,658 men and women who received a doctorate (Ph.D. or Ed.D.) in 1950, 1960, or 1968 revealed that 91 percent of the women and 97 percent of the men were in the labor market immediately after receiving the degree.[127] From that time until 1973, the women were unemployed 7 percent to 8 percent of the time, while the men were unemployed only 0.4 percent of the time. Women were also more likely to have worked part-time and to have interrupted their careers. Fifty-seven percent of the reasons cited for such interruptions were related to marital and parental responsibilities, including pregnancy, lack of suitable jobs available in their husband's locale, lack of competent domestic help or day care for children, and an anti-nepotism policy of husband's employer. Nevertheless, over 60 percent of the women worked full-time without interruption since receiving their degree, and the overwhelming majority of others spent most of their postdoctoral years in the labor market. Women who receive the Ph.D. or Ed.D. are much more likely to be unmarried and childless than women in the general population. However, once a woman receives her degree, she is likely to be working and pursuing her career, whether married or not.

Centra also asked his respondents about the number of hours they worked each week. Women worked a median of 50.4 hours per week, with married women working 49 hours and single ones working 52. Men worked an average of 52.1 hours per week, with married men working 53 and single men working 51. The magnitude of these differences is small, but their pattern is consistent with several we have already discussed: Marriage seems to free men to work, but slow women down. When single, however, women work longer hours than comparable men. It may also be true, of course, that married men and single women feel the greatest economic pressure to succeed and are therefore more motivated than others.

Of course, as we indicated in our discussion of gender, men and women have somewhat different career patterns. In Centra's study, two-thirds of the men and 70 percent of the women were employed in colleges or universities, but women were concentrated at two-year colleges and (nondoctoral granting) four-year colleges. In 1978, women made up less than 30 percent of the faculty at four-year colleges and universities but approximately 44 percent of the faculty at two-year colleges.[128] Faculty at four-year colleges and universities work more hours per week than faculty at two-year colleges.[129] This may account for some of the differences Centra reported in the workweek of men and women. In general, women find it more difficult to get initial full-time academic appointments; are less likely to be hired in prestigious colleges and universities, even when they have the Ph.D.; are promoted more slowly; and receive lower salaries than men, even when they are in the same faculty rank. Factors such as intelligence, years of experience, research productivity, or dedication do not explain these differences.[130]

Changes in the academic marketplace may well be affecting the degree of commitment of college and university faculty. At present most faculty members look forward to a series of promotions: instructor, assistant professor, associate professor, and full professor. Each promotion brings more material rewards, status, and influence within their institutions. As job opportunities for young faculty have declined, many find that they can obtain only temporary employment, with little hope for promotions or tenure. Lortie points out that one reason for the low commitment of public school teachers is that they cannot look forward to promotions or increased rewards for continued effort.[131] Currently some college and university faculty face a similar lack of incentives. Consequently, there is an increased interest in careers outside of academia. There, professional status is based solely on disciplinary expertise and research ability. General commitment to teaching among insecure young faculty who might have to leave academia for employment is not likely to be high.

The work of college professors, like that of schoolteachers, is often stressful and lonely. This is especially true for untenured junior faculty and senior faculty who feel trapped in their positions. Thus, it should not be surprising to find that burnout is also a problem in academia. Although the phenomenon is more and more widely recognized, to date it has not been the subject of much research.[132]

One exception is a major research project recently sponsored by the Carnegie Foundation for the Advancement of Teaching.[133] Results indicate that many faculty members are unhappy with their jobs. Nearly one-fourth of those sampled were considering entering another line of work, and close to 30 percent felt "trapped" in their jobs. More than half would "seriously consider" a different academic job if one were available. Over 20 percent would not become college teachers if they had the choice again, and 40 percent had become less enthusiastic about their careers than they once were. Many faculty members were unhappy with the quality of their students, their lack of job security, and their relatively low salaries.

## Rewards and Satisfactions

### Public School Teachers

The rewards associated with any occupation can be classified as either *material* or *psychic*. When asked about the major rewards offered by their occupation, the vast majority of public school teachers focus on the psychic satisfactions experienced in the classroom. That is probably because the financial rewards are meager. In 1983 it was found that the average salary *after 12 years of teaching* was only $17,000 per year.[134] When inflation is taken into account, teachers actually earned less, on the average, than they did in 1976. Most teachers had to depend on income from spouses, moonlighting, and/or summer work to supplement their wages.[135] Of course, teachers enjoy material rewards beyond salary. These include generous fringe benefits, frequent and lengthy vacations, time compatibility, and an unusual level of job security. Still, the salient rewards are psychic, not material.

Students, rather than material benefits, colleagues, administrators, parents, facilities, or the community, are the teacher's primary source of reward.[136] Consequently, distractions from the work of the classroom are almost universally judged negatively. Interruptions from visitors, administrators, or "extra duties" are resented, and a "good day" is one in which the teacher's time is devoted solely to the class.[137]

The precise goals that teachers have for their students are, however, rather vague and ambiguous. Among those frequently mentioned are improving the students' character, teaching academic skills, and developing an interest in learning. Many teachers aspire to helping all of their students, voicing a strong commitment to universalistic treatment in the classroom. Nevertheless, when teachers are asked about their greatest source of pride, they tend to describe successes with individual students rather than with groups of students. Particular cases in which the teacher feels responsible for substantial behavioral or intellectual improvement on the part of a child are the most commonly cited examples. In relating these stories, teachers often talk about giving special attention to some children who seem to be in greater need than the rest.[138]

The teacher's actual success in accomplishing classroom goals is difficult to measure. Many teachers report anxiety about not knowing whether they are effective. "Is anything *really* happening in my classroom?" they seem to ask. Certainly, teachers can and do use examinations to measure academic learning, but their more general goals of improving character or inspiring an interest in learning are more elusive. Changes that they do manage to detect may be only transitory, and a student can "slip back" at any moment. Furthermore, the teacher is only one of many influences in a child's life. Just why a student shows improvement at any particular time is difficult to determine—events outside the classroom may be as responsible as events inside.

Lortie sees these problems as creating a series of "endemic uncertainties" with which teachers must learn to cope. For the most part, teachers learn to cope on an individual basis, each facing these dilemmas alone and in the privacy of the classroom. To be sure, teachers sometimes turn to each other for support. They share stories about their successes and failures and assure each other that no teacher can reach every student and that some classes are just too troublesome for any teacher to manage well. In general, though, teachers as an occupational group do not have collective strategies by which they can define goals or measure accomplishments. Each teacher struggles more or less independently to maximize psychic rewards and overcome "recurrent doubts about the value of their work with students."[139]

### College and University Professors

Much less is known about the rewards experienced by college and university professors. Some professors are clearly more interested in research than in teaching. For these, the classroom may be a source of annoyance rather than satisfaction, taking time away from activities that are both personally preferred and more highly rewarded by their institutions. A survey of college and university professors asked its respondents whether their interests were primarily in teaching or research.[140] The answers varied considerably from one type of institution to the next. At one extreme were the highly select universities—those that admit only extremely competent undergraduates. At these institutions, 50 percent of the faculty said that their interests were either very heavily in research or leaning in that direction. The remainder said that their interests were either very heavily in teaching or leaning in that direction. At the other extreme were the two-year colleges. At these institutions, only 5 percent of the faculty were heavily interested in research or leaning in that direction, and the remaining 95 percent were, of course, more interested in teaching than research. As we saw earlier, the actual amount of contact between faculty and students also varies with the type of institution in a way that is consistent with these results.

It would seem, then, that faculty at universities receive fewer of their rewards from students than faculty at two-year colleges—and perhaps even most four-year colleges; but teaching is clearly important to the majority of faculty members at all types of institutions. Of course, the level of teaching important to each might be different. For example, university professors might find graduate teaching more rewarding than undergraduate teaching, although we do not know for sure.

Professors, like many other workers, often complain of being overworked and underpaid. What are the facts? According to their own accounts, professors do work long hours: a quarter of those at 4-year colleges and universities work 60 hours per week.[141] But this is not unusual among professionals in other fields. Further, only about half of the work time is dedicated to teaching, advising, and administrative activities.[142] The rest is discretionary time, which can be used for keeping up with developments in their fields, scholarly research, writing, and consulting activities outside the university. Moreover, college classes are in session for relatively short periods of time; thus, professors have even more time outside the classroom than school teachers. However, discretionary time is not the same as leisure time. Indeed, many professors feel they have little or no leisure time at all because the demands of scholarship are so great and open-ended. They find it hard to enjoy guiltless leisure in the evenings, on the weekends, and even between terms and semesters.

The base salary of college professors is low in comparison to many other professionals with comparable amounts of professional training. Furthermore, inflation eroded the purchasing power of that salary by nearly 20 percent between the early 1970s and the early 1980s.[143] Thus, it is not surprising that most professors supplement their base salaries by teaching during the summer and moonlighting. In fact, four out of every five professors augment their salary through some form of additional professional activity, raising their income by 21 percent on the average.[144] Table 6–1 reports data comparing the 1983 income of professors to that of individuals in selected other occupations. Professors earned significantly less than lawyers, engineers, and economists. But they earned significantly more than editors and reporters, librarians, teachers, social workers, and clergy.

**TABLE 6–1 Average Weekly Earnings of Wage and Salary Workers in 1983**

| Occupation | Earnings |
|---|---|
| Lawyers and judges | $650 |
| Engineers | $603 |
| Economists | $600 |
| Managers (marketing, advertising, public relations) | $559 |
| Mathematical and computer scientists | $546 |
| Pharmacists | $509 |
| Natural scientists | $508 |
| College faculty | $502 |
| Editors and reporters | $385 |
| Librarians | $383 |
| Teachers | $365 |
| Social workers | $327 |
| Clergy | $308 |

*Source:* Earl F. Mellor, "Weekly Earnings in 1983: A Look at More than 200 Occupations," *Monthly Labor Review,* 108 (January, 1985), p. 55.

## Professional Organizations and Unions

### Public School Teachers

Since the 1930s, increasing percentages of public school teachers have become members of professional organizations and unions. Today, teachers are among the most highly organized of American public employees. Sixty-five percent of our teachers nationwide are members of a labor organization,[145] and in many states virtually every teacher belongs. The major organizations of teachers are the National Education Association (NEA) and the American Federation of Teachers (AFT). The NEA has approximately three times as many members (1.3 million) as the urban-based AFT.[146] Both organizations are unions. That is, both the NEA and AFT attempt to improve the wages and working conditions of their members through collective bargaining, and both organizations endorse the use of strikes as part of the bargaining process.

Teachers' militance has increased as inflation has eroded their puchasing power. The most conspicuous evidence of this militancy is the teacher strike. In the period from 1959 to 1965, there were no more than ten work stoppages by teachers in any one year, but 1969, 1970, and 1973 each witnessed over one hundred,[147] and in 1980 there were 252 walkouts![148] In addition to striking, however, both organizations lobby for legislation favorable to their interests, support sympathetic political candidates, and occasionally even try to elect school teachers to political office.[149]

These activities represent a major change in the policies of the NEA. As late as the 1960s, the NEA was firmly opposed to work stoppages and tended to be party-neutral in political campaigns.[150] Many teachers considered unions and their activities to be "socialistic." Others approved of unions and strikes for blue-collar workers, but viewed them as incompatible with "professional" status, and therefore, inappropriate for teachers. After all, they argued, teachers and their boards of education do not have a conflict of interests, as do managers and workers. Teachers and board members are all public servants, dedicated to the welfare of students and their communities.[151] Consequently, the NEA confined its concerns to raising standards of teacher training, ethics, and practice, and to promoting public respect for teaching as a profession.

The AFT considered itself a union from the start, though. It emphasized the position of the teacher as an employee, and like other unions, pressed hard for improvements in salary, benefits, and working conditions. The eventual successes of the AFT, combined with many broader changes in American society, prompted greater recognition of these concerns by the NEA.

Today, the goals and activities of the two organizations have converged to a considerable extent. Although the controversy surrounding militant activity and professionalism has not entirely disappeared, the majority of teachers now approve of strikes—at least as a last resort,[152] and both organizations are concerned with the interests of teachers as a professional group. Indeed, studies of militant teachers reveal that those teachers who are most militant tend also to be those who are most concerned with their professional status.[153]

One area in which the activities of the NEA and the AFT are clearly compatible with professionalization concerns teacher autonomy. One characteristic of professionals is that they are not subject to the judgments or control of outsiders when practicing their profession. Teachers, however, are routinely judged and controlled by others.[154] For example, teachers do not have control over their own training or the procedures by which they are licensed. Furthermore, school boards, not teachers, have formal control over curriculum, textbooks, and even teaching methods. Additional formal constraints exist in the form of state and federal laws, policies established by local and state boards, administrative decisions handed down by superintendents, and informal pressures exerted by parents and community-based groups. Still, as we learned in our earlier chapter on bureaucratization, informal social norms have developed that tend to neutralize many of these constraints. In practice, most teachers enjoy considerable freedom and autonomy within their classrooms.

Many people have argued that teaching will not become a profession until teachers attain control over their own occupation, and in recent years the NEA and the AFT have increasingly concerned themselves with this issue. Teachers are now pressing for control over policy decisions, curriculum content, class size, book selection, and so on. This means, of course, that teachers are often opposed to a variety of other groups who may also be seeking increasing control over these decisions. For example, militant teachers are not likely to support increases in either student or community power if these increases are made at the teachers' expense. Teachers are now beginning to say that they—as professionals—are better able to judge what should go on in the classroom than other community members. In response to charges that parents should make these decisions and that schools should reflect the values of parents rather than teachers, NEA former executive secretary Terry Herndon expressed the new confidence of the militant teacher:

> There is a notion in many communities that the purpose of the school is to perpetuate the culture, to indoctrinate the children in the predominant attitudes of the community . . . . We do not accept that as the role of the schools . . . . In most places, the traditional values have included racism, sexism, white-male dominance, Protestantism, and things like that. Some of these values should not be preserved . . . . There has been a dramatic change in the values of American society . . . . We reflect that. We also reflect a better educated, more professional group of teachers. They are not interested in being dictated to by a school board or a school administration.[155]

The concern with professionalization among teachers is evident as well in their demands for improved salaries and material benefits. These demands are now placed in the context of the needs of the profession. For example, the NEA and the AFT argue that improving salaries will attract more qualified people to teaching, allow educational requirements to be raised, encourage people to stay in teaching for a longer period of time, and permit teachers to spend their time improving relevant skills rather than seeking supplementary income through second jobs and summer employment.

### College and University Professors

Until recently, college and university faculty relied almost exclusively on the American Association of University Professors (AAUP) to represent their interests as a profession. The AAUP committed itself, particularly, to the preservation of academic freedom and the protection of faculty members from arbitrary and capricious dismissal. The AAUP has been a staunch defender of academic tenure, and over the years has issued a series of guidelines regarding promotion and dismissal procedures. Institutions that violated these guidelines were censored by the AAUP and members were urged not to accept employment with them until the situation was corrected. The AAUP has also been concerned with improving faculty salaries and working conditions. It has published salary and benefit scales, publicizing the salaries and benefits offered at various colleges and universities and rating each institution according to how satisfactory its scale is.

During the last several years, the AAUP has moved gradually in the direction of more militant activity. As late as 1972, the outgoing president of the AAUP issued a statement in which he strongly disapproved of collective bargaining at the college and university level.[156] His statement reflected the views of many professors who believed—and still believe—that collective bargaining is not appropriate for academics. Their arguments, like those offered by the NEA in the past, are that collective bargaining creates an adversary relationship between faculty, administrators, and governing boards, polarizes interests, and involves outsiders (such as arbitrators) in issues that should be decided by the faculty. In the case of strikes it is also argued that "the educational mission" is deliberately harmed "in order to promote the personal employee interest, in contradiction to the service ideal. . . ."[157]

Nevertheless, in May 1972 the AAUP voted by an overwhelming margin "to pursue collective bargaining as a major additional way of realizing [our] goals in higher education."[158] Since that time, the AAUP has served as an official agent of collective bargaining at a number of colleges and universities in which the faculty has selected it for this role.

The AAUP is not the only organization serving as a bargaining agent, however. The NEA and the AFT have both expanded to include college and university faculty, and, in fact, represent more campuses that have official bargaining agents than does the AAUP.[159]

Collective bargaining among college faculty has developed unevenly. As Figure 6–2 indicates, unionization has been most common in public, as opposed to private, institutions, and in two-year, as opposed to four-year, colleges and universities. Faculty organizing activity slowed after 1981 as a result of legislative inaction and a key judicial decision. In order for organizing to proceed in public institutions, state legislatures must pass enabling legislation. But most Southern and Rocky Mountain states have refused to pass such legislation. Unionization in private institutions was slowed dramatically by a 1980 Supreme Court ruling (the *Yeshiva* case), which stated that private college faculty did not have collective bargaining rights because they were managers, not employees.[160]

**FIGURE 6–2.** Number of Collective Bargaining Agreements.

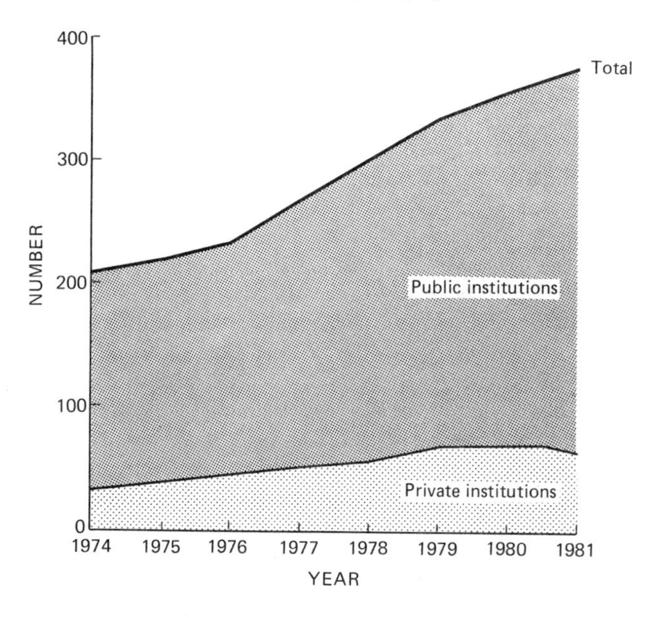


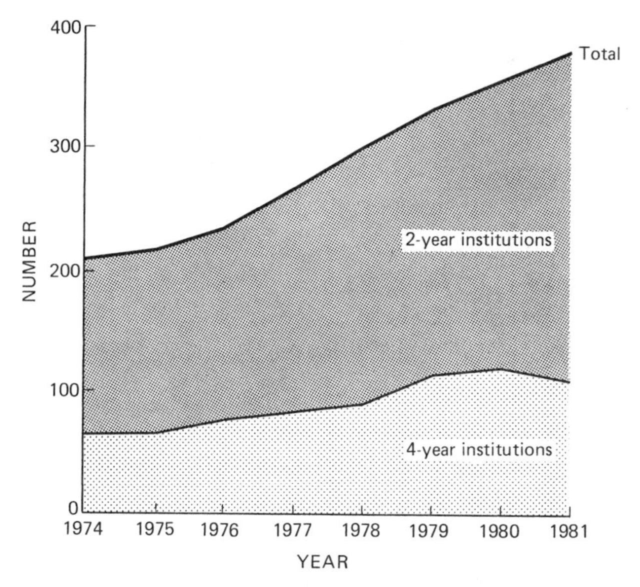


*Source:* Valena White Plisko, National Center for Education Statistics, *The Condition of Education: 1983* (Washington, D.C.: Government Printing Office, 1983), p. 105.

Campus activism tends to be concentrated in institutions that have traditionally been lowest in prestige, financial resources, and economic benefits. University faculty and those at the most prestigious four-year institutions have been more resistant.

There are several explanations for this pattern. The two-year colleges are closest to public school systems in terms of the relationships among faculty, administrators, and boards of governors. Many of these institutions are even under the same governing boards as the kindergarten through twelfth-grade system in their area. Their faculty are much more likely to regard themselves as "employees" rather than as professionals. It was natural, then, that the AFT and the NEA activities of the public school teachers came to encompass this group as well. At the opposite extreme are the faculties at highly prestigious institutions. These faculty have enjoyed a rather strong position relative to their administrators and boards of governors, maintaining a great deal of influence over academic and faculty affairs. Further, these faculty tend to be more cosmopolitan and find it is easier to move from one institution to another when they are dissatisfied. Consequently, they have felt less need to organize. This pattern of resistance among relatively "elite" faculty exists within campuses as well as between them. An extensive analysis by Lipset and Ladd has revealed that faculty members with research grants, high scholarly productivity, high salaries, and tenure are more resistant to collective bargaining than others.[161]

This is not surprising. Many people have suggested that collective bargaining will do little to enhance the position of "elite" faculty, and that it might even weaken their bargaining position. One effect of collective bargaining is likely to be a "leveling" of the differences among faculty teaching within the same bargaining unit.[162] Unions tend to be egalitarian. For the most part, they oppose merit increments and other benefits that are unequally distributed among members. Currently, faculty members who have national reputations, attract grant money, and receive competitive job offers from other universities receive the highest salaries and best working conditions. Faculty who work part-time, or who are still graduate students, or working on short-term contracts receive the lowest salaries. This latter group is often denied medical and other fringe benefits, lacks any semblance of job security, and is required to teach heavier course loads than senior faculty. Similar differences often exist between faculties of different campuses or schools within large multi-institutional systems. For example, faculty at the State University may be better off than faculty at the State Colleges. Available data indicate that thus far the greatest gains from faculty unionism "have accrued to the teaching faculty on the margin of the core faculty . . . . The core faculty 'haves' have shored up some of their benefits from possible attack but otherwise gained the least from bargaining."[163] In fact, Lipset and Ladd believe that the AFT and NEA have already made appeals "to the resentment against the prestigious faculty of those with little power by complaining about academic 'elitism,' the 'academic entrepreneur,' 'the "star" scholar.' . . ."[164] and the "elites" may be reacting protectively in return. For example, the Association of American

Law Schools has recommended that law faculties exclude themselves from university-wide bargaining units whenever possible, hoping, perhaps, to make a better deal on their own and to avoid the leveling that might otherwise result.[165]

Given the tightening academic job market, more and more faculty will find it advantageous to support collective bargaining. This will be particularly true of young, untenured faculty. Many colleges are making promotion and tenure much more difficult to obtain, citing declining student bodies, fiscal crises, and the abundance of candidates among their reasons. The unions are generally opposed to dismissals for these reasons, except under real emergency circumstances.

Some people have argued that unionism will result in a decline in the quality of institutions in which it is successful.[166] They point out that unions will make it difficult to dismiss "merely satisfactory" professors in order to find truly superior ones, and that they will destroy the meritocratic distribution of rewards that now encourages maximum development of faculty talent. Not everyone would agree with these predictions. There are real questions about the degree to which the current system of rewards in academia is genuinely meritocratic. We have seen repeated examples of discrimination against certain groups of faculty—such as against females and members of minority groups. It may well be that these and many others are simply exploited by a system that rewards only one kind of success and then systematically distributes the assets necessary for that success to only a limited few. For example, research, rather than teaching, is most highly rewarded, yet many faculty are burdened by heavy teaching loads, given no facilities or money for research, and excluded from important communications networks through which ideas for research, information about grants, and connections with publishers circulate. Those who do not publish are then told that they receive fewer rewards because they have not earned any more. Apparently, many faculty members are skeptical about the meritocratic basis of academic rewards. The 1969 Carnegie Commission data showed that almost half of all college and university faculty agreed that "Many of the highest paid university professors get where they are by being 'operators' rather than by their scholarly or scientific contributions."[167]

In addition to being concerned with material benefits, working conditions, and tenure, unions are also involved with issues of professional autonomy and the voice of faculty in campus affairs. Among the issues now considered negotiable by the NEA, AAUP, and AFT are: "admissions, class size, workload, calendar, procedures for budget formulation, participation in institutional planning and allocation of resources, procedures for the selection of certain administrators and department chairmen, traditional economic items, and tenure matters."[168] During this period of economic retrenchment, centralization, and consolidation on the college campuses, the position of faculty members is likely to be weakened unless they join together and bargain on a collective basis. The unions will attempt to formalize faculty influence over academic policy as their traditional claims to this power are eroded by these changing conditions.

## SUMMARY, CONCLUSIONS, AND POLICY ISSUES

In this chapter we traced the increasing professionalization of teaching from the colonial period to the present. During most of the colonial period, and continuing into the nineteenth century, teaching was an occupation of low status and even lower material benefits. Most teachers had little education beyond that of their students, with no knowledge of teaching methods or child psychology. For the most part, teaching was thought of as a temporary or supplementary occupation, something to do until a better job or a proposal of marriage came along.

The nineteenth and twentieth centuries witnessed substantial changes in the nature of teaching as an occupation. Normal schools were established for teacher training, and special courses were added to college and university programs. Research and academic publications in education and psychology improved the knowledge base upon which courses in teaching methods and classroom management could be developed. In-service programs, journals of education, and teacher organizations were established. Teachers gained a sense of professional identity and slowly improved their working conditions and status in the general community.

In spite of these substantial gains, though, teaching is clearly not as professionalized as a number of other occupations. Relative to law and medicine, for example, teaching might be classified only as a "semiprofession."[169] Teaching at the primary and secondary levels is neither a lucrative nor a prestigious occupation. The power and autonomy that characterize both law and medicine are absent, and teachers are, at least in a formal sense, constrained by school board policies and administrative regulations. Teachers, unlike physicians, for example, do not control their own training or licensing, nor do they have final say over curriculum and methods (although, as was pointed out previously, teachers do have informal, de facto control over their classrooms).

Furthermore, the training required to become a teacher is not particularly challenging or costly. The body of expertise upon which this training is built and upon which teachers' claims to professional autonomy must be based is relatively weak. There is little in the way of shared technical culture or systematized solutions to routine classroom problems available to teachers.

For these and other reasons, some sociologists have suggested that teaching is not (and perhaps never will be) fully professionalized. At minimum they suggest that several important changes would have to occur before professionalization could be fully accomplished.[170] For example, teacher training would have to be extended and improved. More systematic programs of on-the-job training, through which new teachers could be taught the classroom techniques perfected by experienced colleagues, would probably be needed. Teachers would have to give up some of their current individuality and concern themselves more with systematizing their knowledge, conforming to professional standards, and incorporating scientific research on education into their daily activities.

Then, as a unified, highly trained and self-disciplined group, they might demand more autonomy from outside control and restrictions.

In 1986 the Carnegie Commission Task Force on Teaching as a Profession issued a multi-faceted package of proposals for restructuring and professionalizing teaching.[171] Among the most important proposed changes are: (1) create a national board, similar to those serving the professions of law and medicine, that would be responsible for establishing high standards of pedagogical practice and certifying those who meet them; (2) eliminate the undergraduate education major and strengthen Masters of Arts degree programs in education; (3) upgrade teachers' salaries to make them competitive with other professions; (4) shift many responsibilities from principals to teachers including selection of instructional methods and materials, class scheduling, staffing structure, and student placement; (5) create a new position, "lead teacher," with responsibility for facilitating collegial interaction among teachers, and (6) increase teacher accountability for student performance in proportion to increased teacher autonomy. The two major teachers' unions (NEA and AFT) have endorsed much of the plan, including the creation of a national board. However, because the report calls for a significant redistribution of power, opposition from groups representing administrators and school boards can be expected. It is too early to determine just how many, if any, of these proposals will actually be adopted.

Although some people continue to think of unions as unprofessional, it is clear that the NEA and AFT will play a major role in the professionalization of education. Teacher strikes are still disapproved of by many teachers and laymen alike, and one adverse effect of such strikes is a frequent loss of parental support and confidence. Also, unionization in many ways increases bureaucratization. Collective bargaining usually results in the formal specification of new regulations governing relationships between teachers, administrators, and lay boards of education. Grievance procedures and a host of other bureaucratic mechanisms for safeguarding teacher rights and defining teacher obligations proliferate. Nevertheless, it is clear from recent developments among teachers at all levels that unions can be used to enhance professional autonomy and control over policy decisions.

Professors, in institutions of higher education, face somewhat different problems. The degree of professionalization among college and university faculty varies considerably from one type of institution to the next. Historically, college faculties became increasingly professionalized as they relied more heavily on specialized bodies of knowledge for their expertise. Today, those faculty members who are specialists in narrow areas, or who do research or other creative work, or publish for the international community of scholars in their fields have the greatest degree of professional autonomy, prestige, and material benefits. Nevertheless, even the position of these "elite" academicians seems threatened by recent developments in higher education. The growing surplus of Ph.Ds, the declining student body at many institutions, and fiscal pressures have resulted in a climate of general belt-tightening. Legislatures and administrators seem increasingly interested in consolidation and centralization, in gaining more control and in pressing for accountability for faculty time and use of resources. At the same time, job opportunities for young, untenured faculty are becoming increasingly scarce.

Given this climate, unionization appears to be growing in popularity. Collective action can obviously strengthen the position of faculty without the "credentials" that provide the basis of autonomy for those in more prestigious schools. But given the current changes in the academic marketplace, it might also be necessary to protect the autonomy of young scholars and those who would have remained relatively independent in the past. Of course, some people have predicted that unionization will destroy a basically meritocratic reward structure in higher education and eventually lower faculty quality. Others believe unionization will result in a more equitable system of rewards, more opportunities for scholarly activity in a wider range of institutions, and recognition of other types of faculty competence, such as teaching.

Unionization at all levels may increase teacher power, but it is also important to ask about the implications of unionization for the power of other groups involved in the education process. Earlier, we mentioned that a number of collective bargaining settlements include references to student evaluations. Increasing militancy on the part of teachers might well result in more frequent confrontations with students, parents, and other groups who want some degree of control over the schools and those who teach in them; for example, some student organizations are now arguing that teacher power and student power are not compatible with one another. On some campuses, students have even opposed unionization of their faculty.[172] Similarly, in an interesting article on the United Federation of Teachers, Myron Brenton points out that the UFT has moved from a traditionally liberal—or even radical—set of interests in social issues to a conservative position in defense of teacher power.[173] He argues that in New York City, for example, the UFT opposed decentralization and community control over the schools because it saw in such control a potential weakening of the teachers' power and position. Of course, as we shall see in Chapter 7, not everyone agrees with this characterization. As our quote from Terry Herndon's comments revealed, community control can be seen as a conservative force, while teachers' unions may be seen as a liberating one. Clearly, the full implications of unionization for the politics of education and the professionalization of teachers are yet to be discerned.

## *NOTES*

[1]See, for example, William J. Goode, "Community Within a Community: The Professions," *American Sociological Review,* XXII (February, 1957), 194–200; Everett C. Hughes, *Men and Their Work* (Glencoe: The Free Press, 1958); Christopher Jencks and David Riesman, *The Academic Revolution* (Garden City, New York: Doubleday & Co., 1968), pp. 201–203; and Eliot Friedson, ed. *The Professions and Their Prospects* (Beverly Hills, Calif.: Sage Publications, 1973).

[2]The historical section of this chapter draws heavily from Paul Monroe, *Founding of the American Public School System: A History of Education in the United States,* Vol. VI (New York: The

Macmillan Co., 1940); R. Freeman Butts and Lawrence A. Cremin, *A History of Education in American Culture* (New York: Henry Holt & Co., 1953); and Raymond E. Callahan, *An Introduction to Education in American Society* (New York: Alfred A. Knopf, 1960).

[3]Monroe, *Founding of the American Public School System*, p. 154.

[4]Ibid., p. 149.

[5]Ibid., p. 156.

[6]Ibid., p. 132.

[7]Walter P. Metzger, "Academic Tenure in America: A Historical Essay," pp. 93–159 in Commission on Academic Tenure in Higher Education (William R. Keast and John W. Macy, Jr., Chairman and Cochairman), *Faculty Tenure: A Report and Recommendations* (San Francisco: The Jossey-Bass Series in Higher Education, 1973), pp. 111–12.

[8]S.E. Morison, *Harvard in the Seventeenth Century* (Cambridge, 1936), Vol. 1, p. 15, as cited in Metzger, "Academic Tenure," p. 112.

[9]Ibid., p. 120.

[10]Monroe, *Founding of the American Public School System*, pp. 235–40.

[11]Ibid., pp. 240–41.

[12]Ibid., p. 241.

[13]Ibid., p. 279.

[14]Ibid., p. 361.

[15]Ibid., p. 361.

[16]Ibid., p. 490.

[17]Ibid., pp. 492–96.

[18]Ibid., pp. 385–86.

[19]Ibid., p. 386.

[20]Ibid., p. 386.

[21]Butts and Cremin, *A History of Education*, pp. 287, 449.

[22]Ibid., p. 451.

[23]Ibid., pp. 450–53.

[24]Ibid., p. 450.

[25]Callahan, *An Introduction to Education*, p. 423.

[26]Butts and Cremin, *A History of Education*, p. 457.

[27]Monroe, *Founding of the American Public School System*, p. 250.

[28]Jencks and Riesman, *The Academic Revolution*, p. 6.

[29]Ibid., p. 15.

[30]Metzger, "Academic Tenure," pp. 135–36.

[31]Dan C. Lortie, *School Teacher: A Sociological Study* (Chicago: The University of Chicago Press, 1975).

[32]Suzanne Gardner, *Status of the American Public School Teacher, 1980-81* (National Education Association, 1982), p. 7.

[33]Ibid., p. 71.

[34]Ibid., p. 71.

[35]Ibid., p. 71.

[36]Ibid., p. 71.

[37]W. Timothy Weaver, "Solving the Problem of Teacher Quality, Part 1," *Phi Delta Kappan*, 66, 2 (October, 1984), pp. 108–15.

[38]Gary Sykes, "Caring About Teachers," *Teachers College Record*, 84, 3 (Spring, 1983), p. 579.

[39]W.T. Weaver, "Educators in Supply and Demand: Effects on Quality," *School Review*, 86, 4 (1978), pp. 452–593.

[40]William W. Falk, Carolyn Falkowski, and Thomas Lyson, "Some Plan to Become Teachers: Further Elaboration and Specification," *Sociology of Education*, 54 (January, 1981),

pp. 64–69; Samuel S. Peng, "Education Attracts Fewer Academically High Achieving Young Women," *NCES Bulletin,* (December, 1982), pp. 1–8; Donna Kerr, "Teaching Competence and Teacher Education in the United States," *Teachers College Record,* 84, 3 (Spring, 1983), p. 526.

[41]See Lortie's discussion on "facilitators" in *School Teacher,* pp. 37–50.

[42]Lortie, *School Teacher,* p. 49.

[43]Ibid., p. 29.

[44]For an overview of the many ways women are discouraged, see Nancy Frazier and Myra Sadker, *Sexism in School and Society* (New York: Harper & Row, 1973).

[45]Victor S. Vance and Phillip C. Schlechty, "The Distribution of Academic Ability in the Teaching Force: Policy Implications," *Phi Delta Kappan,* (September, 1982), pp. 22–27.

[46]Saul D. Feldman, *Escape from the Doll's House: Women in Graduate and Professional School Education* (New York: McGraw-Hill Book Co., 1974), p. 129.

[47]Gardner, *Status of the American Public School Teacher,* p. 36.

[48]*Statistical Abstract of the United States* (Washington, D.C.: Government Printing Office, 1986), p. 140.

[49]Georgia Dullea, "Women in Classrooms, Not the Principal's Office," *New York Times* (July 13, 1975), Section 4, p. 7.

[50]Gardner, *Status of the American Public School Teacher,* p. 16.

[51]U.S. Equal Employment Opportunity Commission, *Minorities and Women in Public Elementary and Secondary Schools* (Washington, D.C.: Government Printing Office, 1981), p. 3.

[52]Judith A. Adkinson, "Women in School Administration: A Review of the Research," *Review of Educational Research* 51, 3 (Fall, 1981), p. 320.

[53]National Education Association, *Higher Education Faculty: Characteristics and Opinions* (Washington, D.C.: National Education Association, 1979), p. 7.

[54]Ibid., p. 7.

[55]Oliver Fulton, "Rewards and Fairness: Academic Women in the United States," in Trow (ed.), *Teachers and Students,* pp. 210–15. Also, NEA, *Higher Education,* p. 18.

[56]Fulton, "Rewards and Fairness," pp. 216–20.

[57]Michael R. Ferrari, *Profiles of American College Presidents* (East Lansing: Division of Research, Graduate School of Business Administration, Michigan State University, 1970), p. 163; *Comment,* v. 9 (Fall, 1976), p. 3. (*Comment* is available through the Office of Women in Higher Education, American Council on Education.); Scientific Manpower Commission, *Professional Women and Minorities: A Manpower Data Resource Service,* 5th ed. (Scientific Manpower Commission. August, 1984), p. 132.

[58]*AAUW Journal* (November, 1970) as cited in Nancy Frazier and Myra Sadker, *Sexism in School and Society* (New York: Harper & Row, 1973), p. 164.

[59]Lortie, *School Teacher,* p. 84.

[60]H. Zeigler, "Male and Female: Differing Perceptions of the Teaching Experience," in H. Zeigler, ed., *The Political Life of American Teachers* (Englewood Cliffs, N.J.: Prentice-Hall, 1972).

[61]Neal Gross and Annie B. Trask, *The Sex Factor and the Management of Schools* (New York: John Wiley & Sons, 1976), pp. 71–73, are able to show that even among those teachers who successfully move into administration, males develop aspirations to administrative posts earlier than women. A full 43 percent of the men—but only 13 percent of the women—had done so before age 25.

[62]Gross and Trask, *The Sex Factor,* pp. 40–44 show that these differences exist even among those who successfully become administrators.

[63]P. Schmuck, "Deterrents to Women's Careers in School Management," *Sex Roles,* 1, 4 (1975), p. 188.

[64]See Cynthia Fuchs Epstein, *Women's Place: Options and Limits in Professional Careers* (Berkeley: University of California Press, 1970); Esther Manning Westervelt, *Barriers to Women's Participation in Postsecondary Education: A Review of Research and Commentary as of 1973–*

*74* (Washington, D.C.: Government Printing Office, 1975); Saul D. Feldman, *Escape from the Doll's House.*

[65]Gross and Trask, *The Sex Factor.*

[66]Ibid., p. 47.

[67]Gardner, *Status of the American Public School Teacher,* p. 92.

[68]Phillip Ross Courtney Elliott, *The Sociology of the Professions* (New York: Herder and Herder, 1972), p. 70.

[69]Everett Carll Ladd, Jr. and Seymour Martin Lipset, *The Divided Academy: Professors and Politics* (New York: McGraw-Hill Book Co., 1975), p. 173.

[70]NEA, *Status,* p. 61.

[71]Fulton and Trow, "Students and Teachers," pp. 6–7.

[72]NEA, *Status,* p. 61.

[73]*Chronicle of Higher Education,* May 16, 1984, p. 1.

[74]*Education Week,* January 19, 1983, p. 1.

[75]W. Lee Hansen, "Surprises and Uncertainties: Annual Report on the Economic Status of the Profession," *Academe,* 68, 4 (July-August, 1982), p. 7.

[76]NEA, *Status,* p. 5.

[77]Valena White Plisko and Joyce D. Stern, *The Condition of Education, 1985* (Washington, D.C.: Government Printing Office, 1985), p. 154.

[78]Seymour E. Harris, *A Statistical Portrait of Higher Education* (New York: McGraw-Hill Book Co., 1972), p. 476, and Fulton and Trow, "Students and Teachers," pp. 6–7.

[79]NEA, *Higher Education Faculty,* p. 7.

[80]Ibid., p. 7.

[81]Lortie, *School Teacher,* p. 58.

[82]Ibid., pp. 69–70.

[83]Ibid., p. 80.

[84]Sam D. Sieber and David E. Wilder, "Teaching Styles: Parental Preferences and Professional Role Definitions," *Sociology of Education* 40 (Fall, 1967), pp. 302–15.

[85]The name of the journal is *Teaching Sociology,* published by Sage Publications, Inc.

[86]Joseph Ben-David, *American Higher Education: Directions Old and New* (New York: McGraw-Hill Book Co., 1972), p. 102.

[87]Ibid., p. 102.

[88]Peter Blau, *The Organization of Academic Work* (New York: John Wiley & Sons, 1973), pp. 158–88.

[89]Lortie, *School Teacher,* pp. 67–70.

[90]Ibid., pp. 70–71.

[91]Lortie, *School Teacher,* pp. 71–72; Kevin Ryan, *Biting the Apple: Accounts of First Year Teachers* (New York: Longman, 1980); W. Robert Houston and B. Dell Felder, "Break Horses, Not Teachers," *Phi Delta Kappan,* 63, 27 (March, 1982), pp. 457–60).

[92]Lortie, *School Teacher,* p. 77.

[93]Ibid., p. 77.

[94]Ibid., pp. 79–81.

[95]James Harvey, *The Student in Graduate School* (Washington, D.C.: American Association for Higher Education, 1972), p. 5.

[96]Joe L. Spaeth, "Graduate Students in History," A report prepared for the American Historical Association (Chicago: National Opinion Research Center, 1963), Survey No. 415, as cited in Harvey, *The Student in Graduate School,* p. 5.

[97]Dan Lortie, "Shared Ordeals and Induction to Work," in *Institutions and the Person,* eds., Howard S. Becker, Blanche Geer, David Riesman, and Robert S. Weiss (Chicago: Aldine, 1968), pp. 252–64.

[98]*Women on Campus,* Proceedings of the Symposium, October 14, 1970, (Ann Arbor: University of Michigan Center for Continuing Education of Women), HE 002 516 (*Research in Education,* January, 1972), and John A. Craeger, *The American Graduate Student: A Normative Description,* ACE Research Reports, v. 6, n. 5 (Washington, D.C: American Council on Education, October, 1971), HE 002 628 (*Research in Education,* March, 1972) as cited in Harvey, *The Student in Graduate School,* pp. 24–25.

[99]Westervelt. *Barriers,* pp. 5–18.

[100]Fulton and Trow, "Research Activity in American Higher Education," in Trow (ed.), *Teachers and Students,* pp. 46, 48.

[101]NEA, *Higher Education Faculty,* p. 10.

[102]Fulton and Trow, "Students and Teachers," pp. 6–7.

[103]NEA, *Higher Education Faculty,* p. 7.

[104]Fulton and Trow, "Research Activity," p. 44.

[105]Donald A. Myers, *Teacher Power—Professionalization and Collective Bargaining* (Lexington, Mass.: D.C. Heath and Co., 1973), p. 50.

[106]W.W. Charters, Jr., "Some Factors Affecting Teacher Survival in School Districts," *Urban Education,* 12 (1977), pp. 15–36.

[107]Jonathon H. Mark and Barry D. Anderson, "Teacher Survival Rates—A Current Look," *American Educational Research Journal,* 15, 3 (Summer, 1978), pp. 379–83.

[108]Gross and Trask, *The Sex Factor,* were able to show that even among those who successfully became principals, men were more ambitious than women, had decided to become principals at an earlier age, and had more often entered teaching as a compromise choice.

[109]Lortie, *School Teacher,* pp. 86–89.

[110]Ibid., pp. 89–90.

[111]Ibid., pp. 89–90.

[112]Gardner, *Status of the American Public School Teacher,* pp. 51–2.

[113]Ibid., p. 65.

[114]Ibid., p. 80.

[115]NEA, *Status,* pp. 5, 21.

[116]Gardner, *Status of the American Public School Teacher,* pp. 30–32.

[117]Ibid., p. 95.

[118]Ann P. Parelius, "Change and Stability in College Women's Orientations Toward Education, Family, and Work," *Social Problems,* 22 (February, 1975), pp. 420–32.

[119]Barry A. Farber and Julie Miller, "Teacher Burnout: A Psycho-educational Perspective," *Teachers College Record,* 83, 2 (Winter, 1981), pp. 235–43.

[120]*Education Week,* March 10, 1982, p. 1.

[121]*The New York Times,* September 19, 1982, p. 52.

[122]Fulton, "Rewards and Fairness," pp. 234–37.

[123]Saul D. Feldman, "External Constraints: Marital Status and Graduate Education," in Trow (ed.), *Teachers and Students,* p. 258. Of course, not all graduate students become college or university teachers. Approximately 70 percent of those who received the Ph.D. or Ed.D. in 1950, 1960, or 1968 and who were working in 1973 were in such institutions, according to John A. Centra, *Women, Men, and the Doctorate* (Princeton: Educational Testing Service, 1974), p. 51.

[124]Feldman, *Escape,* p. 9.

[125]Ibid., pp. 103–23.

[126]Ibid., pp. 125–36.

[127]Centra, *Women, Men, and the Doctorate.*

[128]NEA, *Higher Education Faculty,* p. 7.

[129]Ibid., p. 10.

[130]Fulton, "Rewards and Fairness," in Trow (ed.), *Teachers and Students* and also Eliz-

abeth L. Scott, "Developing Criteria and Measures of Equal Opportunities for Women," in *Women in Academia: Evolving Policies Toward Equal Opportunities,* eds. Elga Wasserman, Arie Y. Lewin, and Linda H. Bleiweis (New York: Praeger Publishers, 1975), pp. 82–114.

[131]Lortie, *School Teacher,* pp. 84–86.

[132]*The Chronicle of Higher Education,* March 24, 1982, p. 1.

[133]Robert L. Jacobson, "Nearly 40 Pct. of Faculty Members Said to Consider Leaving Academe," *The Chronicle of Higher Education,* 31, 8 (October 23, 1985), pp. 1, 22. According to this article, data from the survey will be used in a forthcoming book by Ernest L. Boyer: *The Undergraduate Experience in America.*

[134]National Commission on Excellence in Education, *A Nation At Risk: The Imperative for Educational Reform,* (Washington, D.C.: Government Printing Office, 1983), p. 24.

[135]*Education Week,* March 10, 1982, p. 1.

[136]Lortie, *School Teacher,* p. 104; *The New York Times,* September 19, 1982, p. 52.

[137]Lortie, *School Teacher,* pp. 168–73.

[138]Ibid., pp. 109–33.

[139]Ibid., pp. 134–86.

[140]Fulton and Trow, "Research Activity," p. 44.

[141]NEA, *Higher Education Faculty,* p. 10.

[142]Herbert W. Marsh and Kristine E. Dillon, "Academic Productivity and Faculty Supplemental Income," *Journal of Higher Education,* 51, 5 (1981), p. 547.

[143]W. Lee Hansen, "Starting the Upward Climb? The Annual Report on the Economic Status of the Profession, 1984–85," *Academe,* 71, 2 (March-April, 1985), p. 6.

[144]*Chronicle of Higher Education,* 21, 13 (November 17, 1980), p. 1.

[145]Unionization and Work Stoppages Characterize Educators: Census Bureau," *Phi Delta Kappan* April, 1982), p. 571.

[146]James Browne, "Power Politics for Teachers, Modern Style," *Phi Delta Kappan,* 58 (October, 1976), pp. 158–64.

[147]Mary A. Golladay, *The Condition of Education: A Statistical Report on the Condition of Education in the United States* (Washington, D.C.: Government Printing Office, 1976), p. 125.

[148]"Unionization and Work Stoppages," p. 571.

[149]Browne, "Power Politics."

[150]Browne, "Power Politics," p. 163, and Myers, *Teacher Power,* p. 98.

[151]Callahan, *An Introduction to Education,* p. 426, and Myers, *Teacher Power,* pp. 98–100.

[152]Myers, *Teacher Power,* p. 98.

[153]Ronald G. Corwin, *Militant Professionalism: A Study of Organizational Conflict in High Schools* (New York: Appleton-Century-Crofts, 1970); William W. Falk, Michael D. Grimes, and George F. Lord, III, "Professionalism and Conflict in a Bureaucratic Setting: The Case of a Teacher's Strike," *Social Problems,* 29, 5 (June, 1982), pp. 551–60.

[154]See Myers, *Teacher Power,* for a good discussion of this issue.

[155]Parents vs. Education: Split Widens Over Schools," *U.S. News and World Report* (January 27, 1975), reprinted in *Readings in Education* 76/77, (Guilford, Conn.: Dushkin Publishing Group, Annual Editions Series), pp. 150–52.

[156]Sanford H. Kadish, "The Strike and the Professoriate," in *Dimensions of Academic Freedom,* eds. Walter Metzger et al., (Urbana: University of Illinois Press, 1969), and "The Theory of the Profession and Its Predicament," *AAUP Bulletin,* 58 (Spring, 1972), pp. 57–61 as cited in Everett Carll Ladd, Jr. and Seymour Martin Lipset, *The Divided Academy: Professors and Politics* (New York: McGraw-Hill Book Co., 1975), pp. 246–47.

[157]Kadish, as cited in Ladd and Lipset, *The Divided Academy,* pp. 246–47.

[158]Ladd and Lipset, *The Divided Academy,* p. 247.

[159]Joseph W. Garbarino, "Creeping Unionism and the Faculty Labor Market," in *Higher Education and the Labor Market,* ed. Margaret S. Gordon, (New York: McGraw-Hill Book Co., 1974), p. 318.

[160]Carlene A. Clarke, "The *Yeshiva* Case: An Analysis and an Assessment of Its Potential Impact on Public Universities," *Journal of Higher Education,* 52, 5 (1981), pp. 449–69; David Kuechle, "*Yeshiva* Shock Waves," *Harvard Educational Review,* 52, 3 (August, 1982), pp. 267–79.

[161]Ladd and Lipset, *The Divided Academy,* pp. 250–57.

[162]Garbarino, "Creeping Unionism," pp. 309–32.

[163]Garbarino, "Creeping Unionism," p. 330; Barbara Guthrie-Morse, Larry L. Leslie, and Teh-wei Hu, "Assessing the Impact of Faculty Unions: The Financial Implications of Collective Bargaining," *Journal of Higher Education,*" 52, 3 (1981), p. 252.

[164]Ladd and Lipset, *The Divided Academy,* p. 262.

[165]Garbarino, "Creeping Unionism," p. 312.

[166]Ladd and Lipset, *The Divided Academy,* pp. 261–65, 290–98.

[167]Commission on Academic Tenure in Higher Education, *Faculty Tenure,* p. 241.

[168]Ibid., pp. 203–204.

[169]For a review of this concept, see Myers, *Teacher Power,* pp. 63–72.

[170]Lortie, *School Teacher,* and Myers, *Teacher Power,* provide good discussions of these issues.

[171]Carnegie Task Force on Teaching as a Profession, "A System of Pay, Autonomy, Career Opportunities," *Education Week,* May 21, 1986, pp. 11–18.

[172]Phillip W. Semas, "Student Evaluations of Professors Limited by Many Faculty Contracts," *The Chronicle of Higher Education,* 13 (January 24, 1977), p. 10.

[173]Myron Brenton, "Teachers' Organizations: The New Militancy," in *The Education Establishment,* eds. Elizabeth L. and Michael Useem (Englewood Cliffs: Prentice-Hall, 1974).

# CHAPTER SEVEN CENTRALIZATION OF POWER

Who controls American public schools? Who pays the bills? Who does the hiring and firing? Who decides what students must learn in order to be promoted or to graduate? Who establishes and enforces disciplinary codes? When conflict develops, who prevails? These are important, but difficult, questions. The struggle for power is complex and ongoing, and the balance of power among contending groups shifts over time. However, one trend does stand out clearly: control over eduation has become increasingly centralized during the past century.

## HISTORICAL PERSPECTIVES

The first American schools were established by small religious communities for both spiritual and vocational purposes. Local residents built, supported, and controlled their own schools just as they built, maintained and controlled their religious institutions. The schools, like the churches, embodied the religious and cultural pluralism that was so central to the founders of this nation. Parochial schools, charity schools, pauper schools, and proprietary schools all prospered in this climate. At that time

> there were few sharp lines between "public" and "private" education. Even in "public" schools parents often paid tuition. . . Schools commonly reflected the

> pluralism of society and tended to perpetuate differences of religion, ethnicity, social class, and occupational status. Americans thought education was a good thing, but they turned mostly to voluntary agencies or families to provide the money and control.[1]

When the Constitution was written, this attitude toward education was reflected in the fact that no provision was made for federal responsibility over education. In line with the American tradition of local control, legal authority over education was left to the states. The states took little initiative in education at first, leaving the prerevolutionary status quo essentially untouched until the nineteenth century.

As we indicated in Chapter 3, the basic institutional structure of the American common or public school was firmly established by the mid-nineteenth century. Reformers persuaded legislators that children from all social groups should attend the same free, tax supported, schools. Once public funds were made available, schools rapidly increased in size and number. States delegated much of the responsibility for operating these schools to locally elected (occasionally appointed) boards. Lay control through school boards and local financial support, based largely on property taxes, became the norm.

Local school committees exercised broad and often arbitrary power over the newly established public schools. This pattern of active lay control persisted into the twentieth century in rural, but not urban, areas. The triumph of the public school movement in the burgeoning cities across the United States dramatically increased the scale, cost, complexity and potential power of formal education. The Progressive reform movement, bureaucratization, professionalization of administration and unionization of teaching soon contributed to the centralization of power over urban education.

During the nineteenth century the public schools in the cities were part of the dynamic hurly-burly of party politics. At the turn of the century it was not uncommon to find thirty or more school boards elected to represent various wards within the boundaries of one large city.[2] The major political parties backed slates of candidates for school boards just as they did for municipal offices. School elections were part of the general elections. This electoral structure resulted in heated campaigns, large voter turnouts, and the election of many candidates from working-class backgrounds. Some contemporary political scientists view this as a golden era in urban school politics, a time when school officials were responsive to grassroots public opinion.

However, the Progressive reformers of the 1920s disapproved. They charged that the schools were caught up in the graft and corruption of urban political machines. School posts were bought and sold or given as rewards to loyal political workers. Merit and competence were at best secondary considerations. The results, as the Progressives saw them, were massive waste, inefficiency, and incompetence. The reform campaigns led by the Progressives were successful in establishing reforms of the school electoral structure in many cities. Among the changes they won were: (1) the establishment of city-wide boards of education; (2) at-large, rather than ward based, elections; (3) reductions in the size of school boards; (4) lengthened terms of office; (5) appointed, rather than elected, boards in many cities; (6) separation of school elections from general elections; and (7) prohibitions on political party competition for board offices.[3] It was their often expressed hope that these "good government" policies would take politics out of the schools for good.

## CONSOLIDATION OF ELITE CONTROL

The success of Progressive reformers can be seen as a triumph of centralization over lay control of education. Several historians and social scientists have agrued that the Progressives were motivated by a desire to reduce the power of local citizens, who were often poorly educated and/or newly arrived immigrants and to increase the power of wealthy business interests and socially prominent elites. For example, Cohen and Lazerson argue that the

> shift away from district control and ward-oriented politicians to centralized agencies was central to the Progressive movement in politics, and it drew heavily on the Progressive ideology of reform: efficiency, expertise, and nonpartisanship. But these ideas are also linked to bigotry and explicit class bias. School centralization in the interests of efficiency had the effect—and in at least some cases the intent—of removing power and influence over schooling from the hands of the poor and culturally different.[4]

Samuel Bowles and Herbert Gintis discuss the results of several studies that indicate ". . . a decisive shift toward elite control [resulting from Progressive reforms]."[5] Prior to these reforms the majority of school board members in St. Louis were either small businessmen (47.6 percent) or wage earners (28.6 percent). After the reforms were implemented the percentage of small businessmen on boards slipped to 16.7 percent, and *no* wage earners served. In Philadelphia the percentage of board members listed among the social elite rose from 12 in 1905 to 76 just one year later, after the reforms. In other words, these reforms are interpreted as being the means through which big businessmen and professionals were able to wrest control over urban education from local parents.

### Class Representation on School Boards

Conflict theorists continue to pay attention to the class backgrounds of those who serve on boards of public schools, colleges, and universities today. The evidence clearly supports their contention that in most cases economically privileged individuals dominate such boards.

In 1985, approximately two-thirds of all school board members had completed four or more years of college; almost half had completed advanced degrees. The average family income of board members was in the $40,000-49,000 range. Slightly over 57 percent of all members reported incomes of $40,000 or more;[6] 8.6 percent reported incomes less than $20,000.[7] Almost 74 precent of male board members held professional or managerial positions; so did 42 percent of the women. The average board consisted of seven members, only two of whom were women. Fourteen out of every fifteen board members were white.[8]

### Recruitment and Selection of School Board Members

If school boards are truly committees representing the interests of a ruling class, then one would expect that existing board members would try hard to assure that vacancies on the board would be filled by other ideologically and fiscally conservative individuals. Various studies of rural communities have shown just that.[9] For example, A. B. Hollingshead found that the school board elections of Elmtown were controlled by wealthy and powerful landowners, businessmen, and professionals who shared a strong commitment to low taxes.[10] Vidich and Bensman found virtually the same pattern in Springdale, New York.[11]

Ziegler and Jenning's comparative study of school boards found mixed evidence on this issue. On the one hand, it appeared rather easy for an individual to be elected to the board without formal backing. Almost a quarter of the board members stated that no individual or group had tried to recruit them to run. And of those who did report having been urged to run, 21 percent said that their encouragement came from friends and neighbors rather than board members, formal citizens' groups, professional school personnel, or governmental and political figures. Thus, at one point, Ziegler and Jennings characterize board recruitment processes as having an "almost happenstance" character.[12] Later, however, they argue that boards do tend to be self-perpetuating.[13] This conclusion is based on their findings that 21 percent of board members first gained office through appointment to fill the unexpired terms of others and that another 29 percent were encouraged to seek office by board members. The self-perpetuation conclusion does not jibe completely with the "happenstance" one—although there is evidence in support of both.

Once candidates are recruited, the problem of selection emerges. In the vast majority of cases, school boards are elected. However, in a small percentage of districts—less than 5 percent—board members are appointed rather than elected.[14] This is most common in large cities in which it is sometimes argued that appointed boards are more likely than elected ones to represent all significant population groups. In rare instances, a proportion of a board's members are appointed, and a proportion elected.

For the most part school board elections are very dull affairs. About one in every five school board members in the Ziegler-Jennings study had no opposition in their first election. The campaigns that do take place are generally low keyed and minimally financed. In fact, 42 percent of the respondents said that their ideas about schools were no different from those of other candidates.[15] Organized groups generally did not campaign on behalf of their candidates.

The character of school board elections varies to some extent with the electoral rules that govern them. In some districts Progressive reforms mentioned earlier were either never instituted or they were repealed. Ziegler and Jennings compared board elections in which political parties sponsored candidates to those which were nonpartisan; and citywide elections to those conducted on a ward basis. Although debate between candidates over issues is rare, it occurs much more frequently in districts that allow partisan competition and/or are conducted on a ward basis. In at-large elections such controversy is generally avoided in an attempt to appeal to as many segments of the electorate as possible. In general, competition for board offices is adequately described as "tepid."[16]

## Class and Governance in Academia

The board of trustees (sometimes called governors or regents) stands at the pinnacle of legal authority in virtually all American colleges and universities. These bodies have broad legal powers closely paralleling those of school boards. However, their attention centers on budgetary and fiscal matters, and they have been accused of being conservative and self-perpetuating. In 1969 Rodney T. Hartnett published a study of a national sample of trustees. His summary of social background factors has a familiar ring to it:

> In general, trustees are male, in their 50s (though nationally more than a third are over 60), white (fewer than two percent in our sample are Negro), well-educated, and financially well-off (more than half have annual incomes exceeding $30,000). They occupy prestige occupations, frequently in medicine, law and education, but more often as business executives. . . . As a group, then, they personify "success" in the usual American sense of that word.[17]

A more recent report using a more representative sample of colleges and universities confirmed Hartnett's conclusions.[18] Thus, trustees are an even more select group than school board members.

Hartnett's report provided some evidence with regard to trustees' positions on issues of academic freedom. When asked if faculty members have a right to express their opinions freely, two-thirds agreed that they do have this right, but 27 percent disagreed or were unable to say. Thus, there is rather strong—but far from total—support for this core aspect of academic freedom. When asked about other issues, such as administrative control over student newspapers, screening of campus speakers, and the requirement of a loyalty oath for faculty members, liberal responses were less common.

Hartnett's study also produced strong evidence that trustees prefer a hierarchical policy-making model; that is, they felt that on a wide range of decisions administrators and/or trustees should have the only major authority. This obviously excludes faculty and students from significant policy input. The trustees claimed the greatest authority for themselves in the process of choosing a college or university president. In many other matters (that is, student housing rules, appointment of deans, and tenure decisions) trustees were content either to cooperate with administrators or allow them to take the lead. The trustees thought that the faculty should have major influence in program and curriculum decisions, determination of admissions criteria, and policies regarding student cheating. There were no issues in which they believed that students should have major control, although in matters of cheating, housing, and fraternity and sorority activities many trustees did feel the students had a legitimate right to policy input.

One final point from Hartnett's study ought to be noted. The trustees' opinions about the allocation of decision-making power varied greatly by type of institution, being most hierarchical in public junior colleges, moderately hierarchical in nonselective public and private institutions, and much more egalitarian in selective private and public institutions.

In general, the available evidence provides at least some support for the idea that policymaking at the institutional level in higher education is dominated by conservative individuals drawn from privileged strata. But the data also indicate that a full understanding of the governance of higher education will require careful attention to the roles of administrative officers and faculty. Further, the considerable variation among institutions must be recognized.

## A Caution

There is no longer much doubt that those who occupy the governing boards of educational institutions are recruited primarily from the upper ranges of the middle class. Too many studies have come up with this result for there to be much room for dispute.

Serious questions can still be raised, however, concerning the extent to which class backgrounds determine people's positions on school issues and whether or not upper-middle-class values are rightfully characterized as conservative. As W. W. Charters pointed out as early as 1953, there has actually been very little empirical study of the relationship between board members' class positions and their voting patterns on specific educational issues.[19] Unfortunately, his observation is still quite pertinent today.

It may well be that those who serve on boards are generally more enlightened and liberal than others from the same privileged strata. For instance, many board members across the nation have led in efforts to desegregate public schools with a minimum of difficulty. In this they have taken positions that are probably more liberal than many other business executives and professionals, and certainly are more liberal than many working class citizens. It is also true that upper-middle-class individuals are often more willing than others to spend money on education. Conflict occurs when expensive housing developments are constructed in rural townships. The wealthy and relatively liberal urbanites attracted to these developments do not share the low-tax ideology of the oldtimers. They want good schools and are willing to pay the costs to obtain them.[20] Hollingshead found that when Elmtown High School was faced with the threat of loss of accreditation due to the delapidated condition of its building, the board members, but not the community, supported a bond issue to finance a new structure.[21] Furthermore, when the bond issue was defeated, most of the board members resigned in protest.

Similar comments can be made about college and university trustees. Hofstadter and Metzger pointed out that although there have been some clear violations of academic freedom by conservative trustees, there have also been many cases in which that freedom has been maintained, even to the benefit of radical professors.[22]

Hartnett's 1969 study of trustees found that boards at the most selective and prestigious institutions had a higher percentage of business executives than those at junior colleges.[23] Yet the trustees of the junior colleges were generally less strongly committed to academic freedom and much more likely to agree that "running a college is basically like running a business" than were trustees of selective private institutions. It is obvious from these data that class background does not wholly determine positions on educational issues. Nevertheless, although elite members of boards of education may sometimes represent the interests of the working-class, it is equally clear that power has shifted out of the hands of the populous at large and into the hands of a narrower, more elite stratum.

## DIMINISHED PUBLIC INPUT

As schools were consolidated into larger educational districts and board elections were separated from local politics, many people lost interest in school governance. As educational decisions came to involve increasing degrees of professional expertise in the areas of fiscal planning, bureaucratic administration and management, collective bargaining, and educational psychology, fewer members of the general public felt qualified to participate in them. The public became apathetic, willing to leave most school matters almost entirely in the hands of the school boards and professional educators.

This public apathy can be seen as an outcome of a general phenomenon, the Iron Law of Oligarchy: "Who says organization, says oligarchy."[24] Michels pointed out that contemporary organizations are increasingly governed by those few members who have access to the critical expertise necessary to keep them going. Power and control tends always to rest in the hands of a few. Leaders develop special expertise by virtue of their experience, their overview of the whole organization, and access to information crucial for policymaking; however, this is only one basis for their power. They also have control over the structure of the organization, its chief offices, its staff, and its communications structure. Most other members of the organization are uninformed and uninvolved. The oligarchical structure is reinforced by their willingness to remain dependent and follow the directions of their leaders. Michels' theory calls attention to relationships between the public and school boards and between school boards and superintendents.

## The Public and School Boards

Here we are concerned with the extent to which available evidence supports Michels' theory as applied to the relationship between school boards and the public. In the following discussion we are fortunate to be able to draw not only upon the work of Ziegler and Jennings, but also upon a research report of the National School Boards Association (NSBA) in 1974.[25] This association commissioned the Gallup organization to conduct a nationwide poll of the public, questioning individuals about their attitudes toward and knowledge about their school boards. The total sample included 1,517 adults and was conducted in such a way that similar proportions of individuals from various size communities were included.

The NSBA survey provides evidence of extensive ignorance among the public regarding the legal role of the school board. Only a little more than one-third of all respondents knew that the basic role of the board is ". . . to set overall policies and goals, but not actually run the schools." In general, more than half of all adults surveyed did not know that the boards have final legal authority (within the restrictions imposed by state and federal laws) in hiring both teachers and administrators, curriculum, discipline, textbook selection, budgeting, determining salaries and negotiating contracts, setting attendance boundaries, construction and maintenance of school buildings, and many other matters.

Inattention and apathy were also very much in evidence. Almost two-thirds of the respondents were unable to name a single action that their school board had taken during the preceding year. Noninvolvement was especially prevalent among childless adults. The survey indicated that half of such adults had had absolutely no involvement of any kind in school affairs within the two years prior to the survey. Only 14 percent of parents reported no such interaction, however.

Subsequent research has supported the basic conclusion that the quality and quantity of public involvement in educational decision making is generally low.[26] Furthermore, public opinions about the seriousness of various educational problems differ dramatically from those of both school board members and officials. For example, in 1985 the public considered discipline, drugs, and poor curriculum/standards to be the most critical issues facing schools, whereas school board members were most concerned with finances, declining enrollments, and collective bargaining. Some major public concerns, such as truancy, were low on the board members' list of concerns and vice versa.[27] Similar differences have been reported between professional educators and the public.[28]

School officials are probably quite content when the public is apathetic because, in the officials' opinion, the public is most likely to protest the least important issues.

When those surveyed by the NSBA were asked whether they had a favorable or unfavorable opinion of their school boards, about one-third said they did not know.[29] Of those who did express an opinion, however, 74 percent were favorable. Thus, boards generally enjoyed a reservoir of good will. Between 1976 and 1984, public confidence in the schools declined. In 1984, satisfaction with local schools, principals, administrators, and school boards was again on the rise. Still, only 42 percent of the public gave their local schools a grade of A or B and only 41 percent gave their local school boards a grade of A or B.[30] Many respondents in the NSBA study did not think that the boards should have as much power as they do. Although about half of all adults responding felt the boards should have full authority over hiring principals and superintendents and over teachers' salaries and contracts, large majorities felt that they should not have the legal authority that boards now enjoy over textbook selection (81 percent), curriculum construction (79 percent), maintenance of discipline (81 percent), and choice of teaching methods (83 percent).

Furthermore, respondents revealed feelings of alienation, or a sense of powerlessness with regard to school affairs. NSBA respondents were asked whether their board would reconsider a decision if asked to do so. Forty-one percent of all adults and 42 percent of parents felt it was not too likely or not at all likely that the board would reconsider in response to their request. The larger the community, the less responsive the board was perceived to be.

Of course, in light of all this, it may be difficult for board members to be responsive to the public. Their constituencies are often loosely defined, uninformed, and uninvolved. Campaigns are largely devoid of interest and the presentation of clear policy alternatives. Furthermore, most citizens apparently do not even want board members to have authority in certain important policy matters. Rather they prefer to delegate considerable authority to professional educators and have the board members concentrate on fiscal matters. Usually this means keeping expenditures (and thus, taxes) low, hard bargaining with the teachers' unions and, in general, getting the most for the taxpayer's dollar. In the mid-1980's, though, after a decade of concern about the declining quality of education, the public was more willing than usual to raise local taxes in order to pay for school improvements.[31]

Relationships between the school board and the public roughly conform to Michels' model. However, the public is somewhat less satisfied with the board's leadership than the model might imply. One reason for this is that alongside the school board sits the superintendent, an individual with the professional expertise that board members lack. The superintendent and his staff also exercise leadership in educational affairs. In many cases the public, and even the members of the board of educaton, look willingly to the superintendent for guidance.

## ADMINISTRATIVE DOMINANCE

Once Progressive reformers gained control of urban school boards, they sought to make public school systems less political and more systematic and businesslike. They relied on the experts, school superintendents and their staffs, to accomplish these goals. Pre-Progressive reform boards often "meddled" extensively in the running of the school and treated superintendents as hired clerks. The new board members treated administrators with respect, allowed them much more autonomy, and supported the expansion of staff positions. As the public school systems grew and became more complex, boards became increasingly dependent upon the school superintendent and the rest of the administrative staff.

In theory, the school board sets the basic policies in response to the demands of local citizens. The superintendent is hired by the board to implement these policies. But in practice the superintendent, rather than the board, often seems to be in control because he or she also has significant power resources.

The chief resource of the board is its legal mandate to represent the interests of the community in school affairs. This is a potent resource, but board members are also aware that the public wants professional educators rather than lay boards making many of the decisions over which the boards have formal authority. Board members are also likely to share this view, feeling less qualified than the superintendent and, therefore, reluctant to challenge the superintendent.

The superintendent's expertise goes beyond knowledge of educational technique, methods, and management. He or she has more expertise regarding the legal framework within which educational decisions must be made. School board members might not even be aware of how extensive their legal authority is, because people have only the vaguest information about school board duties. Kerr has suggested that superintendents may contribute to this confusion by presenting new board members with piles of legal documents regarding school governance and suggesting that these rules must be mastered in order to be an effective board member.[32] Campbell, Cunningham, and McPhee give a specific example of the complexity of school law:

> The laws providing for one class of school district, the community unit district in Illinois, for example, take four full pages in the codebook of that state and these sections of the law relate to only such matters as the authorization for organization, the petitioning process, election regulations, and powers and duties of the school board.[33]

The vast majority of new members would be intimidated by such complex legalistic material. At least one handbook for new board members (prepared by a superintendent) encourages board members to accept a definition of the situation in which almost all matters are simply too complex for the layperson and are therefore best left to the experts—the superintendents.[34]

Once elected to the board, a new member is socialized to his or her position by the oldtimers on the board and by the superintendent. The clear expectation is that the newcomer will remain silent and be content to learn by quiet observation. Hostile newcomers may be given an intensive indoctrination in order to blunt their hostility. An example is given by Kerr of a fiscal conservative who, after being given a tour and introductory lecture by the superintendent, became a spokesperson for the board to his disaffected constituents.[35] In Kerr's terms, the school board operates as an "agency of legitimation" of established school practices. The individual board member comes to empathize with the school establishment and to share its view that the public is too ignorant, uninformed, and apathetic to play a meaningful role in school decision making.

The basic resource of the superintendent is his or her expertise in educational matters.[36] These officials argue, often successfully, that extensive education and expertise are necessary to make most educational decisions. We have seen that this position seems to be widely accepted among the general public. Under such circumstances most decisions are defined as technical rather than political and are, therefore, left to the administrators and teachers.

But expertise is not the only resource available to the superintendent. He or she may cultivate the support of influential members of civic groups, the larger community, and members of the Parent-Teachers Association to mobilize support if needed. The superintendent also derives some leverage by virtue of the fact that it is the superintendent's responsibility to draw up the agenda for board meetings. At times, superintendents have crowded the agenda with routine details, making it difficult or impossible to have an adequate discussion of controversial issues. Cunningham studied the operation of one five-person board intensively for eight months. During that time they made 187 decisions. About one-third of these were classified as dealing with housekeeping, another 59 percent with administrative decisions, leaving less than 10 percent to be classified as policy decisions.[37]

Even more important, perhaps, than any of the sources of power mentioned thus far are those resources that are directly available to superintendents by virtue of their position as the chief administrative officer within the schools. Time, assistants, and information are resources generally unavailable to the board, which typically has little or no staff of its own. Furthermore, most board members are unpaid volunteers who must earn their livings in other ways and who, therefore, work under severe time limitations.

One study found that school board members and superintendents usually did not disagree over the educational program. Exactly half of the respondents said there was never any such disagreement and only 38 percent said there definitely was. On another measure, dealing with estimates of board success in opposing the superintendent, board members were rather evenly divided, with 54 percent saying board victory was very or fairly likely.[38]

Interesting variations in the frequency of opposition and estimates of board victory were found between city, suburban, and small-town districts. Opposition was much more common in city and suburban districts than in small towns. But estimates of success were considerably lower in city districts, especially in comparison with small-town districts. The investigators interpret the findings regarding city districts in this way:

> The only logical explanation for these anomalous results relates to the complexity of the districts involved. The large city board, which is more politicized than others, reacts to expressions of public dissatisfaction over the

> educational program by advocating policy changes in order to maintain public political support. It is most likely to oppose the superintendent, who is the person most visibly associated with the existing program. The complexity of the educational system in larger cities, however, makes it virtually impossible for the lay board to master its intricacies. Therefore, despite the board's attempt to change the system, its complexity renders it almost impervious to challenge. The technical resources of the superintendent are required to bring about change. Board opposition notwithstanding, the superintendent's chance of prevailing is great in the complex environment of the city school district.[39]

Suburban, and especially small town, board members apparently achieve tighter control and are more self-confident in their dealings with their superintendents.

## Administration in Academia

We would like to trace public-trustee relations in the same detail that we have treated public-school board relations. However, there is to our knowledge no systematic evidence on these important matters. It is our suspicion that surveys comparable to that of the NSBA would indicate that the public is even less informed and involved regarding the governance of higher education. An exception might be found in the alumni of elite private colleges and universities, however. In such institutions alumni are often a major source of funds and, therefore, a major potential source of influence. But such speculation is not terribly useful. So let us turn to other relationships about which more is known, namely trustee-president relations and president (administration)-faculty relations. These are crucial to the process of governance in academia.

### Trustee-President Relations

The trustee-president relationship is closely analogous to the board-superintendent relationship. Boards of trustees and school boards are the bodies legally empowered to oversee the operations of their educational institutions. As the representatives of the public interest, they enjoy broad legal authority. They are the final decision-makers in the selection of administrators and faculty, finance, physical facilities, student affairs, and educational programs. Yet as laypersons and part-time volunteers, these board members generally do not attempt to run their institutions directly. Rather, they delegate administrative responsibility to administrative experts and professional educators. The larger and more complex the educational enterprise involved, the more heavily dependent the board is upon its chief administrative officer. Thus, the power of the administrator based on expertise balances or outweighs the power of boards that is based on law.

Thus, despite their broad legal powers, trustees

> . . . find themselves (1) dependent on others for the formulation and effective making of many decisions for which they are ultimately responsible, (2) inadequately informed about the basic operations for which their institution

> exists, and (3) unable to influence decisions that determine the basic character of the institution as an educational enterprise for which they (influenced by tradition) have delegated authority to the faculty.[40]

These limitations are so severe that trustees often substantially limit their activities to selecting a president and watching over fiscal affairs. Given the business and professional backgrounds of so many trustees, that would seem to be a logical choice. Some might wish at times to involve themselves in more interesting and significant policy decisions, but they are constantly reminded not to meddle in areas beyond their expertise. In any case, from this perspective trustees are hardly the arbitrary wielders of power in academia that a conflict perspective might lead one to expect.

### President-Faculty Relations

Although the president is an expert vis-à-vis trustees, he or she is unable to assume that stance in relations with the faculty. Especially in prestigious colleges and universities, the faculty is composed of highly skilled professionals operating within narrow fields of specialization. In this relationship the president, who can only be a recognized scholar in one or two areas, must generally take the part of the amateur. Professors have been effective in achieving autonomy and control in key areas. They legitimately argue that their scholarship and teaching should be evaluated only by other specialists in their field, and that they and their departmental colleagues should make key decisions regarding graduate and undergraduate course offerings and appointments and promotions of others in their fields.

The differences between various types of colleges and universities in terms of the latitude trustees are willing to grant faculty in policymaking are almost certainly tied to variations in the amount of expertise the trustees perceive the faculty to possess. As we noted in Chapter 6, the most productive (in terms of research) faculties have the most power vis-à-vis administrators and trustees. The less specialized and teaching-oriented faculty enjoy much less autonomy. As Blau put it: "A faculty interested in research and capable of making research contributions has bargaining power that enables it to demand freedom from domination by centralized authority and to command greater influence in academic affairs. . . ."[41] Of course, unions may also press for increased faculty involvement in policy making. In such cases, however, different power resources (numbers of members, unity, and solidarity) may be crucial—not levels of scholarly expertise.

## STATE AND FEDERAL INTERVENTION

Until recently, local school boards enjoyed extensive autonomy within broad limits set by state and federal laws. Today, however, the situation has changed greatly. Legislatures, courts and education agencies at both state and federal levels have intervened extensively in areas that have traditionally been under local control. In seeking to equalize educational opportunities, external authorities have limited local options. Efforts to desegregate schools and to reform educational financing have clearly contributed to the centralization of power over education. The campaign for community control of public schools was a significant, but limited, countermovement toward decentralization.

### Formal Bases for State and Federal Intervention

Because the Constitution of the United States does not list the provision of education as a federal responsibility, final legal authority over educational institutions rests with the legislatures of the individual states. This, however, does not mean that the federal government is without influence.[42] State systems are obliged to operate within the constraints imposed by the Constitution. An important example of the impact of the Constitution involves the place of religion in the schools. The First Amendment to the Constitution establishes the principle of separation of church and state. From this, the Supreme Court has ruled that it is unconstitutional for public school systems to require prayers or give students released time for religious instruction.[43] This clearly frustrates the desires of many parents, teachers, and school officials. Thus, one form of federal influence is in the form of limiting options regarding school programs.

But the greater federal influence may be in increasing, rather than decreasing, the program options available to educators. Through its power to tax the entire population in order to promote the general welfare, the federal government has been able to provide funds for a variety of education projects. For example, federal money has been made available for preschool programs (such as Head Start), subsidization of school lunch costs, and support of educational research and development projects. Clearly, these are all potentially beneficial programs that probably would not have been possible without federal funding. From a legal viewpoint, as long as state and local officials are not compelled to accept or reject funding for such projects, the federal government is not interfering in state prerogatives.

However, as most people probably recognize, for those who do accept federal funds, strings always come attached:

> . . . the government is within its authority in prescribing the framework within which the program will operate. Thus, it has been held that if any state, school district, or other agency receiving federal funds fails to comply with the statutes the federal government may terminate all future aid and assistance to the program. If a school board accepts funds for the maintenance and operation of schools after the passage of the Civil Rights Act of 1964, it is bound by the provisions of the act. To hold that the federal government did not have this authority would violate accepted principles of fiscal accountability. Sound fiscal administration requires that the unit of government responsible for allocating tax revenue must exercise some responsibility for determining the objectives to be attained by the expenditure and the procedures by which such objectives are to be reached.[44]

Government threats to withhold funds become potent levers of social change in certain instances, such as efforts to compel desegregation of schools and to insure equal employment opportunities. From all this it follows that the more heavily dependent an educational system is upon federal funding, the more vulnerable that system is to federal intervention if questions are raised about the legality of basic procedures.

As we have noted, state legislators have ultimate responsibility over all schools, colleges, and universities within their states. However, because they have many other responsibilities and concerns, legislators delegate much operational authority to boards of education. All states have state level boards of education responsible for elementary and secondary education. All but Hawaii also have local district boards. Hawaii has only one state-wide school district and, therefore, only a state level board.[45] However, beyond these very basic points, provisions for school governance vary widely from state to state. Many states, especially those in the South, have county boards that occupy an intermediate position between the state and district levels of governance, and some large cities have district as well as city-wide boards.

In higher education the formal structure is similar. There is a state level board to govern or coordinate the activities of all institutions of higher education.[46] In addition, each individual college or university has its own board of governors. The intermediate, county level board is absent in higher education. Since private colleges and universities are so important in American higher education, it is worth noting here that all our American private colleges and universities are chartered by the individual states. Further, it is legally possible for such charters to be revoked if the operations of private colleges or universities fail to conform to basic state guidelines.[47] Still, it is undoubtedly true that the public has more extensive control over state colleges and universities. This is because the statutory and administrative guidelines concerning such schools are more extensive and, even more importantly, because public institutions depend upon tax funds for their support. Through control over funding levels and budgetary procedures, state legislators can strongly influence the operations of public colleges and universities.

These, then, are some of the basic legal constraints with which governing boards of educational institutions must contend. During calm, quiet times, all these legal technicalities probably fade into the background as these bodies consider small, narrow and routine issues. But in times of extreme controversy, as we shall see, these laws, rules, and regulations are often brought quickly and dramatically to the attention of board members by representatives of social movement organizations, by judges, and by law enforcement officers.

## Desegregation in Southern Schools

Prior to the Civil War there was little public schooling for either blacks or whites, and the question of segregation in the schools rarely arose. Advantaged white children either went to private schools or were tutored in their homes. Most poor whites and virtually all black children were entirely unschooled. In some states it was illegal to teach a slave to read or write.[48]

Once the Civil War ended and slavery was abolished, however, public schools gradually spread throughout the South. For the first time black children had the opportunity to learn—but only in segregated schools. Strict segregation of blacks and whites was customary in the use of all public facilities—from drinking fountains and toilets to schools. This pattern of segregation was officially sanctioned by the Supreme Court in the case of *Plessey v. Ferguson* (1896).[49] Though the case actually concerned the practice of segregation in railroad transportation, the decision that the provision of "separate but equal" facilities was constitutional was extended to cover other public facilities including educational institutions.

The fight to overturn that decision was a long and hard one. It was led by the National Association for the Advancement of Colored People (NAACP), an interracial organization founded in 1909 by white liberals to press for equal rights for all citizens.[50] Beginning in the midst of the depression of the 1930s, the NAACP began to press for the admission of black students into southern white graduate and professional schools. Since many states had not provided such schools for blacks, clear violations of the "separate but equal" doctrine existed. Success in these cases paved the way for the historic *Brown v. Board of Education* decision of 1954. At that time the Supreme Court broke precedent and ruled that "separate educational facilities are inherently unequal." In *Brown* 2 (1955) the justices ordered that the segregated school systems of the South be desegregated with "all deliberate speed." Black Americans were elated by the decisions, hoping that they would finally clear the path for improved educational and economic opportunities. The frustration of these rising aspirations was one of the major causes of the civil rights and, later, black power movements.

Robert Crain has identified four distinct stages in the effort to gain the compliance of southern states with the Supreme Court ruling.[51] The first stage (1954 to 1956) was one during which there was voluntary desegregation in many of the border states. It was also a time during which politicians from the Deep South began to speak of defiance of the Supreme Court, although they generally adopted a "wait and see" attitude. The second stage (1957 to 1959) was that of "massive resistance" to federal court orders. It was during this period that segregationists throughout the South learned the lessons of efforts to defy the will of the Supreme Court in Little Rock, Arkansas. These lessons were that massive resistance had extreme costs in terms of bad publicity, heightened racial tensions, decreased business activity, lost school time, and even federal intervention. When the nation witnessed the spectacle of federal troops, armed with fixed bayonets, guarding against mob violence outside the desegregated Central High School, it became crystal clear that massive resistance was not only terribly costly, but also, ultimately, ineffective. During the third phase (1960 to 1962) much more integration took place as the tactic of massive resistance was discarded and boards sought ways to limit desegregation to token levels. Finally, resistance virtually collapsed in the face of the passage of the Civil Rights Act of 1964. This act empowered the Department of Health, Education and Welfare to withhold all federal funds from districts that practiced racial discrimination and also gave the United States Attorney General power to intervene on behalf of individual citizens in civil rights cases.

State legislatures throughout the Deep South devised a multitude of laws that served to confuse the situation and delay implementation of desegregation.[52] Central among these were "pupil-placement laws." These explicitly gave local (rather than state) boards responsibility for pupil placement. This had the effect of requiring civil rights activists and their lawyers to file separate lawsuits in each district rather than allowing for one sweeping statewide desegregation order. The laws also gave detailed instructions regarding the factors (that is, transportation available, student/teacher ratios, student aptitudes and attitudes, possibilities of violence, home environment of the pupil, and so on) that needed to be taken into account in making assignments and transfers. In addition, the laws set up elaborate administrative procedures for board actions in these matters. These were designed to delay and frustrate efforts by black parents to have their children transferred to white schools. Ultimately, the great majority of these laws were struck down by federal judges who viewed them as efforts to frustrate the order of the Supreme Court.

Throughout much of this period the civil rights protests and white resistance received extensive national media coverage. The news was filled with stories and pictures of nonviolent protestors being beaten, shocked with electric cattle prods, tear gassed, hosed down by fire hoses, and threatened by snarling police dogs. Shootings, bombings, and burnings were also widely reported. Such coverage helped to mobilize public opinion outside the South in support of the Civil Rights Act of 1964. Protest politics were successful. Members of a minority group, led by a charismatic leader, Martin Luther King, Jr., were able to capture the attention of national media, sway public opinion, and pressure federal legislators to act on their behalf. These tactics enabled them to overcome the resistance of southern white politicians, civic business elites, white Citizens Councils, the Ku Klux Klan, most educators, and most school boards. Ultimately, the Brown decision of 1954 was implemented—but only after a decade of struggle.

During this decade of crisis both the symbolic centrality and actual impotence of school boards were revealed dramatically. Robert Bendiner has provided an accurate description of the situation:

> The irony was that for federal judges bent on implementing the Supreme Court's directive, it was the board that was responsible for the mechanical arrangements of the school district and it was to the boards that they addressed themselves. It was the board that built schools, assigned pupils, provided transportation, and interpreted school laws on the local level—where it became a reality. So it was the board that received the federal government's injunctions and enjoyed the attentions of its marshals, just as it was the board that received counterorders from the state house and enjoyed the attentions of the state police.[53]

The boards in the Deep South were only able to act after it became clear to everyone that the Supreme Court's ruling would have to be implemented.

In some cities (Little Rock and New Orleans, for example), desegregation was accomplished only after a long and damaging period of struggle and violent resistance by mobs of angry whites. In others, however, the process was much smoother. Crain has hypothesized that the reason that New Orleans, and perhaps other cities as well, had such a difficult time handling the crisis was because there was ". . . a general failure of community leadership, resulting in a breakdown of social control over the masses. The school board, the mayor, and the civic elite all shied away from taking action."[54] When these individuals and groups took quick, affirmative action on integration, the opposition did not have adequate time to organize. Once in operation, the desegregation programs gradually gained grudging acceptance.

### Desegregation in Northern Schools

As desegregation was rapidly disappearing in the South, it continued to increase in the North. In light of this fact it is not surprising that civil rights leaders soon brought the issue of school desegregation to the North. But there the effort has been much less successful and, over time, many have given up the fight.

A crucial legal distinction was drawn between segregation southern style and the northern version of the same phenomenon. In the South, segregated schooling was mandated by law. This kind of segregation is called *de jure* segregation. In the North, it appeared to most observers that segregation had come about due to housing patterns, rather than through official actions. Thus, it was called *de facto*, rather than *de jure*, segregation. The pattern was familiar. First, one or more black families would be successful in their search for better housing in a white community at the edge of the ghetto. Whites might then attempt to defend their territory by a variety of tactics including harassment of black neighbors and organization of community defense groups. But the efforts at defense generally failed as homeowners became fearful, sold their houses, and moved to "safer" communities. Because it appeared that school boards and school administrators had no role in the process, the Brown decision did not seem applicable.

Still, given the obviously high degree of segregation in schools outside the South and the success experienced by civil rights leaders in attacking the problem in the South, it was natural that school desegregation would become a prime political objective. In the years from 1963 to 1969 the school boards and superintendents in metropolitan areas throughout the North and South were pressured by a variety of means, including quiet diplomacy, demonstrations, sit-ins, and school boycotts, to admit that segregation was a problem requiring action.

However, in the great majority of cases school officials initially ignored demands to desegregate, or took only procedural or symbolic actions, such as appointing a study commission or preparing a policy statement. In general, they denied responsibility either for the development or alleviation of segregation in their public school systems,[55] and since it did appear that segregation was *de facto* rather than *de jure* in nature, the courts were of little help.

In what is certainly the most comprehensive empirical study of desegregation politics in northern cities to date, David J. Kirby and his associates have been able to capture much of the complexity of the politics of school desegregation in the North, and changes in that process over time from 1955 to 1968.[56] Their procedure involved interviewing key respondents in ninety-one cities selected as being representative of northern cities with significant black populations. They set out to interview individuals who occupied key statuses at differing points in time. For example, they interviewed the city editor of a major local paper, a member of both the 1955 and current school board, a moderate and a militant civil rights leader, a black politician, the school superintendent, and so on. There were eighteen interviews and one self-administered questionnaire scheduled for each of the cities. The researchers were able to achieve a near-perfect response rate, due largely to the fact that they did not set out to interview particular individuals, but rather occupants of key positions. Thus, if one black businessman was not available, another could be substituted in his place. A massive amount of complex data was generated, so only a few of the findings can be reported here.

Responses of school boards were classified as general or specific. General responsiveness was indicated by initiation of a wide variety of programs to improve black education (that is, reduce overcrowding, introduce black studies, hire more black teachers), but not desegregation. The specific responses were the development and implementation of school desegregation plans. General responses were common; desegregation was not.

As had occurred in desegregation efforts in the South, action to desegregate was most common when external authorities made it imperative. However, here state boards of education and state superintendents were the relevant authorities rather than the Supreme Court and federal judges. Desegregation was also more likely in cases where prestigious civic-minded businesspeople were persuaded through quiet diplomacy that desegregation was just and appropriate for school boards to undertake. It was also important that the school superintendent cooperate since the concrete development of desegregation plans—as well as their implementation—depended upon the superintendent. Desegregation was found to be less likely when civil rights groups engaged in direct action. Researchers interpreted this as indicating that sit-ins and boycotts served only to generate extreme controversy and to alienate potentially supportive individuals and groups such as business organizations, school boards, and mayors. Local black elected officials apparently played a key role. They often failed to endorse school desegregation, preferring instead programs aimed at improving the quality of ghetto schools. When they took that position it made it much easier for white board members and superintendents to ". . . dismiss demands for desegregation as being a minority opinion."[57]

This study indicated that on the issue of desegregation school boards played a more important role than in most school matters. The authors argue that this is because the decision to desegregate is a policy issue par excellence. It could not have been defined by superintendents as a purely technical issue even if they had wanted to do so—which, of course, they generally did not. Furthermore, in the great majority of instances, the mayors and the state departments of education were reluctant to act. The issue was too hot for those who would ordinarily control the situation. They were content to let the school board be the center of controversy.

In the final chapter of their book, Kirby and his colleagues develop and present data about the extent of desegregation accomplished.[58] They found that by 1971 almost two-thirds of the cities studied had taken some significant action to desegregate schools. These actions have not affected large numbers of students, but they do indicate that the civil rights movement was not a total failure. Nevertheless, Kirby and his associates were able to point to several critical failures:

1. Nonviolent direct action by the civil rights movement succeeded in dramatizing the issue of school desegregation, but it was unable to go beyond that and make the school systems develop desegregation plans.
2. The civil rights movement failed because its potential allies did not support its demands:
   a. Many black political leaders deserted the cause of school integration.
   b. The white community leaders failed to endorse school desegregation wholeheartedly, and the national elite of educators and intellectuals gave it less support than they might have.
   c. The courts, by failing to rule in favor of desegregation in a consistent fashion, failed to support the issue.
3. Beyond this failure to build a powerful coalition in favor of school integration was an ideological failure. The proponents of school desegregation were not able to present a consistent and compelling rationale why schools should be desegregated.[59]

A final assessment of success or failure is premature. The courts have continued to take a consistent stand against *de jure* segregation and have ruled a wide variety of activities illegal. For example, the courts have recognized that existing segregation is often the product of official decisions—such as those establishing school district boundaries in certain locations, rather than because of housing patterns. In other words, segregation in the North is also often *de jure*, rather than *de facto* although the regulations involved are more subtle than the old southern ones.

Close examination revealed that boards have often engaged in a number of activities designed to promote racial segregation in schools. In Boston, for example, the federal court held that the School Committee had produced *de jure* segregation through a variety of strategies including ". . . student assignments, feeder patterns, open enrollment, utilization of facilities, use of portables, construction of new schools, busing to segregate, and faculty discrimination in hiring, assignment, and promotion. . . ."[60] One example of the kind of tactics used must suffice. The Boston School Committee purchased a Catholic school located in the middle of a white section of the city. It then proceeded to assign black students to that school, many of whom could have been accommodated in predominantly white schools closer to their homes. In this manner the Boston School Committee created a 93 percent black school in the midst of a 98 percent white community. Furthermore, most of the 7 percent white students in that school suffered from visual handicaps. As redress for this and other such discriminatory procedures, the federal court ordered that an extensive busing program be implemented in order to desegregate Boston schools. That decision was met with violent protests and heightened racial tensions reminiscent of the southern experience.[61] The Boston School Committee was so recalcitrant that a federal judge assumed control of the school system himself and remained in charge for more than a decade.[62]

While the goal of racial integration is still supported by many,[63] some original supporters came to reject it as either unfeasible or ideologically repugnant. White liberals became concerned with the plight of urban white ethnic communities and the problem of "white flight" to the suburbs in reaction to court-ordered busing for racial integration. Many blacks and whites became more sympathetic to appeals to the neighborhood school tradition, seeing the schools as potential instruments for building ethnic solidarity, strength, and pride (as well as a source of jobs). Many came to see the issue of community control of education as more critical than the issue of integration.

### The Drive for Community Control: A Countermovement

One of the most dramatic popular movements to redistribute power over educational affairs in recent times has been the community control movement. Now the boycotts, teachers' strikes, and public demonstrations are past and hindsight allows for a clearer perception of the events. The issues were extraordinarily complex, the coalitions of participants shifting, the rhetoric and conflict exceedingly sharp, but the results have been inconclusive.

The community control movement was predicated on the belief that big city school systems had grown into huge, rigid, unresponsive, and, above all, ineffective bureaucracies. Many felt that if only school teachers and administrators were more sensitive to the distinctive needs and aspirations of inner-city communities, education would be improved quickly and dramatically. The surest way to insure responsiveness seemed to be to allow impoverished minority and other communities greater control over the public schools which served them.

It was felt that this could be accomplished by breaking up the massive, city-wide school systems and creating many small districts in their place. These newly created districts would serve communities which were relatively homogeneous in terms of social class and ethnicity. Each district would have its own elected school board. Such boards would be able to insure that the school teachers, administrators, policies and curriculum were both sympathetic and effective. They would have the power to change personnel, practices and materials which were not to their liking. Thus, community control would produce urban schools which were more responsive, diverse, democratic and effective.

Critics of community control argued that if put into practice it would reinforce and accentuate ethnic hostilities.[64] Instead of contributing to an integrated society, the schools would become bastions of separatism, ethnic chauvinism, and ethnocentrism. Furthermore, there would be pressures to erode professional prerogatives in the classroom and to evade the bureaucratic administrative guidelines established by city, state, and federal officials. Some critics seemed to fear that there would be a return to the bad old days in urban school politics with graft and patronage being widespread. Others pointed out that community control would not increase the revenues available to city schools—a basic and worsening problem.

Many of those who most strongly advocated community control of urban schools came to their positions reluctantly. As Fantini reports, the policy was adopted out of frustration.[65] Many of the activists were worn out by the fight for desegregation of big city schools. Relentless patterns of bureaucratic resistance, ghetto expansion, and white flight wiped out progress toward integrated schools almost as soon as it was accomplished. Meanwhile, the pattern of educational failure in big-city school systems persisted. In the face of these realities, many turned to community control as the only viable alternative. Many white liberals and others committed to an integrated society parted company with this new leadership, feeling that their ideals had been rejected in favor of cultural separatism. However, at least some advocates of community control argued that in the long run the goal of societal integration would be furthered by community control. In the short term there might be further separatism, with white and black and Puerto Rican communities becoming even more distinct. But decentralization would bring strength through ethnic identity, reverse patterns of educational failure, and improve political clout. If integration was then desired, ethnic communities would be in a better position to influence ensuing events.

Community control as a goal must be sharply differentiated from administrative decentralization.[66] The latter had been widely advocated by specialists in public administration, educators, and sociologists for some time. Decentralization entails dividing massive urban districts into smaller districts and strengthening the position of local district superintendents. The central board and superintendent would, however, remain the top-level decision-makers. Decentralization means delegation of authority within the ongoing structure. Community control means much more, establishing local school boards with wide discretion in personnel policies, curriculum development, and budgetary matters. It entails extensive redistribution of power, with central school boards and professional organizations of teachers and administrators losing influence relative to local board members.

Probably the most spectacular battle in the struggle for community control erupted in New York City in 1967 and lasted until 1969.[67] It began when the school board of an experimental community control district, Ocean Hill-Brownsville, ordered the involuntary transfer of some twenty white teachers. Though such transfers had often been used in isolated cases in which the community was highly dissatisfied with individual teachers, this group transfer provoked retaliations by the strong teachers' union.

When the issue was not resolved to the union's satisfaction, it called a strike in the fall of 1968. This strike continued for thirty-six days, polarized positions, and heightened tensions and hostilities between the predominantly white and Jewish union and the predominantly black and Puerto Rican community organizations. During the strike, and for some time thereafter, intensive lobbying was going on in the state legislature, where various proposals for reorganization of the New York City school system were being developed.

On this issue the teachers' union and the organization representing school administrators joined forces to block community control legislation. Although these two groups had often been at odds with one another on many issues, both feared that their common professional interests would be compromised by community control. These groups effectively utilized their considerable organizational and financial resources in support of a decentralization, rather than a community control, law. The compromise law created thirty-one community districts, each with its own elected nine-member board. Although the local boards were given control over many important district operations (i. e., superintendent selection, hiring employees, shaping the curriculum and building maintenance), the central board retained control over high schools, budgets, and key personnel matters.[68] Advocates of community control considered the new law so inadequate that they boycotted the first community school (CSB) elections in the hope of forcing the adoption of a more sweeping redistribution of power. The tactic failed. Further, the boycotts made it easy for organized interests including the teachers' union, political clubs, antipoverty agencies, and parochial school groups to gain control of the new boards. Thus, the CSB often became "political" in the old-fashioned sense of being controlled by local power brokers. These individuals represented the narrow special interests of particular groups rather than the educational concerns of parents and students. Such boards often clashed with superintendents, "meddled" in administrative matters, and used the schools as sources of patronage jobs.[69]

Rogers and Chung conducted in-depth field work in eight decentralized school districts in New York City. Despite the problems mentioned above, the researchers found many positive developments. They conclude that decentralization "has provided for enough social peace, local-level flexibility, and openness so that schools can be more effectively responsive and accountable to their local constituencies."[70]

Big city school systems across the United States (among them Boston, Chicago, Philadelphia, Saint Louis, Los Angeles, Washington, and Detroit in addition to New York) were decentralized during the last two decades. To date only one comparative study of the decentralization process has been published, *The Politics of Decentralization* by George R. LaNoue and Bruce L. R. Smith.[71] Their study of decentralization efforts in St. Louis, Los Angeles, Washington, Detroit, and New York does not lend itself to easy summary. They argue that although the issue was quite similar in each city, the participants in the conflict and their positions were tied to the unique history and political structure of each city. In general, however, they found that decentralization was so hot and divisive an issue that big-city mayors and even state-level politicians feared entering the fray. They had too much to lose, because this issue pitted supporters of the union movement (AFT) against black urbanites. This threatened a major split in the New Deal coalition of minorities and labor, which, although already shaky, still formed the basis for the Democratic party. Yet federal officials from the Office of Economic Opportunity and the Office of Education also actively promoted the community-control concept in several cities, and private foundations also played a major part in the community control movement, especially by providing funds in support of experimental districts.

> Locally, the school decentralization issue has been largely fought among the traditional school interest groups, emerging neighborhood leaders, teachers' organizations, and the school bureaucracy. Administrators have opposed the community control version of decentralization everywhere and have been either lukewarm or ambivalent in occasionally supporting administrative decentralization plans. Public school leadership has been precarious. Not one of the superintendents in our case study cities survived the three-year period of the study. Teachers have tended to back decentralization in principle and to be suspicious or even hostile in practice. Some black teachers, however, have had firm ideological commitments or pragmatic incentives, and have supported decentralization. Generally, school-parent groups and blue-ribbon school associations have favored decentralization, though often only after overcoming internal divisions. . . . Since the issues of what is a "community" and who speaks for it are so difficult in the complex urban setting, the coalitions favoring decentralization have tended to be unstable.[72]

### Federal Attempts to Promote Equal Educational Opportunity

Largely in response to pressures brought to bear by the civil rights movement, President Lyndon Johnson launched the War on Poverty in the middle 1960s. Equalization of educational opportunity was one central goal of this new, very optimistic, and very costly federal initiative. In addition to desegregation, programs were developed to provide compensatory educational experiences for socially and economically disadvantaged children (Title I of the Elementary and Secondary Education Act, ESEA), to eliminate sexual discrimination (ESEA, Title IX), to extend services to ethnic minority children with limited English-speaking abilities (ESEA, Title VII), and to finance special educational experiences for children with mental, physical, or emotional handicaps (P.L. 94–142). Because federal officials did not trust local officials to spend this new money wisely, they set up a complicated and expensive bureaucracy to coordinate and regulate program finance and implementation.

> To operate its complicated Rube Goldberg administrative structure, [the Education Department] employs a staff of 6,000. Additional thousands, also paid from federal funds, handle administrivia at the state and local district levels. Federal bureaucrats directing categorical programs in Washington need counterparts in state education agencies and school districts. As a result, the federal impact on state departments of education is so great that as much as 80% of their payrolls is paid from federal grant money.[73]

Thus, federal efforts to improve educational equity stimulated the growth of both federal and state education bureaucracies. These agencies developed and enforced detailed guidelines for the implementation of the new programs, allowing little or no discretion to local school boards. For example, P.L. 94–142 *mandates* that an individualized educational program (IEP) be developed for each handicapped child and also that such children be mainstreamed (taught in the least restrictive environment). Legislative attempts to achieve equity and standardization accelerated the process of the centralization of power in education.

### State Financing Reforms

From the beginning, local control of public education has been linked with local support. Because local property taxes originally provided the great bulk of the schools' operating funds, it seemed appropriate that local residents should oversee those schools. However, during the last two decades it has become clear that heavy reliance on local property taxes to support schools commonly produces marked inequities. Communities with strong tax bases can raise large amounts of educational funds with low tax rates, whereas deteriorated cities can raise less money even with much higher tax rates. Lekachman provided a dramatic example by comparing the financial situations of two neighboring communities on Long Island, New York—Levittown and Great Neck. In the 1968–69 school year, the true value of assessed property in the wealthy community of Great Neck was $64,400 per pupil. In Levittown the comparable figure was $16,200. Both communities had the same tax rate, $2.72 per $100 of assessed valuation. Thus, in Great Neck the local property tax raised $1,684.07 per pupil as compared to $410.31 in Levittown. Although Levittown received more state education aid, Great Neck was still able to spend $2,077.52 per pupil as compared to only $1,189.37 in Levittown.[74]

The issue of school finance reform is being fought in the courts. An important breakthrough in the battle came with the 1972 decision of the California Supreme Court in the case of *Seranno v. Priest*.[75] The court held that the state's heavy reliance upon local property taxes resulted in such great inequalities from one community to the next that the school finance plan violated the equal protection clause of the state constitution. Because many other states used similar mechanisms to raise school funds, the case was of national interest. The result has been reform in the direction of increased state funding and decreased use of local property taxes for schools. An attempt to establish that property-tax-based systems of school finance violated provisions of the *federal* Constitution (*Rodriguez v. San Antonio School District*) was rejected by the U.S. Supreme Court in 1973,[76] so that now battles are being fought primarily at the state level across the nation.

As of 1985, seven states have had their school finance systems ruled unconstitutional under state law: Arkansas, California, Connecticut, New Jersey, Washington, West Virginia, and Wyoming. Eight others, including Arizona, Colorado, Georgia, Idaho, Maryland, New York, Ohio, and Pennsylvania have had their systems upheld. Litigation is underway in several other states.[77]

In most of these cases, the courts have considered two major issues in their decisions. First, they have considered whether or not the school finance system violated the equal protection clause in the state's constitution. Second, they considered whether or not the language in the state constitution made education a "fundamental interest" of the state. By requiring that a "thorough and efficient" or "general and suitable" education be provided, for example, a state might indicate such an interest. This means that school finance systems can be overturned if they do not provide an adequate level of funding, even if that funding is distributed in an equitable way.[78]

In general, the courts have been reluctant to specify remedies when ruling systems unconstitutional. Trying to refrain from interfering in the educational process, the courts have left the task of reform to legislators. At times this has resulted in prolonged political and legal battles.[79]

In several cases, the courts have upheld a state's school finance system. An important factor in these cases was often the court's acceptance of the argument that the state had adequately fulfilled its responsibility for education by delegating that responsibility to local school districts. This decentralization of authority was seen as the intent of those who had written the constitutions.[80] Thus, the traditionally high value placed by Americans on local control over education was upheld over questions of equal educational opportunity in these cases.

The impact of school reform efforts is clearly visible in Table 7–1. Beginning in 1970, the percentage of public school funds provided by state governments has increased steadily. Table 7–1 also shows the rapid expansion of federal funding from 1965 to a peak in 1980.

Even if states acted to eliminate local funding entirely, great inequalities between states would remain. That is because states vary widely in wealth and willingness to support public education. Full federal funding would be required to equalize educational expenditures for all Americans. Constitutional, fiscal, ideological, and political restrictions make this quite unrealistic.

## THE GROWING POWER OF UNIONS

During the last two decades, unions composed of schoolteachers and college professors have become powerful forces to be reckoned with in educational affairs. Governing boards, local administrators, legislators, government bureaucrats, and even protest groups have come to appreciate the value of union support and cooperation as well as the dangers associated with union opposition. The National Education Association (NEA), the American Federation of Teachers (AFT), and the American Association of University Professors (AAUP) have turned to collective bargaining and other organized labor tactics, including slowdowns and strikes, to improve the wages and working conditions of their members.

American public schoolteachers negotiated their first major collective bargaining agreement in 1962.[81] Since then about two-thirds of the states

**TABLE 7–1 Revenue Receipts of Public Elementary and Secondary Schools from Federal, State, and Local Sources: United States, 1919–20 to 1978–79**

| | | PERCENTAGE DISTRIBUTION | | |
|---|---|---|---|---|
| School Year | Total $ Value (× 1,000) | Federal | State | Local (including intermediate districts) |
| 1919-20 | $ 970,120 | 0.3 | 16.5 | 83.2 |
| 1929-30 | 2,088,557 | 0.4 | 16.9 | 82.7 |
| 1939-40 | 2,260,527 | 1.8 | 30.3 | 68.0 |
| 1949-50 | 5,437,044 | 2.9 | 39.8 | 57.3 |
| 1959-60 | 14,746,618 | 4.4 | 39.1 | 56.5 |
| 1963-64 | 20,544,182 | 4.4 | 39.3 | 56.3 |
| 1965-66 | 25,356,858 | 7.9 | 39.1 | 53.0 |
| 1969-70 | 40,266,923 | 8.0 | 39.9 | 52.1 |
| 1975-76 | 71,206,073 | 8.9 | 44.6 | 46.5 |
| 1977-78 | 81,443,160 | 9.4 | 43.0 | 47.6 |
| 1979-80 | 96,881,165 | 9.8 | 46.8 | 43.4 |
| 1980-81 | 105,904,908 | 9.3 | 47.4 | 43.3 |
| 1981-82 | n.a. | 7.4 | 47.6 | 44.9 |
| 1982-83 | n.a. | 7.1 | 48.3 | 44.6 |

Source: W. Vance Grant and Thomas D. Snyder, *Digest of Education Statistics,* 1983-84, National Center for Education Statistics, U.S. Department of Education (Washington, D.C.: Government Printing Office, 1983), p. 77; Valena White Plisko and Joyce D. Stern, U.S. Department of Education, National Center for Education Statistics, *The Condition of Education, 1985* (Washington D.C.: Government Printing Office, 1985), p. 36.

have adopted legislation permitting teachers (along with other public employees) to organize and bargain collectively, and membership in the NEA and AFT has increased rapidly. Teachers are now among the most heavily unionized public employees, and the NEA may be the nation's largest union. The NEA's political activities extend far beyond negotiating local contracts to include lobbying, support of state and federal political candidates, and electioneering during local school board contests. Teachers involved in these political activities are protected from management reprisals both by civil service regulations and state statutes. Given the size, strength, and political savvy of the NEA, its political influence is not surprising. Unfortunately, the body of sociological theory and research regarding the impact of teacher unionization is minimal.

However, Douglass Mitchell and his associates conducted some interesting exploratory research designed to elucidate changes in school management brought on by collective bargaining.[82] They studied eight diverse school districts intensively for one year. The research team interviewed school board members, superintendents, teacher organization presidents, negotiating team members, school principals, central office administrators, rank-and-file teachers, and even community group leaders. They also observed bargaining sessions, analyzed contracts, and reviewed the social histories of each district. Use of multiple and diverse data sources yielded rich and detailed findings, only a few of which can be mentioned here.

Mitchell and his associates concluded that collective bargaining alters the balance of power between administrators and teachers. It increases teacher autonomy and decreases administrative discretion. Through collective bargaining, teachers' unions gain specific and elaborate rules limiting the scope of administrators' ad hoc, unilateral decision-making authority. Naturally, administrators resist and resent being constrained by formalized and centralized rules. The authors claim that ". . . this conflict between managerial discretion and teacher autonomy or security is a real, permanent, and serious problem."[83] Take, for example, the formalization of work rules that distinguish between "regular" and "extra" duties. These new rules restrict the range of routine duties associated with the teachers' role. Union contracts specify that teachers should be paid for extra work such as supervising extracurricular activities, meetings after-hours, and parent conferences. Despite union efforts the rate of pay is often so low that teachers are not motivated to participate. The activities decline as a result. Bargaining also results in the institution of grievance procedures, which allow teachers who believe they have received arbitrary and capricious treatment to seek review by the school board or other agency. These rules have the effect desired by unions; they encourage uniformity in principal-teacher relationships.

Collective bargaining agreements also specify in detail the procedures by which teachers are to be evaluated. The rules typically limit the number of formal evaluations and specify that teachers must be notified in advance of classroom visits. Regularization may reduce the anxiety that both teachers and principals often experience during evaluations, but both parties are dubious about the validity or effectiveness of such procedures. Finally, the researchers found that when negotiations were not going well, labor-management tensions increased. Teachers were less inclined to cooperate and often minimized their teaching efforts. In labor relations terms, they resorted to work slowdowns. However, once the contracts were signed, relations improved noticeably.

Unions have provided teachers with a counterbalance that restricts what administrators refer to as "appropriate discretion" but which teachers characterize as "arbitrary and capricious behavior." Teacher loyalty is now often primarily to the union rather than to the school or district. As a result, collective action based on shared concerns is more common and effective. Experienced administrators and board members understand that the countervailing power of teachers' unions can be used to undermine or veto new policies or programs that the union leadership considers threatening. Although they often find unions distasteful, board members and administrators must learn to live and work with the unions if they are to get things done.

Local unions are affiliates of state and national organizations. So it is not surprising that items from bargaining agendas formulated at the state or even national level arise during district-level negotiations. Furthermore, union lobbying efforts to achieve favorable state and even federal legislation often directly impact upon local decision making. In sum, unionization contributes not only to the regularization, but also the centralization, of power in education.

Professors, like schoolteachers, turned to collective bargaining during the 1970s. Six hundred and eighty-one college and university faculties had selected collective bargaining agents by 1981, and more than one-fourth of faculty and staff members had joined a union. As noted in Chapter 6, unionization was most prevalent in public, two-year institutions. At present the momentum of the unionization process has been stalled because half the state legislatures have resisted efforts to enact enabling legislation and because of a 1980 Supreme Court decision that apparently bars the faculty in many, if not all, private institutions from collective bargaining.[84]

The NEA and AFT are the primary actors in the unionization of higher education, with the AAUP playing a relatively minor role, except in the relatively few four-year colleges and universities that have organized. We have seen that these unions were centrally concerned with protecting the security and autonomy of teachers, especially through the elaboration and codification of grievance procedures. Thus, it should come as no surprise that the same procedural emphasis is evident at the higher education level. Personnel relationships have been standardized and formalized as a direct result of collective bargaining. Many observers expected that unions would displace faculty senates as the centers of faculty input to academic decisions, and they may well be correct. In 1981 Baldridge and associates reviewed the research literature and concluded, "Unions appear to be able to live with senates, and vice versa."[85] But just one year later he asserted, "The real effectiveness of senates seems to be at an all-time low as faculty unions undercut some of their authority and central administrations steal the rest."[86] All that is clear is that the situation is in flux. Power often shifts upward to the state level once the faculty begin to bargain collectively. This occurs because the faculty of different colleges combine forces into a single unit, which bargains with state officials. The unions also lobby at the state level, sometimes achieving victories through legislation that they might not have been able to achieve otherwise. For example, in Illinois the union was able to get a bill passed (over the governor's veto) that granted public community college professors tenure after three consecutive years of employment. Unionization has spurred the centralization of power.

## SUMMARY, CONCLUSIONS, AND POLICY QUESTIONS

Who governs American educational institutions? Although it is still a difficult question, some things do seem relatively certain. School boards, the traditional bastions of local control, have lost much of their autonomy. Local boards have been pushed around and swept aside by larger forces at the local, state, and federal levels.

Administrators and union leaders contend with board members at the local level. Both groups present themselves as professional, as experts in contrast to the amateur board members. Especially in the larger and organizationally complex consolidated districts, board members must rely heavily upon administrators to keep the schools running. But administrators complain that boards have given the "keys to the store" to the unions. Collective bargaining has, in fact, limited administrative discretion. And unions have effectively used slowdowns, strikes, and electioneering to blunt local board initiatives.

But local board members, administrators and union activists are all small players on the contemporary education stage. Largely as a consequence of pressures generated by nationwide social protest movements and taxpayers' revolts, the big decisions regarding curriculum, graduation requirements, and finances are made at higher levels—by legislators, government bureaucrats, and judges. Local school boards are faced with increasing regulations, mandates, and court orders that they cannot ignore.

The Reagan administration is ideologically opposed to expansion of federal influence in education. So administration officials have tried to reduce federal funding and to simplify and deregulate aid programs. However, liberal politicians and others who support active federal involvement in education oppose these moves. They see them as evidence of a diminished commitment to fairness and equal educational opportunity. It remains to be seen whether or not the Reagan administration can turn back the tide of centralization.

Whatever the commitments of federal education officials may be, there is no indication of state efforts to strengthen local control over education. Quite to the contrary, state legislators and state boards of education are ever more willing to exercise powers which they had traditionally delegated to local school boards. The increasingly intrusive posture of state education authorities comes in response to strong pressures for fiscal reform and accountability, on the one hand, and for educational excellence, on the other. State agencies have become impatient in seeking changes. They consider school boards incapable of taking effective action in the face of pressing problems. Thus, instead of being content to exert influence by issuing minimal, basic guidelines and offering technical assistance, those agencies now seek direct control through curricular and testing mandates coupled with strict compliance procedures. Mandated tests are increasingly popular means of remote control over education. By forcing local districts to eliminate social promotion and ensure minimal competency through establishing promotion and graduation gates, state officials effectively shape the local curriculum. The local school boards have no choice but to perform the onerous work of implementing the mandates and absorbing the anger they generate.

We have described the part unionization plays in the centralization of power. Lobbying and electioneering are important means of political influence. From the union point of view a statewide legislative victory is obviously much more important than the same victory achieved through collective bargaining with a local school board. Legislators have occasionally attempted to bypass unions in the same manner that they have recently bypassed school boards. In New Jersey, for example, the state legislature has passed a bill setting a statewide minimum starting salary for teachers of $18,500. The unions opposed the measure because it did not provide for increases for experienced teachers as well. In the next bargaining rounds, New Jersey school boards will have to face the nearly impossible task of meeting union demands for across-the-board raises while not exceeding state-imposed spending caps and preserving curricular diversity. Teachers' unions have also opposed governors' proposals to introduce merit pay. Union veto powers are tested whenever state legislators pass bills that are opposed by teachers' unions.

Americans value diversity, freedom, efficiency, and equality. School boards can be seen as institutional embodiments of the nation's founders' primary concern with the freedom of small, relatively homogeneous communities to socialize their youth as they saw fit, without government interference. But in recent times, questions have been raised about the ability of such boards to provide enlightened, efficient, and equitable education. Power has shifted away from local communities. These developments summon up basic and important policy questions. Does centralization of power pose a threat to educational freedom and diversity or does it provide critical protection for the handicapped, the poor, and the minority student? Has outside intervention by politicians, courts and bureaucrats facilitated educational innovation, efficiency, and effectiveness, or has it been counterproductive, leading to rigidity, wastefulness, and lowered morale?[87] Should the federal government pull back from educational involvement, as Reagan has proposed, or should it push forward toward a national system of education?

## NOTES

[1]David B. Tyack, "Governance and Goals: Historical Perspectives on Public Education," in Don Davies, ed., *Communities and Their Schools*, (New York: McGraw-Hill Book Co., 1981), p. 14.

[2]Joseph M. Cronin, *The Control of Urban Schools: Perspectives on the Power of Educational Reformers* (New York: Free Press, 1973), pp. 1–89.

[3]Cronin, *The Control of Urban Schools*, pp. 90–147.

[4]David K. Cohen and Marvin Lazerson, "Education and the Corporate Order," *Socialist Revolution* v. 2 (March/April 1972), p. 66.

[5]Samuel Bowles and Herbert Gintis, *Schooling in Capitalist America* (New York: Basic Books, 1976), p. 189.

[6]In 1983, only 22.5 percent of all families in the United States had incomes this high, according to Bureau of the Census, *Statistical Abstract of the United States 1986* (Washington, D.C.: Government Printing Office, 1986), p. 451.

[7]In 1983, 39.4 percent of all families had incomes in this range. Ibid., p. 451.

[8]Donald T. Alvey, Kenneth E. Underwood, and Jimmy C. Fortune, "Our Annual Look at Who You Are and What's Got You Worried," *The American School Board Journal*, 173 (January, 1986), p. 27. In the South, and perhaps other areas of the country as well, a system of "tight, white" control of local school boards persists, even in districts serving predominately black student populations. *The New York Times*, June 23, 1986, Sec. 1, p. 10.

[9]Ray E. Jongwald, "The School Board in the Rural Community," in *Understanding School Boards: Problems and Prospects*, ed. Peter J. Cistone, (Lexington, Mass.: Lexington Books, 1975), pp. 173–87.

[10]A. B. Hollingshead, *Elmtown's Youth and Elmtown Revisited* (New York: John Wiley & Sons, 1975).

[11]A. J. Vidich and J. Bensman, *Small Town in Mass Society* (Princeton, N.J.: Princeton University Press, 1968).

[12]L. Harmon Ziegler and M. Kent Jennings, with G. Wayne Peak, *Governing American Schools: Political Interaction in Local School Districts* (North Scituate, Massachusetts: Duxbury Press, 1974) p. 35.

[13]Ibid., p. 51.

[14]National School Boards Association, *The People Look at Their Schools* (Evanston, Ill.: National School Boards Association, 1975), p. 19.

[15]Ziegler and Jennings, *Governing American Schools*, p. 43.

[16]Ibid., p. 71.

[17]Rodney T. Hartnett, "College and University Trustees: Their Backgrounds, Roles and Educational Attitudes," in Elizabeth L. Useem and Michael Useem, *The Educational Establishment* (Englewood Cliffs, N.J.: Prentice-Hall, Inc., 1974), p. 147

[18]Irene L. Gomberg and Frank J. Atelsek, *Composition of College and University Governing Boards*, Higher Education Panel Report No. 35 (American Council on Education, 1977), pp. 4–5.

[19]W. W. Charters, Jr., "Social Class Analysis and the Control of Public Education," *Harvard Educational Review*, 23 (Fall, 1953), pp. 268–83.

[20]William M. Dobiner, *Class in Suburbia* (Englewood Cliffs, N.J.: Prentice-Hall, Inc., 1963), pp. 127–40.

[21]Hollingshead, *Elmtown's Youth and Elmtown Revisited*, p. 353.

[22]Richard Hofstadter and Walter P. Metzger, *The Development of Academic Freedom in the United States* (New York: Columbia University Press, 1955), p. 438.

[23]Hartnett, "College and University Trustees," p. 153.

[24]Robert Michels, "The Iron Law of Oligarchy," in *Power in Societies*. ed. Marvin E. Olsen, (New York: The Macmillan Company, 1970), p. 149.

[25]NSBA, *The People Look at Their School Boards, pp. 1–47.*

[26]Robert H. Salisbury, *Citizen Participation in the Public Schools* (Lexington, Mass.: D.C. Heath & Co., 1980); Harvey J. Tucker and L. Harmon Zeigler, *Professionals Versus the Public: Attitudes, Communication, and Response in School Districts* (New York: Longman, Inc., 1980).

[27]Alvey, Underwood, and Fortune, "Our Annual Look," pp. 23–6.

[28]Tucker and Zeigler, *Professionals Versus the Public.*

[29]NSBA. *The People Look at Their School Boards, p. 36.*

[30]Edward B. Fiske, "Poll Finds Rising Confidence in Schools," *New York Times*, August 5, 1984, Sec. I, p. 20.

[31]Ibid., p. 20.

[32]Norman D. Kerr, "The School Board as an Agency of Legitimation," in *Governing Education: A Reader on Politics, Power, and Public School Policy*, ed. Alan Rosenthal (Garden City, N.Y.: Anchor Books, 1969), p. 153.

[33]Roald F. Campbell, Luvern L. Cunningham, and Roderick F. McPhee, *The Organization and Control of American Schools* (Columbus, Ohio: Charles E. Merrill, 1965), p. 89.

[34]Lloyd W. Ashby, *The Effective School Board Member* (Danville, Ill.: Interstate Printers and Publishers, 1968), p. 48.

[35]Kerr, "The School Board as an Agency of Legitimation," p. 153.

[36]Ziegler and Jennings, *Governing American Schools*, p. 150.

[37]Campbell, Cunningham, and McPhee, *The Organization and Control of American Schools*, p. 178.

[38]Ziegler and Jennings, *Governing American Schools*, p. 164.

[39]Ibid., p. 177.

[40]John J. Corson, *Governance of Colleges and Universities* (New York: McGraw-Hill Book Company, 1960), p. 49.

[41]Peter M. Blau, *The Organization of Academic Work* (New York: John Wiley & Sons, 1973), p. 169.

[42]LeRoy J. Peterson, Richard A. Rossmiller, and Marlin U. Volz, *The Law and Public School Operation* (New York: Harper & Row, 1969), p. 4.

[43]David L. Kirp and Mark G. Yodof, *Educational Policy and the Law: Cases and Material* (Berkeley, California: McCutchan Publishing Company, 1974), pp. 94–105.

[44]Peterson, Rossmiller, and Volz, *The Law and Public School Operation*, p. 5.

[45]Campbell, Cunningham and McPhee, *The Organization and Control of American Schools*, p. 93.

[46]Lyman A. Glenny and Thomas K. Dalgish, "Higher Education and the Law," in *The University as an Organization*, ed. James A. Perkins, (New York: McGraw-Hill Book Company, 1973), pp. 179–81.

[47]E. O. Duryea, "Evolution of University Organization," in *The University as an Organization*, ed. J. Perkins, pp. 16–20.

[48]Stanley M. Elkins, *Slavery: A Problem in American Institutional and Intellectual Life*, 2nd ed. (Chicago: The University of Chicago Press, 1968), p. 60.

[49]Kirp and Yudof, *Educational Policy and the Law*, pp. 281–91.

[50]Ibid., pp. 289–307.

[51]Robert L. Crain, *The Politics of School Desegregation* (Chicago: Aldine Publishing Company, 1968), pp. 226–36.

[52]Reed Sarratt, *The Ordeal of Desegregation: The First Decade* (New York: Harper & Row, 1966), pp. 31–33.

[53]Robert Bendiner, *The Politics of Schools* (New York: Harper & Row, 1969), pp. 44–45.

[54]Crain, *The Politics of School Desegregation*, p. 298.

[55]Larry Cuban, *Urban School Chiefs under Fire* (Chicago: The University of Chicago Press, 1976).

[56]David J. Kirby et al., *Political Strategies in Northern School Desegregation* (Lexington, Mass.: Lexington Books, 1973).

[57]Ibid., p. 163.

[58]Ibid., pp. 171–202.

[59]Ibid., p. 158.

[60]Roger I. Abrams, "Not One Judge's Opinion: Morgan v. Hennigan and the Boston Schools," *Harvard Educational Review*, 45, 1 (February, 1975), p. 7.

[61]Alan Lupo, *Liberty's Chosen Home: The Politics of Violence in Boston* (Boston: Little, Brown and Company, 1977).

[62]*New York Times*, September 4, 1985, sec. 1, p. 14.

[63]U.S. Commission on Civil Rights, *Statement of the United States Commission on Civil Rights on School Desegregation* (Washington, D.C.: Government Printing Office, 1982), p. 154; Christine H. Rossell and Willis D. Hawley, eds. *The Consequences of School Desegregation* (Philadelphia: Temple University Press, 1983); Jennifer L. Hochschild, *The New American Dilemma* (New Haven: Yale University Press, 1984).

[64]See Albert Shanker, "The Cult of Localism," and Amitai Etzioni, "The Fallacy of Decentralization," both in *School Policy and Issues in a Changing Society*, ed. Patricia Cayo Sexton, (Boston: Allyn & Bacon, 1971), pp. 198–204, 213–24.

[65]Mario Fantini, Marilyn Gittell, and Richard Magat, *Community Control and the Urban School* (New York: Praeger Publishers, 1970), pp. 22–42.

[66]Sexton, *School Policy and Issues*, pp. 195–96.

[67]Fantini, Gittell, and Magat, *Community Control and the Urban School*, pp. 141–72.

[68]Roald F. Campbell, Luvern L. Cunningham, Michael D. Usdan, and Raphael O. Nystrand, *The Organization and Control of American Schools, Fourth Edition* (Columbus, Ohio: Charles E. Merrill, 1980), p. 146.

[69]David Rogers and Norman H. Chung, *110 Livingston Street Revisited: Decentralization in Action* (New York: New York University Press, 1983), pp. 216–17.

[70]Ibid., p. 207.

[71]George R. LaNoue and Bruce L.R. Smith, *The Politics of School Decentralization* (Lexington, Mass.: Lexington Books, 1973).

[72]Ibid., pp. 228–29.

[73]George Neill, "Washington Report," *Phi Delta Kappan*, 62, 5 (January, 1981), p. 396.

[74]Robert Lekachman, "Schools, Money and Politics: Financing Public Education," in *Emerging Education Issues*, eds. Julius Menacher and Erwin Pollack, (Boston: Little, Brown and Company, 1974), p. 51.

[75]Mary A. Golladay, *The Condition of Education: 1976 Edition* (Washington: Government Printing Office, 1976), p. 145.

[76]Ibid., p. 145.

[77]Michael W. LaMorte and Jeffrey D. Williams, "Court decisions and School Finance Reform," *Educational Administration Quarterly*, 21 (Spring, 1985), pp. 59–89.

[78]Ibid.

[79]Ibid.

[80]Ibid.

[81]Myron Lieberman, *Before, During and After Bargaining* (Chicago: Teach 'em, 1979), p. 8.

[82]Douglass E. Mitchell and others, "The Impact of Collective Bargaining on School Management and Policy," *American Journal of Education*, February, 1981), pp. 147–88.

[83]Ibid., p. 167.

[84]The following discussion draws heavily upon one comprehensive literature review. J. Victor Baldridge, Frank R. Kemerer, and others, *Assessing the Impact of Faculty Collective Bargaining* (American Association for Higher Education, 1981), pp. 1–57.

[85]Baldridge, Kemerer, and others, *Assessing the Impact*, p. 46.

[86]J. Victor Baldridge, "Shared Governance: A Fable About the Lost Magic Kingdom," *Academe*, 68, 1 (January-February, 1982), pp. 12–15.

[87]For further discussion, see Arthur E. Wise, *Legislated Learning* (Berkeley: University of California Press, 1979) and Paul Seabury, ed., *Bureaucrats and Brainpower: Government Regulation of Universities* (San Francisco: Institute for Contemporary Studies, 1979).

# CHAPTER EIGHT
# EDUCATION AND STRATIFICATION

When sociologists discuss social stratification, they are concerned with valuables (such as wealth, power, and prestige) that are unequally distributed among members of society. In most societies, some individuals have great accumulations of wealth, wield considerable power, and are held in high esteem; others have barely enough money to survive, have little control over their lives, and are generally looked down upon as inferior.

For the most part, individuals who are similar in wealth, power, or prestige have other characteristics in common and tend to associate with each other in their places of residence, business, recreation, and worship. In the United States, for example, elites are disproportionately white, male, and Protestant. Many have large accumulations of inherited wealth and are influential in business and political circles. Elite families live in exclusive urban neighborhoods and suburbs, send their children to private schools, and tend to remain isolated from those who are substantially less privileged than they. At the other extreme, the most disadvantaged Americans live in urban or rural slums. These families have few material possessions, live in dilapidated, overcrowded housing, and must often depend on social services such as welfare or food stamps to survive. Although the majority of America's poor are white, blacks and other minorities are disproportionately concentrated in this group. Located between the elites and the poor is a wide spectrum of individuals, from upper-middle-class professionals to working-class laborers, who also tend to associate with others of similar income, education, and social status in their communities and on the job.

It is possible, then, to view societies as hierarchical arrangements of layers, or strata, with the wealthy at the top and the poor at the bottom. The shape of the hierarchy formed by these layers, or the proportion of the total population that falls at the top, in the middle, and at the bottom varies from one society to another and varies over time within any one society. So, too, do the bases upon which people come to be located in one particular stratum or another, and the mechanisms, if any, by which they can move from one layer to the next. Some societies are rigidly stratified into relatively closed layers called castes. Individuals born into a particular caste have little or no opportunity to move into another. Their position in the stratification system is determined for life. Most societies are more open than this. An individual's talents, achievements, and even luck can result in mobility out of one stratum and into another. Mobility can be either up or down: People can improve their socioeconomic standing relative to that of their parents or fall below it.

For any particular society, it is important to know the extent to which social mobility is possible and the means through which individuals can become successfully mobile. In the United States, as in most advanced technological societies, education is a key element in the process of social mobility. As we described in Chapter 3, industrialization gradually tightens the relationship between education and occupational placement. In the United States, for example, educational attainment, or the number of school years completed, is the single most important determinant of occupational and income attainment.[1] This is not to say that education explains all or even most of the variation in people's income. Factors such as family background, race, gender, intelligence, and even luck are also important. Whatever else individuals may have working for or against them, though, educational credentials are necessary for entering virtually all lucrative and prestigious occupations. As the data presented in Chapter 3 clearly show, the incomes of year-round, full-time workers vary directly with education.

It is for these reasons that "equality of opportunity" is usually discussed in the context of education. "Equality of opportunity" exists when each person, regardless of such ascribed characteristics as family background, religion, ethnicity, race, or gender, has the same chance of acquiring a favorable socioeconomic position. This is not to say that equality of opportunity implies a system based only on random luck, such as a lottery; rather, it requires that socioeconomic status be achieved in a fair and open contest—one in which the winners are those who work hardest and demonstrate the most ability. Education is an obviously important part of that contest in contemporary societies. If access to education is not equal for all, then access to occupations, financial success, and prestige will not be equal either.

Notice that the way in which we defined "equality of opportunity" still permits considerable inequality to exist within society as a whole. Some people can still be wealthy and influential, while others can be poor and powerless. Our definition requires only that this inequality be based on differences in achievement in a fair and open system. However, it is also possible to define "equality of opportunity" as a guarantee that all individuals in a society will have similar levels of wealth, power, and prestige and that no person or group of people will be significantly deprived relative to others. This alternate view raises important issues for educational policy, and we will return to it again at the end of this chapter.

For now, we will explore the relationship between education and stratification in the United States, keeping the issue of equality of opportunity in mind. We will begin by looking at the patterns of educational achievement in the United States, at who does well in school and who does not. We will then consider various explanations of these patterns and evaluate the extent to which our educational system does or does not offer equality of opportunity to all Americans.

## PATTERNS OF EDUCATIONAL ATTAINMENT AND ACHIEVEMENT

There are many correlates of educational attainment and achievement that we could look at in this chapter, but we will concentrate on three that have been found to be particularly important in affecting educational outcomes—socioeconomic status, race or ethnicity, and gender. Children who differ from one another in these three characteristics tend to have different types of educational experiences and different degrees of success and failure in school. Children vary, especially, in their levels of educational attainment as measured by the number of school years completed, and educational achievements, as measured by such items as grades, standardized test scores, and school program completed.

### Socioeconomic Status

Socioeconomic status or social class can be measured in a number of different ways. Most commonly, it is measured by father's education, occupation, or income, either separately or together. Sometimes, mother's education or occupation, family income, or household possessions are used, especially in combination with each other or with father's characteristics. Whatever the measure, however, socioeconomic status is positively correlated with both educational attainment and achievement: The higher a student's socioeconomic status, the greater his or her educational accomplishment is likely to be.

Innumerable studies have documented this relationship between socioeconomic status and education. Whether we look at scores on standardized ability or achievement tests, classroom grades, participation in academic rather than vocational high school programs, involvement in extracurricular activities, number of years of schooling completed, or enrollment in or completion of college and professional school, children from more socioeconomically advantaged homes outperform their less affluent peers.

These relationships can be illustrated by data collected by the Department of Health, Education and Welfare as part of its national longitudinal studies of high school students. These studies were initiated in 1972 with a national sample of 18,143 high school seniors.[2] Since then, follow-up data on these students have been collected at regular intervals so that their postsecondary educational and occupational experiences could be analyzed. In 1980, the then senior and sophomore classes of high schools throughout the country were added to the study. These, too, have been followed in subsequent research.

One variable looked at closely in these studies was socioeconomic status. Socioeconomic status was measured by an index constructed from father's education, mother's education, parents' income, father's occupation, and household items, such as possession of a color television set. The sample of students was classified into three socioeconomic categories.

The National Longitudinal Studies revealed several direct positive relationships between educational success and socioeconomic status. One such relationship was found between the students' socioeconomic statuses and their scores on various standardized tests administered as part of the study. These tests measured vocabulary, associative memory, reading, inductive reasoning, mathematical skills, and perceptual speed. On each test, students in successively higher socioeconomic categories received better mean scores. For example, among 1980 seniors, the mean scores of the three socioeconomic categories on the reading test were 6.62, 8.98, and 11.13; on the mathematics test, they were 6.66, 9.27, and 11.79.[3] The highest mean scores were those of the most socioeconomically advantaged group and the lowest mean scores were those of the least advantaged group.

Similar relationships were found between socioeconomic status and other measures of educational accomplishment. Seniors at the highest socioeconomic level had a mean grade point average of 3.07 (A = 4, B = 3, C = 2, D = 1) as compared to 2.85 and 2.68 at the middle and lower levels.[4]

Not surprisingly, educational plans were also related to socioeconomic status. Among 1982 seniors only 28 percent of the least advantaged students planned to attend a four-year college as their major activity during the year after high school, whereas 74 percent of the most advantaged students had such plans.[5] Indeed, when the 1980 seniors were questioned two years after graduation, it was found that only 46 percent of the lowest socioeconomic group, but 86 percent of the highest socioeconomic group, had actually attended some type of postsecondary school or college. Overall, 19 percent from the lowest socioeconomic group, but 61 percent from the highest group, were in four-year colleges and universities.[6] It is clear that those from socioeconomically advantaged families will ultimately reach higher levels of educational attainment than those who are disadvantaged.

Previously unavailable data indicate that scores on the Scholastic Aptitude Test (SAT) also vary with social class. White students from families with 1980 incomes of less than $6,000 had median verbal and math scores of 404 and 435, respectively, whereas those from families earning

$50,000 or more had median scores of 461V and 509M. The same direct relationship between parental incomes and SAT scores also existed within ethnic minority groups.[7]

### Race and Ethnicity

Some racial and ethnic groups in the United States have higher levels of educational accomplishment than others. Japanese, Chinese, and Jewish children tend to do particularly well, for example. The academic accomplishments of most other minority groups, such as blacks, Puerto Ricans, Mexican-Americans, and American Indians, are lower than that of whites.

The HEW studies mentioned earlier included the achievements of black, Hispanic, Asian, and white students. The Hispanic category included all students who identified themselves as Mexican-American, Chicano, Puerto Rican, or of other Latin American origin.

On each of the standardized tests used in the study of 1982 seniors, the mean scores of white and Asian students were highest, and the mean score of black students was lowest; Hispanic students fell in between. For example, on the verbal skills test the mean for white students was 33.1. Asian students followed closely behind with a mean of 31.6. The mean for Hispanic students was 20.4 and for black students 19.8. Corresponding scores on the mathematics test were 17.4, 20.2, 8.9 and 8.5.[8]

When the grades of these students were examined, a similar, but not identical, pattern was revealed. In all subjects, including English, mathematics, science, social science, business, arts, and trade and industry courses, Asian students outperformed all other groups. In English, for example, 25.6 percent of the Asian students received an A grade as compared to 19.2 percent of the whites, 10.1 percent of the Hispanics, and 9.7 percent of the black students. In mathematics, the gap between the Asian and white students was even greater, with 27.6 percent of the Asian students but only 18.4 percent of the whites getting A grades. The largest concentration of low grades was found among Hispanic and black students. Almost a third of these students received D or F grades in such basic subjects as English, mathematics, and science.[9]

Racial and ethnic patterns can also be found in Scholastic Aptitude Test (SAT) scores. Asian students outscore whites in mathematics, but whites score higher on the verbal section of the test. Hispanic students' scores fall between those of the white and Asian groups, on the one hand, and those of black students, on the other.[10] These findings fit the general pattern consistently reported in the education literature. When achievement is measured by standardized tests or classroom grades, white students tend to do better than non-Asian minority students.[11]

Many studies have shown that the educational attainment of whites is greater than that of blacks and most other minorities, but this picture is changing. Traditionally, whites far outdistanced minority students in educational attainment. Blacks born at the turn of the century, for example, attained a median of 5.1 years of education as compared to 8.9 years for whites.[12] This gap is easy to understand in light of the history of black education in the United States. As we indicated in earlier chapters, blacks and other minorities have often been systematically denied equal access to education.

The gap between black and white educational attainment has narrowed considerably in recent years, however. In 1975, the median level of education attained by blacks who had been born between 1946 and 1950 was 12.5 years; for whites born in the same period, it was 12.8.[13] In 1984, the median number of school years completed was 12.6 for whites, 12.2 for blacks, and 11.3 for those of Spanish origin.[14]

Differences in rates of high school graduation have, of course, shown a parallel decline. Sixty percent of whites born from 1913 to 1922 graduated from high school, whereas only about one-quarter of black and Hispanic youth graduated.[15] By 1982, 84.7 percent of white twenty to twenty-four year olds had completed high school, as compared to 77.3 percent of blacks and 59.6 percent of Hispanics.[16] The higher dropout rate among minority students is clearly evident in these percentages.

Similar long term trends have occurred in higher education. By 1970, 11.3 percent of all whites had completed four or more years of college; so had 4.4 percent of all blacks and 6.0 percent of those of Spanish origin. In 1984 these figures were 19.8, 10.4, and 8.2 respectively.[17]

Data on students who were seniors in 1982 suggest that these patterns are likely to continue into the future. The educational plans of these seniors showed that 75 percent of the Asian students, 52 percent of the whites, 46 percent of the blacks, and 35 percent of the Hispanics were planning to attend college in the year after high school.[18] Two years after the 1980 class had graduated, 86 percent of the Asians, 64 percent of the whites, 60 percent of the blacks, and 52 percent of the Hispanics were actually enrolled in some type of postsecondary education. Asian and white students were more likely than black and Hispanic students to be in four-year colleges or universities.[19]

### Gender

The relationship between educational accomplishment and gender varies strikingly according to what measure of educational success is being used. In this respect, the pattern differs considerably from those observed for socioeconomic and ethnic variables.

If we look at school adjustment and classroom performance, we find that girls have many fewer problems than boys. Beginning with kindergarten and continuing through the public school years, girls are less likely than boys to get into trouble for misbehaving or to require special remedial programs.[20] Girls' grades in both elementary school and high school tend to be higher than boys'. The mean grade point average of females in the class of 1982 was 2.7; for males, it was 2.5.[21] Almost 28 percent of the females, as compared to 22 percent of the males, had straight A averages. In fact, the females received more A grades in every subject, including mathematics, science, business, and trade and industry. In English, foreign language, and the arts, approximately ten percent more females than males received A grades.[22]

Although girls get better grades, boys often score higher on standardized tests. Among 1982 seniors, boys outperformed girls on the mathematics skills test, 16.2 to 14.5, and the science test, 10.8 to 9.5. Girls did better on the combined verbal skills tests of reading, writing, and vocabulary, scoring 31.0 to the boys' 29.0.[23] However, boys had a slight edge on the reading subtest.[24] The National Assessment of Educational Progress has consistently shown that females achieve higher reading scores than males. However, when it comes to SAT scores, males have outperformed females in verbal as well as quantitative skills since 1972. The gap between the SAT scores of males and females has increased over the years. In 1972, boys outperformed girls by two points in verbal ability and forty-four points in mathematics. By 1985, these differences were twelve and forty-seven points respectively.[25]

Turning to educational attainment rather than achievement, we continue to find mixed results. The median number of years of schooling completed by men and women is now approximately equal: 12.7 for men and 12.6 for women in 1984.[26] However, men still continue to obtain a disproportionate share of doctor's and first professional degrees.

Throughout most of the twentieth century, women graduated from high school in greater proportions than men. Among young people in 1950, for example, 53.6 percent of the men, but 60 percent of the women, were receiving a high school diploma.[27] This gap has narrowed in recent years, but females are still more likely than males to complete high school.[28]

In spite of higher rates of high school graduation among women, the overall level of educational attainment of men has traditionally been greater than that of women. This is because women have been less likely than men to go on to college and obtain advanced degrees. Women showed impressive gains in college attendance during the 1970s, however, and since 1979, women have comprised the majority of college students.[29] Beginning with the 1981-82 academic year, women received slightly more than 50 percent of all bachelor's degrees.[30] This trend is likely to continue. Among 1982 seniors, 55 percent of the women, but only 45 percent of the men planned to attend college immediately after graduation.[31] Among 1980 seniors studied in 1982, 66 percent of the females, but only 59 percent of the males, were actually enrolled in postsecondary education.[32]

Women have also shown spectacular gains at the master's level. A milestone was reached in 1981 when for the first time women received over half of all master's degrees awarded.[33] This figure is projected to hover slightly below 53 percent at least into the mid-1990s.

Although women have also made gains at the most advanced educational levels, they still lag behind men. Women are currently receiving approximately one third of all doctor's degrees. This figure has risen from only 14 percent in 1970.[34] Women are also receiving approximately 30 percent of all first professional degrees, up from only 6.3 percent in 1970.[35]

## EXPLAINING PATTERNS OF EDUCATIONAL SUCCESS

Sociologists looking at statistics on educational success often disagree on how to interpret them. Consensus theorists focus on convergences in educational attainment and achievement between various groups and on the large numbers of poor, minority, and female students who attend institutions of higher learning. These data are cited as evidence that educational opportunities are no longer substantially tied to ascriptive characteristics and that allocation into occupational categories is based on competence rather than accidents of birth.

An example of this type of argument can be found in Hauser and Featherman's 1976 discussion of educational attainment.[36] Hauser and Featherman analyzed cohorts of males born during the first half of the twentieth century and concluded that there has been an overall decline in inequality of schooling since the turn of the century. They base their conclusion on three central facts. First, the mean or average number of years of schooling completed by each succeeding cohort has steadily increased. Among those born in 1897 to 1901, the mean number of years of schooling completed was 8.9; among those born in 1947 to 1951, it was 12.8. Second, the variability of years of schooling completed is considerably lower in later-born cohorts than in earlier ones. In later cohorts, the educational attainment of individuals is clustered closer to the mean level attained by their entire cohort. Fewer people attain either exceptionally low or exceptionally high levels of education. Third, the negative impact that certain ascribed characterisics had on educational attainment earlier in the century has, according to their analysis, declined. For example, coming from a broken home or being black were greater handicaps to educational attainment in the past than either is now.

Unlike Hauser and Featherman, conflict theorists focus on the continued educational differentials between ascriptive groups. The educational differentials referred to earlier in this chapter are cited as evidence that educational institutions perpetuate present patterns of socioeconomic, racial, and sexual inequities. In looking at the Hauser and Featherman data, for example, conflict theorists might point out that although variability in educational attainment has decreased over this century, the importance of remaining variability has probably increased. Early in the century, differences in educational attainment had less significance for one's socioeconomic future than they do today. Furthermore, as Hauser and Featherman themselves report, and as conflict theorists such as Bowles and Gintis reiterate,[37] the effects of such ascriptive factors as father's education and occupation on educational attainment have remained stable over the course of this century.

Whatever theoretical orientation is used, however, it is clear that a statistical description of educational attainment and achievement is necessary but not sufficient for a real understanding of the functioning of our educational system. The important question of why some groups do better in school and stay there longer than other groups is still unanswered. We will turn now to some possible explanations of these patterns and to a more thorough evaluation of the educational process.

Attempts to explain patterns of educational attainment and achievement can be classified into two general categories: those that focus on the characteristics of students and their families, and those that focus on the characteristics of the schools and the broader society.

## Children and their Families

Explanations that focus on the characteristics of children and their families stress that children are several years old by the time they enter school, and that they are already the complex products of their genetic endowments and social experiences. They come to school with a variety of talents and handicaps that already predispose them toward school success or failure, and as they move through school they continue to be influenced by these factors and by others that are beyond the control of educational institutions. Let us look more closely at some of these factors.

### Mental Ability

Most of us assume that mental ability plays a major role in how successful we are in school. Indeed, studies have consistently shown that, all other things being equal, individuals with high scores on mental ability tests tend to receive higher grades in school and to complete more years of schooling.

Although mental ability is often measured by I.Q. tests, it can also be measured in other ways. The longitudinal high school studies we have been discussing combine achievement test results into a cognitive ability score. Among 1980 seniors, higher ability students received higher grades. Those in the highest quartile on ability had a mean grade point average of 3.37; those in the lowest quartile had a mean average of 2.43.[38] Among 1982 seniors, 42 percent of those in the highest ability quartile had A averages, compared to only 13 percent in the lowest ability quartile.[39] A similar pattern is observed when we turn to college plans and attendence. Over 76 percent of the highest ability 1982 seniors were planning to attend college immediately after graduation; only 25 percent of the lowest ability students had similar plans.[40] Two years after graduation, 86 percent of the highest ability students in the class of 1980 were in postsecondary education, as compared to 46 percent of the lowest ability students.[41]

Of course, all other things are not usually equal. People vary on many different dimensions and several of these can affect the relationship between mental ability and both educational achievement and attainment. Gender is a good example of such a variable. There is still considerable debate about the possible existence of gender linked ability differences. The most frequently cited finding is that girls excel in verbal ability and boys excel in quantitative skills and visual-spatial ability, especially after adolescence. Even if this were the case, however, it could not explain the fact that males now outperform females on the verbal section of the SAT or that girls receive higher grades than boys in mathematics as well as in English. Neither would it explain the long history of lower educational attainment among women. In the past, when men and women with similar scores on mental ability tests were compared, the similarity in their ability did not result in similarity of educational attainment. Men received more education than women of equal talent. Consequently, it was once estimated that 75 percent of all intellectually qualified youngsters who did not enter college were girls, and that female brainpower was one of our nation's most wasted resources. We have already pointed out that women now receive more than half of all bachelor's and master's degrees, but they are still underrepresented among those receiving doctor's and first professional degrees.

If we turn to socioeconomic variables, we find that individuals from more socioeconomically advantaged backgrounds have higher levels of measured ability than those from less advantaged backgrounds. For example, the typical I.Q. difference between the children of professional fathers and those of working-class fathers has been estimated as twenty points.[42] This difference is consistent with the higher levels of educational achievement found among students from middle- and upper-middle-class homes, and sociologists have made repeated efforts to determine whether these intelligence score differences can account for all the social class variations in educational achievement.

Christopher Jencks has estimated that overall, "about a third of the discrepancy in educational attainment between economically advantaged and disadvantaged students is explained by differences in their test scores."[43] This still leaves much to be explained. In other words, if we look only at children with similar scores on mental ability tests, those from privileged backgrounds still manage to acquire more years of schooling than their less affluent peers. Differences in educational achievement among various socioeconomic groups can only be partially accounted for by differences in mental ability among these groups.

Neither can differences in measured ability scores totally explain the patterns of educational achievement associated with racial and ethnic groups, although they make a contribution to this understanding. Blacks and most other minority groups have average mental ability scores that are lower than those of whites: The average I.Q. difference between black and white children is approximately 15 points.[44] Within minority group populations, mental ability scores are related to socioeconomic status in much the same way as they are for whites; the higher the socioeconomic status of a member of a minority group, the higher his I.Q. is likely to be.[45]

The lower average mental ability scores of black and minority children is consistent with their lower levels of educational achievement, but some interesting findings were uncovered when black and white children of similar ability were compared: Black children outperformed whites in grades and in number of school years completed.[46] The first follow-up data from the 1970 national longitudinal study reflected this fact. Among each of the three ability groups tested, higher proportions of both black and Hispanic-American students were enrolled in college a year and a half after high school graduation than were white students. Among the highest ability group, 70 percent of the whites, but 79 percent of the blacks and 78 percent of the Hispanic-Americans, were enrolled. The parallel figures for the lowest ability group were 14 percent for whites and 24 percent for both blacks and Hispanics.

Similarly, Jencks pointed out that data gathered during the decade of the sixties showed blacks to be obtaining more education than whites when ability and socioeconomic status were taken into account.[47] Such findings indicate that black-white differences in the number of years of schooling completed can be explained primarily in terms of the overall lower ability test scores of black students and the concentration of blacks among the poor.

However, black-white differences in educational achievement are less well explained by mental ability scores and socioeconomic factors. As late as 1976, Gordon found that when black and white children with similar I.Q. scores and socioeconomic backgrounds were compared, blacks tended to have lower achievement test scores than whites.[48] These lower scores must be explained by factors other than the lower average I.Q. of blacks or their concentration among the poor. We will be looking at possible explanations throughout the remainder of this chapter.

In summary, differences in ability scores account for some, but not all, of the differences in educational achievement and attainment among socioeconomic and racial groups. They do not account for differences in the educational achievement and attainment of men and women.

Before looking at some other sources of explanation for these differences, one further important question about mental ability must be answered, however: Why is it that mental ability test scores are so clearly related to socioeconomic and racial factors? Why do children born into minority groups and economically disadvantaged families receive lower ability test scores than others?

*The Meaning of Intelligence Test Scores.* Although many people view intelligence as a generalized ability to think logically and to solve mental problems, research has shown that there is no single, unidimensional trait that can be reasonably labeled "intelligence." What we normally regard as intelligence is actually made up of several distinct types of mental abilities, which are not necessarily highly correlated with each other. For example, Maccoby and Jacklin distinguish spatial, verbal, analytic, conceptual, and reasoning abilities as a minimum classification, and then subdivide each of these.[49]

Most commonly used measures of intelligence, including standardized I.Q. tests, are oversimplified in that they tap only a few of the many facets and styles of intellectual functioning. Children who are weak in the specific dimensions being tested will get low overall intelligence scores, although their abilities along other dimensions might be average or even superior.

Some researchers believe that intelligence tests do not fairly sample all varieties of intellectual skills, but that they favor the kinds of skills at which white middle-class children excel. For example, intelligence tests rarely measure how individuals solve practical problems requiring long-term planning and involvement. Instead, they emphasize the ability to work rapidly at solving brief abstract problems. Reissman has suggested, however, that economically disadvantaged children are particularly weak on short speed-oriented items.[50] Studies have also indicated that at least some racial and ethnic groups show distinctive patterns of strengths and weaknesses in their ability profiles.[51] For example, blacks tend to be stronger in verbal skills than in quantitative skills, whereas the pattern for Asians is reversed. Within each particular ethnic or racial group, ability test scores rise along with socioeconomic status, but the overall pattern of abilities stays the same. For example, middle-class Asian-Americans receive higher scores than working-class Asian-Americans, but within each of these two groups averages on quantitative tests are higher than on verbal tests. It is clear, then, that the specific items included on an intelligence test can favor one group of children and handicap another.

There is another way in which intelligence test scores deviate from our conception of them as reliable measures of overall mental ability. Intelligence test scores can vary for the same individual at different times. Scores are affected by a person's mood, anxiety about test-taking, hostility toward the examiner, or practice in taking similar tests. Children who are already failing in school or who belong to a different ethnic or racial group than the examiner might be especially likely to score low because of such factors. Riessman considers the issue of rapport and motivation to be crucial for understanding the test scores of disadvantaged children, and evidence supporting the effects of improved rapport on verbal scores is dramatically described by William Labov.[52]

A number of studies have focused on the effects of practice on intelligence test scores. As early as the 1950s, Ernest Haggard was able to show that the I.Q. scores of disadvantaged children improved sharply with only three hours of practice.[53] Later, programs were developed that successfully raised the I.Q. scores of preschool children.[54] Although these improvements in I.Q. were not always permanent, they clearly illustrated the relevance of experience for how well individuals score on such tests.

The success of some of these experiments in raising I.Q. scores encouraged researchers to focus on the early experiences of children, and especially on the interaction between children and their mothers for explanations of children's scores. Racial and social class differences in intelligence test scores do not emerge until children are one or two years of age, but they are clearly delineated by the age of three.[55]

Evidence for the importance of parent-child interaction in shaping early I.Q. scores can be found in a series of studies conducted as part of the Harvard Pre-School Project.[56] Toddlers between the ages of one and three were observed in their home environment over several months and interaction between mothers and children carefully observed. Major differences in levels of competence began to emerge when the children were somewhere between ten months and one-and-one-half years of age, with some children going on to develop into well-adjusted, intelligent youngsters and others lagging far behind.

Burton White attributed these differences to how mothers interacted with their children. The most talented children had mothers who provided many toys and much freedom of movement. These mothers did not spend much time directly interacting with their children and many of them worked; however, they structured the child's environment so as to stimulate and encourage curiosity and exploration, and they acted as "consultants" when they did interact with the child, building in language skills, adding ideas related to what the child was doing, and teaching that adults are good resources for information. Mothers of less successful children tended to restrict their child's physical movement and seldom encouraged their children's attempts to make sense of the world.

Another set of studies were conducted specifically on the children of poor black women whose own I.Q. scores were less than 75.[57] The children were visited at home from infancy and their mothers instructed in baby care, homemaking, and nutrition. From three months of age, the children were brought to educational centers and provided with perceptual, motor, and language stimulation on a one-to-one basis. At two, each child was put in a class with five other youngsters and three teachers. The classes were enlarged as the children grew older. All classes met on a full-time daily basis. At the age of five, these children had an average I.Q. of 124, with some testing as high as 135. A comparable group of children not receiving the experimental treatment had average I.Q. scores that were 30 points lower.

Not every similar study has been this successful. The Mother-Child Home Program provided forty-six twice-weekly home visits to mothers of two year olds. The visits were designed to improve mother-child verbal interaction. Although the mothers did significantly improve their verbal interaction with their children, the children showed only modest I.Q. gains. No lasting effects on first grade school adjustment or achievement were demonstrated.[58]

An analysis of a large number of childhood intervention projects suggests that the most successful projects have started with young children, have actively instructed and involved the mother in the teaching of her own child, have moved the child out of the home and into a group program on a daily basis, and have continued extra support services after the child has been moved into a regular school classroom.[59] Such studies highlight the contribution of early childhood experiences to intellectual devlopment, but also show that intervention must be substantial to make a difference.

Sociologists have known for a long time that there are social class variations in child-rearing practices.[60] Middle-class parents, both black and white, tend to encourage curiosity, initiative, and independence. Working- and lower-class parents tend to encourage obedience, neatness, honesty, and docility. Even in their preferences for types of teachers, middle-class mothers are much more likely than working-class mothers to prefer teachers who emphasize encouraging creativity and self-initiative as opposed to teachers who stress discipline or mastery of subject matter.[61] The child-rearing preferences and practices of middle-class families seem to facilitate the kind of intellectual development that leads to high I.Q. scores. Preferences and practices of economically disadvantaged families seem to inhibit it.[62]

Because minority children are disproportionately poor, social class differences in child-rearing practices can also explain some of the gap between blacks and whites on mental ability tests. Indeed, some studies have shown that the closer the family characteristics of black and Chicano children are to those of white middle-class children, the closer are the I.Q. scores of all three groups.[63]

Considerable confusion exists in the sociological literature regarding the extent of these differences in child-rearing practices, how they should be interpreted, and what, if anything, might be done about them. The consensus perspective tends to stress the degree to which child-rearing practices among widely divergent segments of American society overlap. For example, there is empirical evidence to suggest that differences in child-rearing practices across social classes is far less today than it was in the past, and that the influence of the mass media will probably diminish these differences even further in the future. To the extent that some groups (such as the poor) may still have substantially different child-rearing practices, consensus theory suggests that these practices are inadequate and maladaptive, retarding the movement of these families into the mainstream of American life. As a solution, consensus theory implies that programs to educate parents in how to stimulate and care for their children would be helpful; so would programs to supplement or even replace parental care with early childhood education—in day care centers, for example.

Conflict theory, of course, focuses on the continued existence of differences among socioeconomic and racial groups. This perspective denies that the child-rearing practices of disadvantaged groups are any less adequate than those of the white middle class. Instead, it emphasizes that the child-rearing practices of disadvantaged groups produce children who are well prepared to cope with the kinds of life experiences they are likely to encounter, and that these children have many talents and abilities lacking in middle-class children. It is only when a middle-class standard of adequate socialization is used, such as that symbolized by the I.Q. test, that these children seem inadequate. From this perspective programs that "impose" middle-class values on disadvantaged youth seem outrageous.[64]

Bowles and Gintis, two conflict theorists mentioned earlier, have taken a somewhat different approach.[65] They argue that the child-rearing patterns of various social classes are a product of their position in the economic structure and that these practices, reinforced by the schools, perpetuate these positions from one generation to the next. Bowles and Gintis argue, for example, that the working-class emphasis on obedience to rules derives from the occupational experiences of working-class parents in jobs requiring subordination and conformity. The family life of these workers also becomes permeated with these values and they are passed on to the next generation. Learning this pattern of behavior prepares children to enter educational and occupational slots similar to their parents. Because they lack such middle-class personality traits as curiosity and independence, these children will find pathways to upward mobility closed to them. From this perspective, only substantial change in the economic structure and the nature of work would reduce class differences in child-rearing practices.

There are many ways other than through child-rearing practices that socioeconomic status, race, and ethnicity affect I.Q. Nutritional deficiencies experienced prenatally and in early postnatal development have been linked to lowered mental ability,[66] as has the neglect of various medical problems, including visual and auditory handicaps.[67] The child who cannot hear clearly can easily become one who cannot speak, read, or manipulate thought through language. Even living in overcrowded, noisy conditions can have a depressing effect on intellectual functioning.[68]

Other experiences unequally distributed among socioeconomic, ethnic, and racial groups are also relevant to performance on intelligence tests; language patterns are an example. I.Q. tests are generally administered in what linguists refer to as Standard English, the language in which this text is written. Yet black children often speak a dialect known as Black English, or Nonstandard Negro English, in their homes and communities. Hispanic children often speak Spanish. Examiners sometimes conclude that children using Nonstandard English language forms lack verbal or reasoning ability, claiming that such linguistic forms do not even permit abstract conceptual thought. Yet, linguists have documented that these dialects are highly structured and complex, and that they are clearly compatible with sophisticated thought and expression.[69]

Exposure to other aspects of American culture also affects test scores. Information items or vocabulary words included on many tests are more familiar to certain groups of children than to others. In a classic study done in 1929, Shimberg showed how items believed to be free of cultural bias actually discriminated against children reared in rural setting, and that this probably accounted for the lower intelligence scores rural children were consistently obtaining on ability tests.[70] More recent analyses have pointed to items that discriminate against children whose experiences differ from those of white middle-class Americans. For example, one analysis described an item on a picture test in which children were expected to pair the picture of a cup with a picture of a saucer. Instead, Mexican-American children paired the cup with a table. These children were not familiar with saucers; in their experience, cups were placed directly on the table.[71] A student in one of our classes gave another interesting example of cultural bias in standardized ability tests. This student's mother was a reading disabilities specialist whose job it was to test children for various types of intellectual impairments. One of the tests she administered orally to elementary school students asked them to define the word "submarine." The only acceptable answer was one referring to a boat that could move under water. Yet many students defined it as a type of sandwich. These children were especially likely to be living in depressed areas where many inexpensive quick-food stores are located. They were, unfortunately, marked down for giving an "incorrect" answer. The bias is clear, and although there have been efforts to remove the most blatant biases from standardized tests, it is generally recognized that no test can be entirely "culture free." It is important to keep this in mind when interpreting intelligence test results.

All of these facts indicate that intelligence tests do not tell us about an individual's overall potential for learning. Rather, they are measures of certain types of achievement and learning that have already taken place.

They are useful in assessing mastery over some highly specific intellectual skills and in predicting children's school success. You recall that researchers have found that variations in educational achievement and attainment can be partially explained by variations in intelligence test scores. This is not surprising. The skills measured on intelligence tests are the same skills required in the conventional classroom. It is important to remember, however, that intelligence tests cannot predict how well individuals will learn in other kinds of settings, how well they will do in the community, or what their potential would be if different educational strategies were introduced into the classroom.

*The Debate over Genetic Determinants.* Some theories attribute I.Q. differences among socioeconomic and racial groups to genetic factors. These theories are based on two central hypotheses, neither of which is currently testable. The first hypothesis is that genetic factors account for a substantial proportion of observed variations in individual I.Q. scores. The second hypothesis is that socioeconomic and racial groups represent different gene pools, each having a greater or lesser abundance of those genes that contribute to intellectual superiority.

Both of these hypotheses have been attacked on several grounds.[72] All the evidence we have presented above concerning the effect of experience on I.Q. scores, the cultural biases built into I.Q. tests, and our inability to measure any kind of "innate" intellectual potential have been cited. In addition, the considerable crossbreeding of racial and socioeconomic groups in the United States are important to consider.

Arthur Jensen,[73] Richard Herrnstein,[74] and others[75] who defend the genetic theory have argued that there is a tendency for individuals to marry others similar to themselves in socioeconomic background and for people to rise or fall in the stratification system according to their natural intellectual abilities. In other words, they argue that the brightest people, endowed with the most superior genetic make-up, will rise to the top of the stratification system and intermarry, passing their favorable genes on to their offspring. Any person inheriting a lower level of intelligence will sink to the appropriate socioeconomic level, and likewise pass on this inferior make-up. Children who inherit levels of intelligence different from their parents' will be downwardly or upwardly mobile in relation to their ability and birth status.

The assumptions underlying this model are readily apparent. At minimum, it assumes a system that accurately assesses and rewards individual ability. Much of this book suggests that American society, at least, is not sufficiently open or equitable to support these assumptions. Further, the frequency of marriages across socioeconomic strata is considerable, working against the assumptions of homogamous in-breeding.

The research and statistical methods used to substantiate the impact of heredity on I.Q. have long been controversial. The whole hereditarian position was badly undercut when it was discovered that one of its major proponents was a fraud. Sir Cyril Burt had been honored as the father of British educational psychology. He had conducted important studies of the

I.Q. scores of identical twins raised apart. These studies provided strong support for the genetic case. However, since Sir Cyril's death in 1971, it has become apparent that his work was largely fraudulent. He not only fabricated his data but he even invented the research assistants who were supposed to have gathered the data.[76]

Nevertheless, hereditarians such as Arthur Jensen, argue that there is still considerable legitimate data to support their position. Jensen argues that black students score lower than whites on nonverbal as well as verbal I.Q. tests, that blacks score significantly higher on tests that are "culture-loaded" than on those that are "culture-reduced," and that I.Q. gains among young children involved in intervention programs usually fade within one to three years.[77] None of these findings proves that there is a genetic basis to differences in I.Q. scores.[78]

We do not have the space to detail all sides of the debate over I.Q. determinants. For our purposes, however, the question seems moot. It is obvious to us all that human intellectual functioning is highly malleable and sensitive to experience. Until we can provide equity to poor and minority children in terms of nutrition, medical care, housing, early childhood stimulation, and other relevant experiences, and until we can devise measures of intelligence that are free of cultural bias, we can only assume that these deprivations represent the most reasonable explanation of intelligence test score differences to date.

There is a real question, though, as to why I.Q. tests continue to be used and why so much time and energy have been devoted to them. Consensus theory suggests that such tests may reflect the more general trend toward increasingly universalistic standards of evaluation and allocation in modern societies. Through the use of standardized tests, talent can be objectively identified. Then, each individual can be given the kind of education and occupational responsibilities most suited to his or her abilities.

Conflict theory suggests that intelligence tests were developed as a mechanism for perpetuating and legitimizing socioeconomic inequalities. At the time that these tests were adopted and developed in the United States, there was considerable concern among some Americans about the inferior genetic quality of immigrants arriving from southwestern European countries.[79] As Kamin points out in *The Science and Politics of I.Q.*, the I.Q. test was used to "prove" this inferiority.[80] The overwhelming majority of recent immigrants who took these tests failed, and this failure was interpreted as "proof" of their inferior genetic stock. Legislation restricting immigration followed soon after. After all, "83% of the Jews, 80% of the Hungarians, 79% of the Italians, and 87% of the Russians" had been shown to be "feeble-minded" by these tests.[81] Similar interpretations were put on the low scores of the poor and working classes. Unemployment, poverty, and crime were interpreted as products of inherited characteristics, destining the "degenerate" races to educational, occupational, and social failure. Thus, Kamin argues that from the beginning I.Q. tests were really political rather than scientific instruments, used to further constrict the opportunities offered to the disadvantaged and justify their position at the bottom of the stratification system.

## Attitudes and Values

As we have seen, differences in educational achievement are only partially accounted for by differences in intelligence test scores, and these scores themselves are forms of educational achievement that must be explained. Sociologists have looked at students' attitudes and values as one possible source of such explanation. Their focus has been on two general sets of attitudes and values: those that directly involve education and those that affect educational achievement in more subtle and indirect ways. Included in the first category are attitudes toward education, achievement, and learning. Included in the second category are attitudes toward the self and toward the future.

A number of studies have looked at the attitudes and values of various racial, ethnic, and socioeconomic groups. One early study, directed by Fred Strodtbeck in the 1950s, set out to explain the high levels of achievement found among Jews.[82] Strodtbeck compared the attitudes and values of Jewish families to those of Catholic Italian families. Although the Italians had immigrated to the United States at about the same time as the Jews, they had not been as educationally and occupationally successful. Strodtbeck found that, in contrast to the Italian Catholic families, Jewish families were more likely to encourage individual achievement, were more willing to have their sons leave home in order to seek success, and were more likely to emphasize planning for the future. Jewish families were also less authoritarian and encouraged independence in their children. Strodtbeck argued that these values directly supported educational and occupational achievement and that they helped explain the superior academic achievement of Jewish students. Strodtbeck's study is consistent with several others that have compared child-rearing practices and attitudes among various socioeconomic groups. As we suggested earlier, middle-class families are more likely than working-class or poor families to encourage independence, self-discipline, creativity, and self-actualization. Working-class families are more concerned with obedience, respect, and cleanliness.

Of course, many children from working-class and poor families do well in school, and one study by Joseph Kahl was interested in what attitudinal differences might exist between the families of these children and those of others who did not achieve well in school.[83] Kahl discovered that the working-class families with sons who were successful in school were more likely than others to stress the importance of getting ahead. These families tended to be dissatisfied with their own situation in life and the parents were anxious that their sons do better than they had. Importantly, these parents also believed that the key to success was education. They took a strong interest in their son's progress in school and rewarded him when he did well. Like Strodtbeck's work, Kahl's study suggests that the attitudes of students and their families are important in shaping educational achievement. Unfortunately, however, these two studies were small, looked only at male children, and were somewhat impressionistic. A more comprehensive study was, however, published in 1966 by a panel of researchers directed by James Coleman.

Coleman's study, *Equality of Educational Opportunity*, was a comprehensive survey of American schools that included information on over 645,000 pupils.[84] Each student was given a series of achievement tests covering verbal ability, reading comprehension, mathematics, general information, and nonverbal ability. Coleman was especially interested in ethnic and racial factors and most of his data are analyzed in terms of the six groups he tested: whites, blacks, Mexican-Americans, Asian Americans, Puerto Ricans, and Indian Americans. Coleman found that the students' scores on these tests were related to race and ethnicity. Whites had higher scores than all but one of the other groups. Asian Americans occasionally scored as high or higher than whites. This conforms to previous findings on patterns of educational achievement. However, Coleman's data also included attitudinal measures, and he was able to relate attitudes to test scores.

Coleman's survey included several items designed to measure interest in learning and motivation. These items asked students how much time they spent studying, how they would feel if they had to quit school, how often they stayed away from school because they didn't want to go, and how high in class rank they wanted to be. In general, those groups with higher achievement test scores showed more positive attitudes toward school—with one major exception. Overall, black students showed the most positive attitudes, surpassing even whites and Asians.

Similar questions were asked in the National Longitudinal Study of the class of 1982. Of all racial/ethnic groups questioned, blacks were least likely to say that they cut classes and less likely than all but Asian students to say that they attended classes without homework completed.[85]

Coleman uncovered a similar pattern regarding educational aspirations. Educational aspirations—or how much education an individual wants to acquire—reflect a combination of attitudes, ranging from general beliefs about the value of schooling to feelings about classroom activities. Research has shown that students from socioeconomically advantaged backgrounds tend to have higher educational aspirations than students from less advantaged backgrounds, but also that black students have exceptionally high levels of educational aspirations. Coleman's data consistently found that fewer black students than white students wanted to end their education with high school. Analyses and research, reported by Jencks and others,[86] Rosenberg and Simmons,[87] and Portes and Wilson[88] have continued to confirm this phenomenon.

What do these findings imply about the relationship between attitudes and educational achievement? In general, positive attitudes toward education are prominent among groups that have high levels of educational achievement, but blacks, whose level of educational achievement is below that of whites, have very positive attitudes and high levels of aspiration. Sometimes, researchers have interpreted the high educational aspirations of black students as "unrealistic," indicating that black students lack either factual knowledge about how difficult it is to obtain higher education, adequate counseling, or the ability to set appropriate life goals. For example, Coleman refers to the "considerable lack of realism in aspirations, especially among Negroes whose responses deviate most from actual rates of college-going and completion of high school."[89] Yet, as we indicated earlier, black educational attainment has increased rapidly over the last two decades, and there is evidence that in comparison to whites of equal socioeconomic status and ability, blacks do, in fact, attain more education. In an interesting article, published in 1976, Portes and Wilson argued that blacks are disadvantaged relative to whites in terms of their lower socioeconomic status and ability test scores, but that the high levels of aspirations expressed by blacks represents a real educational advantage for them.[90] In fact, Portes and Wilson hypothesized that personal aspirations, motivation, and willingness to work hard may be especially important in facilitating the educational success of groups that are not yet fully integrated into the mainstream of American life.

*Self-Concept.* Among the more indirect attitudinal influences on education that have received attention in the literature is self-concept, that is, an individual's attitudes toward oneself. Do you think of yourself in a positive way, as competent, attractive, likeable, intelligent, and so on, or in a negative way, as awkward, ugly, dumb, or belligerent, for example? Social psychologists have long argued that once people develop a particular view of themselves, they behave in ways which are compatible with that view. People who believe they have no aptitude for science, for example, will avoid taking science courses, get extremely anxious when taking tests in science, and simply stop making any real effort to master scientific material. As a result, they will, in fact, do poorly in science and demonstrate little scientific aptitude. Their original self-concept will become a self-fulfilling prophecy.

Many people have argued that negative self-concepts might be particularly prevalent among children who have experienced discrimination or economic deprivation, and that this might explain why these groups do less well in school than others. There is some evidence that at least partially supports this hypothesis—but some does not.

First, a number of studies have shown that self-concept varies systematically with social class, at least for whites.[91] Children who come from more affluent backgrounds tend to have a more positive view of themselves than other children, and as you know by now, they also do better in school. On the other hand, this relationship between socioeconomic status and self-concept does not seem as definite if we look only at black students. A study conducted in 1971 by Rosenberg and Simmons on a random sample of 2,625 students in the Baltimore area found a positive correlation between self-esteem and socioeconomic status for white, but not black, students.[92]

There is even more confusion surrounding the relationship between race and self-concept. A number of sociologists and psychologists have argued persuasively that black children display more negative self-concepts than whites.[93] To support their arguments, they cite the results of surveys, interviews, studies in which black children choose to play with white dolls rather than black ones, and experiments in which black children seem to believe that they are less beautiful than whites. At least two large sample studies, those of Coleman, and of Rosenberg and Simmons, do not support these findings, however. Coleman found that white and black children had similarly positive self-concepts. Rosenberg and Simmons found that black children had higher levels of self-esteem than whites. For example, 33 percent of the white students, but 46 percent of the black students in their sample had high self-esteem.

One problem with all this research is that the way in which self-concept is measured varies from one study to the next, so we cannot be certain that all the studies are actually talking about the same thing. For example, whereas Coleman's measures focused on school achievement, Rosenberg and Simmons' measures were much broader in scope. For example, Coleman asked students to agree or disagree with the statement: "I sometimes feel that I just can't learn." Rosenberg and Simmons asked students to indicate whether or not they ever felt like "I'm not much good at anything." Studies involving the choice of dolls or playmates would be even more dissimilar. Also, there may have been changes in black self-concepts over time, with the civil rights movement and the black power movement having positive effects on at least some, if not all, groups of blacks. Age, too, is an important but often neglected variable. What may be true of the self-concepts of young children may not be true for older ones.

What about the relationship between self-concept and academic achievement? Is it true that children with more negative self-concepts do less well academically than others? Again, the answer is less than clear, and seems to depend upon the race of the child we are discussing. For whites, self-concept seems to be one of the most powerful attitudinal variables affecting achievement, at least when it is measured by achievement test scores.[94] For blacks, however, self-concept does not seem to consistently affect academic achievement as measured by similar test scores. Instead, a second attitudinal variable, the sense of control an individual has over his or her environment, affects black achievement in a much more powerful way.[95]

*Sense of Control over the Environment.* Coleman's research indicated that the attitudinal variable that accounted for the largest proportion of variation in test scores for blacks and most other minority groups was their sense of control over the environment. This variable measures how confident a person is in his or her own ability to shape the future through planning and active initiative. Coleman measured this sense of control by asking students to agree or disagree with each of three statements: (1) Good luck is more important than hard work for success; (2) Every time I try to get ahead, something or someone stops me; and (3) People like me don't have much of a chance to be successful in life.

Although only a minority of students agreed with these statements, those blacks, Puerto Ricans, Indian Americans, and Mexican-Americans who did had lower verbal achievement scores than those who did not. On the whole, also, each of these groups answered yes more often than did either whites or Orientals. In other words, those children who assumed that they could affect their environment were higher achievers than those who felt that luck, fate, or other uncontrollable factors were responsible for what would happen to them.

Coleman summarized his results this way:

> For children from advantaged groups, achievement or lack of it appears closely related to their self-concept: what they believe about themselves. For children from disadvantaged groups, achievement or lack of achievement appears closely related to what they believe about their environment: whether they believe the environment will respond to reasonable efforts, or whether they believe it is instead merely random or immovable . . . children from advantaged groups assume that the environment will respond if they are able enough to affect it; children from disadvantaged groups . . . assume that nothing they will do can affect the environment—it will give benefits or withhold them but not as a consequence of their own action.[96]

It would seem logical to assume that these differences can be traced to the daily experiences of disadvantaged children. The overwhelming nature of employment, housing, health, and other problems faced by the poor, the discrimination experienced by minority groups, and the general unresponsiveness of our society to the economically disadvantaged must certainly convey to children the feeling of relative helplessness indicated in this and other studies. Indeed, Coleman found that for all groups a consistent relationship existed between the economic level of a child's home and his or her sense of control over the environment.

## Schools

Until now, we have tried to account for group differences in educational achievement by focusing on the characteristics of children and their families. We have seen that ascriptive characteristics, such as socioeconomic status, race, ethnicity, and sex have powerful impacts on educational achievement and that group differences in measured abilities, socialization experiences, attitudes, and values help explain some, but not all, of these impacts. We will now turn to a different set of variables and ask how schools contribute to group differences in educational achievement.

### Characteristics of Schools and Differences among Them

Most of us assume that some schools are better than others. If asked what makes a school good, we would probably answer in terms of the credentials of its teachers, the adequacy of its facilities, the size of its budget, and, perhaps, even the characteristics of its students. If asked about the benefits of attending a "good" school, we would probably answer in terms of higher levels of academic achievement and subsequently higher levels of educational and occupational attainment.

For many years, sociologists shared the assumptions of the general public regarding school quality, as measured by these factors, and its relationship to achievement. Sociological research did not question popular definitions of school quality and effectiveness, but, instead, focused on documenting disparities between schools attended by various groups of children. Sociologists were anxious to show that those groups whose average level of educational achievement was low attended schools that were inferior to those schools attended by groups whose average level of achievement was high. In this way, they hoped to attribute differences in educational achievement to differences in educational opportunity.

A classic example of this type of research was conducted in Detroit by Patricia Sexton in the late 1950s.[97] Sexton classified Detroit's schools according to the average income of the families whose children attended them. She then obtained information about the schools' facilities, teachers, special programs, and students' achievement. Her findings were striking documentaton of inequality in the distribution of educational resources. First, Sexton was able to document the by now familiar relationship between income and scores on standardized achievement tests. She found that all of the elementary schools whose average family income was above $7,000 performed above grade level on the Iowa Achievement tests; all schools whose average family income was below $7,000 performed below grade level. Furthermore, as children moved through school, the gap between rich and poor on these tests increased. Whereas the difference between the lowest income schools and the highest income schools was 1.36 years in the fourth grade, this difference grew to 1.9 years in the eighth grade.

Second, Sexton found that the higher income schools were superior to the lower income schools on a variety of dimensions. The higher income schools had smaller classes, better qualified teachers, newer school buildings, and better facilities. For example, there were no, or only substandard, science facilities at 47 percent of the below $7,000 schools but at only 2 percent of the above $7,000 schools. Similar findings pertained to the high schools. The average age of the below $7,000 schools was approximately twenty years greater than that of the above $7,000 schools. The implications of this study seemed clear. Poor children attended inferior schools and these inferior schools contributed to and perpetuated their academic inferiority. It was only one small step to extend this argument to minority children as well. Because we know that minority children come disproportionately from lower-income families, it was clear that they, too, must be attending inferior schools in disproportionate numbers.

Further evidence of the inferiority of schools in economically disadvantaged neighborhoods was gathered in Howard Becker's study of teachers' career patterns.[98] Becker's study of Chicago public school teachers documented the teachers' preference for white middle-class children. His data showed that new, inexperienced teachers were appointed to schools that served poor and minority students. These were the schools with many openings and few voluntary applicants. As these teachers gained experience, credentials, and seniority, they applied for transfer and moved on to schools serving higher income groups. Thus, the schools serving black and other economically disadvantaged children had high rates of teacher turnover and a disproportionate number of inexperienced and uncommitted teachers. Similar findings were reported in other more recent studies as well.[99]

Similarly, we know that there have been, and still are, wide disparities in the amount of money that school districts have to spend on their students. As we pointed out in chapter 7, the traditional source of most educational funds has been local property taxes. Some communities, such as wealthy suburbs or areas with valuable industrial properties, have a large tax base. Others, such as poor rural communities or overcrowded inner-city slums, have a small tax base, at least relative to the numbers of children that tax base must support. Even if these areas all charge the same tax rate, some will have many more dollars per pupil available than others. This situation is further complicated by the fact that communities with large numbers of students from poor families and communities in urban areas have additional costs—for special remedial and other programs in the former case and municipal overhead in the latter. In spite of the changes in funding discussed earlier, inequalities in resources still exist in many areas of the country, both between school districts and within them.

## The Coleman Report: Findings and Controversies

All these facts about differences among schools were well known in 1964, but surrounding these facts were a series of as yet untested assumptions. Among these assumptions were that: (1) children of minority racial and ethnic groups attended schools that were generally inferior to those attended by white children; (2) this inferiority could be measured in terms of such factors as school facilities, teachers' credentials, and the characteristics of children attending these schools; and (3) these school characteristics were systematically related to children's academic achievement. Not many people doubted the validity of these assumptions. In 1964, the President and the Congress commissioned a report for the purpose of surveying "the lack of availability of equal educational opportunities for individuals by reason of race, color, religion, or national origin in public educational institutions. . . .[100] The report, published in 1966, was titled *Equality of Educational Opportunity*. Most people, including both the legislators who commissioned the survey and the social scientists who conducted it, believed that the report would provide clear proof of the inequality of educational opportunity in our nation's public schools. Instead, the Coleman Report, as it is popularly called, challenged some of our most unquestioned assumptions about American education and sent shock waves through government, schools, and academia. Since the publication of the Report, there have been criticisms of its methods and conclusions. Several social scientists have reanalyzed various portions of the data. Nevertheless, the basic findings of the Report have, for the most part, been confirmed by these other efforts.[101] Let us look more carefully at some of these findings as they relate to issues of academic achievement.

*1. Segregation in the Schools.* On the fundamental question of whether or not children from different racial groups attended different schools, Coleman was able to confirm what most people had expected and what other researchers had found before: "The great majority of American children attend schools that are largely segregated."[102] This is particularly true for black children, although it holds for other racial and ethnic minorities as well. It also extends to teachers. Black teachers are concentrated in schools serving black students; white teachers in schools serving whites. To the extent that integration has occurred among teachers, white teachers teach minority children, but few minority teachers teach whites.

2. *Differences in Academic Achievements.* As we mentioned earlier, Coleman measured academic achievement in terms of students' scores on a series of achievement tests his group sent to participating schools. Some of the results of his survey might have been different if he had used grades, I.Q. tests, or other measures of either intelligence or school success. However, one finding would probably have remained the same: white children outperformed all others, except Asian Americans. This finding was not surprising. As we indicated earlier, it has been confirmed many times before and since.

Coleman also confirmed another common finding, the gap between majority and minority achievement increases the longer children remain in school. In other words, the achievement scores of white and black children, for example, get further apart as they grow older. You may recall that Sexton found a similar phenomenon in Detroit when she compared achievement levels at schools serving different socioeconomic groups.

Likewise, the more recent study of the class of 1982 showed that Asian and white students improved their verbal skills, mathematics, and science achievement scores more than black and Hispanic students as they moved from their sophomore to their senior years. Since these groups already had higher scores, the differential increase widened the gap further. Socioeconomic variables worked the same way. The gap between lower and higher status students increased over the last two years of high school.[103] Many people have suggested that this indicates the failure of schools to compensate for preschool factors leading to achievement differences between socioeconomic and racial groups. In fact, they have charged that schools add further handicaps to those that poor and minority children already experience outside of school. The Coleman Report was expected to document these additional handicaps and some of the ways the schools created them.

3. *Differences in School Characteristics.* It is here that the Coleman Report begins to get controversial. Coleman reported that although minority and majority children attended different schools, they did not attend schools that were as substantially different as had been assumed. Of course, Coleman did not measure all possible sources of variation between schools, and we will talk about some of these other sources later. Also, Coleman got his information from the schools themselves. For example, the availability of a chemistry laboratory was determined by whether or not the principal of the school claimed that one was available. Furthermore, participation in Coleman's survey was voluntary, and many of those selected for participation refused. These factors may well have biased his results. In addition, the manner in which Coleman presented his statistics and analyzed them has been criticized for obscuring some of the extreme differences that exist

within and between individual schools located in the same school districts. Nevertheless, efforts to refute Coleman's findings have not been very successful.[104]

Basically, Coleman found that on a number of factors that seem to be relevant to academic success, black students were disadvantaged relative to whites. For example, whites had greater access to physics, chemistry, and language laboratories; there were more books per pupil in their libraries; and their textbooks were in more sufficient supply. Furthermore, whites had greater access to college preparatory curriculae and to accelerated programs. Also, the average white child attended a school in which teachers had higher mean scores on verbal tests, had more advanced educational degrees, and received higher salaries.

Nevertheless, the advantages were relatively small, and not all in one direction. For example, 94 percent of blacks and 98 percent of whites attended secondary schools with a chemistry laboratory. Both groups attended elementary schools that were about as likely to have a remedial reading teacher; and blacks had the advantage when it came to elementary schools with a full-time librarian.

There were also very sizeable regional differences, with the differences between children of the same racial group who live in various parts of the country being often greater than the differences between racial groups living in the same part of the country. Sometimes, the findings were even reversed. For example, for the nation as a whole, 29 percent of all black children in elementary school attended a school with an accelerated curriculum; so did 40 percent of comparable whites. However, in the nonmetropolitan North and West, 47 percent of blacks and 26 percent of whites attended such a school. In the metropolitan Southwest, 34 percent of blacks and 76 percent of whites attended such schools. In other words, the national figures alone failed to reveal the substantial variations within and between racial groups from one part of the country to the next; thus, a simple statement about black disadvantages could be deceptive.

The school characteristic that showed the greatest variation according to race in Coleman's study was student body make-up. As we already indicated, schools in the United States were and still are highly segregated racially. In addition, though, they are segregated socioeconomically. The average black child "has fewer classmates whose mothers graduated from high school; his classmates more frequently are members of large rather than small families; they are less often enrolled in a college preparatory curriculum; they have taken a smaller number of courses in English, mathematics, foreign language, and science."[105]

Coleman did not ask students about their subjective perceptions of the students in their schools or about the general learning environment. The national longitudinal high school studies did. Among 1980 seniors, white and high socioeconomic status students rated their schools higher on both quality of academic instruction and teacher interest in students than did minority and lower socioeconomic students.[106] Among 1982 seniors, black and Hispanic students were more likely than white and Asian students to say that their schools had a problem with poor attendance, student fighting, and threats or attacks on teachers. Lower socioeconomic groups reported these problems more often than higher groups. Lower socioeconomic groups were also more likely to say that they felt unsafe at school; all minority groups were more likely to feel unsafe than whites.

*4. The Relationship between School Characteristics and Achievement.* It is here that Coleman's findings have been most hotly debated and scrutinized. Most succinctly, Coleman found that the characteristics of the schools children attended accounted for very little of the variation in their levels of achievement. The characteristics that counted least were those involving curriculum and facilities. The characteristics that counted most were those involving the make-up of the student body. The characteristics that fell between these in influence were those involving teachers' academic training, verbal test scores, and the educational level of the teachers' mothers.

Note that the more important of these factors were the ones on which whites and blacks differed most. Black-white differences were greatest when it came to student body make-up, somewhat less when it came to teacher characteristics, and least in terms of curriculum and facilities. Furthermore, Coleman found that whites and blacks had varying degrees of sensitivity to these characteristics of schools. Having better qualified teachers, for example, made more of an impact on the educational achievement of black children than it did on the achievement of white children.

Nevertheless, the most startling conclusion was that so little of the variation in academic achievement among children could be explained in terms of differences in their schools. There are several explanations for this finding. One important explanation is that Coleman found that most of the variation in children's achievement occurred within, rather than between, schools, so that differences between schools could not possibly account for this variation. In other words, if we look at any particular school, we are likely to find that there are enormous differences in achievement level between the top and the bottom students in that school. On the other hand, if we compare schools with each other, the average level of achievement of students at one school will not be as distinctly different from the average level of achievement of students from another school. There are greater differences, or more variation in achievement scores within than between schools. Differences between schools cannot be expected to explain any of the variation that occurs within them. For example, the fact that a particular school has better teachers than others cannot explain why some children in that school have high levels of achievement and others do not. Therefore, even if we combine all of the variables that measure differences between schools in Coleman's study, they cannot explain the bulk of the overall variation in achievement test scores.

In Coleman's study, the variables that did explain this variation best were those related to differences among students, rather than differences among schools. These variables were the students' home background, self-concept, and sense of environmental control, which we discussed earlier in this chapter.

## The Social Composition of Schools and the Question of Integration

As we have already indicated, children in the United States generally attend racially segregated schools. They also attend schools that are socioeconomically segregated, and over the years sociologists have focused considerable attention on the effects of attending schools with varying types of student bodies.

A number of studies have suggested that children are affected by the socioeconomic status of the other children who attend the same school.[107] In general, these studies have found that a working-class child who attends a predominantly middle-class school is more likely to have higher levels of achievement and to go on to college than is a working-class child who attends an overwhelmingly working-class school. Some studies have also found that a middle-class child who attends a predominantly working-class school is less likely to receive high achievement test scores or go on to college than is a middle-class child who goes to a predominantly middle-class school. The Coleman Report arrived at conclusions consistent with this viewpoint. Coleman suggested that one way to improve the academic achievement of poor and minority children was to integrate them with children who were more socioeconomically advantaged than they. The general assumption in these cases is that the attitudes, aspirations, work habits, and so on of the middle-class children in a school will create a climate conducive to achievement, and also that middle-class children can act as role models for others.

However, there have also been some studies that seem to contradict these conclusions. For example, a study by Alexander and Eckland suggested that the presence of high ability students in a school may actually lower the educational aspirations, attainment, and preparation of other students when ability and socioeconomic status is controlled.[108] This is because students compare themselves to these high ability peers and conclude that they are not sufficiently intelligent to have similar aspirations. In addition, several reanalyses of Coleman's data have suggested that the effect of other students' characteristics on academic achievement is either negligible or undeterminable from Coleman's data.[109] Among the difficulties here is the fact that children and their families might select themselves into different schools. In other words, a working-class family that moves into a middle-class community, or otherwise arranges for its children to attend a middle-class school, may be different from other working-class families in important ways.

These issues are even more complex and controversial when racial rather than socioeconomic integration is involved. Studies of racial composition and its effects on children have resulted in contradictory and confusing findings.[110] One reason for this is that they do not always control for all of the other ways in which schools differ from each other. For example, because minority children come disproportionately from poor families, racial integration also means socioeconomic integration in many cases, but some studies do not take these socioeconomic factors into account and attribute all observed effects to racial variables. Also, minority children, on the average, have lower achievement test scores so that racial integration may often involve integration in terms of achievement scores as well; however, studies do not often take this into account.

Another problem with these studies is that they often look at racial integration that is the result of a variety of circumstances. Some integration is achieved without planning or conscious effort. Some is the result of voluntary acton. Other times, integration occurs only after a long and bitter legal battle. Clearly, the impact of integration on school achievement might vary according to these circumstances. Effects might also vary with the age of the children involved, whether the schools are located in rural or urban areas, or with the part of the country we are looking at. In short, one reason why studies of the effects of racial composition have come to such diverse conclusions is that they are often looking at very diverse phenomena. The methods used to study desegration have also varied widely from one study to another, making consistent results less likely.

Nevertheless, in a meta-analysis of ninety-three desegregation studies, Mahard and Crain conclude that a number of clear desegregation effects emerge from the data.[111]

First, Mahard and Crain found that desegregation had a consistent positive impact on the achievement scores of black students. Second, they found that this positive impact was strongly dependent upon the grade in which the students first experienced desegregation. Only when students were desegregated from the earliest grades, preferably kindergarten or first grade, was this positive impact observed. Apparently, desegregation "creates a sudden burst of achievement growth" in the early elementary years that is then merely maintained rather than increased later on. Third, the key subject area in this improved achievement seems to be language arts. If a desegregated school can help minority students improve their language skills, improvement is then observed across all subject areas. If language skills do not improve, neither do other skills. Fourth, desegregation also improves the I.Q. scores of black students. The average estimated gain is four I.Q. points. Fifth, desegregation plans in metropolitan areas, where both central-city and suburban schools are involved, have the greatest positive effect on black achievement. This finding is clearly consistent with Coleman's contention that desegregation must be socioeconomic as well as racial to be effective. Sixth, desegregation is most effective when the number of black students in a school constitutes a "critical mass." Too few black students, or too many, reduces the positive impact of desegregation. Mahard and Crain found that the size of this "critical mass" was different for Southern and Northern schools. In the South, achievement peaked in schools that were between 19 and 29 percent black. In the North, it peaked at 9 to 18 percent black.

Little research has been done on the effect of desegregation on high school students and results appear mixed. Mahard and Crain suggest that high school experiences have little impact on overall reading and mathematics performance, something they feel is shaped primarily in the earlier grades. However, desegregation can have a positive effect on achievement in subjects such as science and history, which are taught primarily at the high school level.[112] In an earlier study, using data from the National Longitudinal Study of the High School Graduating Class of 1972, Crain and Mahard demonstrated that Northern black students attending predominantly white high schools did better on achievement tests, attended college more often, and stayed in college longer than their counterparts who attended segregated high schools. However, in the South the achievement of black students was not better in predominantly white high schools, and their rates of college attendance and persistence were actually lower than those of black students who attended segregated high schools.[113]

Desegregation affects, in important ways, many other characteristics of children besides their academic performance. Among the factors that have been looked at are self-esteem, aspirations, and interracial attitudes. For example, Rosenberg and Simmons reported that although blacks attending integrated schools were receiving higher marks than those in segregated schools, they had lower levels of self-esteem.[114] Other studies, too, have reported drops in minority children's level of self-confidence or self-concept, and also drops in levels of aspiration.[115] On the other hand, several studies indicate that minority children who attend integrated schools are more likely to get better jobs when schooling is completed, and receive higher incomes in the first few decades after leaving school.[116]

Mahard and Crain hypothesize that desegregation affects black students' perceptions of their ability to influence their environment.[117] Earlier, we spoke of Coleman's finding that black students who felt that their actions could control their environment had higher levels of achievement. Mahard and Crain suggest that the experience of desegregation may convey "symbolic messages" to black children about personal efficacy, increasing their faith that effort can result in an improved future.

Data on racial attitudes have not been conclusive. Whether desegregation reduces or exacerbates interracial prejudice and hostility seems to depend a great deal on the context within which that desegregation has occurred. For example, desegregation is more likely to lower interracial hostility and prejudice when young, elementary-aged children are involved than when older, high-school-aged students are desegregated.[118]

It is obvious that we do not yet know enough about the effects of desegregation. More longitudinal studies, in which children can be followed for a long period of time, are needed. The effects of desegregation may be different over a long period than they are immediately after desegregation has been accomplished. Also, only longitudinal designs, with such factors as socioeconomic status, ability, community context, and so on carefully taken into consideration, can give us definitive results.

### The Internal Life of the School and Variations in Achievement

We indicated that very little of the variation in educational achievement among various groups of children can be explained in terms of differences between schools. Earlier in this chapter we looked at some alternative sources of explanation, the children themselves, and their families.

There remains, however, at least one other important set of explanatory variables. These involve the internal life of the schools, and focus on the differential educational experiences of various groups of children who may, in fact, be attending the same schools and may even be sitting in the same classrooms. We have mentioned some of these issues at other times, but we will review them here from this new perspective.

*The Expectations of Teachers and Other Personnel.* Few factors have received more attention in the educational literature than this one. The issues involved are complex, but can be summarized by two central questions. First, do teachers and other school prsonnel have different educational expectations for children from various socioeconomic, racial, and gender groups? Second, do these differential expectations affect children in such a way that they become self-fulfilling prophecies, with success from children expected to do well, and failure from children expected to fail?

A number of studies have shown that teachers do in fact have different expectations for different children, but the bases upon which these different expectations are formed is still somewhat unclear.[119] In some studies, teachers' expectations have been successfully manipulated by giving them false information about their students' potential for academic achievement, but these studies do not tell us much about how teachers form their expectations on a normal day-to-day basis in the classroom. Other studies have assessed teacher expectations without any artificial manipulation and have concluded that these expectations are influenced by a number of factors. Some of these are more educationally relevant than others. For example, teachers have been found to be influenced by students' I.Q. scores, achievement test scores, previous school records, and so on. However, teachers' expectations are also importantly influenced by students' physical attractiveness, socioeconomic status, race, gender, names, and older siblings.[120] In other words, teachers have been found to expect less achievement from students who belong to minority groups, come from economically disadvantaged homes, have unusual names, are physically unattractive, or have older siblings who were unsuccessful in school. Teachers also expect these children to display particular types of personality characteristics and particular types of behavior. For example, teachers often expect greater aggressiveness, leadership, and independence from boys than from girls.

If teachers do have such systematically different expectations for children, do these expectations affect the students' performance in school, and if so, how does this effect take place? Some cues are provided by the numerous studies done on these phenomena.

The study that has received the most publicity in this area and that precipitated much of the work that has come after it was conducted by Rosenthal and Jacobson in an elementary school in San Franciso.[121] Rosenthal and Jacobson administered a standard intelligence test to all the children in grades one through six. However, the teachers in the school were told that the test was a special one, designed to predict intellectual "blooming." Approximately 20 percent of the children of each class were randomly selected and identified as students who would "bloom" during the course of the school year. The children were all retested several months later, at the end of the school year, and again the following year. According to Rosenthal and Jacobson, their results showed that those children who were expected to show intellectual gains were more likely to improve their test scores than those children who were not expected to show such gains.

The Rosenthal and Jacobson study caused a considerable stir in both the academic and nonacademic world. It seemed that experimental proof of the effect of teacher bias had been obtained. However, there were many important weaknesses in this study.[122] First, the results themselves were very inconsistent. Most of the predicted intellectual gains were confined to younger children, with the older ones showing no significant change. Second, there was some possibility that results were contaminated by the fact that some teachers—who knew which children were supposed to "bloom"—administered the second tests, and may have influenced them. Third, the intelligence levels of the students in the school were so extremely low as to cast serious question on the validity and reliability of the tests they were using. In addition, the numerous efforts to replicate Rosenthal and Jacobson's findings have been inconsistent in their results: Many studies have failed to support the findings of the original study, though others have provided at least some degree of support.

Among the reasons for these inconsistent findings is the fact that the effect of teacher expectations is far more complex than originally suspected. For example, it is now known that the various characteristics that any particular student has interact in influencing teacher expectations.[123] A teacher might generally expect minority children to do less well than whites, but if the minority children involved are middle class and the whites are working class, this expectation might be modified. Also, the teacher's own characteristics are important.[124] Male and female teachers have been found to form different expectations for the same categories of children; the same has been found for black and white teachers, and for those who do or do not believe in the validity of standardized tests. Even the teacher's own training and sensitivity to the issues involved is influential in shaping expectations. For example, educating teachers about Nonstandard English can affect their reactions to students who speak this way.[125] Finally, the number and complexity of factors that affect teacher expectations have been found to be much greater than originally assumed. Many fewer teachers than originally believed are substantially influenced by students' test scores and more are influenced by their actual experiences with the children.[126]

In a synthesis of eighteen studies of teacher expectancy effects, Raudenbush found that the better teachers knew their students at time they were furnished with such test scores, the smaller the expectancy effect actually was. When teachers had had an opportunity to work with students for several months, they were simply not pursuaded by the information experimentors gave them.[127] Of course, teachers' experiences with students themselves can be shaped by their expectations. People tend to interpret their observations in ways consistent with their original beliefs.

If teachers do have differential expectations, and if these are sometimes based on ascribed characteristics or factors that are not really relevant to achievement, how do these expectations actually affect children? One answer is that teachers might subtly affect children's self-concept, communicating to some that they are competent and to others that they are not. One way in which this might work is through the quantity and quality of the interaction between teachers and students. For example, it has been found that teachers give more attention to boys than girls in elementary school.[128] This attention is both positive and negative. Boys are in trouble more often, but they are also praised more often; in comparison, girls are expected to be quiet and teachers tend to overlook them. In a recent study of more than one hundred fourth–, sixth–, and eighth–grade classrooms, Sadker and Sadker found that boys were involved in more interactions with teachers than were girls. Boys received more attention, more praise, more criticism, and more remediation (help to correct or improve their responses).[129] Boys demanded more attention by calling out answers, and teachers tended to respond by accepting these answers. When girls called out, teachers were more likely to tell them to raise their hand. Most of the classrooms observed were internally sex-segregated, and teachers spent more time near the boys. Similar results were obtained when Sadker and Sadker looked at college classrooms. Overall, they concluded that classrooms are divided into the "haves" and the "have nots," with "students in the same classroom, with the same teacher, studying the same material . . . experiencing very different educational environments."[130]

It has also been reported that teachers praise, support, and interact verbally more with high achievers than with low achievers; the comments of low achievers are more often simply ignored.[131] Of course, once teachers begin actually encouraging only certain children—perhaps by answering the questions of some, while ignoring others—they are also affecting the opportunities that different children have to learn.

In addition, teacher expectations may lead to children being tracked or grouped in a particular way in the classroom or school. For example, Rist found that kindergarten teachers sometimes grouped children after only a few days or weeks with them.[132] This grouping was supposedly based on the children's potential for learning, though it was clear that it was heavily influenced by the children's socioeconomic background. The "slow" group was made up entirely of the most socioeconomically disadvantaged children in the class. All the children in Rist's sample were black, so there were no racial differences among groups. Once the grouping had been made, the brightest groups were placed closest to the teacher and the blackboard. The other children were farther away, given less opportunity to participate in learning experiences, and praised less often. As might be expected, the group expected to do best did so, and the group expected to do worst did so too. As the children were promoted into higher grades, the way in which they were classified in kindergarten continued to affect their treatment in higher grades.

In other words, teachers seem to expect more from some children and then behave in ways that elicit more from them. When these children do indeed achieve at high levels, they are then disproportionately praised (or reinforced) for their success. We need more research to tell us precisely how these mechanisms operate and what variables affect them. It is clear, though, that children going to the same school and sitting in the same classroom may be receiving very different kinds of educational experiences.

*Instructional Materials.* In addition to the messages students might be receiving from teachers regarding their academic potential and the differential treatment they may be experiencing, children are affected by the instructional materials provided by their schools. These materials can affect various types of children differently.

For one thing, textbooks, films, and other materials provide role models with which children can identify and shape their own aspirations and expectations. For many years, instructional materials almost completely omitted references to minority groups or their experiences in the United States. Few minority persons were depicted in these materials and the lifestyle presented as ideal was clearly that of middle-class white Americans. Since the 1960s, however, there has been greater responsiveness to minority groups on the part of the producers of instructional materials. Urban environments are routinely presented in children's textbooks, and principal characters belong to a variety of racial and ethnic groups. Still, the settings rarely present life as the inner-city slum child or the inhabitant of a depressed rural community really experiences it. Furthermore, there has been gross negligence regarding the treatment of women in these materials. Several analyses have shown that virtually all instructional materials used in our public schools are heavily biased in their presentation of men and women.[133] In general, these materials portray the two genders only in very stereotypical and traditional roles. Males are brave, intelligent, adventurous, creative, ambitious, and natural leaders; females are shy, dependent, dull, fearful, and good followers. Males live exciting lives and grow up to be any of dozens of types of workers; females stay mainly in the home or close to it, and grow up to be wives, mothers, or occasionally, teachers, librarians, or nurses. Women are underrepresented in biographical anthologies and almost absent from history textbooks. Even when special efforts are made to include women in the curriculum, through Women's History Week, for example, the message may still be that women are peripheral to history rather than an integral part of it.[134]

The effects of these materials on children have not been directly and experimentally studied. We do not know, for example, whether children using different books would find it easier to learn from them, develop more positive self-concepts, or have higher levels of aspiration. However, these materials often serve to reinforce the messages children are already receiving from teachers and other school personnel. They consistently tell some groups that they are important and that much is expected of them, while at the same time they tell others they should remain in the background or that they have nothing really important to contribute. Although all children in a school may be using the same materials, the messages each group receives might be substantially different.

*Tracking and Curricular Divisions* In chapter 3 we discussed how children are grouped according to various standards of ability or accomplishment. Can ability grouping and tracking explain some of the within-school variation in students' educational achievement and attainment? There are good reasons to think that they might. Grouping and tracking are likely to affect the quality and character of educational experiences. At minimum, students assigned to different groups will be exposed to different subject matter. Academic track students take subjects such as Physics and Calculus that are not usually available to vocational and general track students. Furthermore, when a subject, such as English, is taken by all students, the instructional content of the course is likely to vary with track. Those who are not taught much beyond general math or basic English are not likely to gain admission into four-year colleges or universities, even if they later decide to attend. Not only will they lack the formal credentials for admission, but they will also lack the factual and conceptual knowledge and skills required for college success. Considerable remedial work would be necessary before they could acquire a higher degree, making that degree particularly costly and time-consuming.

It may also be that higher ability groups and upper track students are advantaged by having more experienced and skillful teachers. As Goodlad points out, "With increasing seniority, many teachers hope to be selected to teach upper track students, who are believed to be more eager to learn and less unruly."[135] Indeed, Goodlad reports that teachers in upper tracks express themselves more clearly, are better organized and are perceived to be more enthusiastic by their students than are teachers of lower track students.[136]

Ability grouping and tracking also tend to affect the learning environment of the classroom by concentrating students "perceived to be immature and inattentive" together.[137] These lower groups then become characterized by more frequent disruptions of academic activities and an environment less suitable for learning.[138] Teachers of lower track courses have been found to spend more time dealing with behavior and discipline problems than teachers of other courses.[139] Compared to other students, those in lower groups report higher levels of discord in their classrooms, and more frequently feel that other students are unfriendly and teachers are punitive.[140]

These types of classroom differences led Bowles and Gintis to suggest that students in different programs are encouraged to develop different intellectual capacities and personality traits. Bowles and Gintis have suggested that "vocational and general tracks emphasize rule-following and close supervision, while the college track tends toward a more open atmosphere emphasizing the internalization of norms."[141]

Goodlad concurs, pointing out that the upper track English teachers he studied encouraged such traits as self-direction, creativity, and critical thinking while lower track English teachers stressed conforming behavior, such as working quietly, punctuality, obeying rules, and getting along with others.[142] Bowles and Gintis believe that such differences in educational atmosphere develop personality characteristics suited to different occupational slots, preparing vocational and general track students for blue-collar and lower level white-collar jobs, and academic track students for upper-level white-collar and professional occupations.

At this time, there is little statistical evidence available to test these possibilities. However, James Rosenbaum's 1975 study of a five-track system in a white, working-class junior high school provides at least some relevant data.[143] Rosenbaum measured the I.Q. scores of the students in this school over a period of three years. He found that the I.Q. scores of students in the upper tracks became more differentiated. He interpreted this as evidence that children in the upper tracks were encouraged to develop as individuals and allowed considerable independence and self-direction. Some became outstanding intellectually; others did not, but the unique abilities and talents of each individual seem to have surfaced. The children in the lower tracks, however, were channeled into greater uniformity. Their learning environment encouraged conformity. Rosenbaum suggested that his findings parallel differences in the opportunities and expectations associated with various socioeconomic strata, in general. Members of the upper strata are permitted more freedom, personal development, and independence than members of lower strata. Of course, Rosenbaum's study contained no direct measure of personality traits or behavior. Considerable research will be necessary before we can determine the relationships, if any, between tracking, curriculum placement, and either cognitive or personality development.

Another way in which tracking and curriculum divisions might affect educational achievement and attainment is through differential access to school facilities and services. As you recall, Coleman's study did not find that school facilities could explain much of the variation in students' educational achievement. However, Coleman's data do not deal with differential access to those facilities within individual schools. The presence of a science laboratory does not mean that all children get to use it. We would suspect that such facilities are differentially used by children classified as high in ability or college-oriented. Similarly, school funds may be spent on programs and facilities that serve certain groups of children more than others. It is well known, for example, that schools have spent much more money on athletic programs for boys than for girls. We know less about differential spending for various socioeconomic or racial groups within schools or about differential spending for ability or curricular groups. In her analysis of data originally gathered for the Coleman Report, Heyns found that students in academic tracks received more counseling than others and concluded that "Curriculum assignment appears, therefore, to be an institutional mechanism within schools for the selective distribution of encouragement and counseling, and perhaps other resources as well."[144]

Dividing students into either ability or curriculum groups also affects their experiences in other important ways. All of the variables upon which such divisions are usually made are correlated with socioeconomic status, race, gender, and other ascribed characteristics. This means that the children in any particular track or program will be more homogeneous on these characteristics than the children in the school taken as a whole. Tracking can be used to segregate a school internally, channeling white, middle-class children into high ability or college-oriented programs, and minority children or those from economically disadvantaged homes into low ability or general programs.[145] This means that the schools create a stratification system within their own walls. Children in each group associate with each other more than they associate with those in other groups, and they are likely to be influenced by and draw their friends from their own academic group. We pointed out that Coleman and others have reported that attending school with middle-class students facilitates educational achievement and attainment. It is therefore likely that because children in upper tracks and academic programs associate disproportionately with high-status peers, they have a distinct educational advantage over others.

A study published by Karl Alexander and Edward McDill in 1976 provides data on this point.[146] Alexander and McDill analyzed data collected in the 1960s from twenty public high schools. They reported that "college preparatory enrollment does indeed provide access to 'highly motivated, academically oriented peers.' "[147] The effects of such access were greatest on students' values and attitudes, resulting in stronger commitments to higher education and intellectual achievement.

Indeed, Alexander and McDill showed that curriculum enrollment had many important effects on students' rank in class, scores on a math achievement test, educational plans, self-concepts, and intellectualism. The exact mechanisms through which these effects occurred are not yet clear. However, students in the academic track achieved better grades and math scores and aspired to more education than other sutdents, even after differences in ability and socioeconomic status were taken into account.

In a later analysis of a longitudinal survey of high school youth, Alexander, Cook, and McDill draw similar but not identical conclusions.[148] They report that placement in an academic track increases students' math achievement, college aspirations, college applications, and college admissions. Academic track placement did not meaningfully affect students' verbal achievement or grades.

It appears from much of the research cited above that ability grouping and tracking bestow advantages on students placed in upper tracks and disadvantages on others. Indeed, many educators and social scientists have drawn that conclusion.[149] However, others report mixed results and some disagree entirely. In a study of reading achievement among fourth grade students, Rowan and Miracle found that *tracking* worked to the disadvantage of students in lower ability classrooms, but *grouping within classrooms* worked in a compensatory fashion.[150] Teachers in heterogeneous classrooms made special efforts to help lower group students catch up with the others. The students in the lower groups were actually paced faster and had more direct interaction with their teachers than those in higher reading groups. Rowan and Miracle also found that although tracking limited some students' access to high ability peers, this limitation did not actually affect student achievement.

After an extensive analysis of 52 methodologically superior studies of ability grouping and tracking in secondary schools, Kulik and Kulik[151] concluded that students grouped by ability made achievement gains slightly greater than those who were not and that high, middle, and low ability groups benefitted equally. Only in programs specifically designed for gifted and talented students were effects greater. Providing "enriched instruction" for these students benefitted them substantially.[152] However, programs specifically designed for academically deficient students did not result in either enhanced or diminished achievement. Kulik and Kulik conclude that "The effect of grouping is near-zero on the achievement of average and below average students; it is not negative."[153]

Kulik and Kulik also looked at the effects of grouping on attitudes. They found that grouped students had more positive feelings about the subjects they were studying and more positive self-concepts: "Students seemed to like their school subjects more when they studied with peers of similar ability, and some students in grouped classes even developed more positive attitudes about themselves and school."[154] Kulik and Kulik conclude that grouping does not negatively affect the attitudes and self-concepts of low ability students.

Although the evidence is still inconclusive, it appears that ability and tracking may at times give some students advantages over others. Does this mean, then, that tracking or curriculum divisions might explain some of the patterns of educational achievement and attainment we have been discussing? Before we can answer this question, we would have to know whether there is a systematic bias in how students are placed into various tracks or curriculum programs. Evidence on the biases built into ability tests and the effects of ascriptive variables on teachers' and counselors' evaluations has been cited.[155] Further evidence of the effects of ascriptive variables on curriculum placement are provided by Alexander and Eckland,[156] and Alexander and McDill.[157] However, all of these researchers have also found that ability is a major determinant of placement, and Heyns found no evidence of class bias in selection operating independently of differential achievement. She concluded that "The principal determinant of curriculum placement and grades is verbal achievement test score, not father's occupation, education, or family size."[158] Of course, the verbal achievement scores, themselves, *were* affected by ascriptive factors.

Davis and Haller's study of tracking in five New York State school districts found track placement "unbiased."[159] Haller and Davis report only a very weak correlation between socioeconomic status and track. Variables such as the student's aspirations and academic ability were the most powerful determinants of track placement. Alexander, Cook, and McDill, in the same study reported above, concluded that "socioeconomic characteristics of students influence curriculum enrollment in high school almost totally through their effects on achievements, goals, and encouragement during junior high school."[160] Nevertheless, they also reiterate that higher status students are still disproportionately found in college tracks and that many of the factors that determine student placement are still unknown.

In view of these findings, we can probably answer our earlier question with a reserved affirmative: tracking and curriculum placement probably explain some of the patterns of educational achievement and attainment we have been discussing. Academic tracking, at least at the high school level, seems to bring at least some long term educational benefits to those placed in the upper track. Although such ascriptive factors as socioeconomic status do not directly affect student placement in a substantial way, they can affect those achieved characteristics that do: academic achievement, goals and aspirations, encouragement, and so on. As Alexander, Cook, and McDill point out, many of the other variables that account for which student is placed in which track are as yet unknown.[161]

Much more research needs to be done on tracking, curriculum enrollment, and other experiences and opportunities offered differentially to various socioeconomic, racial, ethnic, and gender groups within the schools before we have definitive answers; but studies of within-school processes are clearly one important key to understanding patterns of success and failure in our schools.

### Effective Schools

Sociologists and educators are keenly aware that most urban schools are ineffective, but they also know that a few schools do succeed with disadvantaged, inner-city students. Researchers have undertaken deviant case analyses, studies of urban schools that do promote learning, in an effort to identify organizational keys to achievement. The "effective schools" studies provide a remarkably consistent, depiction of the characteristics that make such schools distinctive.[162] These include: focused goals, normative consensus, active administration, and collegial cooperation.

The principals and teachers focus their efforts on cognitive growth, limiting their concern with alternative social and emotional goals. Consensus is relatively easy to reach regarding these narrow academic goals. In addition, progress toward the accomplishment of such goals is relatively easy to assess. Faculty and staff of effective schools are convinced that disadvantaged children can and will learn under the proper conditions. Teachers tend to be relatively demanding with regard to student behavior and diligence. Formalized policies and regulations regarding student discipline help ensure that there is consensus on this key issue. The principals of effective schools are active leaders who involve themselves in goal-setting; faculty recruitment and selection; monitoring, evaluating, and providing technical assistance to teachers; protecting teachers from bureaucratic disruption of classroom activities; and promoting collegial relationships. It is highly unusual in the field of education for teachers to work together—*loose-coupling* is the norm. But in effective urban schools, teachers routinely consult and cooperate with their colleagues.

Unfortunately, many of the effective schools studies are methodogically weak, not really comparing schools to each other in a systematic and precise way. Considerably more work will have to be done before we can determine whether or not specific school characteristics are linked to greater success in teaching children who typically have high rates of academic failure.

## SUMMARY AND CONCLUSIONS: THE QUESTION OF EQUALITY

We began this chapter by asking whether or not we have equality of educational opportunity in the United States today. In building toward an answer to this question, we have learned a number of relevant facts. Both educational achievement and attainment vary systematically with a number of ascribed characteristics. Children from most minority groups in the United States do less well in school and complete less education than children of the majority, and children who come from economically deprived families do less well and complete less education than those who come from more economically secure families. As a matter of fact, there is virtually a straight line relationship between socioeconomic status and educational success. Also, although girls get better grades in school than boys, their long-term attainment of doctor's and first professional degrees is lower.

Many explanations for these phenomena have been offered. They range from explanations focusing on children and their families to explanations that focus on schools and the context within which children are educated.

Consensus and conflict theorists differ both in their assessment of how much inequality exists in the system and in what explanatory factors they stress in their assessment. Consensus theorists focus on the extent to which the educational system does provide opportunities for upward mobility. Over time, a larger proportion of our nation's youth have been provided with an increasingly lengthy publicly financed education. Minorities, the poor, and women have particularly benefitted from these changes. Consensus theorists also focus on the fact that none of the correlations between educational success and ascribed variables are perfect. In fact, even with all ascribed variables taken into account, a considerable amount of variation exists in educational success that cannot be explained. Many studies have also shown that ability is an important determinant of educational success, predicting grades, curriculum placement, and college attendance well, for example. In short, consensus theorists argue that the schools do admit all children and treat them relatively universalistically. Failure on the part of some groups to do as well as others might be traced to minor problems remaining in the system, inadequate socialization experiences in the home, or an as yet not quite completed integration of all groups into the mainstream of American life.

Conflict theorists, on the other hand, stress the relationships between ascribed characteristics and educational success, and the fact that these relationships have remained persistent over time. They have little faith that the system is improving. Conflict theorists tend to explain this persistence in terms of the power relationships among diverse groups within our society. They argue, for example, that those groups whose children do well in school are precisely those that control the schools. These groups control the criteria for success, the allocation of resources, the content of curriculum, and the ways in which ability and achievement are measured, and they attempt to assure success for their own offspring while discouraging others. For example, Bowles has pointed out that our current set of educational priorities rewards educational achievement with economic subsidies.[163] These subsidies are in the form of generous public funding provided for colleges and universities. To get a share of these funds, you must be a successful student. Because middle-class children are disproportionately successful, they get a disproportionate share of this educational subsidy. Suppose, however, we changed our priority. If a higher value was placed on developing as yet unfulfilled educational potential, then those who are doing *least* well in school might be offered *more* in terms of school service and opportunities. The poor, working classes, and minority groups would benefit more than the middle class. But Bowles argues that middle- and upper-middle-class interests set educational policies, and that they would not support policies that work to their own detriment.

The empirical data that might be used to answer questions about equality of educational opportunity or sources of inequality are confusing and at times contradictory. A few things seem to be emerging fairly consistently, however. For example, school characteristics, including funding, seem to explain much less about educational success than we previously believed. On the other hand, the internal dynamics of educational institutions seem capable of explaining much more. The expectations of teachers and counselors, role models provided in instructional materials, and tracking or curriculum divisions have been studied, but not extensively enough to provide definitive answers. Finally, the home environment and early socialization experiences of youngsters are clearly important. Why this is provokes considerable controversy. Explanations range from the incompatibility of home and school expectations, to inadequacies in the family, to the impact of work roles on child socialization.

Another complicating factor has been that our conceptions of "equality of educational opportunity" have changed over time. Some of these changes have been in response to empirical information we have acquired about educational processes. Coleman has given an interesting overview of these changes.[164] He points out that early in our history social reformers defined equality of opportunity in terms of providing all children with a chance to attend school and exposing them to the same curriculum once they got there. A second definition was accepted later on; this definition focused on the fact that children are destined for a variety of futures, and they should be able to acquire the type of education most suitable for their own particular case.

For example, James Conant recommended providing vocational education for students with "less than average abilities." These students, he pointed out, are concentrated in the slums and will enter the labor market directly after school. On the other hand, Conant emphasized the importance of "rigorous academic programs" for the "bright" children concentrated in wealthy suburbs. These children will go on to colleges and professional schools. However, Conant also stressed that not-so-bright students living in suburbs also need such academic programs, because their parents will see to it that they, too, go on to higher education.[165]

With increasing sophistication about educational outcomes, it became apparent that policies that permitted students to attend different schools or to be tracked into different types of programs often resulted in self-fulfilling prophecies. Poor and minority children were more often placed in vocational programs or in ones that were of inferior academic quality, regardless of their potential. In addition, the schools attended by different groups of children often differed in terms of their resources and facilities. In time, then, an additional element entered our conception of equality of educational opportunity. This was that schools should be equal in terms of the *inputs*, or the resources that they had available to them. At first, inputs were viewed only in terms of facilities, teachers, and so on, but soon other kinds of inputs were shown to be educationally relevant. For example, the social composition of the students attending a school was not traditionally thought of as an educational input. However, when evidence of the effects of composition on educational *output*, or results, began to accumulate, composition was considered a relevant variable. The decision of the Supreme Court in the 1954 *Brown* case exemplified this newer thinking when it ruled that schools that were racially segregated could not be "equal"—even if their facilities were.

It was just a short step from this thinking to an increasing emphasis on measuring the results or effects of education on students instead of simply measuring school inputs. Some inputs may be of greater importance to certain groups of children than others. The new definition of equality of education was, then, that schools are equal when the educational *outcomes* of these schools are essentially the same for children of equal backgrounds and abilities. This means equalizing such intangible factors as teachers' attitudes, school morale, and anything else that might affect the achievement of different types of students.

But, of course, children are not all equal in their backgrounds or their abilities, as this chapter has so vividly pointed out. A further issue regarding equality must therefore be raised. Is it the responsibility of the schools to assure equality of educational output even when the characteristics of students vary as much as they do? In other words, do we have equality of opportunity only when we have equality of results for all children? Coleman uses an interesting graph to illustrate this dilemma. Looking at Figure 8–1, which set of lines, if any, illustrates equality of educational opportunity? Clearly not the rural South, where blacks and whites end school even further apart than when they began it. But what about the urban Northeast? Here students end school about as far apart as when they began it. Is it the responsibility of the schools to effect a covergence between these two groups? But what about factors that the school cannot influence? Can the school be expected to counter the effects of prejudice and discrimination in the larger society, for example, or differences in early childhood socialization? If so, how can this be done?

This leads us directly into one last point we wish to make here. There is a real question, still, about the relationships between educational experiences and the future adult lives of students. Recent studies have suggested that even if we eliminated all inequalities in schooling, there would still

**FIGURE 8–1.** Patterns of Achievement in Verbal Skills at Various Grade Levels by Race and Region.

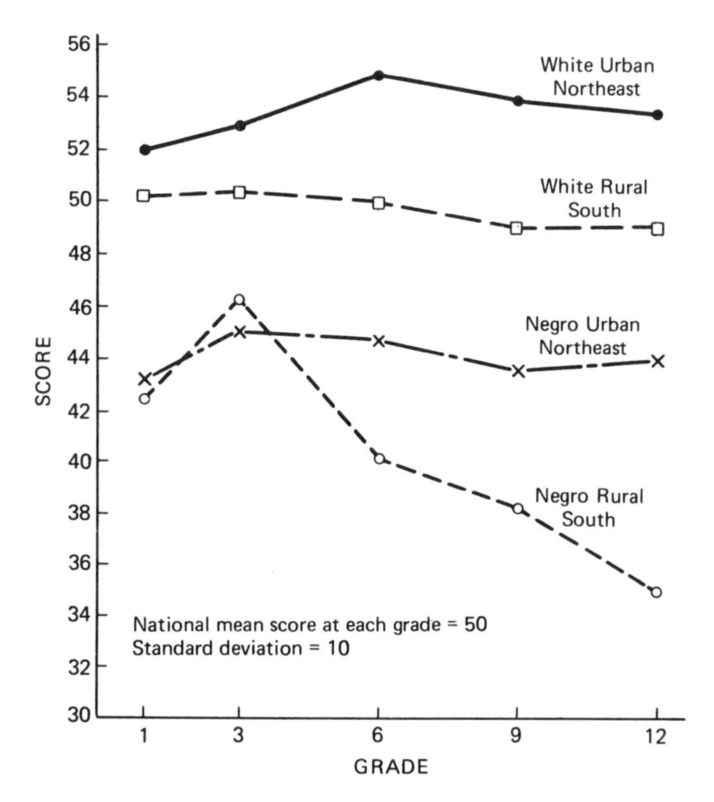


*Source:* James S. Coleman, "The Concept of Educational Opportunity," *Harvard Educational Review,* 38, No. 1 (Winter 1968), 20.

remain considerable inequalities in occupational opportunities and income in peoples' adult lives.[166] Figure 8–2, for example, shows that between 1950 and 1970 educational inequality declined, while income inequality remained essentially the same. You may recall that in the introduction to this chapter we mentioned that equality of educational opportunity does not necessarily mean equality in the distribution of money, power, or status. However, if such general social equality is one's goal, educational reform alone will not achieve it. Too many factors other than education play a major role in determining success in adult life. Figure 8–3 gives a good example of this. The chart shows the probability of a man being in the top fifth of the income distribution in the United States if he acquires an average number of years of schooling and has an average childhood I.Q. As you can see, with the effect of gender, I.Q., and educational attainment removed, socioeconomic status still plays a major role in determining adult income. For the population as a whole, gender, age, motivation, personality, and a host of other variables are important influences on adult in-

FIGURE 8–2. Equalization of Education Has Not Been Associated with Equalization of Income.

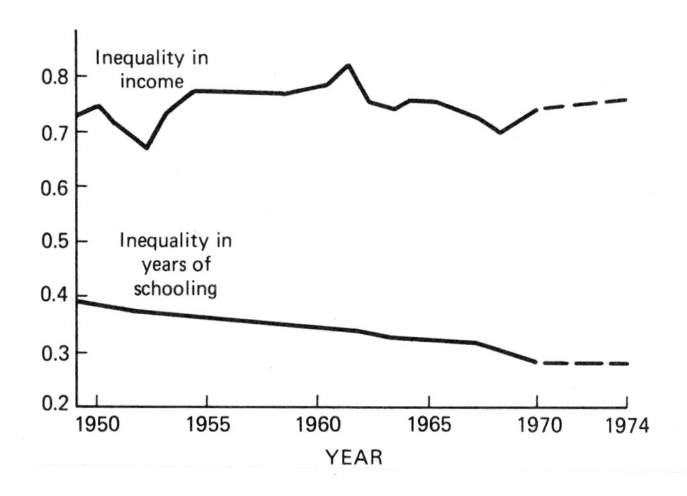


FIGURE 8–3. The Effect of Socioeconomic Background on Economic Success Is Strong Even for Individuals with Equal Education and I.Q.

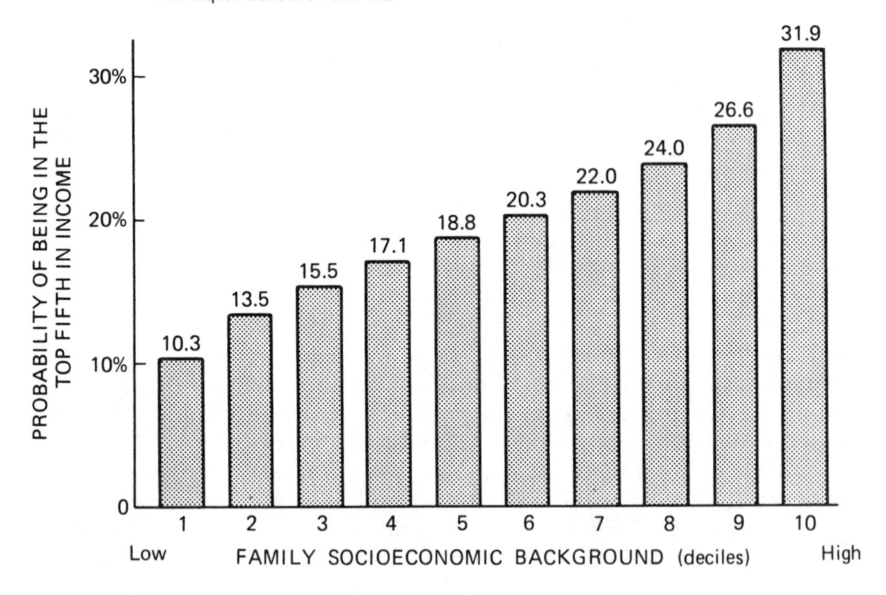


come and occupational attainment. As yet, sociologists do not know or understand the full range of factors involved.[167] However, to the extent that schools do affect future rewards, there are further complications. Some types of educational experiences increase success in certain areas, but not in others. For example, an analysis by Jencks and Brown on a sample of 90 high schools showed that the "estimated effectiveness of a given high school will vary dramatically according to the measure of success one chooses to emphasize."[168] The authors summarize their results as follows:

> High schools that are unusually effective in boosting student performance on one standardized test are only marginally more effective than average in boosting performance on other tests. Those that are notably effective in boosting test scores across the board are no more effective than average in getting their students to finish high school, attend college, graduate from college, or enter high-status occupations. High schools that are unusually effective in increasing the amount of education a student gets are also appreciably more effective than average in boosting a student's eventual occupational status. However, high schools that are unusually successful in getting males into high-status occupations are no more successful than average in getting females into high-status occupations, and vice-versa.[169]

In general, they found that high school quality accounts for only 1.0 to 3.4 percent of the variance in twelfth-grade test scores, 0.2 to 2.4 percent of the variance in educational attainment, and 2.5 to 4.8 percent of the variance in occupational status and career plans of students. Reducing inequalities between schools, they argue, will do little to reduce inequalities among adults.

Because all these analyses have been done only on schools as they currently exist and only with certain variables in mind, it is impossible to really tell at this time how much difference schools can make. It seems to us, however, that a firm commitment to equality of educational opportunity is necessary if we are ever to find out. Furthermore, such commitments are, in our opinion, moral imperatives. It may also be, however, that without substantial reform in other institutions in American society, the schools will not be able to bring us very much further in the direction of equality of *socioeconomic* opportunities. Inequalities in the distribution of wealth, power, and status, in the availability of housing and jobs, and in the distribution of societal resources are inseparable from questions about inequalities in education.

## NOTES

[1]Alejandro Portes and Kenneth L. Wilson, "Black-White Differences in Educational Attainment," *American Sociological Review,* 41 (June, 1976), pp. 414–31; Christopher Jencks, Susan Bartlett, Mary Corcoran, James Crouse, David Eaglesfield, Christopher Jencks, Gregory Jackson, Kent McClelland, Peter Meuser, Michael Olneck, Joseph Schwartz, Sherry Ward, and Jill Williams. *Who Gets Ahead? The Determinants of Economic Success in America* (New York: Basic Books, 1979), p. 230.

[2]William B. Fetters, National Center for Education Statistics, *National Longitudinal Study of the High School Class of 1972; Student Questionnaire and Test Results by Sex, High School Program, Ethnic Category, and Father's Education* (Washington, D.C.: Government Printing Office, 1975).

[3]William B. Fetters, George H. Brown, and Jeffrey A. Owens, National Center for Education Statistics, *High School Seniors: A Comparative Study of the Classes of 1972 and 1980* (Washington, D.C.: Government Printing Office, 1984), p. 39.

[4]Ibid., p. 39.

[5]National Center for Education Statistics, *Two Years in High School: The Status of 1980 Sophomores in 1982* (Washington, D.C.: Government Printing Office, 1984), p. 25.

[6]National Center for Education Statistics, *Two Years after High School: A Capsule Description of 1980 Seniors* (Washington, D.C.: Government Printing Office, 1984), p. 8.

[7]College Board, *Profiles, College-Bound Seniors, 1982* (Princeton, N.J.: College Entrance Examination Board, 1982), p. 14.

[8]National Center for Education Statistics, *Two Years in High School*, p. 10.

[9]Valena White Plisko and Joyce D. Stern, eds., *The Condition of Education, 1985* (Washington, D.C.: Government Printing Office, 1985), p. 50.

[10]College Board, *Profiles, College-Bound Seniors, 1981* (Princeton, N.J.: College Entrance Examination Board, 1982), p. 16.

[11]There is evidence that the gap between the standardized scores of black and white students on the SAT as well as on other achievement tests is narrowing; see Lyle V. Jones, "White-Black Achievement Differences: The Narrowing Gap," *American Psychologist*, 39 (November, 1984).

[12]Christopher Jencks, Marshall Smith, Henry Acland, Mary Jo Bane, David Cohen, Herbert Gintis, Barbara Heyns, and Stephen Michelson, *Inequality: A Reassessment of the Effect of Family and Schooling in America* (New York: Basic Books, 1972), p. 21.

[13]U.S. Bureau of the Census, *Current Population Reports*, Series P–20, No. 295, "Educational Attainment in the United States: March 1975," (Washington, D.C.: Government Printing Office, 1976), pp. 9–12.

[14]U.S. Bureau of the Census, *Statistical Abstract of the United States 1986* (Washington D.C.: Government Printing Office, 1986), p. 133.

[15]Nancy W. Burton and Lyle V. Jones, "Recent Trends in Achievement Levels of Black and White Youth," *Educational Researcher*, 11, 4 (April, 1982), pp. 10–11.

[16]Plisko and Stern, *The Condition of Education*, p. 74.

[17]U.S. Bureau of the Census, *Statistical Abstract*, p. 133.

[18]National Center for Education Statistics, *The Status of 1980 Sophomores*, p. 25.

[19]National Center for Education Statistics, *Two Years After*, p. 18.

[20]Pauline S. Sears and David H. Feldman, "Teacher Interactions with Boys and with Girls," in *And Jill Came Tumbling After: Sexism in American Education*, eds. Judith Stacey, Susan Bereud, and Joan Daniels, (New York: Dell Publishing Co., 1974), pp. 147–58; and Eleanor E. Maccoby and Carol N. Jacklin, *The Psychology of Sex Differences* (Stanford, Calif.: Stanford University Press, 1974), p. 119.

[21]National Center for Education Statistics, *The Status of 1980 Sophomores*, p. 18.

[22]Plisko and Stern, *The Condition of Education*, p. 50.

[23]National Center for Education Statistics, *The Status of 1980 Sophomores*, p. 10.

[24]Plisko and Stern, *The Condition of Education*, pp. 56–7.

[25]Glen Harvey, "Finding Reality Among the Myths: Why What You Thought About Sex Equity in Education Isn't So," *Phi Delta Kappan*, 67 (March, 1986), p. 510.

[26]U.S. Bureau of the Census, *Statistical Abstract*, p. 134.

[27]Mary A. Golladay, *The Condition of Education: 1976 Edition* (Washington, D.C.: Government Printing Office, 1976), p. 33.

[28]National Center for Education Statistics, *The Status of 1980 Sophomores*, p. 3.

[29]Plisko and Stern, *Condition of Education*, p. 79.

[30]Ibid., p. 124.

[31]National Center for Education Statistics, *The Status of 1980 Sophomores*, p. 25.

[32]National Center for Education Statistics, *Two Years After*, p. 8.

[33]Plisko and Stern, *The Condition of Education*, p. 124.

[34]Ibid., p. 128.

[35]Ibid., p. 128.

[36]Robert M. Hauser and David L. Featherman, "Equality of Schooling: Trends and Prospects," *Sociology of Education*, 49 (April, 1976), pp. 99–120.

[37]Samuel Bowles and Herbert T. Gintis, *Schooling in Capitalist America: Educational Reform and the Contradictions of Economic Life*, (New York: Basic Books, 1976), p. 33.

[38]Fetters, Brown, Owens, National Center for Education Statistics, *High School Seniors*, p. 39.

[39]Plisko and Stern, *The Condition of Education*, p. 50.

[40]National Center for Education Statistics, *The Status of 1980 Sophomores*, p. 25.

[41]National Center for Education Statistics, *Two Years After*, p. 8.

[42]J. McV. Hunt, "Heredity, Environment, and Class or Ethnic Differences," in *Assessment in a Pluralistic Society: Proceedings of the 1972 Invitational Conference on Testing Problems* (Princeton: Educational Testing Service, 1972), pp. 3–36.

[43]Jencks and others, *Inequality*, p. 139.

[44]Ibid., p. 142.

[45]John C. Loehlin, Gardner Lindsey, and J. N. Spuhler, *Race Differences in Intelligence* (San Francisco: W. H. Freeman and Co., 1975), pp. 168–74.

[46]Portes and Wilson, "Black-White Differences," pp. 420–23.

[47]Jencks and others, *Inequality*, p. 142.

[48]Margaret T. Gordon, "A Different View of the I.Q.—Achievement Gap," *Sociology of Education*, 49 (January, 1976), pp. 4–11.

[49]Maccoby and Jacklin, *The Psychology of Sex Differences*, pp. 176–7.

[50]Frank Riessman, *The Culturally Deprived Child* (New York: Harper & Row, 1962), p. 55.

[51]Loehlin, Lindsey, and Spuhler, *Race Differences in Intelligence*, pp. 178–85.

[52]Riessman, *The Culturally Deprived Child*, pp. 53–54. See also similar points made by William Labov, "The Logic of Nonstandard English," in *The Myth of Cultural Deprivation*, ed. Nell Keddie, (Harmondsworth, Middlesex, England: Penguin Education, A Division of Penguin Books, Ltd., 1973), pp. 21–66.

[53]Ernest A. Haggard, "Social Status and Intelligence," *Genetic Psychology Monographs*, 49, (1954), pp. 141–86, and personal communications cited in Riessman, *The Culturally Deprived Child*, pp. 52–54.

[54]Carl Bereiter and Siegfried Engelmann, *Teaching Disadvantaged Children in the Preschool* (Englewood Cliffs, N.J.: Prentice-Hall, Inc., 1966).

[55]Loehlin, Lindsey, and Spuhler, *Race Differences in Intelligence*, pp. 149–51.

[56]Burton L. White, "Growing Up Competent: How Families Make the Difference," *Carnegie Quarterly*, 21 (Summer, 1973), pp. 6–8.

[57]Rick Heber as cited in Arthur Whimbey, "Something Better than Binet?," *Saturday Review/World*, (June 1, 1974), pp. 50–53.

[58]John Madden, John O'Hara, and Phyllis Levenstein, "Home Again: Effects of the Mother-Child Program on Mother and Child," *Child Development*, 55 (April, 1984), pp. 636–47.

[59]Urie Bronfenbrenner, "Is Early Intervention Effective?," in Marcia Guttentag and Elmer L. Struening, eds., *Handbook of Evaluation Research* v. 2 (Beverly Hills: Sage Publications, 1975), pp. 519–603.

[60]Melvin Kohn, *Class and Conformity: A Study in Values* (Homewood, Ill.: Dorsey Press, 1969). See also James D. Wright and Sonia R. Wright, "Social Class and Parental Values for Children: A Partial Replication and Extension of the Kohn Thesis," and Melvin L. Kohn, "Comment on Wright and Wright: Social Class and Parental Values: Another Confirmation of the Relationship," both in *American Sociological Review*, 41 (June, 1976), pp. 527–37 and 538–48.

[61]Sam D. Sieber and David E. Wilder, "Teaching Styles: Parental Preferences and Professional Role Definitions," *Sociology of Education*, 40 (Fall, 1967), pp. 302–15.

[62]J. McVicker Hunt, "Black Genes—White Environment," *Trans-action*, 6 (June, 1969), pp. 12–22.

[63]Jane R. Mercer, "Pluralistic Diagnosis in the Evaluation of Black and Chicano Children: A Procedure for Taking Sociocultural Variables into Account in Clinical Assessment," Paper presented at the meetings of the American Psychological Association in Washington, D.C., September, 1971 as cited by J. McV. Hunt, "Heredity, Environment, and Class or Ethnic Differences," p. 22.

[64]For two different views of early childhood intervention programs, see J. McV. Hunt, "Parent and Child Centers: Their Basis in the Behavioral and Educational Sciences," and

Edmund W. Gordon, "An Invited Critique" both in *American Journal of Orthopsychiatry*, 41 (January, 1971), pp. 13–42. Also, Keddie, *The Myth of Cultural Deprivation* contains diverse evidence on the adequacy of non-middle-class culture.

[65]Bowles and Gintis, *Schooling in Capitalist America*, pp. 125–48.

[66]Loehlin, Lindsey, and Spuhler, *Race Differences in Intelligence*, pp. 196–231.

[67]Loehlin, Lindsey, and Spuhler, *Race Differences in Intelligence*, pp. 271–280 reviews the relationships between cultural experiences and sense perception.

[68]Hunt, "Black Genes," p. 19.

[69]William Labov, "The Logic of Nonstandard English," and J. L. Dillard, *Black English: Its History and Usage in the United States* (New York: Vintage Books, 1972).

[70]Myra E. Shimberg, "An Investigation into the Validity of Norms with Special Reference to Urban and Rural Groups," *Archives of Psychology*, No. 104, Columbia University, 1929 as cited in Loehlin, Lindsey, and Spuhler, *Race Differences in Intelligence*, pp. 67–70.

[71]Irving E. Sigel, "How Intelligence Tests Limit Understanding of Intelligence," *Merrill-Palmer Quarterly*, 9 (January, 1963), pp. 39–56.

[72]See, for example, Leon J. Kamin, *The Science and Politics of I.Q.* (New York: John Wiley & Sons, 1974), or J. V. Hunt, "Black Genes."

[73]Arthur R. Jensen, "How Much Can We Boost I.Q. and Scholastic Achievement?" *Harvard Educational Review*, 39 (Winter, 1969), pp. 1–123.

[74]Richard J. Herrnstein, *I.Q. in the Meritocracy* (Boston: Little, Brown, 1973).

[75]See Loehlin, Lindsey, and Spuhler, *Race Differences in Intelligence*, pp. 167–77.

[76]L.S. Hearnshaw, *Cyril Burt, Psychologist* (Ithaca, N.Y.: Cornell University Press, 1979).

[77]Arthur R. Jensen, *Straight Talk About Mental Tests* (New York: The Free Press, 1981), pp. 128–67, 184–90.

[78]Brian Mackenzie, "Explaining Race Differences in IQ: The Logic, the Methodology, and the Evidence," *American Psychologist*, 39 (November, 1984), pp. 1214–33.

[79]Of course, the first widely used intelligence test was developed by Alfred Binet in France. We are referring to modifications and further elaborations in the United States

[80]Kamin, *The Science and Politics of I.Q.*, pp. 15–32.

[81]Ibid., p. 16.

[82]Fred L. Strodtbeck, "Family Interaction, Values, and Achievement," in *Talent and Society*, eds. David C. McClelland, Alfred L. Baldwin, Urie Bronfenbrenner, (Princeton, N.J.: D. Van Nostrand Company, 1958), pp. 135–94.

[83]Joseph A. Kahl, "Educational and Occupational Aspirations of 'Common Man' Boys," *Harvard Educational Review*, 23 (Summer, 1953), pp. 186–203.

[84]James S. Coleman and others, *Equality of Educational Opportunity* (Washington, D.C.: Government Printing Office, 1966).

[85]Pliska and Stern, *The Condition of Education*, p. 66.

[86]Jencks and others, *Inequality*, pp. 141–43.

[87]Morris Rosenberg and Roberta Simmons, *Black and White Self-Esteem: The Urban School Child* (Washington, D.C.: Arnold M. and Caroline Rose Monograph Series, American Sociological Association, 1971), p. 145.

[88]Portes and Wilson, "Black-White Differences," pp. 420–23.

[89]Coleman and others, *Equality*, pp. 280–81.

[90]Portes and Wilson, "Black-White Differences," pp. 420–30.

[91]Rosenberg and Simmons, *Black and White Self-Esteem*, p. 71; and National Center for Education Statistics, *High School Seniors*, p. 41.

[92]Ibid., p. 71.

[93]Kenneth B. Clark, *Dark Ghetto* (New York: Harper & Row, 1965); Jean D. Grambs, "The Self-Concept: Basis for Reeducation of Negro Youth," and "Discussion, Comments, and Issues," in William C. Kvarsceus, John S. Gibson, Franklin Patterson, Bradbury Seasholes, and Jean Grambs, *Negro Self-Concept: Implications for School and Citizenship* (New York: McGraw-Hill Book Co., 1965); and Rosenberg and Simmons, Black and White Self-Esteem, pp. 1–10.

[94]Coleman and others, *Equality*, pp. 319–25.

[95]Ibid., pp. 319–25.

[96]Ibid., p. 321.

[97]Patricia Sexton, *Education and Income* (New York: Viking Press, 1961).

[98]Howard S. Becker, "The Career of the Chicago Public School Teacher," *American Journal of Sociology*, 57 (March, 1952), pp. 470–77.

[99]Marvin J. Berlowitz, "Institutional Racism and School Staffing in an Urban Area," *The Journal of Negro Education*, 43 (Winter, 1974), pp. 25–29.

[100]Coleman and others, *Equality*, p. iii.

[101]Frederick Mosteller and Daniel P. Moynihan, *On Equality of Educational Opportunity* (New York: Random House, 1972).

[102]Coleman and others, *Equality*, p. 3.

[103]National Center for Education Statistics, *Two Years in High School*, p. 12.

[104]Mosteller and Moynihan, *On Equality*.

[105]Coleman and others, *Equality*, p. 20.

[106]National Center for Education Statistics, *High School Seniors*, p. 37.

[107]Alan B. Wilson, *The Consequences of Segregation: Academic Achievement in a Northern Community* (Berkeley: The Glendessary Press, 1969); U.S. Commission on Civil Rights, *Racial Isolation in the Public Schools* (Washington, D.C.: Government Printing Office, 1967), pp. 84–91.

[108]Karl Alexander and Bruce Eckland, "Contextual Effects in the High School Attainment Process," *American Sociological Review*, 40 (June, 1975), pp. 402–16.

[109]Marshall S. Smith, "Equality of Educational Opportunity: The Basic Findings Reconsidered," *On Equality*, eds. Mosteller and Moynihan, pp. 230–42.

[110]Nancy H. St. John, *Desegregation: School Outcomes for Children* (New York: John Wiley & Sons, 1975).

[111]Rita E. Mahard and Robert L. Crain, "Research on Minority Achievement in Desegregated Schools," in *The Consequences of School Desegregation*, eds. Christine H. Rossell and Willis D. Hawley (Philadelphia: Temple University Press, 1983), pp. 103–25.

[112]Ibid., p. 114.

[113]Robert L. Crain and Rita E. Mahard, "School Composition and Black College Attendance and Achievement Test Performance," *Sociology of Education*, 51 (April, 1978), pp. 98–99.

[114]Rosenberg and Simmons, *Black and White Self-Esteem*, pp. 99–102.

[115]Rosenberg and Simmons, *Black and White Self-Esteem*, pp. 24–26, and St. John, *Desegregation*, p. 119.

[116]Robert L. Crain, "School Integration and Occupational Achievement of Negroes," *American Journal of Sociology*, 75 (January, 1970), pp. 593–606.

[117]Mahard and Crain, "Research," pp. 121–124.

[118]St. John, *Desegregation*, pp. 64–86.

[119]Carl Braun, "Teacher Expectation: Sociopsychological Dynamics," *Review of Educational Research*, 46 (Spring, 1976), pp. 185–213.

[120]Ibid., pp. 192–95.

[121]Robert Rosenthal and Lenore Jacobson, *Pygmalion in the Classroom* (New York: Holt, Rinehart & Winston, 1968).

[122]Elyse S. Fleming and Ralph G. Anttonen, "Teacher Expectancy or My Fair Lady," *American Educational Research Journal*, 8 (March, 1971), pp. 241–52.

[123]Braun, "Teacher Expectation," pp. 193–95.

[124]Ibid., pp. 195–97.

[125]William H. Agee and William L. Smith, "Modifying Teachers' Attitudes Towards Speakers of Divergent Dialects through Inservice Training," *The Journal of Negro Education*, 43 (Winter, 1974), pp. 82–90.

[126]Jerome B. Dusek, "Do Teachers Bias Children's Learning?" *Review of Educational Research*, 45 (Fall, 1975), pp. 661–84.

[127]Stephen W. Raudenbush, "Magnitude of Teacher Effects on Pupil IQ as a Function of the Credibility of Expectancy Induction: A Synthesis of Findings from 18 Experiments," *Journal of Educational Psychology*, 76 (February, 1984), pp. 85–97.

[128]Sears and Feldman, "Teacher Interactions with Boys and with Girls," pp. 148–49.

[129]Myra Sadker and David Sadker, "Sexism in the Classroom: From Grade School to Graduate School," *Phi Delta Kappan*, 67 (March, 1986), pp. 512–15.

[130]Ibid., p. 513.

[131]Braun, "Teacher Expectation," pp. 199–202.

[132]Ray C. Rist, "Student Social Class and Teacher Expectations: The Self-Fulfilling Prophecy in Ghetto Education," *Harvard Educational Review*, 40 (August, 1970), pp. 411–51.

[133]Terry N. Saario, Carol Nagy Jacklin, and Carol Kehr Tittle, "Sex Role Stereotyping in the Public Schools," *Harvard Educational Review*, 43 (August, 1973), pp. 386–416.

[134]Charol Shakeshaft, "A Gender at Risk," *Phi Delta Kappan*, 67 (March, 1986), pp. 499-503.

[135]John I. Goodlad, *A Place Called School* (New York: McGraw-Hill, 1984), p. 151.

[136]Goodlad, *A Place Called School*, p. 155. See also Jeannie Oakes, *Keeping Track: How Schools Structure Inequality* (New Haven: Yale University Press, 1985).

[137]Donna Eder, "Ability Grouping as a Self-Fulfilling Prophecy: A Micro-Analysis of Teacher-Student Interaction," *Sociology of Education*, 54 (July, 1981), p. 154.

[138]Ibid., pp. 151–162.

[139]Goodlad, *A Place Called School*, p. 155.

[140]Ibid., p. 155.

[141]Bowles and Gintis, *Schooling in Capitalist America*, p. 132.

[142]Bowles and Gintis, *Schooling in Capitalist America*, p. 155.

[143]James E. Rosenbaum, "The Stratification of Socialization Processes," *American Sociological Review*, 40 (February 1975), pp. 48–54.

[144]Barbara Heyns, "Social Selection and Stratification within Schools," *American Journal of Sociology*, 79 (May 1974), pp. 1434–51.

[145]Janet Eyler, Valarie Cook, Rachel Tompkins, William Trent, and Leslie Ward, "Resegregation: Segregation within Desegregated Schools," in Rossell and Hawley, eds., *Desegregation*.

[146]Karl Alexander and Edward McDill, "Selection and Allocation within Schools," *American Sociological Review*, 41 (December, 1976), pp. 963–80.

[147]Alexander and McDill, "Selection and Allocation within Schools," p. 973.

[148]Karl L. Alexander, Martha Cook, and Edward L. McDill, "Curriculum Tracking and Educational Stratification: Some Further Evidence," *American Sociological Review*, 43 (February, 1978), pp. 47–66.

[149]R.C. Rist, *The Urban School: Factory for Failure* (Cambridge, Mass.: MIT Press, 1973); J.E. Brophy and T.L. Good, *Teacher–Student Relationships: Causes and Consequences* (New York: Holt, Rinehart & Winston, 1974); R. Barr and R. Dreeben, "Instruction in Classrooms," in L.S. Schulman, ed., *Review of Research in Education*, 5 (Itasca, Ill., 1977); Diana Felmlee and Donna Eder, "Contextual Effects in the Classroom: The Impact of Ability Groups on Student Attention," *Sociology of Education*, 56, 2 (1983), pp. 77–87.

[150]Brian Rowan and Andrew W. Miracle, Jr., "Systems of Ability Grouping and the Stratification of Achievement in Elementary Schools," *Sociology of Education*, 56 (July 1983), pp. 133–44.

[151]James A. Kulik and Chen-lin C. Kulik, "Effects of Ability Grouping on Secondary School Students," *American Educational Research Journal*, 19, 3 (Fall, 1982), pp. 415–28.

[152]Ibid., p. 422. See also James A. Kulik and Chen-lin C. Kulik, "Effects of Accelerated Instruction on Students," *Review of Educational Research*, 54, 3 (Fall, 1984), pp. 409–25.

[153]Kulik and Kulik, "Effects of Ability Grouping on Secondary Students," p. 426.

[154]Ibid., p. 426.

[155]Aaron V. Cicourel and John I. Kituse, *The Educational Decision-Makers* (Indianapolis: Bobbs-Merrill, 1963). James E. Rosenbaum, *Making Inequality: The Hidden Curriculum of High School Tracking* (New York: John Wiley & Sons, 1976).

[156]Karl L. Alexander and Bruce K. Eckland, "Sex Differences in the Educational Attainment Process," *American Sociological Review*, 39 (October, 1974), pp. 668–82.

[157]Alexander and McDill, "Selection and Allocation within Schools."

[158]Heyns, "Social Selection and Stratification within Schools," p. 1449.

[159]Emil J. Haller and Sharon A. Davis, "Teacher Perceptions, Parental Social Status and Grouping for Reading Instruction," *Sociology of Education*, 54 (July, 1981), pp. 162–74. See also R.A. Rehberg and E.R. Rosenthal, *Class and Merit in the American High School* (New York: Longman, 1978); R.M. Hauser, W.H. Sewell, and Duane F. Alwin, "High School Effects on Achievement," in W. Sewell and Robert M. Hauser, eds., *Schooling and Achievement in American Society* (New York: Academic Press, 1976).

[160]Alexander, Cook, and McDill, "Curriculum Tracking and Educational Stratification," p. 47.

[161]Alexander, Cook and McDill, "Curriculum Tracking and Educational Stratification," p. 64.

[162]This literature is too large and scattered to review here, but some of the key references follow. Wilbur Brookover, Charles Beady, Patricia Flood, John Schweitzer, and Joe Wisenbaker, *School Social Systems and Student Achievement: Schools Can Make a Difference* (New York: Praeger, 1979); Larry Cuban, "Effective Schools: A Friendly but Cautionary Note," *Phi Delta Kappan*, 9 (1983), pp. 695–96; Gary Natriello and Sanford M. Dornbusch, "Pitfalls in the Evaluation of Teachers by Principals," *Administrator's Notebook*," 29, 6 (1980–81); Phi Delta Kappa, *Why Do Some Urban Schools Succeed?* (Bloomington, Ind.: Phi Delta Kappa, 1980); Susan J. Rosenholtz, "Effective Schools: Interpreting the Evidence," *American Journal of Education* 93, 3 (May, 1985), pp. 352–88; Michael Rutter, Barbara Maugham, Peter Mortimore, Janet Ousten with Alan Smith, *Fifteen Thousand Hours: Secondary Schools and Their Effects on Children* (Cambridge, Mass.: Harvard University Press, 1979).

[163]Samuel Bowles, "Unequal Education and the Reproduction of the Social Division of Labor," in *Schooling in a Corporate Society: The Political Economy of Education in America*, ed. Martin Carnoy, (New York: David McKay, 1972), pp. 38–66.

[164]James Coleman, "The Concept of Equality of Educational Opportunity," *Harvard Educational Review*, 38 (Winter, 1968), pp. 7–22.

[165]James B. Conant, *Slums and Suburbs: A Commentary on Schools in Metropolitan Areas* (New York: McGraw-Hill Book Co., 1961), pp. 33–49, 71–94, 125–28.

[166]Jencks and others, *Inequality* pp. 176–265; and Bowles and Gintis, *Schooling in Capitalist America*, pp. 26–36.

[167]Jencks and others, *Inequality*, pp. 176–246.

[168]Christopher S. Jencks and Marsha D. Brown, "The Effects of High Schools on Their Students," *Harvard Educational Review*, 45 (August, 1975), pp. 273–324.

[169]Ibid., p. 311.

# CHAPTER NINE SOCIOLOGY AND EDUCATIONAL POLICY

Most of this book has been devoted to outlining in sociological terms the basic structure and processes of American educational institutions. What has emerged is a portrait of a highly complex system that is closely tied to other institutions such as the family, economy, and polity, and to large-scale societal trends. The system sometimes seems too complex, too interrelated, too entrenched to permit planned change. For those who see our educational institutions as fundamentally flawed or misdirected, a growing sense of frustration is likely to develop as they learn more about how these institutions operate. The constraints seem so formidable that there is a strong temptation to simply give up hope for improvement.

Yet our intent has not been to stifle the urge to alter and change our educational system. On the contrary, we have advocated a policy-oriented approach that has institution building as its fundamental goal. Thus far, we have described the present workings of our system with the hope that such knowledge will be helpful in devising realistic and workable alternatives to present practices. Clearly, we have isolated many fundamental difficulties: lack of metropolitan planning, tendencies toward blind credentialism, both looseness and rigidity in bureaucratic organization, mechanistic processing of students, inadequate definitions and realizations of professionalism, low levels of participation in educational politics, and class, sex, and racial biases, to name a few. But up until now there has been relatively little discussion of major proposals for alteration of the present system. During the past two decades, many innovative proposals have been widely debated, if not widely implemented. We shall describe some of the most important of these briefly. Then, in conclusion, we shall return to the fundamental question, "What specific roles can sociologists play in bringing about a new and better educational system?"

## THE CRITICS AND THEIR ALTERNATIVES

It should be obvious by now that there are many bases upon which American educational institutions can be criticized. Those committed to libertarian educational philosophies charge that the schools are too rigid and constraining and that they teach students to be passive and docile. These critics advocate more freedom and democracy in the classroom and school. Those committed to the political liberation of the poor and minorities believe the schools to be biased instruments of oppression. They advocate politically oriented and community-controlled schools. Those who value diversity and competition often criticize contemporary public education as too bland, homogeneous, and monopolistic. They espouse policies designed to encourage the development of alternate kinds of schools. Some would have us broaden our conception of education and extend it throughout the life cycle. Others would have us narrow present conceptions of schooling in order to concentrate on the development of basic, pragmatic skills. Some have even advocated the total elimination of formal education.

These criticisms are raised by people with diverse values, including independent personalities, political freedom and equality, diversity, competition, self-improvement, and pragmatic knowledge. Virtually all believe that if their policies were fully implemented a new and better society would develop. Since these values and the policies growing out of commitments to them are not mutually exclusive, it should come as no surprise that there is a considerable diversity, overlap, and confusion among the many proposals for change in American education. We shall discuss only a few of these; open classrooms, free schools, alternate public schools, voucher plans, lifelong education, back-to-basics, and deschooling. Although in our discussions we shall try to draw rather sharp distinctions between these various policy proposals, it should be borne in mind that real-life programs often combine features of more than one of them.

### Open Classrooms

One of the most popular innovations during the 1970s was the open classroom. This reform came to the United States through the process of cultural diffusion, having been previously widely heralded in Great Britain as a new and promising approach to early childhood education.[1] Yet the philosophical and psychological principles underlying open classrooms are similar to those of the Progressive education movement of the 1920s and 1930s in the United States. Proponents of this type of educational experience make frequent references to Rousseau, Dewey, and Piaget among others. As Charles Silberman noted, the chief differentiating characteristic between this and the earlier Progressive movement is ". . . the . . . hard-headed recognition of and indeed insistence on the teacher's central role."[2]

As in traditional classrooms, the teacher-student relationship is central; the roles, however, are defined quite differently. The student is expected to acquire knowledge primarily through encounters with the rich variety of learning materials present in an open classroom. Among these are scales, weights and measures, musical instruments, tools of various sorts, paints, writing materials, watertables, math problem sets, science experiments, and comfortable places to read. The idea is that virtually any normal child, when placed in such a rich learning environment, will find many items of interest. They will learn easily as they encounter these diverse learning tools. The child enjoys broad latitude in determining which projects she or he will undertake and how long they will be continued.

But the materials by themselves are not enough. The teacher plays an active role as guide, monitor, and interpreter of the materials. As a guide the teacher helps show the way to important goals—especially reading, writing, and arithmetic. But rather than attempting to lead all students in rote memorization of basic facts, the teacher allows them to learn more casually as they deal with the rich classroom environment. The teacher, of course, has control over the structure and materials of the classroom and can arrange them so that the emphasis is on basic skills. In such classes the teacher is constantly in motion, talking with small groups of children about what they are doing, suggesting further projects, and observing the strengths and weaknesses of individual students. When progress appears slow in one area, special help will probably be provided, but always with the recognition that children display differences in their rates of cognitive development. These variations are seen as normal and are to be expected. Although there may be certain common exercises in phonics, physical education, music, and other subjects, the emphasis is *not* upon these communal activities in which the teacher is clearly the leader and the children are followers. Instead, the teacher acts more as a facilitator of child-initiated, though teacher-structured, learning activities.

Proponents of open classrooms claim that they are superior to traditional classrooms in many ways. First, they are much more enjoyable for students. This follows from several features of such learning situations. Among the most important of these are: Students can generally do things that interest them; arbitrary age-grade and classroom divisions can be overcome so that teachers and students from several different grades can interact easily; the emphasis is upon monitoring individual progress rather than on competitive testing and grading; children do not experience failure as frequently—a feature that may be especially important to poor or minority students; and, finally, the classroom is more comfortable, even though it is noisier and may seem chaotic to an outsider. Second, open classrooms are claimed to be superior in that they encourage student initiative and the inquisitive spirit rather than docility and parroting of teachers' lessons.

However, superiority of the method on a third crucial dimension—actual learning of basic subject matter—has yet to be demonstrated. Early evaluations suggested that open classrooms were equally as effective as traditional ones in teaching reading but slightly less effective with regard to arithmetic.[3] Later evaluations have been more negative. Nevill Bennett has reported on his research comparing informal (open), mixed, and traditional classrooms. His results were that in English, reading, and mathematics the formal approach was superior to the informal. Although he found that children in informal classrooms were more positively oriented toward school, they also showed more anxiety (presumably due to the lack of structure). His results also indicated that the differences among the various kinds of classes may be primarily due to the amount of time the children spend on basic lessons. For example, he found one teacher with an informal class that did match the achievement gains of the traditional classes, but this teacher made certain the students spent as much or more time on the basics as did the traditional teachers.

It is important to reserve judgment on this approach until more conclusive evidence is available. Further, the moral lessons of different classroom structures need to be recognized and evaluated. Clearly, the student is expected to assume a more subordinate, passive, and docile role in the traditional classroom. Just as clearly the students' joy in learning is less highly valued in such classes. Anecdotal and observational accounts of open classrooms suggest that they are strikingly different from traditional ones because they teach that learning can be fun, that students can take more responsibility for their learning, and that initiative and movement are encouraged.

Additionally, there is danger that this *innovation will be spread too quickly*, before administrative and teaching personnel fully understand their new roles. If forced into situations in which teachers or principals are unconvinced of the value of open classrooms, the results may be disastrous because so much depends upon motivated and competent teachers. At present, many teachers who would like to cooperate in implementing changes of this type simply have not been sufficiently trained to do so.

If given a choice between effectiveness in teaching the basics and developing joy and self-initiative among students, most Americans would probably choose the former. Working-class individuals tend to be especially dubious about such libertarian pedagogical methods, perhaps because they recognize that schooling is preparation for adult work and so many jobs are dull and constrained rather than self-actualizing. Still, let us hope that joy, creativity, and high levels of achievement do prove to go together. Then it will not be necessary to make a choice between these goals, all of which are considered desirable by a broad range of Americans.

### Alternate Educational Institutions

In contrast to advocates of open classrooms who seek to reform established educational institutions, there are those who advocate the development of new, alternate institutions. They argue that too many obstacles (in the form of rules, traditions, habits, conservative personnel, and school boards) exist to reform ongoing public schools. Alternate institutions may be developed from scratch with new structures, committed personnel, and students who freely choose to participate in them. In this way, the necessity of overcoming the resistance of those with vested interests in the status quo is avoided.

Radical critics of American public schools believe that it is impossible to work "within the system," so they seek to establish their own private schools in which greater freedom is possible. These are often referred to as *free* schools, with the adjective being used in its political, rather than financial, sense.[4] These institutions have been based upon what establishment educators reject as extreme and unrealistic philosophies. We shall describe briefly the Summerhill school of A. S. Neill that has served as a model and inspiration for many contemporary American free schools,[5] and we shall also sketch the main characteristics of other newly founded free schools in the United States.

But there are other critics of traditional public schools who take the more optimistic position that alternate *public* schools are possible. These may be seen as experiments in institutionalizing educational methods and philosophies that differ from the traditional, compulsory, age-graded, teacher-dominated, test- and grade-oriented school or college. But in order to be acceptable to the public it is necessary that these not be seen as crazy, dangerous, or extravagant experiments. In fact, as we shall see, such alternate programs are not only possible, but many of them actually exist.[6]

### Free Schools

Summerhill is a small, private residential school located in the village of Leiston, England. Since its founding in 1921 it has been oriented toward providing students with a maximum of freedom in the belief that they will become happy, fulfilled adults through this experience. It offers a full program of classes from elementary through high school, but attendance at classes is purely voluntary. Many students arrive at Summerhill only after having prolonged negative experiences with traditional schools. Such students often avoid classes for months, sometimes years. Instead, they spend their time in a variety of other activities including play, loafing, or working on projects in wood, metal, or art workshops; but when they do resume their studies it is on a completely voluntary basis—and they learn quickly.

There are rules at Summerhill to cope with problems of group living and the health and safety of the students, but these rules are established in a democratic fashion with each teacher and student having one vote. The result is a nonauthoritarian, highly egalitarian environment that affords students much more freedom than in the typical public school. At this school the formal curriculum is of secondary importance to the task of learning to live a happy and involved life.

Much to the surprise of many skeptics, graduates typically adjust well to life outside the school. Many students go on to higher studies, but others simply take very average jobs. Yet Neill reports that their employers describe them as unusually committed and happy workers.

But it should be noted that this is a small school with fewer than fifty very atypical students. Since it is far from free in the financial sense, most students come from privileged backgrounds. Many students have had a history of trouble and failure in traditional schools. Thus, they represent a highly selective clientele for whom such a free experience may be particularly appropriate. Furthermore, the school maintains a 10:1 student-teacher ratio, one that would be much too expensive for all but the richest of public school systems. In addition, it must recruit rare, dedicated faculty who not only believe in the school's philosophy but who are also willing to work for the minimal wage offered. Finally, the parents are unusual in their acceptance of the freedom of the school, including the freedom to loaf. Given these characteristics, it is difficult to imagine large-scale school systems based on this model.

There have long been a few private schools in the United States that were explicitly modeled after Summerhill. But in the period of student and civil unrest between 1966 and 1971, there was a dramatic proliferation of diverse private schools.[7] The alternative school movement apparently continued to expand into the early 1970s, but thereafter growth was slowed by declining enrollments, inflation, ideological disagreements among parents, the conservative trend in national politics, and the creation of alternative public schools. By 1980 the alternative school movement seemed "moribund."[8] Even so the movement was significant. It symbolized the depth of dissatisfaction with traditional public schools among some parents and teachers, and it demonstrated that there was significant demand for alternatives. The alternative private schools stimulated the creation of alternative public schools.

Allen Graubard, the foremost student of the American free school movement, identified four distinct types among such private schools. The first of these is the *classical free school* in the tradition of Summerhill. Many are boarding schools that endeavor to create a warm, sensitive community of equals. Personality development and self-actualization are considered more important than cognitive achievement, which is understandable given the fact that the clientele is almost entirely composed of white children from economically privileged families.

A second, and closely related type, is the *parent-teacher cooperative elementary school.* These are organized by white, liberal, middle-class parents who dislike the highly structured program of traditional public schools. Parents work closely with dedicated teachers who agree to work for low wages. Although tuition is often based upon ability to pay and efforts are made to recruit minority pupils, these schools are not explicitly designed to meet the needs of an underprivileged clientele.

The third type is the *free high school.* There are several variants depending primarily upon the social class of the clientele. Some are ". . . oriented toward the white middle-class and hip youth culture." Participatory democracy is a key value. Students and teachers work together to define and carry out a politically and pedagogically radical education.

There are working-class versions oriented toward youth who are very hostile to public high schools and may have already dropped out. These are much more vocationally oriented than their middle-class counterparts, and in addition, they are often explicitly concerned with developing a proud working-class consciousness. Finally, there are street academies, such as Harlem Prep, that represent attempts on the part of concerned adults to salvage the education of impoverished minority group students who have come to hate normal public schools. Discipline, rather than freedom, is stressed, but here discipline is accepted and relations between staff and students are close.

Graubard's fourth type is the *community elementary school.* These schools are founded by adults who believe in community control of public schools. They are explicitly political in orientation, with stress on the development of ethnic consciousness as well as on the acquisition of basic skills. Although some such schools are pedagogically innovative, many are rather traditional and practice strict discipline. Once again, however, discipline—when enforced by those obviously in sympathy with the aspirations of oppressed minorities—seems to be accepted by students as appropriate rather than oppressive.

From these brief descriptions it is clear that the term "free school" is a broad and inclusive one. In actuality, these differences in definition of the school role, pedagogical approaches, clientele, and structures of governance are quite considerable and are the basis of much conflict among free school advocates. Although all the individuals involved may be sincere in their desire to change education and, through it, society, their visions of the ideal future differ extensively. Firestone has argued that commitments to ill-defined or contradictory goals, as well as to intense social relations and participatory democracy among parents, teachers, and students, are causes of much conflict in such schools.[9] These problems, in addition to those of funding and staffing, make it easy to understand why free schools seem to be rather unstable organizations. This instability, combined with small size, seems to limit the potential of these models as alternatives for mass education.

### Alternate Public Schools

It is simply a fact that many parents and students have found the standard educational program of our public schools to be ineffective and oppressive. A majority may well be satisfied, but a significant minority is not. Now many critics are arguing that the dissatisfied should be provided with publicly supported options.

Kenneth Clark, a widely respected black social psychologist and educator, has condemned present urban school systems as segregated, inefficient, incompetent, and destructive,[10] and he has gone on to suggest that alternative public schools be established to compete with the present failing systems. Specifically he proposes: (1) state support of regional schools that could draw students from both the inner city and the suburbs, (2) federal government support of residential schools that would serve students in regions composed of several states, (3) schools supported by colleges and universities associated with their teacher training programs and open to outsiders as well as to faculty children, (4) schools sponsored and run by industries and labor unions, and (5) Defense Department schools that could serve to train those not reached in regular school settings and that might recruit volunteers for military careers. Given the facts that his proposals require new forms of federal and state support, are in potential conflict with established systems and personnel, and would violate the neighborhood school tradition, it is not surprising that these controversial proposals have not received much serious consideration from educational planners.

Still, the free school movement and general public dissatisfaction has apparently made some impact upon the educational establishment. This is evidenced by the fact that a diversity of alternate schools have been established within public school systems across the nation. There were only about 100 public alternative schools in 1970, but a decade later over 10,000 such schools, serving 3,000,000 students, existed. [11] Urban school systems across the United States found alternative schools useful in promoting reform, dealing with student violence and vandalism, and desegregation.[12] Alternative public schools have been initiated by administrators, teachers, parents, students, and university professors. Like free schools, they come in a multitude of types. Smith delineated some of these.[13]

There are open schools organized around interest centers located either within individual classrooms or in certain parts of the building, serving the entire school. There are "schools without walls," which use zoos, museums, factories, newspapers, and other community facilities as places of learning. There are learning centers (educational parks, magnet schools, career-education centers, specialized vocational and science schools) that draw from all parts of a city, not just particular neighborhoods. Continuation schools have been developed to help dropouts, pregnant teenagers, and adults complete high school. Multicultural and bilingual schools also exist in which every effort is made to assure an ethnically diverse student body. There are alternate schools within traditional schools. There are even public free schools that approximate Summerhill's ideals in many ways. Further, not only the structure but also the content of alternate schools is different, so that the usually tabooed topics of sexuality, corruption, and quality of life can be openly explored. Ironically, one of the most popular types of public alternative schools, the back-to-basics school, is repugnant to libertarian ideals. This fundamental school emphasizes teacher authority, formality, traditional subjects, and such old-fashioned instructional strategies as recitation and rote memorization.[14] Conservative as well as liberal parents are seeking alternative educational experiences for their children.

### Voucher Plans

Many conservative educational policy analysts and politicians believe that parents do not now have sufficient choices regarding their children's schooling. As they see it, the tax-supported public schools have a virtual monopoly. Even when parents have good reason to doubt the effectiveness of their local public schools, private school tuition costs are often prohibitive. The poorer the parent, the fewer the options. Educational *voucher plans* offer a means to enhance parental choice and promote competition and diversity in the educational marketplace at the same time.

The basic idea behind voucher plans is quite simple. Instead of channeling public funds directly to public school districts, funds are given in the form of vouchers, to parents who can then choose the educational program that is best for their child. The parent may choose to use the voucher to obtain educational services from a public or a private school.

Because schools must depend on tuition payments for their financial survival, each would be encouraged to develop strong and attractive programs to meet the demands of parents. Competition between schools for voucher funds would result in the most popular programs growing in size while the unpopular ones shrink and ultimately fold entirely.

The chief administrative unit in such a system would be the Educational Voucher Agency (EVA), which either could be an established school board or a new, separate body representing larger or smaller jurisdictional areas. The EVA would have responsibility for receiving funds, disbursing them, deciding which schools would be eligible for participation in the program (within certain mandatory guidelines), and auditing expenditures by individual schools. All voucher schools would have to meet the minimum state standards existing for private schools. These tend to be considerably less restrictive than those set for public schools. In order to encourage socioeconomic integration, schools taking disadvantaged students would receive incentive payments over and above the standard voucher amount.

There are several variations of such plans, but all have proven highly controversial. In fact, they have been opposed by virtually all organized groups in the education establishment including the National Education Association, the American Federation of Teachers, the National School Boards Association, the National Association of School Boards of Education, and the Council of Chief State School Officers. In addition, the American Civil Liberties Union has taken the position that such programs undermine the goals of public education. The National Association of Colored People is opposed because it fears that voucher plans will perpetuate segregation. These opposing groups believe that voucher plans will

> . . . destroy the public schools; play havoc with the stabilizing factors in our democratic society; bring religious, economic, social, and political divisiveness; encourage racism; become educational hucksterism; create an unmanageable bureaucracy; dilute educational opportunites; make a farce of constitutional separation of church and state; encourage parents to choose schools based on prejudices; and contradict traditions of local support and control.[15]

On the other hand, advocates of voucher plans argue that they will

> . . . promote general improvement in education through competition; promote democratic freedom of choice; increase educational diversity; give parents some control and responsibility; promote accountability; overcome racial and economic limitations of neighborhood schools; drive bad schools out of

business; improve the education of the disadvantaged; improve equity among taxpayers; and increase total expenditures for education.[16]

We cannot detail the reasoning behind all these assertions, but it should be clear that the controversy is great.

Only one experimental voucher program was ever put into operation and it was highly modified. This program was tried only in Alum Rock, California. The Alum Rock demonstration program deviated from the ideal of a free market in education because it included only public schools.[17] In addition, it included guarantees that staff would not be dismissed and schools would not be closed. However, even this modified plan was successful in promoting diversity in public education. During the 1974–75 school year the 14 voucher schools (which represent 58 percent of all the schools in the system) offered 55 mini-schools among which parents were free to choose. Teachers were enthusiastic about the program because they were able to teach in ways consistent with their different educational philosophies. Informal norms developed that protected the mini-schools from the discomfort of all out competition for students. Finally, the achievement scores in voucher schools were essentially identical to those in nonvoucher schools.

Voucher plans have been debated for a long time. They were unpopular in the relatively liberal Carter administration, which won the backing of the NEA, but President Reagan continues to endorse voucher plans. The most recent version would distribute federal remedial education funds via vouchers.[18] Although legislation setting up voucher plans is narrowly targeted for what is clearly a needy group, opponents view it as a threat to public schooling, as endangering the separation of church and state, and as a policy which is likely to bring about socioeconomic and racial segregation. The idea remains controversial and ideological, and thus unlikely to be put into practice soon.

### Lifelong Education

The proposals we have discussed so far are primarily youth oriented. They share the basic assumption that education is something experienced and completed during the first two or three decades of life, and rarely supplemented in any serious way after that. As a result, they concentrate on issues of classroom management, curriculum design, and psychological, social, or intellectual development with only the child in mind.

Several major policy reports written during the last few years have challenged this basic model.[19] They recommend restructuring education so that it is a continuous process, experienced during all stages of the life cycle. According to this model, the traditional division of the life cycle into a period of preparation and a period of participation is artificial and no longer suited to the pace of contemporary life. Social change is now so rapid that individuals need to be in almost constant touch with new scientific and technological information, as well as with new developments in other spheres, in order to remain in the mainstream of economic, political, and social life.[20] Without continuous learning, the gap between the generations can grow increasingly greater, with older people finding themselves unprepared for either the latest demands of the labor market or for the adjustments required by new styles of living.

Consequently, these reports recommend that schools, particularly at the college and university level, be open to adult students of all ages and that changes that encourage adult enrollment be instituted. In fact, many of these recommendations have already been realized in several parts of the United States as well as in Great Britain, France, and several other nations. In the United States, programs embodying these recommendations are generally referred to as "external degree programs," although there is considerable variation among them.[21] The theme common to all these programs, however, is increased flexibility and diversity. In each program, students are able to obtain at least some college credit without coming onto the college campus to attend regularly scheduled courses.

### Flexibility of Time and Space

One way in which external degree programs provide flexibility for their students is by dispersing the college through both time and space. Courses may be offered at unusual hours, on weekends, and during what are normally vacation periods. In this way, course schedules are made compatible with work and family responsibilities.

Furthermore, faculty and students may meet for courses or consultations on campus or in the community, with special resource centers, libraries, museums, and other local facilities being favored choices for these purposes. This reduces commuting time and, simultaneously, permits the use of rich sources of information and learning not generally tapped in traditional settings. Indeed, the use of decentralized locations and community resources for educational purposes is such an important element in external degree programs that several institutions now offering such degrees do not even have a campus of their own.[22]

External degree programs also make use of on-the-job locations. Many companies now offer in-service courses and other educational opportunities to workers. These are offered at the workplace rather than at a formal school, though professional faculty are generally hired to teach them. Such programs obviously reduce commuting and scheduling problems to a minimum and also facilitate a better integration of education and work.

### Credit for Competency

Another way in which external degree programs introduce flexibility is by granting credit on the basis of competence rather than on the basis of courses completed. Most students are familiar with CLEP, the College-Level Examination Program, through which students can gain college credit by taking standardized examinations. In many external degree programs, credit can also be obtained through examinations arranged with individual faculty members. Students do not necessarily take formal courses. They may, for example, only consult with faculty members about reading material or other experiences through which learning can occur. When ready, they take an examination and receive appropriate credit if they pass. Indeed, the trend away from formal courses and toward credit by examination is so great that some external degrees are now granted by institutions that do not offer courses or formal instruction at all. The Illinois Board of Governors Bachelor of Arts degree program and Thomas A. Edison College in New Jersey are examples.[23]

A number of programs have gone one step further, though, and have also dispensed with examinations. In these programs, credit is granted on the basis of an assessment of the students' experiences and competencies. This assessment may be relatively standardized—so that four years of military service may be automatically converted to fifteen college credits, for example—or highly individualized. It is the *proof* of competency and not the *means* through which it was acquired that is important, however. As the president of one such program put it, "Potential students can offer anything which makes sense to them to achieve this equivalency [of two years college credit]: formal or informal educational experiences, work, hobbies, reading, innate genius.[24] Obviously, such a policy has many advantages, particularly for adults. Not only are their past experiences acknowledged as valuable, but they find that much less than the traditional four years of study will be needed to complete their degree.

Some programs have also been innovative in their definitions of competencies. For example, Minnesota Metropolitan State College required students to acquire competency in five areas.[25] Competency was defined as a combination of skill or knowledge, understanding, and attitudes. The five areas were: (1) basic learning and communication, which included reading, speaking, writing, listening, and computation, as well as attitudes that facilitate communication; (2) civic involvement, which included a positive attitude toward participation in community decision making as well as understanding and competence in such participation; (3) competence in a profession or career, including the ability to obtain and hold a job; (4) competence in leisure and recreation, or an ability to use leisure time comfortably; and (5) personal growth and maturation, which included the capacity to "confront with a minimum of trauma the fact that people die, lose jobs, have children—all unexpectedly. It includes . . . knowledge of what it means to be human and a capacity to act on that knowledge."[26] It is clear that these competencies are not those normally required for a college degree, nor those usually acquired in the traditional classroom setting.

### The Impact of Lifelong Education

It is clear that the changes occurring to facilitate adult participation in educational experiences will also have far-reaching effects on the educational opportunities of the traditional college-age population.[27] First and most obviously, they will also have increasingly flexible and diverse programs available to them. Second, they will experience more of their education in age-heterogeneous settings. The isolation of adolescents and young adults in age-homogeneous schools will diminish, and so might the influence of the peer group and the strength of adolescent subcultures. At the same time, young people will not be pressured into moving through their educational experiences in a "lockstep" fashion, forced to make important educational and occupational decisions when they may not yet be ready, or to continue on with their education when they might prefer a period of work or other experience instead.

Those who cannot afford education at an early age might benefit particularly, since it will be acceptable and relatively easy to return to education after several years in the work force or to continue studies on a part-time basis.

Some proposals for the financing of education through the life cycle would be especially advantageous to this group. Such proposals involve vouchers similar to those we discussed earlier. Under this plan, each individual would be entitled to a certain number of years of education, which he or she can use at any time in the life cycle. At the same time, employers would be required to grant time off for a return to education or learning.

A number of important questions about lifelong education are still unanswered. We know relatively little about the educational needs of adult students or the learning environments most appropriate for people of various ages. In addition, a number of specific criticisms have been leveled against external degree programs.[28] Central to these criticisms is the question of quality and standards. Traditional methods of evaluating and accrediting college programs must be revised to accommodate the new, diverse formats and purposes. Meanwhile, many fear the proliferation of diploma mills that turn out credentialed but undereducated graduates.

Some of these problems will be worked out in time, but other questions will be debated for years. For example, is learning that occurs as a by-product of life experience really equivalent to the kind of learning that occurs in the classroom? What does it mean to award a college degree on the basis of such competencies as leisure and recreation, personal growth and maturation? Will these changes promote greater equality of educational opportunity between the rich and poor, men and women, and old and young? Or will they simply water down these opportunities so that, while they are more readily available, they are also of less worth? Or is it about time that we recognized that meaningful learning does not only take place from 8 to 4 on weekdays in age-homogeneous classrooms utilizing textbooks and lecture notes?

Finally, it is important to note that much progress toward lifelong learning has already been made even within traditional colleges and universities. The changes have been driven by demographic realities. The cohorts of traditional-age students have begun to decline and will continue to do so for many years. American colleges and universities have offset the shrinkage of younger cohorts by enrolling increasing numbers of older students, especially women, who study on a part time basis. In 1985, 43 percent of all college students were twenty-five or older and 45 percent attended classes part time.[29] Age heterogeneity is, and will remain, a reality of the college classroom.

## Back to Basics

Whereas advocates of lifelong learning would have us broaden our conceptions of education, others would have us narrow and refine those conceptions. In recent years a new wave of conservative criticism of American elementary and secondary education has developed. These critics feel that schooling should center on the development of basic skills[30] and competencies in the traditional areas of reading, writing, and arithmetic. In order to refocus on these fundamentals, they propose that schools drop programs in guidance and counseling as well as courses dealing with sex, drugs, race relations, art and music appreciation, physical education, and driver training. Obviously, proponents of back-to-basics disagree with the progressive educators' conception that the school should be concerned with the "whole child," including physical, emotional, and aesthetic (in addition to intellectual) development.

These conservative critics feel that progressive schools have been overburdened by "social service" projects to such an extent that they have failed in their primary function—to assure that children have mastered fundamentals in order that they may function effectively as adults. They cite the downward trend in aptitude and achievement test scores, high dropout rates, and high rates of functional illiteracy as proof of this failure. In addition, they feel that several liberal school policies have been responsible for the failures of the children to learn to read. Among these are the following:

1. *Social promotion.* The liberal educators' concern with the social adjustment of their pupils has led them to adopt a policy whereby virtually all students are promoted from grade to grade along with their classmates. This occurs even when the skills necessary for success in the next grade have not been acquired. These new critics of American schools believe that children should only be promoted when they have mastered those fundamentals necessary for adequate work at the next level.
2. *School discipline.* These critics do not believe in democratic, child-oriented classrooms. They believe education should be teacher centered; discipline should be strict; tests should be frequent and demanding; and grading should be frequent and quantitative. In addition, they advocate the reinstatement of codes regulating hair styles and dress.
3. *The Discovery Method.* Open classrooms may be all right for some children, but these parents do not want a permissive, self-discovery approach for their own children. They believe that rote memorization and drill should play a prominent part in education. What good is the new math, they ask, if their children do not know that $9 \times 7 = 63$?

Although these critics often speak of a total reorientation of American education, they sometimes only demand that at least one "fundamentals school" be added to each district and be available to all who want it. But even where there is not demand for total reconstruction of a school system, many teachers and administrators are understandably disturbed by this groundswell of reactionary sentiment. Still, for the moment at least, it seems that this antiestablishment movement is on the rise.

School boards have been generally reluctant to make the changes that conservative parents demand. Quite apart from ideological and philosophical considerations, such a total reorientation would involve tremendous amounts of time and energy. One board member made an insightful observation when he noted

> Consider what it would mean to policy development to go all the way back to the basics as partisans demand. . . . It would mean restructuring the board's policy statements on philosophy, goals, instructional program, discipline, homework, study halls, retention, promotion, graduation, report cards, counseling, extra-curricular activities—to mention but a few topics. No board is about to do that.[31]

State legislators and boards of education responded to public pressure for accountability and increased emphasis on basics by mandating the use of minimum competency tests. The popularity of these standardized tests which were designed to ascertain whether or not students had mastered very basic material, may have peaked in 1983 at which time they were required in forty states.[32] Two states dropped the requirement during the following year. In 1984 the tests were most often used to identify students who needed remedial work and to strengthen graduation requirements. Only seven states expected to use minimum competency test scores as a basis for determining whether or not a child should be promoted from one grade to another.[33]

Under *merit* (as opposed to *social*) *promotion* policies, only those students who exceed minimum scores on standardized tests continue to the next grade. Those who fail are retained in grade and are given remedial help until they are able to pass the promotion test. At present, no one can be sure whether utilizing minimum competency test scores as promotion gates actually increases educational achievement. An early claim to success came from Greensville County, Virginia.[34] In 1973 that district abandoned its social promotion policy in favor of one that used minimal standards of competency for grade promotions. During the first three years after the inception of the new policy, the numbers of students retained in grade dropped dramatically, significant gains were made in achievement, and I.Q. test scores and attitudes toward testing both improved. However, the larger and more rigorously evaluated New York City promotion-gates program apparently failed. Students in that experimental program made the same gains in California Achievement Test reading scores as did those in a comparison group educated under the old social promotion policy.[35]

As we have pointed out before, scores on standardized tests do not necessarily reflect understanding, creativity, or an ability to learn on one's own. A truly satisfactory evaluation would also take into account their moral, as well as cognitive, impact. If back-to-basics raises test scores at the cost of developing more authoritarian and even more submissive students, most educators would oppose them even more strongly than they now do. Conservatives, however, might interpret such changes as improvements in self-discipline and respect for adult authorities. Thus, such changes might please them greatly.

## Deschooling

Ivan Illich goes further than any of the previously discussed critics by arguing for the elimination of schooling rather than its reform or radical alteration.[36] This is because Illich believes that all schools share certain fundamental characteristics that make them destructive to individuals and to societies. From this perspective, traditional schools and permissive schools, schools in democratic societies and schools in socialist societies, schools for adults and schools for children, are merely variations of the same basic theme.

According to Illich the central theme or message taught by the "hidden curriculum" of the schools is "that only through school can an individual prepare himself for adulthood in society, that what is not taught in school is of little value, and that what is learned outside of school is not worth knowing."[37] This message alienates the individual from his own spontaneous interests and learning experiences outside the classroom. It gives the school, the teachers, and the administrators who control the schools a monopoly over learning. Only learning delivered by a person certified to teach is considered valuable; only learning that is recognized through course credits and diplomas is meaningful. Learning becomes transformed into a commodity to be purchased and consumed. Schools control how this commodity will be packaged, in what units and sequences. They also determine how scarce or abundant these units will be and to whom they will be accessible.

Under this system, the number and types of educational packages you accumulate determines your "knowledge stock." Your knowledge stock, in turn, can be used to acquire special privileges such as higher income, occupational status, and access to more powerful tools of production. Illich refers to this as "knowledge capitalism." He believes that knowledge capitalists control scientific know-how and the media of communication, thus exercising a disproportionate influence over others and making participatory democracy impossible. For Illich, this is a new class structure controlled by vested interests with a monopoly over schooling and its distribution.

As a solution to these problems and a means to greater equality Illich recommends the abolition of schooling and the establishment of a series of "networks" or "opportunity webs" that will enable anyone to learn whatever he or she wants to learn. In proposing these arrangements, Illich makes a number of basic assumptions about learning. Most centrally, he assumes that people learn best from direct experience, and that even today, most important learning occurs outside school rather than in it. People learn from books and from friends, from observation and from solving practical problems. He also assumes that if people are sufficiently motivated to learn they will seek out learning experiences without any degree of compulsion or constraint. Illich proposes four specific "opportunity webs."

### Reference Services to Educational Objects

The purpose of this network would be to provide individuals with the objects or "things" they need for learning. This would include access to such materials as books, maps, and scientific equipment as well as to materials used in various manufacturing processes. These would be provided by establishing resource centers and also by encouraging companies to invite interested persons to observe their operations. People could use these resources whenever they wished, rather than waiting until reaching the "proper" grade in school or the hours put aside for these materials in the school curriculum.

### Skill Exchanges

Illich believes that a wide range of skills from speaking Spanish to performing surgery can be learned simply by watching someone who already has those skills and receiving some instruction from them. Consequently, he recommends establishing networks through which people who have a skill they are willing to teach and others who wish to learn that skill are put in contact with each other. Illich is opposed to certifying certain people as teachers and believes that "the right to teach any skill should come under the protection of freedom of speech." According to Illich, certification only creates an artificial shortage of both teachers and skilled practitioners.

### Peer Matching

Peer matching would involve people who were interested in meeting others with similar skills and interests so they could share these with one another. Illich argues that schools artificially restrict those with whom we come in contact and therefore violate our rights to free assembly. Illich recommends registering people in large computer banks that would then match them with each other when peers were desired.

### Professional Educators

Illich proposes that three types of professional educators might arise under his system. The first would be administrators who concentrate on building and maintaining the resources and networks discussed above. The second would be pedagogues who help guide students to their goals. For example, the pedagogue might suggest what books would be most helpful to a student desiring to learn a particular skill or tell him how he could make use of the skill exchange network. The third would be educational initiators or masters. These masters would be great teachers who lead their pupils on to advanced learning and insights. Such great teachers would attract students and form master-disciple relationships with them.

Illich's proposals have been soundly criticized on a number of important points. First, he is rather vague in many of his proposals and gives little detail on exactly how the transformation to his deschooled society might actually take place. Second, he is extremely negative about contemporary schooling and makes a number of statements about how little students learn in school and how much they learn outside it with little, if any, empirical data to back up his claims. As Sidney Hook put it, "Despite the extremism of his position, Illich writes with an astonishing confidence and dogmatism, piling one questionable statement upon another in reckless disregard of evidence, logic, and common sense."[38]

Many of the criticisms directed at Illich's proposals focus on his objection to anyone directing the education of others. Critics have pointed out that children, especially, do not always know what is important to learn. If given total freedom to experience and learn what they wish, children might expose themselves to harmful influences, such as drug use or delinquency, and might not acquire the skills they need to properly evaluate their own talents and opportunities. Furthermore, some skills may be best learned in youth or in an orderly sequence. In particular, habits of discipline and study may be critical to later success, but people do not usually appreciate them until adulthood when acquiring them may be difficult or impossible.

Other criticisms focus on the issue of equality and whether or not Illich's proposals will promote more or less opportunity for the disadvantaged.[39] Many argue that they would produce less, that the poor would not use educational resources as effectively as the rich, and that experiences would be even more class-stratified than they are now. Given free choice, people may choose not to mix with others of different races, religions, or ethnic groups. They may also choose not to teach them or learn from them. Contrary to Illich's view, these critics believe that it is compulsory schooling that guarantees everyone an opportunity to learn. Abolishing schooling will also abolish the freedoms and opportunities it protects. More, not less, inequality would result.

Critics have also challenged Illich's opposition to the certification of teachers. As Hook points out, "His open society . . . would be an open society for . . . educational quacks without safeguards for their victims . . . ."[40] To be fair, Illich also recognizes this as a problem, but he rejects the alternative of certifying as worse than the problems it might solve.

Finally, Illich has been criticized for not recognizing that any society, in order to exist, presupposes a certain communality of values. All schools promote continuity of tradition, moral insight, and a minimum level of cognitive literacy because these are essential for holding society together and having people interact meaningfully with one another.[41] These critics, in a sense, are returning to the theme of consensus theorists mentioned in the first pages of this volume; that is, unless we are all educated to some minimal set of core values, society will dissolve into anarchy. This is precisely where they believe Illich's proposals might lead.

## OPPORTUNITIES FOR SOCIOLOGISTS IN EDUCATIONAL INSTITUTION-BUILDING

In the first chapter, we indicated that institution-building in education involves critical examination of the schools, clarification of educational goals, and the development of new models of learning. The criticisms and proposals just reviewed contribute to improving education in all these respects, but institution-building is a much larger enterprise. It is an enterprise that offers sociologists many different roles. We shall describe a few of these below.

### The Traditional Social Scientific Role

Many sociologists are primarily concerned with building their discipline by adding to its body of theory and research. Traditionally, this has meant activities that approximate the ideals of the natural sciences. These activities include the derivation of hypotheses from general theories, testing hypotheses through empirical research, modifying theories on the basis of research findings, replication of the work of others and, in general, working toward the accumulation of a general and abstract body of knowledge. "Value neutrality" has also been basic to this approach: The researcher makes every effort to avoid the influence of personal bias on the research process.

Sociologists who adhere to these ideals may prefer doing "basic" research, but are often found doing research with a "practical" application instead. This is primarily because funds for "relevant" projects are more abundant. However, these sociologists are not advocates of particular proposals, although they recognize that their research may be useful to policymakers as well as academics. Indeed, their attempts to remain unbiased and objective may render the work of such traditional scholars more credible and influential than usual.

The quality of educational research is widely perceived to be extremely low. The National Institute of Education (NIE) was created in 1970 as a bureaucratic embodiment of the federal government's commitment to research and development in the field of education. Unfortunately, political and organizational shortcomings rapidly lead to its failure and extinction.[42] Chester Finn, in 1986 the top federal official directly concerned with such research, gave a blunt, negative appraisal of the situation, "Education research has failed entirely [for at least two decades] to prove either to educators or to the general public that it deserves support or even attention."[43] In light of this widely shared assessment, it is not surprising that the federal government allocates only .5 percent of its education budget to research. Virtually all of the federal education funds are allocated to a handful of national centers and regional laboratories. State and local governments offer practically no support for research. Sociologists interested in studying educational institutions can seek funding from other federal agencies (most notably the National Science Foundation) and private foundations, but the competition for the limited and declining research funds is fierce. So individual investigators have little hope of securing grants to do research. Without substantial federal support for basic research, the educational knowledge base appears doomed to remain weak.

### Monitoring Educational Institutions

One problem faced by anyone wishing to improve American education is to keep track of its main features and how these change over time. Given what you now know about the size and diversity of the educational enterprise, you can appreciate just how difficult this basic task might be. Only the availability of high quality descriptive statistics and sophisticated means for analyzing and interpreting them make such monitoring of educational institutions a possibility.

Statistics are currently available that describe a great many aspects of education in the United States. These have been collected and analyzed by a variety of groups; included among these groups are state and federal agencies, professional associations such as the NEA and AAUP, private foundations such as the Carnegie Commission on Higher Education, and corporations such as the Educational Testing Service. Some of these statistics have been more useful than others. One reason is that some organizations are merely repositories for data routinely collected and submitted, such as administrative reports, whereas others design studies and collect their own data to answer explicit policy-oriented questions.

To date, most of the routinely submitted statistics have had major shortcomings. Although they have dealt comprehensively with such matters as school expenditures, class size, and achievement test scores, they have neglected such important issues as student satisfaction, moral development, values, and creativity. Furthermore, these statistics are often cross-sectional rather than longitudinal. Longitudinal data involve observations of the same individuals or institutions at different points in time. They are expensive and more difficult to gather, but they are crucial for assessing change and discerning clear cause-and-effect relationships.

Probably the most important step toward more effective monitoring of American Education to date occurred in 1974 when the National Center for Education Statistics was established. In addition to gathering traditional statistics on education in the various states, the Center was given specific ". . . mandates calling for (1) conducting and publishing specialized analyses, (2) reviewing and reporting on educational activities in foreign countries, and (3) providing assistance to state and local educational agencies in improving their statistics."[44] Unlike many other government agencies, the NCES has been gathering longitudinal data and sponsoring research that will be helpful in monitoring changes in the educational process.

Sociologists can and do contribute to these monitoring activities. As employees, consultants, and individually funded project directors, sociologists use their skills to design studies, collect data, and analyze findings. Their expertise in statistics and methods is particularly important for monitoring purposes, but their firm grounding in sociological theory enables them to pinpoint which variables and relationships are worth investigating. We can expect continuing improvement in the statistical monitoring of education as sociological participation in this enterprise increases.

### The Sociologist as Program Evaluator

One of the few areas in which there is a relatively strong demand for sociologists is in the area of program evaluation. Up to this point, sociologists have been sought to help in this process primarily because of their methodological and statistical expertise, rather than because of their powerful theoretical insights.

Ideally, the evaluator's role would be that of the impartial outside expert, but in reality the evaluator is often under pressure from various interest groups and caught in a political process. A negative evaluation may result in a program reorganization, cutback, or cutoff.

Jobs, contracts, and services are at stake. As it happens, however, the potential impact of the evaluator has often been blunted because studies have yielded ambiguous or contradictory results. A good example of the complexities of the evaluator's role can be found in attempts to demonstrate the effectiveness of various preschool and early childhood education programs, specifically Head Start, Follow Through, and Head Start Planned Variation. (HSPV).[45]

Head Start was a key program in the War on Poverty that was launched in the mid-1960s. Its thrust was to fund preschool programs for children from impoverished homes. Social research had documented the fact that cognitive development is extremely rapid in the first several years of life. However, there was also evidence that poor children lagged behind middle-class children in terms of cognitive development during the preschool years and, therefore, entered school at a disadvantage. Politicians and educators both had high hopes that the provision of compensatory preschool education to the poor would make a significant contribution toward the goal of equalizing educational opportunity. Head Start was so politically popular that it was immediately translated into a large-scale national program without the benefit of careful pretesting. In 1966, only a year after the program was launched, evidence began to accumulate that, although Head Start programs often produced substantive gains in achievement and I.Q. test scores, these gains tended to fade out when the children entered the regular public schools. Proponents of the early childhood education concept felt that the fade out problem could be handled if only the federal government followed through in its commitment to the education of the poor. This could be accomplished by providing supplementary assistance for Head Start pupils after they entered public schools.

However, by this time legislators had become aware of the diversity of theories and lack of consensus among educational researchers about how to conduct successful compensatory education programs. Instead of rushing a new national program into operation, the decision was made to support a number of Head Start and Follow Through experiments in order to identify particularly effective approaches. This was Head Start Planned Variation (HSPV). A university-based research institute was given the major responsibility for developing the design of the planned variation experiment and collecting data for evaluation. By 1973, twenty-two models had been tried out under HSPV auspices. Among the diverse techniques tried were rapid-fire drills, individualized diagnosis of children's strengths and weaknesses, bilingual and culturally relevant instruction, systematic provisions of rewards and punishments, use of educational games, efforts to build positive self-images, enlistment of parents as tutors and aides, sophisticated technological tools (such as the Talking Typewriter), fostering close school-home cooperation and open classrooms. In the end, the general conclusion was:

> Children in Head Start Planned Variation showed substantially greater test score gains than would have been expected if they had not been enrolled at all. They did not, however, do significantly better, on the average, than the comparison children in the regular Head Start program, nor did particular Planned Variation models emerge as significantly better than others. Some models were associated with significantly higher scores on particular tests—one with substantial I.Q. gains—but when several output measures were considered, there were "no overall winners or losers."[46]

After it had become clear in 1973 that HSPV would soon end, the Brookings Institution sponsored a conference in an attempt to understand why the project and the evaluation efforts had proven to be disappointing.

Perhaps the most basic problem was a lack of time and money necessary to develop the programs adequately. Pressures to get the programs out into the field were intense. In some cases there simply was not enough time to do a careful and precise job of translating theory into action. Haste also contributed to a number of methodological inadequacies including lack of randomization, samples too small to be meaningful, and the utilization of inappropriate and/or unreliable measures of output. One conference participant offered the opinion that adequate research, development, and dissemination of only one kind of program would require twelve years and more than $6,000,000.[47] Obviously, this kind of funding was simply not forthcoming, and is not in the foreseeable future.

In addition to limitations of time and money, there were political problems that prevented some plans from being carried out as they were intended. The HSPV program fell under the War on Poverty guidelines. These called for extensive community participation in the implementation of this federal program. Researchers had to work with parents and activists whose concerns, quite naturally, were with results, not the niceties, of experimental research and design. This often required important modifications in the projects.

It appears that HSPV was successful as an educational enterprise in spite of its shortcomings:

> For academic researchers and curriculum developers who became sponsors, [these] were trials by the sword. Participation in the programs forced them out of the laboratory and into the classroom, where they faced the problem (often under extreme pressure) of translating theories and hypotheses into specific directions for teachers and children. Without question, the programs both hastened the development and elaboration of models that would otherwise have remained much longer on the drawing boards, and altered the models in the process. For program evaluators and policy analysts the programs also provided an invaluable education. They learned about the difficulties of doing social action research in the face of complex political and bureaucratic pressures. They found out, late and the hard way, about the costs that design flaws and compromises (for example, lack of random selection procedures) exact in the form of weak or uninterpretable results.[48]

However, it was an expensive lesson, and one which has made legislators reluctant to support significant new evaluation research efforts. Limited post-HSPV evaluations have failed to end controversy over the efficacy of governmentally supported early childhood education programs.[49]

### The Role of Policy Advocate

In recent years sociologists have with increasing frequency assumed the role of advocate, that is, one who speaks out in behalf of a particular client or policy. When sociologists do this as private citizens and amateurs, no particular difficulties arise, but when they speak out as experts who claim scientific support for their positions, controversy is likely to follow. On the one hand, their claim to expertise may draw the interest of the mass media and the courts. On the other hand, it may also draw the hostility of other social scientists with opposing views, and equal claims to expertise.

For example, in the mid-1970s, James Coleman took a stand in opposition to court-ordered busing for the purpose of desegregating urban schools. He believed that he had developed solid empirical evidence that court-ordered busing accelerates the loss of whites to suburbia and increases "white flight."[50]

Coleman's critics, many of whom were advocates of alternative policies such as the creation of metropolitan school districts to promote integration, roundly criticized his research methods and, most importantly for this discussion, his professional behavior in an ethical sense. For example, Pettigrew and Green charged him with making policy pronouncements that were unsupported by his data, with failing to differentiate clearly and consistently between his research evidence and personal beliefs, and with mounting a media campaign designed to legitimize opposition to court-enforced integration.[51] He, in return, made similar charges against his critics.[52]

The fact that the mass media are increasingly interested in social research, though not generally very sophisticated about its methods and limitations, raises special problems. Apparently this particular controversy was exacerbated by misquotes, misinterpretations, and misdirected attention (for example, toward *ad hominem* attacks) by journalists. Within the context of professional meetings and media, it is likely that research evidence will be treated with appropriate caution and skepticism, but the mass media invariably oversimplify and often exaggerate. There is need for clarification of professional norms regarding the publication of research in these media and need for continued primary reliance upon professional meetings and journals.

Though the role of advocate is highly controversial and is disdained by many in academia, it does involve people in the political process, and it does increase the probability that their views will be taken into account by policymakers. Furthermore, the fact that one expert will frequently disagree with another often has the virtue of clarifying issues and increasing the probability that more definitive research will be undertaken in the future.

### Teaching and Institution-Building

Of all the possible roles sociologists can play in educational institution-building, teaching is by far the most widely available to them. As teachers, sociologists have the opportunity to influence the next generation of professors, researchers, teachers, administrators, board members, and voters; that is, they have the chance to affect those who will directly make and enact educational policy in the future.

There appear to be wide variations among sociologists in terms of the way they handle their potential influence over the policy preferences of their students. Some try to ignore this potential influence, concentrating on basic theory and research and spending little or no time discussing applications and policies. Others, who believe that theory and practice should be interwoven, have little hesitance in making full use of their persuasive powers to influence students' opinions. At one extreme, some may view teaching as a subversive activity, a means through which they can undermine the existing educational and social structure.[53] At the other, some may use their knowledge to construct a "warrant of legitimation," or defense of the status quo.[54] In either case, the teaching role is being used to shape policy and decision-making processes.

Perhaps the most common position taken on this ethical issue is that professors should resist the temptation to make political use of their position. Even though students may press the professor to take a stand and lead them in pursuit of a particular goal, that pressure should be resisted. According to this view, because sociology professors are no better equipped than any other individual to decide what values should be given top priority, they should insist on remaining detached and analytical, going only so far as to help students understand the probable consequences of various political alternatives. In any case, dissension on this aspect of the professorial role is widespread.

### Curriculum Development

Curriculum development, and especially textbook publishing, are natural extensions of teaching and research activities. These are means by which one's theoretical perspectives and research findings can achieve broad dissemination and practical application, as well as being a means through which professors can exert influence upon educational policy.

Some of our most celebrated mathematicians, biologists, and physicists have participated in major efforts to improve the science curricula of high schools. Their materials have been researched, developed, and disseminated with the help of the federal government through the National Science Foundation. These improved curricula have been widely adopted and praised.

However, a similar sort of effort in the social sciences, designed for fifth and sixth graders, has run into significant opposition and controversy. This curriculum is entitled, Man: A Course of Study (MACOS).[55] One aim of the course is to illustrate the uniqueness of the human animal by contrasting human behaviors with those of other species. Some organized interests, most notably the "Scientific Creationists," have objected to the teachings about evolution that underlie these contrasts. The Scientific Creationists are college graduates who have formal organizations, journals, and research projects, such as those of organized science. They are dedicated to proving that all life on earth was created by God during seven days as described in the Bible.

But probably the most controversial part of the course involves the study of the Netsilik Eskimo tribe and its adaptations to modern society and technology. The traditional practices of this tribe have included some activities abhorrent to our society, including infanticide and senilicide. It seems clear to most observers that these practices are presented as adaptations to a harsh environment, although the developers of MACOS are careful to point out that the materials are primarily designed to provoke serious discussion rather than to provide a set of pat answers. Critics charge that these materials are too potent for ten-, eleven-, and twelve-year-olds and that it is inappropriate to introduce youngsters to such profound issues as cultural relativity. Furthermore, they argue that the fundamental lessons of value relativity and environmental determinism are either misguided or wrong. Additionally, the federal government's support of the project has raised the perennial question of the extent to which the government should intervene in local education. The charge was made that this is part of an effort to achieve a uniform national curriculum, a charge based on the observation that federally subsidized new materials have typically swept aside all competing curricula. Given what we have discovered in our previous chapters on education in various rural and urban communities and on the dynamics of local control, it should come as no surprise that this negative reaction on the part of some conservative communities would develop.

However, it should be noted that teachers and students alike have praised the materials.[56] Evaluation studies have indicated that children develop empathy and understanding of another culture without losing their attachment to their own. Furthermore, the children develop an enthusiasm for social studies not evident previously. Teachers are often similarly enthusiastic. In adapting to a heavy use of films and discussions many have altered their teaching styles from a teacher-centered to a child-centered one.

The decentralized nature of public school finance and control places real limits on the ability to establish strong social science programs in conservative communities. Many parents are threatened by the central process of examining and comparing value systems. In particular, many perceive a direct contradiction between the scientific belief systems underlying such programs and their traditional religious beliefs. But this, of course, does not imply that sociologists and educators must abandon their efforts to improve social science education in elementary and high schools. It just means that the task will be difficult.

Another part that sociologists can play in curricular development is the use of careful content analyses in order to expose various forms of bias.

Sociologists concerned with race relations have called attention to the omission and distortion of the social history of black Americans, and, more recently, sociologists committed to equality between the sexes have called attention to the conservative, traditional, passive, and unrealistic roles female characters play in children's books.[57]

Finally, sociologists have made an important contribution in calling attention to the hidden curriculum: the norms and values embodied in the rules, regulations, and requirements of organizational procedure that students typically learn in school. Durkheim, Parsons, Dreeben, and Coleman are among the sociologists who have called attention to these factors.[58] For example, Coleman has argued that the emphasis upon interscholastic sports in high schools promotes anti-intellectualism. To countract this he has proposed interscholastic academic competitions as a means of letting youth know that brains, not just muscles, are valued.

## PROSPECTS FOR A POLICY-ORIENTED SOCIOLOGY OF EDUCATION

It should be obvious by now that there is no one universally accepted method for sociologists to involve themselves with the formation of public policy. There are many roles they can, and do, play, each of which has a potential impact on educational institutions. However, it should also be obvious that the ability of sociologists to contribute successfully to policy-making depends as much on others beyond their profession as it depends on themselves. The receptivity of politicians, other professionals, and practitioners is of critical importance.

Unfortunately, this receptivity is often lacking. Boards of education, administrators, and faculty are often defensive and resistant to the types of research that are most urgently needed. For example, the educational establishment was unified in its opposition to testing voucher plans. Decreased defensiveness and increased willingness to cooperate, experiment, and question current practice are badly needed.

Some people are skeptical that research can ever make an important contribution to institution-building in education. Certainly, the impact of research on educational policy to date has not been impressive. Politics as well as shortcomings in the research itself forestalled such contributions. Furthermore, some people are skeptical that educational processes can ever be analyzed "scientifically." Education, they argue, will always be more of an art than a science.

In summary, we would not expect a policy-oriented sociology of education to have a rapid and dramatic impact on education, but we would be optimistic about its long-range effects. If nothing else, research can promote the ". . . slow erosion of old assumptions and pieties."[59] It can undermine the popular myths supporting current practices and stimulate fresh ideas and paradigms for the future. To the extent that sociologists consciously seek to have an impact on educational institutions, these effects will occur more rapidly; but the diffusion of meaningful ideas from academia into the public domain will occur with or without such conscious efforts.[60]

## *NOTES*

[1]Lady Bridget Plowden and others, *Children and Their Primary Schools: A Report of the Central Advisory Council for Education*, Vol. 1 (London: Her Majesty's Stationery Office, 1966); Charles E. Silberman, *Crisis in the Classroom* (New York: Random House, 1970); Joseph Featherstone, *Schools Where Children Learn* (New York: Liveright, 1971); Charles H. Rathbone, *Open Education: The Informal Classroom* (New York: Citation Press, 1971); Ewald B. Nyquist and G.R. Haws, *Open Education: A Source Book for Parents and Teachers* (New York: Bantam Books, 1972).

[2]Silberman, *Crisis in the Classroom*, p. 210.

[3]Nevill Bennett, *Teaching Styles and Pupil Progress* (Cambridge, Mass.: Harvard University Press, 1976).

[4]Allen Graubard, *Free the Children: Radical Reform and the Free School Movement* (New York: Pantheon Books, 1972); John C. Carr, Jean Dresden Grambs, and E G. Campbell, eds., *Alternative Schooling in American Education: Pygmalion or Frankenstein?* (Reading, Mass.: Addison-Wesley, 1977): Cornelius J. Troost, ed., *Radical School Reform: Critique and Alternatives* (Boston: Little, Brown, 1973).

[5]A.S. Neill, *Summerhill: A Radical Approach to Child Rearing* (New York: Hart Publishing Company, 1960); Harold H. Hart, ed., *Summerhill: For and Against* (New York: Hart Publishing Company, 1970).

[6]Mario D. Fantini, *Public Schools of Choice* (New York: Simon & Schuster, 1973); Kenneth B. Clark, "Alternative Public School Systems," in *School Policy and Issues in a Changing Society*, ed. Patricia Cays Sexton, (Boston: Allyn & Bacon, 1971); pp. 411–26.

[7]The following description of American free schools is based primarily upon Allen Graubard, "The Free School Movement," *Harvard Educational Review*, 42, 3 (August, 1972), pp. 351–70.

[8]Allan A. Glatthorn, "Alternative Schools," *Review of Education*, 6, 1 (Winter, 1980), p. 59.

[9]William A. Firestone, "Ideology and Conflict in Parent-Run Free Schools," *Sociology of Education*, 49 (April, 1976), pp. 169–75.

[10]Clark, "Alternative Public School Systems," pp. 411–26.

[11]Mary Anne Raywid, "The First Decade of Public School Alternatives," in Fred Schultz, ed. *Education 82/83* (Guilford, Ct.: Dushkin Publishing Group, 1982), p. 52.

[12]Robert D. Barr, "Alternatives for the Eighties: A Second Decade of Development," in Schultz, ed. *Education 82/83*, pp. 56–58.

[13]Vernon H. Smith, *Alternative Schools: The Development of Options in Public Education* (Lincoln, Neb.: Professional Educators Publications, Inc., 1974).

[14]Raywid, "The First Decade," p. 52.

[15]Rita Hegedus, "Voucher Plans," in *Handbook of Contemporary Education*, ed. Steven E. Goodman (New York: Bowker, 1976), pp. 128–31.

[16]Ibid., pp. 130–31.

[17]Jim Warren, "Alum Rock Voucher Project," *Educational Researcher*, 5 (March, 1976), p. 13.

[18]*Education Week*, December 4, 1985, p. 11.

[19]U.S. Department of Health, Education and Welfare, *Report on Higher Education* (Washington, D.C.: Government Printing Office, 1971); the Carnegie Commission on Higher Education, *Less Time, More Options* (New York: McGraw-Hill Book Co., 1971); Ann Heiss, *An Inventory of Academic Innovation and Reform* (Berkeley: The Carnegie Commission on Higher Education, 1973); Theodore M. Hesburgh, Paul A. Miller, and Clifton R. Wharton, Jr., *Patterns of Lifelong Learning* (San Francisco: Jossey-Bass, 1973); and Organization for Economic Co-operations and Development, *Recurrent Education: A Strategy for Lifelong Learning* (Paris, 1973).

[20]Margaret Mead, "Thinking Ahead," *Harvard Business Review*, 36 (November-December, 1958), pp. 23ff.

[21]For an overview of these programs, see John R. Valley, "External Degree Programs," in Goodman, *Handbook of Contemporary Education*, pp. 599–605.

[22]Valley, "External Degree Programs," p. 601.

[23]Ibid., p. 600.

[24]David E. Sweet, "A Model for an Upper-Division Urban College," in *The Expanded Campus: 1972 Current Issues in Higher Education*, ed. Dyckman W. Vermilye, (San Francisco: Jossey-Bass, 1972), pp. 211–24.

[25]Ibid., pp. 215–16.

[26]Ibid., p. 216.

[27]For a discussion of the impact of lifelong education, see Ann P. Parelius, "Lifelong Education and Age Stratification: Some Unexplained Relationships," in *Age in Society*, ed. Anne Foner, (Beverly Hills: Sage Publications, 1975), pp. 75–92.

[28]Stephen K. Bailey, "Flexible Time-Space Programs: A Plea for Caution," in Vermilye, *The Expanded Campus*, pp. 172–76, and Valley, "External Degree Programs."

[29]Norbert J. Hruby, "MIA: The Nontraditional Student," *Academe*, 71, 5 (September-October, 1985), p. 27.

[30]Ben Brodinsky, "Back to Basics: The Movement and Its Meaning," *Phi Delta Kappan*, 58 (March, 1977), pp. 522–27; James K. Wellington, "American Education: Its Failure and Its Future," *Phi Delta Kappan*, 58 (March, 1977), pp. 527–30; Samuel A. Owen and Deborah L. Ranile, "The Greensville Program: A Commonsense Approach to Basics," *Phi Delta Kappan*, 58 (March, 1977), pp. 531–34.

[31]Brodinsky, "Back to Basics," p. 524.

[32]Valena White Plisko, *The Condition of Education, 1984* (Washington, D.C.: Government Printing Office, 1984), p. 178.

[33]Valena White Plisko and Joyce D. Stern, *The Condition of Education, 1985* (Washington, D.C.: Government Printing Office, 1985), p. 16.

[34]Owen and Ranile, "The Greensville Program," pp. 531-34.

[35]David L. Larabee, "Setting the Standard: Alternative Policies for Student Promotion," *Harvard Educational Review*, 54, 1 (February, 1984), p. 81.

[36]Ivan Illich, *Deschooling Society* (New York: Harper & Row, 1972).

[37]Ivan Illich, "The Alternative to Schooling," *Saturday Review* (June 19, 1971) pp. 44–48.

[38]Sidney Hook, "Illich's De-Schooled Utopia," in *Radical School Reform: Critique and Alternatives*, ed. Cornelius J. Troost, pp. 67–74.

[39]See also, Manfried Stanley, "Illich Defrocked," in Troost, *Radical School Reform*, pp. 74–80.

[40]Hook, "Illich's De-Schooled Utopia," p. 73.

[41]Stanley, "Illich Defrocked," P. 77.

[42]Lee S. Sproull, Stephen S. Weiner, and David Wolf, *Organizing an Anarchy* (Chicago: University of Chicago Press, 1978).

[43]Charles T. Kerchner, "Educational Research Is in Trouble," *Politics of Education Bulletin*, 13, no. 3 (Spring, 1986), p. 6.

[44]O. Jean Brandes, *Projects, Products, and Services of the National Center for Education Statistics* (Washington, D.C.: Government Printing Office, 1973), p. 1.

[45]Alice Rivlin and Michael Timpane, *Planned Variations: Should We Give Up or Try Harder?* (Washington: The Brookings Institution, 1975).

[46]Alice M. Rivlin and P. Michael Timpane, "Planned Variation in Education: An Assessment," in Alice M. Rivlin and P. Michael Timpane, ed., *Planned Variations*, pp. 10–11.

[47]David P. Weikart and Bernard A. Banet, "Model Designs in Follow Through," in Alice M. Rivlin and P. Michael Timpane, eds., *Planned Variations*, 73–75.

[48]Alice M. Rivlin and P. Michael Timpane, "Planned Variation in Education: An Assessment," p. 11.

[49]For a positive assessment see D.P. Weikart and Lawrence J. Schweinhart, *Changed Lives: The Effects of the Perry Preschool Program on Youths Through Age 19* (Ypsilanti, Mi.: High Scope, 1984). A negative assessment is given in Arthur R. Jensen, "Compensatory Education and the Theory of Intelligence," *Phi Delta Kappan*, 66, 8 (April, 1985), pp. 554–58.

[50]James S. Coleman, Sara D. Kelly, and John A. Moore, "Recent Trends in School Integration," paper presented at the Annual Meeting of the American Education Research Association, Washington, D.C., April 2, 1975.

[51]Thomas F. Pettigrew and Robert L. Green, "School Desegregation in Large Cities: A Critique of the Coleman White Flight' Thesis," *Harvard Educational Review*, 46 (February, 1976), pp. 1–53.

[52]James S. Coleman, "Response to Professors Pettigrew and Green," *Harvard Educational Review*, 46 (May, 1976), pp. 217–24.

[53]Neil Postman and Charles Weingartner, *Teaching as a Subversive Activity* (New York: Dell Publishing Company, 1969).

[54]Geraldine Joncich Clifford, "A History of the Impact of Research on Teaching," in *Second Handbook of Research on Teaching*, ed. Robert M. Travers, (Chicago: Rand McNally, 1973), p. 27.

[55]George Weber, "The Case Against Man: A Course of Study," *Phi Delta Kappan*, 57 (October, 1975), pp. 81–82.

[56]Peter B. Dow, "The Case for Man: A Course of Study," *Phi Delta Kappan*, 57 (October, 1975), pp. 79–81.

[57]Judith Stacey, Susan Bereaud, and Joan Daniels, eds., *And Jill Came Tumbling After: Sexism in American Education* (New York: Dell Publishing Company, 1974).

[58]Emile Durkheim, *Moral Education*, trans. Everett K. Wilson and Herman Schaurer, (New York: The Free Press, 1961); Talcott Parsons, "The School Class as a Social System," *Harvard Educational Review*, 29 (Fall, 1959); Robert Dreeben, *On What Is Learned in Schools* (Reading, Mass.: Addison-Wesley, 1968); James S. Coleman, *The Adolescent Society: The Social Life of the Teenager and Its Impact on Education* (Glencoe, Ill.: The Free Press of Glencoe, 1963).

[59]Martin Trow, "Some Factors Which Affect the Use of Social Science Reserch in Higher Education," paper presented at the meetings of the American Sociological Association, Washington, D.C., August 1962, p. 22.

[60]Geraldine Joncich Clifford, "A History of the Impact of Research on Teaching," pp. 24–25.

# INDEX